A History of Race in Muslim West Africa, 1600–1960

The mobilization of local ideas about racial difference has been important in generating – and intensifying – civil wars that have occurred since the end of colonial rule in all of the countries that straddle the southern edge of the Sahara Desert. From Sudan to Mauritania, the racial categories deployed in contemporary conflicts often hearken back to an older history in which blackness could be equated with slavery and nonblackness with predatory and uncivilized banditry. This book traces the development of arguments about race over a period of more than 350 years in one important place along the southern edge of the Sahara Desert: the Niger Bend in northern Mali. Using Arabic documents held in Timbuktu, as well as local colonial sources in French and oral interviews, Bruce S. Hall reconstructs an African intellectual history of race that long predated colonial conquest, and which has continued to orient inter-African relations ever since.

Bruce S. Hall is an assistant professor at Duke University. His work appears in the *Journal of North African Studies* and the *International Journal of African Historical Studies*. Professor Hall previously held positions as an assistant professor at the University at Buffalo (SUNY) and as an Andrew W. Mellon postdoctoral fellow at Johns Hopkins University.

AFRICAN STUDIES

The African Studies Series, founded in 1968, is a prestigious series of monographs, general surveys, and textbooks on Africa covering history, political science, anthropology, economics, and ecological and environmental issues. The series seeks to publish work by senior scholars as well as the best new research.

A list of books in this series will be found at the end of this volume.

A History of Race in Muslim West Africa, 1600–1960

BRUCE S. HALL
Duke University

CAMBRIDGE
UNIVERSITY PRESS

CAMBRIDGE
UNIVERSITY PRESS

32 Avenue of the Americas, New York NY 10013-2473, USA

Cambridge University Press is part of the University of Cambridge.

It furthers the University's mission by disseminating knowledge in the pursuit of education, learning and research at the highest international levels of excellence.

www.cambridge.org
Information on this title: www.cambridge.org/9781107678842

First published 2011
Reprinted 2012 (twice)
First paperback edition 2014

A catalogue record for this publication is available from the British Library

Library of Congress Cataloguing in Publication data

Hall, Bruce S.
A history of race in Muslim West Africa, 1600–1960 / Bruce S. Hall.
p. cm. – (African studies ; 115)
Includes bibliographical references and index.
ISBN 978-1-107-00287-6
1. Blacks – Africa, West – History. 2. Black race – History. 3. Slavery – Africa, West – History. 4. Islam and culture – Africa, West – History. I. Title.
DT15.H23 2011
305.800967′0903 – dc22 2010046888

ISBN 978-1-107-00287-6 Hardback
ISBN 978-1-107-67884-2 Paperback

Contents

Maps and Figures

MAPS

FIGURES

Acknowledgments

There are many people who helped me over the course of this project. Certainly the largest contribution was the many conversations I had in Mali with people whom I can only recognize here in a very general way. These discussions often helped shape my thinking about the history of northern Mali and pointed me in directions that I would not have followed otherwise. That being said, I cannot pretend that those people would necessarily recognize their ideas and suggestions in what follows.

This book is based on three main types of primary source material. First, I conducted interviews with people in northern Mali, mostly in the Songhay language. Second, I used Arabic documents held at the Institut des Hautes Etudes et de Recherches Islamique – Ahmed Baba (IHERIAB) in Timbuktu. Third, I carried out research on colonial documents held at the Archives Nationales du Mali in Bamako, the archives of the Ministry of the Interior in Bamako, and in the local administrative offices in Timbuktu and Goundam. My work with Songhay language materials was assisted by Aldiouma Amadou Cissé dit Diadié, who also undertook the difficult task of teaching me the Songhay language. At IHERIAB, I thank Dr. Mohamed Gallah Dicko, Sidi Mohamed ould Youbba, Bouya Haidara, Noury Mohamed Alamine Al-Ansary, Hammay Bania, Ali Koina, San Shirfi Alpha, and Alfadoulou Abdoulahi. I owe a special appreciation to Djibril Doucouré who permitted me to work freely with the collection. At the Archives Nationales du Mali, I thank Dr. Aly Ongoïba, Alyadjidi Almouctar Baby, Lamine Camara, Abdallahi Traoré, Timothé Saye, Adama Diallo, and Siaka Koné for all of their assistance. The Haut Commissaire of the Region of Timbuktu in 2002, Colonel Mahamadou Maïga, opened the doors of local government offices in Timbuktu and

Goundam for me. I also thank Amadou Dolo, Mahamane Sidiya, Baye Konaté, and Mahamadou M. Touré.

An incomplete list of people to whom I owe a debt of gratitude is as follows: Badou Ababa, Mohamed ag Ahassane dit Halice, Alassane Alkalifa, Nicole Anderson, Abbas Benmamoun, Jeremy Berndt, Sara Berry, Dirk Bonker, Dinie Bouwman, Brandon County, Yacine Daddi Addoun, Roger Des Forges, Stephanie Diakité, Laurent Dubois, David Eltis, Damien Emonet, Peter English, Janet Ewald, Jennifer Gayner, Garett Gietzen, Alessandra Giuffrida, Jonathon Glassman, Jane Guyer, Abdalkader Haidara, Ismaël Diadié Haidara, Michael Hainsworth, John Hanson, Chouki el Hamel, Jeffrey Heath, Engseng Ho, Valerie Hoffman, Jochen Höttcke, John Hunwick, Jean-Marie Huon, Azarak ag Inaborchad, Peter Kagwanja, Hassan Kamal, Martin Klein, Anna Krylova, Pier Larson, Baz Lecocq, Christian Lenz, Paul Lovejoy, Ghislaine Lydon, Patrick McDevitt, Abba Bomoye Maiga and family, Mahamane Mahamoudou Dadab dit Hamou, Gregory Mann, Shahid Mathee, Leben Nelson Moro, Muhamed Nouhi, Cynthia Radding, Seraphima Rombe-Shulman, Jonathon Sears, Erik Seeman, Robert Shenton, Michael Sherfy, Ali ould Sidi, Aisha Sobh, Jérôme Soci, Ramya Sreenivasan, Philip Stern, Phillips Stevens, Maria Todorova, Seydou Togola, Boubakar Alkaya Touré dit Garba, Simone van Vugt, Liana Vardi, Claude Welch, and Jason Young. This book began as a dissertation and as such I owe a special note of thanks to the members of my dissertation committee (Jean Allman, Kenneth Cuno, Donald Crummey, and Charles Stewart). I am especially grateful to my dissertation advisor, Charles Stewart, whose advice has been indispensible to me as a graduate student and since. I thank Kathryn Mathers for doing the index.

My research in Mali was supported by the Institut des Sciences Humaines in Bamako. I thank the CNRST for research authorization in Mali. The research undertaken for this book was supported by fellowships from the Social Science and Humanities Research Council of Canada (SSHRCC) and by the Social Science Research Council (SSRC). I also thank the University of Illinois for awarding me the Scott Dissertation Completion Fellowship. I owe a debt of gratitude to former and present colleagues at Johns Hopkins University, University at Buffalo (SUNY), and Duke University.

To my partner Sima, my sister Sarah, and to my parents, Susan and Harry Hall, I am especially thankful for all the support that they have offered me over the different stages of this long process.

Note on Orthography

The spelling of all place names follows official conventions in Mali and elsewhere, with the following exceptions: I use Timbuktu instead of Tombouctou, as it is spelled in Mali, Azawad instead of Azaouad, Arawan instead of Araouane, Masina instead of Macina. Otherwise, I use French orthography for place names in Mali, Senegal, and Niger, and Arabic for Algeria, Morocco, Mauritania, Libya, and Tunisia. Arriving at a consistent system for personal names has been more difficult. In general, I have tried to follow the individual spellings used by the people themselves. In the period before the establishment of colonial rule, I have followed Arabic orthographic conventions; in the colonial period, I have sometimes used French spellings where this is the only source, although not always where there are Arabic sources. For the colonial period, I have used French orthography in most cases even when Arabic sources suggest different spellings. For the pastoralist confederacy and lineage names, I have used a hybrid system to make it easier on the reader, following where possible the past practice of academic writing and contemporary Malian usage while trying to reflect the actual pronunciation as much as possible.

For transliterations of literary Arabic words, I have followed the system used by the *International Journal of Middle East Studies*. I have avoided the unnecessary use of diacritics in Arabic words and names to the greatest extent possible. I have transliterated spellings using diacritics the first time a term, person, group, or Arabic word is introduced, but these have been dropped in all subsequent invocations. After the first mention, Maḥmūd ould Daḥmān is subsequently spelled Mahmud ould Dahman, Barābīsh becomes Barabish, and "ḍurūra" becomes "durura." For words drawn from Hassaniyya Arabic, Tamashek, and Songhay, I have followed the orthographic conventions found in Jeffrey Heath's work on these language families.[1] For Fulfulde, I have relied on the lexicon of Donald W. Osborn et al.[2] It should be noted that within these language families, there are significant dialectical differences. I have privileged the versions of Songhay, Tamashek, Hasaniyya Arabic, and Fulfulde spoken in the area around Timbuktu.

[1] Jeffrey Heath, *Hassaniya Arabic (Mali)-English-French dictionary* (Wiesbaden: Harrassowitz, 2004); Heath, *Dictionnaire touareg du Mali: tamachek-anglais-français* (Paris: Karthala, 2006); Heath, *Dictionnaire songhay-anglais-français, vol. 1, Koyra chiini* (Paris: L'Harmattan, 1998).

[2] Donald W. Osborn, David J. Dwyer, Joseph I. Donahue, *A Fulfulde (Maasina)-English-French Lexicon: A Root-Based Compilation from Extant Sources Followed by English-Fulfulde and French-Fulfulde Listings* (East Lansing: Michigan State University, 1993).

Abbreviations used in References

ACG	"Archives," Cercle de Goundam, Mali
ACT	"Archives," Cercle de Tombouctou, Mali
AHR	*American Historical Review*
ALA II	John Hunwick et al., *Arabic Literature of Africa, vol. II: The Writings of Central Sudanic Africa* (Leiden: Brill, 1995)
ALA IV	John Hunwick et al., *Arabic Literature of Africa, vol. IV: The Writings of Western Sudanic Africa* (Leiden: Brill, 2000)
AMI	Archives de la Ministère de l'Intérieur, Bamako, Mali.
ANM	Archives nationale du Mali
Ar.	Arabic
ART	Archives, Région de Tombouctou, Mali
b.	(Ar.) "son of" (for "ibn/bin")
BCEHS-AOF	*Bulletin du Comité d'études historiques et scientifique de l'A.O.F*
BSOAS	*Bulletin of the School of Oriental and African Studies (SOAS)*
CEA	*Cahiers d'études africaines*
CJAS	*Canadian Journal of African Studies*
CSSH	*Comparative Studies in Society and History*
Fr.	French
Fu.	Fulfulde
GAL	Carl Brockelmann, *Geschichte der arabischen Literatur*, 3 volumes, 2 Supplements (Leiden: Brill, 1937–1942).
HA	*History in Africa*

HAr.	Hassaniyya Arabic
IHERIAB	Institut des Hautes Etudes et de Recherches Islamiques – Ahmed Baba, Timbuktu, Mali
IJAHS	*International Journal of African Historical Studies*
JAH	*Journal of African History*
JOSF	*Journal Officiel du Soudan Français*
Kahhala	ʿUmar Riḍā Kaḥḥala, *Muʿjam al-muʾallifīn: Tarājim muṣannifī ʾl-kutub al-ʿarabiyya*. 4 volumes (Beirut: Muʾassasat al-risāla, 1993)
MLG	Ulrich Rebstock, *Maurische Literaturgeschichte*. 3 volumes (Würtburg: Ergon, 2001).
OCRS	Organisation commune des régions sahariennes
PSP	Parti Progressiste Soudanais
RBCAS	*Research Bulletin, Centre of Arabic Documentation, University of Ibadan*
SA	*Sudanic Africa*
So.	Songhay
Ta.	Tamashek
US-RDA	Union Soudanaise-Rassemblement Démocratique Africain

Glossary

ʿabīd (sing. ʿabd)	(Ar.) slaves
Adrar	mountainous area, often spelled "Adagh;" it refers to the Adrar-n-Ifoghas unless otherwise specified
ʿahd	(Ar.) pact or treaty
amān	(Ar.) granting of mutual security
amenokal	(Ta.) political leader or "chief" of a Tuareg confederacy
Arma	Songhay-speaking descendants of Moroccan soldiers; elite group in certain Niger valley towns such as Timbuktu
azalaï	(Fr./HAr.) salt caravan
Azawad	desert region north of the Niger Bend (French spelling "Azaouad")
Barābīsh	Arabophone warrior-status lineage based north of the Niger Bend
bellah-iklan	(So.) servile "blacks" in Tuareg society
bīḍān	(Ar.) "whites"
Bilād al-sūdān	(Ar.) "Land of the Blacks"
borochin	(So.) noble-born people, free people
gaabibi	(So.) servile "blacks"
goum	(Fr./HAr.) camel-mounted military police
goumier	(Fr.) camel-mounted military policeman
Gourma	right bank of the Niger River
ḥarāṭīn (sing. ḥarṭānī)	(Ar.) servile "blacks"

harbibi	(So.) servile "blacks"
ḥassān	(HAr.) warrior-status lineage
Haoussa	left bank of the Niger River
iderfan (sing. edaraf)	(Ta.) freed slaves
Ifoghas	a Tuareg clerical-status lineage based in the Adrar-n-Ifoghas
Igawaddaran	a Tuareg warrior-status confederation based in the Niger Bend
ighawelan (sing. eghawel)	(Ta.) slaves living freely
iklan (sing. akli)	(Ta.) male slaves (female slaves: "tiklaten," sing ."taklitt")
ilallan (sing. elall)	(Ta.) noble-born people, free people
imghad (sing. amghid)	(Ta.) tributary groups
imoshagh (sing. amashagh)	(Ta.) members of Tuareg warrior-status lineages, sometimes understood more broadly as "nobles" (a dialectical variations of the spelling is "imajagh")
inesleman (sing. anaslemen)	(Ta.) clerical-status lineage
Irreganatan	a Tuareg warrior-status lineage based in the Niger Bend
Iwellemmedan	a Tuareg warrior-status confederation based in the eastern Niger Bend
Kel Ahaggar	a Tuareg warrior-status confederation based in the Hoggar Massif
Kel Ajjer	a Tuareg warrior-status confederation based in the Tassili-n-Ajjer
Kel Entsar	a Tuareg clerical-status confederation, based in the Niger Bend
Kel Essuk	a Tuareg clerical-status lineage based in the Niger Bend
Kel Ewey	a Tuareg warrior-status confederation based in the Aïr Massif
Kel Temulayt	a Tuareg warrior-status confederation based in the Niger Bend
Kissou	region southwest of Timbuktu
Kunta	an Arab clerical-status confederation based in the Niger Bend and Mauritania.
Masina	the inland "delta" of the Niger River to the southwest of the Niger Bend

Massūfa	a Berberophone group prominent in the medieval Sahel and southern Sahara
méhariste	(Fr.) desert camel corps under French command
mustaghraq al-dhimma	(Ar.) "he whose assets are consumed"
Shur Bubba	a seventeenth-century conflict in southwestern Mauritania said to have completed conquest of clerical-status lineages by Arab, warrior-status lineages
Sorko	Songhay-speaking fishers
Soudan Français	French colonial territory that gained its independence as the Republic of Mali
sūdān	(Ar.) "blacks"
Tādmakkat	a medieval town in the Adrar-n-Iforghas
Takrūr	imprecise term for Sahelian West Africa
Tengeregif	a Tuareg warrior-status confederation based in the western Niger Bend
walāya	(Ar.) "saintliness"
zwāyā	(HAr.) clerical-status lineage

Introduction

> [I]f race is socially and historically constructed, then racism must be reconstructed as social regimes change and histories unfold ... [W]e [must] recognize that a new historical construct is never entirely new and the old is never entirely supplanted by the new. Rather the new is grafted onto the old. Thus racism, too, is never entirely new. Shards and fragments of its past incarnations are embedded in the new. Or, if we switch metaphors to an archaeological image, the new is sedimented onto the old, which occasionally seeps or bursts through. Our problem then, is to figure out how this happens and to take its measure.
>
> Thomas C. Holt[1]

RACE IN NORTHERN MALI

The language of racial difference has become a common feature of political discourse in many parts of postcolonial Africa, especially in the countries of the Sahel, the Horn of Africa, and the Great Lakes. Yet understanding how Africans have come to deploy idioms of race to describe intra-African differences has often been handicapped by academic scholarship that insists on race being understood as an exclusively European-American ideology. Mahmood Mamdani's well-known book on the Rwandan genocide is illustrative of this larger problem. He frames African uses of racial language as a kind of false consciousness derived from the colonial experience: "At the core of the ideology of Hutu Power was the conviction that the Tutsi were a *race* alien to Rwanda, and not an

[1] Thomas C. Holt, *The Problem of Race in the Twenty-First Century* (Cambridge, MA: Harvard University Press, 2000), 20–1.

indigenous *ethnic group*. The shift in political vocabulary was a return to the vision of the colonial period." Hutu Power propagandists "claimed to be radical nationalist and populist. Yet, in defining the Tutsi as a foreign race, even if without knowing it, they were reaffirming the colonial legacy and construing themselves the same way that Belgian colonialism had construed them prior to independence."[2] For Mamdani, the appearance of racial language stands as an indictment of the wider failure of postcolonial Africa to liberate itself from the effects of the colonial experience. As such, the Rwandan genocide is presented as an ironic tragedy; ironic because Rwandans employed the same tools as the colonizers – "even if without knowing it" – in their contests for power.

This book offers a different perspective, arguing instead that there are African histories of race that do not obey colonial logics. Along the Sahel in West Africa, a long history of racial language is evident in the writings of Muslim intellectuals well before the arrival of Europeans. Sahelian writers made a fundamental distinction between "whites" (Ar. bīḍān), for those who claimed Arab pedigrees, and "blacks" (Ar. sūdān). In these texts, "blackness" worked as a marker of inferiority that created significant legal disability for people who could be labeled in this way. When the Sahel was colonized by France beginning in the late nineteenth century, the colonial administration used these existing local conceptions of racial difference in the organization of its rule, in part because they corresponded to European denigrations of people defined as black. If we wish to understand the ways that racial languages work today in the countries of the African Sahel, we must explore the intellectual history of this region in much greater depth. Only then will we be able to evaluate the influence that European racial ideologies had in shaping postcolonial political language, and the extent to which Mamdani's evaluation of Rwanda – or more recently Darfur[3] – offers a convincing explanation of this history.

Among the most important flashpoints of racial conflict along the Sahel are the northern regions of Mali and Niger. In 1990, simultaneous revolts were launched by ethnically-Tuareg militias against the authority of the Malian and Nigerian governments. These actions began a conflict that came to be known as the Tuareg Rebellion (1990–1995). Small in scale compared to other African civil wars, these events nonetheless

[2] Mahmood Mamdani, *When Victims Become Killers: Colonialism, Nativism, and the Genocide in Rwanda* (Princeton, NJ: Princeton University Press, 2001), 190. Italics in original.

[3] Mamdani has made an almost identical argument for Darfur (Mamdani, *Saviors and Survivors: Darfur, Politics, and the War on Terror* [New York: Pantheon, 2009], 147–52).

degenerated quickly into violence defined by locally understood categories of racial difference. The Tuareg – and later Arab – rebels identified themselves as "non-blacks" who were fighting against "black"-dominated governments and armies in Mali and Niger. The expressed objective of the rebellion was the creation of independent or autonomous territories for Tuareg and Arab people, where they would constitute the racial and ethnic majority.

Rebel grievances were often expressed in racial terms. Tuareg intellectuals presented a picture of themselves as an oppressed racial minority forced to fight brutal and corrupt regimes that targeted them because of historically driven racial animus. In a book published by the Nigerian Tuareg intellectual Mano Dayak in 1992 at the height of the conflict, he accused the governments of Niger and Mali of an explicit policy of terrorizing the Tuareg people as vengeance for the Tuareg history of enslaving blacks: "The Republic of Niger decided to make the Tuareg pay dearly for their 'insolence' and for their past as 'slave' masters."[4] In a document published in 1994 by Tuareg rebels in Niger outlining their political demands for the creation of a "Tuareg zone," control was demanded over all areas of Niger that had once been "administered" by the Tuareg before the arrival of the French colonial state at the end of the nineteenth century. As such, the rebels claimed land in which Tuareg populations were quite small. In this "Tuareg zone," the rebels demanded that the future electorate exclude all non-Tuareg populations not considered (by the Tuareg rebels) to be autochthonous. In the Nigerian press, this was understood as an attempt to reimpose Tuareg domination over local blacks.[5] In the words of André Salifou, a southern Nigerian intellectual close to the government at the time, "certain Tuareg have decided to recall their pre-colonial past, which consisted of raids and other pillaging essentially at the expense of the sedentary populations. They want to play the most important role in the Sahel which has been abandoned by the European colonialists for thirty years and where power is exercised by the Blacks, which is to say, in their eyes, by inferior beings."[6]

Rebel demands in Mali for the "liberation" of the Azawad region (the Saharan area immediately north of the Niger Bend) as a Tuareg and Arab homeland met with similar responses. In a pamphlet published during

4 Mano Dayak, *Touareg, la tragédie* (Paris: Editions Jean-Claude Lattès, 1992), 63.

5 Dominique Casajus, "Les amis français de la cause touarègue," *CEA* 137, XXXV–1, (1995): 243–4.

6 André Salifou, *La question touarègue au Niger* (Paris: Karthala, 1993), 11.

the conflict by sympathizers of the loyalist black militias created during the war, the territorial claims made by rebel groups were mocked: "The Azawad is free. It is not occupied by any Songhay, or by any Fulbe, or Sarakollé. No black sedentary people claim the Azawad [which is nothing but] an expanse of desert." The real aim of the rebel movement, the pamphlet claimed, was the "recognition of a right to the villainous appropriation of the land of the regions, the property of the sedentary peoples." The rebels "are racists and enslavers. They consider all blacks to be slaves, inferior beings." They "want recognition of the right to dominate the black people." The Tuareg "have always been bandits, living from theft, raids and brigandage. The people of the North have a foreign body in the social tissue."[7]

The language of slavery was central to the racial framework of the conflict and, as we will see, to the larger history of racial ideas in the wider region. In Mano Dayak's book, he attempted to downplay the history of slavery in Tuareg society: "In times of war, the winner took his booty. The Tuareg frequently took prisoners whom they brought back with them to their camp. But after that, these slaves integrated into Tuareg families." Instead of being treated as slaves, these captives "were treated practically in the same manner as everyone else." They could acquire livestock and gain their freedom. Dayak argued that even using the term "slaves" was a mischaracterization of history, and of the racial situation in the present. They were "more domestic servants than slaves. Their descendants are the black-skinned Tuareg that we find amongst us today." For Dayak, "[t]he theme of slavery has been, and continues to be, used to stir up the hatred of the people of the South against us. The harsh policy which the governments of Mali and Niger have adopted towards the Tuareg represents nothing more than the continuation of vengeance. They … speak to us again and again about this past in which they were the servants and we were the masters."[8]

The writers of the anti-Tuareg pamphlet had an answer to claims made by those like Dayak: "Co-citizens of the North, let us sweep all of the nomadic presence from our towns and villages, from our lands, even the uncultivated lands! Tomorrow the nomads will settle there as a dominating people. Black sedentary peoples, from Nioro to Meneka, let

[7] Anonymous, "La Voix du Nord, no. 00" (no date). See also Hélène Claudot-Hawad, "Touaregs au Mali: 'Négrafricanisme' et racisme," *Le Monde diplomatique* (April 1995): 30.

[8] Dayak, *Touareg*, 21–2.

us organize ourselves, and let us arm ourselves for the great battle which is brewing. Let us drive the nomads back into the sands of the Azawad." To end the rebellion, the pamphlet writers proposed a full race war: "The only way to put an end to the war is for the black sedentary peoples to rise against the nomads. The authorities and the military know it. The nomads know it also ... We must not be naïve. The white Tamachek are not our 'brothers.' They know it and we know it."[9]

I began the research for this book in 1999, four years after the end of the Tuareg Rebellion. At that time, it seemed to me that racial language and racial tension permeated social intercourse in northern Mali. People used racial labels to talk about themselves and others as a matter of course. Yet it was the competing claims of racial oppression that struck me as especially ubiquitous. Understanding why racial arguments were so common in political contexts became a focus of my research. As the following story of my visit to a village called Tin Aicha indicates, finding answers to my questions was far from straightforward.

I visited Tin Aicha in the course of oral research that I carried out in the autumn of 2002. It is a small settlement on the north shore of a large seasonal lake called Lake Faguibine (approximately 100 km west of Timbuktu). I went there to investigate an ongoing conflict over land ownership. I had been given the names of two individuals who lived in the town: a "white" Tuareg man and the "black" chief of the village who was identified to me as a "bellah," a term used to refer to people of slave origin in Tuareg society (and whom I will call "bellah-iklan," combining the Songhay and Tamashek terms for this status category). These two men, I was told, would be able to give me the different perspectives on problems associated with land tenure.

Tin Aicha is an otherwise unremarkable place of sand dunes, acacia trees, sheep, goats, and scattered compounds with straw shelters and the rare adobe structure. In good years, Lake Faguibine fills with water from the annual rise of the Niger River floodwaters. When this happens, the land in the lake basin becomes agriculturally rich and can be farmed. In the early years of the colonial occupation in the 1890s, French officials considered the region to be the breadbasket of northern Mali, its grain markets the most important in the subregion. But when I visited, many decades had passed since the lake had last filled with enough water to reach the shores of Tin Aicha; instead of crops, the lake bed was thickly covered with trees and bushes. Located in the high Sahel, the land is

[9] "Voix du Nord."

barely able to support a sparse population engaged mostly in a pastoral economy across the hot, dry sands that stretch between Timbuktu to the east and the Mauritanian border 150 km to the west. The people who live in Tin Aicha speak Tamashek, the Berber language of the Tuareg people in northern Mali. But whereas the village is linguistically homogeneous, it is divided racially. The majority of villagers are black, although there is a significant minority who are Tuareg of noble – or at least nonslave – descent. They consider themselves, and are recognized by most others in northern Mali, to be nonblack; depending on the language being used, they describe themselves, and are described, as white or red.[10]

When I arrived in the village, I found my way to the home of the village chief. Word of my arrival spread and soon everyone with a local political interest came to see what had brought me to the village. That I was a researcher and not a development worker caused some disappointment, but as the issues of my research were revealed in the ensuing discussion, interest increased and I became embroiled in a heated conversation with several of the white Tuareg about the "traditional rights" of land ownership in the area. My main interlocutor turned out to be the man I had been directed to meet. He was a retired teacher who had settled in the village and become something of a local historian and political agitator on behalf of his faction of the community. At one point, he invited me to come with him to his home so that he could show me some of the historical materials he had collected.

At his house, he showed me an array of documents in French and Arabic relating to the history of his community – the Kel Entsar – as well as copies of colonial documents relating to land tenure, relations with other groups, and copies of letters and petitions he had written to Malian governmental authorities concerning various grievances. He showed me an incomplete history of the Kel Entsar that he was himself writing, and I offered him some advice on where he might find additional sources that would interest him. The combination of material was not at all unusual for someone in his position. The documents that were of most interest to him, however, were colonial conventions drawn up by the French administration to regulate rights to land in the fertile basin of Lake Faguibine. He had several of these and he wanted my assistance in helping him locate others. We both knew that in these conventions, the

[10] Throughout the book, I will often use the terms "black," "white," and "race." It will be understood, I hope, that even when not indicated by quotation marks or parentheses, these terms are not meant as objective descriptors of physical or "racial" difference, but as social and cultural constructions.

French colonial state had assigned the land rights of the northern half of Lake Faguibine, including the land around the village of Tin Aicha, to the Tuareg nobles of the Kel Entsar. Slaves – or bellah-iklan – who until the very end of the colonial period remained in servile relationships with their Tuareg masters and overlords, provided the labor. The colonial state and Tuareg political leaders made it impossible for the bellah-iklan to own land because of their status as slaves. The retired teacher hoped that through his campaign he would be able to reclaim the agricultural land of Tin Aicha for his community, not so that they could work it but in order to return to a sharecropping relationship with bellah-iklan who would farm it for them. The great act of treachery in the teacher's eyes lay at the feet of the "black" Malian government that had turned the land around Tin Aicha over to a group of bellah-iklan in the first place, thus depriving his community of its "traditional" rights and undermining the natural social hierarchy in Tuareg society.

When I was later able to interview the village chief, he told a different story. In his version of events, the land around Tin Aicha had been unoccupied when bellah-iklan, displaced by the Sahelian famine of 1973, had first settled there in 1976. No one owned the land then. The Malian government, with the assistance of an American Quaker nongovernmental organization had rightly given them access to the unused land and supported the new settlement by providing seeds and livestock, and by building a school and a health center. The village chief employed the commonly understood agriculturalist version of traditional land tenure rights in northern Mali by claiming that since the bellah-iklan were the cultivators who had put the land into use, it belonged to them. These bellah-iklan, he claimed, were not the former slaves of the noble Tuareg in the village; they had full rights to the land as freemen. The village chief told me that the white Tuareg had only arrived in the village after the end of the Tuareg Rebellion, and they had been attempting to dispossess the local black inhabitants of their land ever since. They had also been trying to unseat the local black officeholders such as the village chief and mayor. Accordingly, these particular Tuareg had absolutely no legitimate claim on the land because they were from a different area and had only come to Tin Aicha after a disagreement with their fellows hundreds of kilometers away.

It was not uncommon in my research to encounter conflicting local accounts of the past and differing claims of grievance and traditional rights. But when I was later able to investigate the history of the Tin Aicha settlement, I discovered that the initial settlers who had been given land in the reconstituted village were mostly white Tuareg who had been living in a local government-run camp for famine victims since 1973. According to a report by the American Quaker organization that had financed the Tin Aicha resettlement project, only 8 of the 200 families settled in the village and living there by 1978 were bellah-iklan.[11] The Tin Aicha project was conceived of as a means of sedentarizing seminomadic pastoralists and putting them to work as farmers – goals shared by the Malian government and international development organizations at the time (and since). The report on the project suggested that the destitute settlers had begun to undertake agriculture for the first time in their lives – work that was dishonorable for them in their cultural terms. However, the hoped-for transformation of these pastoralists into sedentary farmers proved illusory. It turned out that they approached farming as only a necessary evil required of them until they could reconstitute animal stocks and return to their former pastoralist lifestyle. When that happened, most of them left Tin Aicha or found bellah-iklan who would sharecrop the agricultural land for them. When the civil war started in the early 1990s, the whole population was forced to flee from the sedentary villages of the Lake Faguibine region.

At the time that I visited Tin Aicha, I failed to understand something that was very important: the racial tensions there were not the product of changed relations between former masters and former slaves; instead, they pitted people who shared no long-term personal connections with each another. Both the black bellah-iklan and the white Tuareg in Tin Aicha made racial arguments in which they presented themselves as the victims of racism. For my bellah-iklan interlocutor, the Tuareg are racists because they perceive and treat blacks as socially inferior, servile, and as slaves by nature. Their true goal is the resubjugation of black people as workers and servants. Their actions in Tin Aicha proved the truth of this yet again. For the white Tuareg teacher, on the other hand, the postcolonial government of Mali, which he described as controlled by blacks for the interests of blacks, had dispossessed his people because they are not black. The Malian government had given land to people of slave origin, and more recently had sought to exterminate or expel his people during the Tuareg Rebellion in the first half of the 1990s. These arguments, made in the small village of Tin Aicha, are instances of much wider uses of racial ideas across northern Mali, in which competing narratives of

[11] The American Friends Service Committee, *Tin Aicha, Nomad Village* (Philadelphia: American Friends Service Committee, 1982), 62.

racial oppression animate social and political relationships and undergird different moral orders.

My visit to Tin Aicha exposed for me the problem of trying to draw too close a connection between a particular local history of relations between groups of people over generations and the articulation of racial arguments. This may appear an elementary sort of problem for historians of race in the United States, where dislocation, migration, and industrialization went hand in hand with the development of racial formation. At the beginning of my research I had hoped to use microhistories of relations between particular groups of people over time as a way of tracing the emergence of racial ideas and racial identities, especially among former slaves and their former masters. But the problem that the Tin Aicha case highlights is that racial arguments are, almost by definition, abstractions that do not adhere well to real places and real people. Race works instead as an argument about the world, as a moral ordering device, even at times as a way of conjuring a utopian vision; it does not work nearly as well in organizing the details of individual relationships. It is precisely the abstractness of race that makes it so effective because it is not easily susceptible to empirical disproof, and it can coexist with social relations that belie the premises of different racial arguments.

This book traces the development of arguments about race in one place along the edge of the Sahara Desert in West Africa over centuries. It demonstrates the ways in which these ideas were deployed by people in this region, and it reveals some of the social, economic, and political "work" that race was made to perform in different contexts. It is, therefore, a book about the particular configurations of the abstraction of race along the West African Sahel, and the concrete effects that racial arguments have had on the social relations of the people who have lived in this place.

WHY RACE?

The use of the term "race" to describe non-European constructions of human difference, especially prior to European colonial expansion, may cause some readers pause. One possible objection is based on the idea that the term "race," or some cognate in local vocabularies, must be present in order to carry the meaning of the modern ideas of racism. There is no meta-term in the Sahelian Arabic sources that I will use in this book, or a particular treatise that I can point to, that clearly articulates a theoretical framework of such a term. In different contexts, certain words (Ar. qawm, qabīla, ʿirq) stand for race, but there was no Arthur de Gobineau or Herbert Spencer of the West African Sahel. However, such an objection is really just a form of nominalism. As David Nirenberg has pointed out, it is as if, in a European context, one were to argue "that because the word *Rasse* did not enter German until the eighteenth century and the word *Anti-Semitismus* until the nineteenth, we need not look for these concepts in the earlier history of German-speaking lands." The nominalist challenge is similar to objections based on narrow definitions of race. As Nirenberg puts it, we should not be surprised that "those who define race as the application of eighteenth- and nineteenth-century vocabularies of biological classification to human populations differentiated by skin color are certain that it cannot be found in earlier periods. Such definitions fail to make sense even of modern racial ideologies, which are themselves not only tremendously diverse but also change a great deal over time."[12]

The common problem with objections based on single terms or narrow definitions based on a modern Western idea of race is that they rest on a fiction that there is a coherent model in European racial thought with which to compare ideas about race elsewhere. Every serious scholar who has attempted to trace the historical development of racial thought in Europe has shown just how diverse these ideas have been.[13] The notion of race has become far too attached to one particular set of historical concepts – that of nineteenth- and twentieth-century "scientific" models of race – as if these were its only "true" manifestation and should somehow be equated with a universal race theory.[14] Even in Europe, racial thought was never especially coherent. At its zenith in the second half of the nineteenth century, famous writers on race such as Gobineau and Paul Broca argued for completely different sets of ideas about what race was and what it meant, disagreeing fundamentally about racial mixing and its consequences. It is just empirically untrue that there was ever a single coherent form of racial thought that could stand as a nominal model for what "real racial thought" is.

[12] David Nirenberg, "Race and the Middle Ages: The Case of Spain and Its Jews," in *Rereading the Black Legend: The Discourses of Religious and Racial Difference in the Renaissance Empires*, ed. Margaret R. Greer, Walter D. Mignolo, and Maureen Quilligan (Chicago: University of Chicago Press, 2007), 73–4.

[13] Two of the clearest examples are Michael Banton, *Racial Theories* (Cambridge: Cambridge University Press, 1987) and Ivan Hannaford, *Race: The History of an Idea in the West* (Baltimore: The Johns Hopkins University Press, 1996).

[14] David Theo Goldberg, *Racist Culture: Philosophy and the Politics of Meaning* (Oxford: Blackwell, 1993), 41.

As Stuart Hall has pointed out, it is impossible to make sense of racial phenomena unless the historical specificity of particular instances of race is accounted for.[15] Focusing on the historicity of race means insisting that there are historically specific "racisms" rather than some singular ahistorical form, and that ideas and practices around race articulate with other social phenomena in different historical contexts. Thomas Holt has argued that "the idea that race is socially constructed implies also that it can and must be constructed differently at different historical moments and in different social contexts."[16] Etienne Balibar has made a similar point: "There is not merely a single invariant racism but a number of racisms, forming a broad, open spectrum of situations."[17]

If we take Hall, Holt, and Balibar's ideas about the historicity of race seriously, it is fairly obvious that there are many historical contexts around the world where racisms have appeared. For heuristic purposes, we can define racism as representations of human difference that posit a direct connection between physical and mental qualities that are constant and unalterable by human will, based on hereditary factors or external influences such as climate or geography.[18] To quote David Nirenberg again, "all racisms are attempts to ground discriminations, whether social, economic, or religious, in biology and reproduction. All claim a congruence of 'cultural' categories with 'natural' ones. None of these claims, not even the most 'scientific' ones of the twentieth century, reflects biological reality."[19] Using these criteria, we encounter ideas about race in premodern China, India, the Muslim-ruled Middle East, and medieval Europe (especially Iberia).[20] These ideas can be easily

[15] Stuart Hall, "Race, Articulation and Societies Structured in Dominance," in *Race Critical Theories: Text and Context*, ed. Philomena Essed and David Theo Goldberg (Malden, MA: Blackwell, 2002), 38–68. Cited in Holt, *Problem of Race*, 20–1.

[16] Holt, *Problem of Race*, 21.

[17] Etienne Balibar, "Racism and Nationalism," in *Race, Nation, Class: Ambiguous Identities*, ed. Etienne Balibar and Immanuel Wallerstein (New York: Verso, 1991), 40. This passage is cited in Eve Troutt Powell, *A Different Shade of Colonialism: Egypt, Great Britain, and the Mastery of the Sudan* (Berkeley: University of California Press, 2003), 16.

[18] Benjamin Isaac, *The Invention of Racism in Classical Antiquity* (Princeton, NJ: Princeton University Press, 2004), 23.

[19] Nirenberg, "Race and the Middle Ages," 74.

[20] Peter Robb, "Introduction: South Asia and the Concept of Race," in *The Concept of Race in South Asia*, ed. Robb (Delhi: Oxford University Press, 1995), 75; Bernard Lewis, *Race and Slavery in the Middle East: An Historical Enquiry* (New York: Oxford University Press, 1992), 42; Frank Dikötter, *The Discourse of Race in Modern China* (Stanford, CA: Stanford University Press, 1992), 1–30; Pamela Kyle Crossley, *Orphan Warriors: Three Manchu Generations and the End of the Qing World* (Princeton, NJ: Princeton University Press, 1990), 5; Kyle Crossley, *A Translucent Mirror: History and Identity in Qing*

compared to the earliest western European racial theories that used race to indicate differences of lineage, tribe, ethnicity, caste, religion, or even "nation."[21] Even before the cognate for the word "race" entered European languages beginning in the thirteenth century in Southern Europe – and not until the sixteenth century in the case of English – what we might call proto-racial ideas were clearly present in notions of outsider groups, among which the Jews were the most prominent.[22] According to Benjamin Isaac's study of racism in antiquity, classical Greek and Latin sources often "attribute to groups of people common characteristics considered to be unalterable because they are determined by external factors or heredity." Isaac calls this "proto-racism" and he finds it to be extremely widespread.[23]

There is perhaps a danger in subsuming too many things under the single label of race. Would it not be better to rely on context-specific terminology? For example, in the Indian case, the Sanskrit term "varna" can be glossed as a marker of differences of skin color and caste.[24] Closer to the concerns of this book, a number of anthropologists of Mauritania prefer to use the Arabic term "bidan," which literally means "whites," to refer to arabophone Mauritanians, rather than invoke the terminology of color and racial difference embedded in the terminology. This can certainly be justified on emic grounds, but very often its purpose is really to obscure for readers the extent to which racial categories are central to

Imperial Ideology (Berkeley: University of California Press, 1999), 14; Jonathan Elukin, "From Jew to Christian? Conversion and Immutability in Medieval Europe," in *Varieties of Religious Conversion in the Middle Ages*, ed. James Muldoon (Gainsville: University of Florida Press, 1997), 171–89; Nirenberg, "Race and the Middle Ages."

[21] See, for example, David Theo Goldberg, "The Semantics of Race," *Ethnic and Racial Studies* 15, no. 4 (1992): 545; Banton, *Racial Theories*, 1–27; E.J. Hobsbawm, *Nations and Nationalism since 1780. Programme, Myth, Reality* (Cambridge: Cambridge University Press, 1992), 65; Pierre H. Boulle, "François Bernier and the Origins of the Modern Concept of Race," in *The Color of Liberty: Histories of Race in France*, ed. Sue Peabody and Tyler Stovall (Durham, NC: Duke University Press, 2003), 12; Charles de Miramon, "Noble Dogs, Noble Blood: The Invention of the Concept of Race in the Late Middle Ages," in *The Origins of Racism in the West*, ed. Miriam Eliav-Feldon, Benjamin Isaac, and Joseph Ziegler (Cambridge: Cambridge University Press, 2009), 215–16.

[22] The Jews are not the only group targeted by this kind of discourse. See, for example, David Goldenburg, *The Curse of Ham: Race and Slavery in Early Judaism, Christianity, and Islam* (Princeton, NJ: Princeton University Press, 2003); John Block Friedman, *The Monstrous Races in Medieval Art and Thought* (Syracuse, NY: Syracuse University Press, 2000).

[23] Isaac, *Invention of Racism*, 38.

[24] John Brockington, "Concepts of Race in the Mahābhārata and Rāmāyana," in *The Concept of Race in South Asia*, ed. Peter Robb (Delhi: Oxford University Press, 1995), 97–108; Romila Thapar, "The Image of the Barbarian in Early India," *CSSH* 13, no. 4 (1971): 408–36.

Mauritanian (or South Asian?) social life.[25] It is of course appropriate to ground particular histories of race in specific, emic accounts of human difference. This is certainly a goal of this book. But it is equally important that the particularity of the case not prevent an analysis of the social work that these ideas perform in the context in which they arise. As such, I use the term race throughout this book where it is analytically appropriate. This fulfills a heuristic value for readers and it makes historical comparison more feasible. There are many particularities to the ways that race works in the West African Sahel, but there are also a surprising number of similarities with other racial formations. My insistence on the use of the term race is designed to help the reader understand where local ideas articulate with wider social phenomena.

It is, I think, almost unnecessary to point out that ideas of race, in whatever form, are constructions of human culture and not an objective reality. Racial ideas are false categorizations because they yoke together much that is dissimilar on the basis of a little that is more or less the same.[26] But these ideas often do reflect something that is recognizably true – often phenotypic differences in skin color – which, although obviously not determinate of moral behavior in any way, provide a foundational basis for the larger constructions of cultural meaning that coalesce to this difference. It would be very difficult to imagine that the historical interactions between North and West Africans along the Sahel, and for that matter on the other side of the Sahara Desert in North Africa, would not have been understood in terms of some form of difference associated with the obvious variations in physical appearance. What is important, though, is not the recognition of difference, but the ways in which it was constructed and reconstructed over time, and the historically specific effects that this had on particular social relationships.

There is an old debate in the historiography of slavery and race in the Americas about whether European racism toward Africans preceded New World slavery or vice versa. In 1944, Eric Williams famously wrote that "Slavery was not born of racism; rather, racism was the consequence of slavery."[27] But the interesting question is surely not just one of

[25] Somewhat absurdly, when using the term "bidan" as an ethnic name, referring to speakers of Hassaniyya Arabic, the former slaves of the bidan are included despite racial markers used to distinguish them from the bidan. For example, Mariella Villasante-de Beauvais, *Parenté et politique en Mauritanie: Essai d'Anthropologie historique. Le devenir contemporain des Ahl Sîdi Mahmûd, confédération bidân de l'Assâba* (Paris: L'Harmattan, 1998), 240.

[26] Robb, "Introduction," 75–6.

[27] Eric Williams, *Capitalism and Slavery* (New York: Capricorn Books, 1965), 7.

origins; all agree that Europeans held negative and prejudicial views of Africans before New World slavery and that such attitudes were intensified by slavery. The important issue concerns the understanding of how the interaction between racial attitudes and structures of power and exploitation worked to produce more elaborate racial ideologies.[28] I have found Thomas Holt's work especially helpful in formulating this idea:

> Recognizing the relative plasticity of race and racism as concepts and their parasitic and chameleonlike qualities in practice, I have suggested that we might do better not to try to define or catalogue their content. Rather, our task might be instead to ask what work race does.... In doing its 'work' race articulates with (in the sense of relating to) and sometimes articulates for (in the sense of speaking for) other social phenomena, like class, gender, and nationality. And through that articulation – in all its forms – it often achieves social effects that mask its own presence, or the presence of other forces, like class.[29]

For the societies of the African Sahel that are the subject of this book, I do not have the luxury of putting aside the task of cataloging the content of racial ideas and the ways in which they adhere to larger systems of thought in that region, because this research has yet to be done. As such, this book will analyze both the intellectual history of the development of racial ideas and then, following Holt, explain some of the social "work" that racial ideas were made to perform.

To address the danger of invoking race so often and in such a diverse array of settings that the term is diluted into meaninglessness, I have been careful to distinguish racial ideas – and the reasons they develop – from ideas about alterity that do not do any obvious social work. As I have argued, there are a large number of historical settings in which perceptions of difference that include proto-racial qualities can be found. However, it is only when these ideas are made to do concrete social work that I think it is appropriate to invoke what Michael Omi and Howard Winant call "racial formation": "[R]ace is a matter of both social structure and cultural representation. Too often, the attempt is made to understand race simply or primarily in terms of only one of these two analytical dimensions." What Omi and Winant call "racial projects" connect "what race means in a particular discursive practice and the ways in which both social structures and everyday experiences are racially organized, based

[28] Banton, *Racial Theories*, 10.

[29] Holt, *Problem of Race*, 27.

upon that meaning."[30] This book explores the various racial projects in the history of the West African Sahel. I am not simply looking for representations of difference, but also for the consequences of those ideas.

In the non-European cases of race discussed earlier, it is only appropriate to talk about a racial formation in contexts where ideas about race came to play an important role in ideologies of domination. In precolonial India, the ideologies of caste structure possessed a "race-like essentialism" that codified social hierarchy.[31] The first explicitly racial constructions of barbarians in China occurred as a reaction to Mongol rule (1279–1368), and were, in a sense, ideologies of resistance to the subjugation felt by intellectuals under foreign rule.[32] Conversely, the establishment of Qing rule in China in the seventeenth century was buttressed by racial ideas about lineage that came to function as an ideology of a conquest state.[33] In the Muslim-ruled Middle East, an identification of blackness with certain forms of slavery developed very early, naturalizing this connection to the extent that the word for slaves (Ar. ʿabīd) came to be applied to all black people, whatever their status, in some Arabic dialects.[34] In each of these cases, historically specific racisms emerged before significant European interventions. These ideas of race did not disappear as the influence of European power and ideas were brought to bear on these regions. They did change, "grafting the new onto the old,"[35] but in

30 Michael Omi and Howard Winant, *Racial Formation in the United States: From the 1960s to the 1990s*, second edition (New York: Routledge, 1994), 56.

31 Robb, "Introduction," 61; The connection between race and caste in precolonial India is contentious in large part because this was the interpretation of many British colonial ethnographers in the nineteenth century. See Susan Bayly, "Caste and Race in the Colonial Ethnography of India," in *The Concept of Race in South Asia*, ed. Peter Robb (Delhi: Oxford University Press, 1995), 165–218; and Crispin Bates, "Race, Caste and Tribe in Central India: The Early Origins of Indian Anthropometry," in *The Concept of Race in South Asia*, ed. Peter Robb (Delhi: Oxford University Press, 1995), 219–59. Among the most prominent scholars who have challenged the idea that caste was a basic tenet of precolonial India are Ronald Inden, *Imagining India* (London: Basil Blackwell, 1990); Bernard Cohn, *Colonialism and its Forms of Knowledge: The British in India* (Princeton, NJ: Princeton University Press, 1996), 16–56; Nicholas Dirks, *Castes of Mind: Colonialism and the Making of Modern India* (Princeton, NJ: Princeton University Press, 2001), 5.

32 Dikötter, *Discourse of Race*, 23–4.

33 Pamela Kyle Crossley, "Thinking about Ethnicity in Early Modern China," *Late Imperial China* 11, no. 1 (June 1990): 1–35.

34 Lewis, *Race and Slavery*, 56. See also Chouki El Hamel, "'Race', Slavery and Islam in Maghribi Mediterranean Thought: The Question of the Haratin in Morocco," *Journal of North African Studies* 7, no. 3 (2002): 29–52; Powell, *Different Shade*.

35 Holt, *Problem of Race*, 20.

many places, including Sahelian West Africa, what was new looked an awful lot like what it was supposed to have replaced.

COLONIALISM AND AFRICAN IDENTITY

I certainly do not wish to imply by this line of argument that the impacts of modern European ideas about race on other, non-European constructions of difference have been anything but profound. But the borrowings from Europeans were not mere imitations. In many colonial situations, a language of race was shared by both colonizer and colonized, albeit in different configurations and meanings for each. Race often functioned as a convenient and available shared idiom, which each side believed to have in common. Borrowing occurred in both directions, imbuing local notions of race with European ideas and influencing European colonial constructions of knowledge about the culture and social structure of the colonized society. One way of thinking about the process whereby colonized people picked up European theories of race is in terms of what Mary Louise Pratt calls "transculturation," in which "members of subordinated or marginal groups select and invent from materials transmitted by a dominant or metropolitan culture."[36] But I also insist that colonial encounter was productive of novelty on both sides, and that European discourses of race in this case were influenced by the dialogues and cross-cultural engagements that accompanied the exercise of colonial power.[37]

Despite the absorption of some European ideas about race during the colonial period and afterward, it is difficult to avoid the impression that Sahelian racial discourses remain, in content and idiom, fundamentally African. I argue in this book that the racial arguments deployed in the contemporary Sahel are much closer to local eighteenth- and nineteenth-century formulations than to twentieth-century European racial frameworks. This, it seems to me, poses a problem for some of the generalizations found in the Africanist literature about the relative newness of ethnic and racial categories in colonial Africa. Rather than look for the construction or invention of racial categories by European colonial officials, this book makes the argument that a particular configuration of race existed in the Sahel long before the arrival of Europeans. The importance of race in the

[36] Mary Louise Pratt, *Imperial Eyes: Travel Writing and Transculturation* (London: Routledge, 1992), 6.

[37] Tony Ballantyne, *Orientalism and Race: Aryanism in the British Empire* (New York: Palgrave, 2002), 4.

colonial Sahel must be understood as the outcome not of a new colonial discourse about race, but as the result of new kinds of dialogue and negotiation that invoked race between French officials and Africans, and between local Africans themselves in the new circumstances of colonial rule. One of the questions that this book sets out to answer is precisely how that dialogue proceeded, and with what stakes.

Much intellectual labor has been exhausted since the rise of anticolonial nationalism in dissecting the various forms of the colonial state in Africa and Asia. Over the last several decades, the attention of many writers interested in the areas formerly ruled by European empires has focused on the problematic of knowledge. This is due in large part to the economic and political crises that developed in many postcolonial countries in the 1970s and 1980s, and their perceived failures to live up to the promises of independence. The renewed attention to the impact of colonialism led to presentations of a much stronger colonial state than had hitherto been described in the tradition of older liberal or nationalist historiographies.[38] This new state was envisioned as a far more powerful hegemon than before, and historians began to focus on themes such as the production of colonial knowledge, which was increasingly understood to be a fundamental component of colonial power. Writers on India such as Bernard Cohn, Ronald Inden, and Nicholas Dirks argued that nineteenth-century European ethnographers, philologists, and officials had constructed a ludicrously flawed understanding of India based on structures of caste that served the British project of colonial domination. To "know" India in the "scientific" European sense was to subjugate it; to name and classify its castes was to fragment a complex and dynamic society and to reinvent it.[39] Dirks, for example, acknowledged that caste was an important part of Indian social organization before the arrival of Europeans in South Asia, but he wrote that:

> [I]t was under the British that "caste" became a single term capable of expressing, organizing, and above all "systematizing" India's diverse forms of social identity, community, and organization. This was achieved through an identifiable (if contested) ideological canon as the result of a concrete encounter with colonial

[38] Tony Ballantyne, "Rereading the Archive and Opening up the Nation-State: Colonial Knowledge in South Asia (and Beyond)" in *After the Imperial Turn. Thinking with and through the Nation*, ed. Antoinette Burton (Durham, NC: Duke University Press, 2003), 103–4; Frederick Cooper, "Conflict and Connection: Rethinking Colonial African History," *AHR* 99, no. 5 (1994): 1516–45.

[39] Cohn, *Colonialism*; Inden, *Imagining India*; See the discussion of these writers in: Bayly, "Caste," 165–6.

modernity during two hundred years of British domination. In short, colonialism made caste what it is today.[40]

Writers on Africa have often gone even further in their arguments about the colonial construction – or invention – of ethnicities (or "tribalism" as it is sometimes termed). New colonial-era "tribal" or ethnic categories, it is suggested, transformed much more fluid and flexible identities of precolonial times into rigid and essentialized categories that lay at the basis of colonial control.[41] Whether in the realm of caste or ethnicity, the colonial state has often been endowed with transformative power in ascribing subjectivities to those it ruled.

There are a number of problems with these formulations, starting with the overstatement of the discursive unity of colonial knowledge, which was, in fact, a much more variegated project with many different strands of thought and knowledge production in the European metropole and in the colonies themselves.[42] Concrete differences often separated the types of knowledge produced in European salons from the formulations of colonial officers, missionaries, and ethnologists on the ground, who, in their desire to find local collaborators, identified and constructed groups of people (often local rulers or nobles) who were seen as exceptions to broader orientalist knowledge because of their perceived or potential "affinities" to Europeans.[43] This occurred along the African Sahel where French administrators identified very strongly with Arab and Tuareg nobles whose "quasi-feudal" social structures, they thought, recalled a lost European past.[44] But even with a more complicated understanding of

[40] Dirks, *Castes of Mind*, 5.

[41] The seminal work on this theme is Terence Ranger, "The Invention of Tradition in Colonial Africa" in *The Invention of Tradition*, ed. Eric Hobsbawm and Ranger (Cambridge: Cambridge University Press, 1983), 211–62. See also Jean-Loup Amselle, *Mestizo Logics: Anthropology of Identity in Africa and Elsewhere*, trans. Claudia Royal (Stanford, CA: Stanford University Press, 1998), 11–12; and Mahmood Mamdani, *Citizen and Subject: Contemporary Africa and the Legacy of Late Colonialism* (Princeton, NJ: Princeton University Press, 1996), 41, 184–5.

[42] David Ludden, "Orientalist Empiricism: Transformations of Colonial Knowledge," in *Orientalism and the Postcolonial Predicament: Perspectives on South Asia*, ed. Carol Breckenridge and Peter van der Veer (Philadelphia: University of Pennsylvania Press, 1993), 250–78; Thomas Trautmann, *Aryans and British India* (Berkeley: University of California Press, 1997), 21–24.

[43] Andrew Barnes, "Aryanizing Projects, African 'Collaborators,' and Colonial Transcripts," in *Antinomies of Modernity: Essays on Race, Orient, Nation*, ed. Vasant Kaiwar and Sucheta Mazumdar (Durham, NC: Duke University Press, 2003), 63–6.

[44] Philippe Loiseau, "L'administration et les rapports nomades/sedentaires," in *Nomades et commandantes. Administration et sociétés nomades dans l'ancienne A.O.F.*, ed. Edmund Bernus, Pierre Boilley, Jean Clauzel, and Jean-Louis Triaud (Paris: Karthala, 1993), 164.

the variety of producers of colonial knowledge, the models of "invented tradition" are not sufficient for understanding the intellectual histories that lay behind these conceptual changes. As Jonathon Glassman suggests, there is a tendency in some of this literature to portray "a one-sided, unidirectional process, in which Europeans 'invented' rigid ethnic categories" that colonized people accepted, "abandoning their older, more flexible conceptions of identity."[45]

One solution to this problem has been to focus on the role of local intellectuals in formulating and propagating new ideas about ethnicity. Although still giving primary place to the colonial state and its agents as the ultimate instruments that provoked change, attention has been paid to the ways that European constructions of ethnic or tribal categories were taken up by members of these "newly" defined communities in shaping and popularizing them. Thus, as John Iliffe famously puts it, "Europeans believed Africans belonged to tribes; Africans built tribes to belong to."[46] Faced with the social and cultural upheavals of colonial occupation, with European codifications of tribal custom in the structures of native rule, and with the examples of nationalism outside of the continent, African intellectuals shaped new ethnic frameworks out of the cultural raw material of their past. These new ethnicities proved useful for those who held "traditional" offices in the colonial structures of indirect rule, and for ordinary people in helping to structure long-distance migration and to ensure control (for men) over land and women left behind.[47] The most sophisticated works on ethnic change have sought to go beyond the realm of intellectuals and trace the ways in which these

[45] Jonathon Glassman, "Sorting out the Tribes: the Creation of Racial Identities in Colonial Zanzibar's Newspaper Wars," *JAH* 41 (2000): 397–8ff. Glassman discusses Terence Ranger's evaluation of some of the shortcomings in the "invention of tradition" literature that he is closely associated with ("The invention of tradition revisited: the case of colonial Africa," in *Legitimacy and the State in Twentieth Century Africa: Essays in Honour of A.H.M. Kirk-Greene*, ed. Ranger and Olufemi Vaughan [London: Mcmillan, 1993], 62–111).

[46] John Iliffe, *A Modern History of Tanganyika* (New York: Cambridge University Press, 1979), 324.

[47] Leroy Vail, "Introduction: Ethnicity in Southern African History," in *The Creation of Tribalism in Southern Africa*, ed. Vail (London: J. Currey, 1989), 14–15. See also Thomas Spear, "Introduction," in *Being Maasai: Ethnicity and Identity in East Africa*, ed. Spear and Richard Waller (London: J. Currey, 1993), 13–14; John Lonsdale, "The Moral Economy of Mau Mau," in *Unhappy Valley, Book 2: Violence and Ethnicity*, ed. Bruce Berman and Lonsdale (London: J. Currey, 1992). On the transformations in "native law," see Martin Chanock, *Law, Custom, and Social Order: The Colonial Experience in Malawi and Zambia* (Cambridge: Cambridge University Press, 1985).

constructions of ethnicity circulated in the larger population, and how the ideas introduced by literate intellectuals were selected, modified, internalized, and transformed.[48] What is sometimes called "identity formation" is understood by most Africanist historians as essentially instrumental, constructed to meet immediate social needs rising out of colonial rule.

Of course, many configurations of ethnicity in Africa can be traced to the colonial period. The construction of colonial knowledge did sometimes provoke a feedback effect whereby Africans themselves appropriated European ideas for their own purposes.[49] Mary Louise Pratt calls this process "autoethnography," in which "colonized subjects undertake to represent themselves in ways that engage with the colonizer's own terms."[50] But to insist on an exclusively instrumentalist approach and on constructions of ethnic belonging that draw much of their logic from the classifications and racial essentialism of the exercise of colonial power creates an overly sharp dichotomy between precolonial Africa characterized by "flexibility" and "pluralism" and the "rigidities" of colonial identities.[51] The unitary discursive power of the colonial state has been overstated, and as such, the discursive continuity – or cultural content – of African arguments about social categories, including the passage between the precolonial and colonial situation, has been downplayed if not ignored altogether.[52] The important point here is that Africans brought rich vocabularies and developed concepts about the social world in which they lived into their relationships with Europeans, just as colonial officials carried a late-nineteenth century conceptual vocabulary of race, nation, and tribe. It was around the concepts that each side thought they shared in common that the most productive initial dialogue occurred. Of course, with time, both colonizer and colonized became more familiar with each other's

[48] Glassman, "Sorting out the Tribes," 400; Steven Feierman, *Peasant Intellectuals: Anthropology and History in Tanzania* (Madison, WI: University of Wisconsin Press, 1990); Richard Waller, "Acceptees and Aliens: Kikuyu Settlement in Maasailand," in *Being Maasai: Ethnicity and Identity in East Africa*, ed. Thomas Spear and Waller (London: J. Currey, 1993), 226–57; Derek Peterson, *Creative Writing: Translation, Bookkeeping, and the Work of Imagination in Colonial Kenya* (Portsmouth, NH, Heinemann, 2004).

[49] Amselle, *Mestizo Logics*, 16.

[50] Pratt, *Imperial Eyes*, 7.

[51] Glassman, "Sorting out the Tribes," 402–3.

[52] On this point, see Thomas Spear, "Neotraditionalism and the Limits of Invention in British Colonial Africa," *JAH* 44 (2003): 3–27; Carolyn Hamilton, *Terrific Majesty: The Powers of Shaka Zulu and the Limits of Historical Invention* (Cambridge, MA: Harvard University Press, 1998), 3–4; Paul Nugent, "Putting the History Back into Ethnicity: Enslavement, Religion, and Cultural Brokerage in the Construction of Mandinka/Jola and Ewe/Agotime Identities in West Africa, c. 1650–1930," *CSSH* 50, no. 4 (2008): 920–48.

conceptual language and framework, and this aided in communication and assimilation of the other's ideas. But it would be a big mistake not to recognize that this was a two-way process, and that European constructions of knowledge about African people evolved as a result.

The part of this book that deals with the colonial era focuses on the relationships and dialogue that occurred between French colonial officials and Africans, and between Africans themselves in the Niger Bend region of what is today northern Mali. It insists that the production of colonial knowledge and the shifts and evolution of ideas about race occurred in this space, as collaboration and negotiation. Colonial rule rested on an ability to obtain information about not only the nature and organization of indigenous societies, but also on the political machinations of local people. For this, the French administration relied on local structures of authority and networks of intellectual production that existed in the Niger Bend before the arrival of Europeans, and that carried over, more or less intact, into the colonial period. This was a partially literate society; existing communities of knowledge, styles of reasoned debate, and patterns of social communication, to borrow C.A. Bayly's phrasing, largely determined the reception and diffusion of European and African ideas.[53] Many people in the Niger Bend were, like in so many other parts of Asia and Africa, "literacy aware."[54] I mean by this that the number of people who participated in larger intellectual conversations connected to literacy was much higher than the five to ten percent of the population that could read and write. As such, even the form of most of the correspondence during the colonial period between the French administration and Africans followed northern Malian idioms and used Arabic. In this book, I will use some of these sources to show how people in the Niger Bend deployed racial arguments with each other and with the agents of the colonial state, and how these ideas changed in the process.

BEYOND IDENTITY

The concept of identity played an important role in the original conception of this project. In early stages of the research, I had thought that I could make the development of racial identity analogous to forms of ethnic

[53] C.A. Bayly, *Empire and Information: Intelligence Gathering and Social Communication in India, 1780–1870* (Cambridge: Cambridge University Press, 1996), 9. Closer geographically, Gregory Mann makes a similar point in *Naive Sons: West African Veterans and France in the Twentieth Century* (Durham, NC: Duke University Press, 2006), 3.

[54] Bayly, *Empire*, 39.

identity that Africanist historians tell us were so important to the negotiation of colonial rule. With time, however, I became less and less comfortable with the paradigm of identity and as such, I have chosen to approach the issue of race differently than many readers might anticipate.[55] This book is not about racial identity, but about the invocation of racial arguments. I am interested in tracing the emergence and changing structures of ideas about racial difference, and the ways in which these ideas were deployed in a variety of contexts over time in the Niger Bend to make arguments about particular social and political matters. Because I am not concerned here with racial identity per se, or the kinds of cultural practice that might go along with such a phenomenon, I am able to show the ways in which racial arguments worked as strategies and claims open to different people, rather than the sole province of specific racially identifying groups. In West Africa and elsewhere, race is an abstraction and a form of argument; it is used for specific and concrete reasons to do particular kinds of social and political work.

Many of the racial arguments discussed in this book invoke an inferiority attached to blacks. It was blackness that rendered one vulnerable to legitimate enslavement, to political domination, and to other kinds of legal disability. As I will show, such racial arguments often provoked explicitly antiracial responses; but it is nonetheless tempting to suggest that what this book seeks to explain is a structural discourse of antiblack racism over a very long period of time. I have tried to avoid posing the problem in this way because, as in possibly analogous contexts of antiblack racism in the Atlantic world and antisemitism in Europe, to do so is to risk teleology. Racial ideas about black inferiority drew their strength and power from historical invocations and enactments, not from an ahistorical structure of ideas. I have found David Nirenberg's formulation of this problem in the context of violence directed at minorities in medieval Spain to be especially helpful. He writes:

> I am not arguing that negative discourses about Jews, Muslims, women, or lepers did not exist, but that any inherited discourse about minorities acquired force only when people chose to find it meaningful and useful, and was itself reshaped by these choices. Briefly, discourse and agency gain meaning only in relation to each other. Even thus delimited, the notion of a "persecuting discourse" requires qualification. Such a discourse about minorities was but one of those available, and its invocation in a given situation did not ensure its success or acceptance. The choice of language was an active one, made in order to achieve something,

[55] See Frederick Cooper, *Colonialism in Question: Theory, Knowledge, History* (Berkeley: University of California Press, 2005), 59–90.

made within contexts of conflict and structures of domination, and often contested. Thus when medieval people made statements about the consequences of religious difference, they were making claims, not expressing accomplished reality, and these claims were subject to barter and negotiation before they could achieve real force in any given situation.[56]

Nirenberg's framework of the active choice of language – what I call argument – is central to my analysis of the history of race in the West African Sahel.

Because this is not a book about identity, I am not especially concerned with the literature on ethnicity or ethno-genesis in Africa. The criticisms of an ethnic paradigm before the advent of colonial rule, which one finds in prominent writers such as Jean-Loup Amselle, are, in effect, critiques of the anachronism of imposing models of ethnic identity and belonging on precolonial Africa. As a way of problematizing essentialized claims about ethnic identity, Amselle is quite convincing; but as an approach to the intellectual history of early colonial Africa – or precolonial Africa – his arguments are extremely impoverishing because they leave little room for the role of African ideas in the formation of colonial categories.[57] One of the most important themes of this book is that large numbers of people in West Africa drew on a wide and largely shared intellectual tradition connected to the wider world through the vehicle of Islamic learning. They made arguments drawn from this tradition that positioned and situated them in relation to the new European colonial power that burst into their lives in the nineteenth century. The Niger Bend is one of the best-endowed regions of Africa for extant written sources produced by Africans during the period before the arrival of Europeans, and under colonial rule. Using these sources, which are almost entirely written in Arabic, the Niger Bend presents an opportunity to empirically test some of these interpretations of the African past.

I have followed a methodology that focused on recovering discrete cases of racial argument in the past. Most instances that I analyze in this book were derived from written sources, in Arabic and French, produced in the Sahel. Almost all of the Arabic materials used in this book are drawn from unpublished manuscripts held in Timbuktu at the Institut des Hautes Etudes et de Recherches Islamiques – Ahmed Baba (IHERIAB). I spent almost two years living in Timbuktu, slowly working through

[56] David Nirenberg, *Communities of Violence: Persecution of Minorities in the Middle Ages* (Princeton, NJ: Princeton University Press, 1998), 6.
[57] Amselle, *Mestizo Logics*, 43–57.

the IHERIAB manuscript collection. Other historians have worked with the manuscript material from Timbuktu – most notably John Hunwick, H.T. Norris, Mahmoud Zouber, Paulo de Moraes Farias, Ismaël Diadié Haïdara, and Elias Saad, on whose works I have relied greatly – but many of the sources that form the empirical base of this book have never been discussed in published form before. Likewise, the richest and most interesting French sources were drawn from the remnants of colonial records held in local government offices in northern Mali. I was very fortunate to gain access to this material, which was almost completely unorganized. Among the things found only at this local level of the chain of colonial document production (and not at the Malian national archives or in France) was much of the correspondence between French officials and northern Malian chiefs and notables, and detailed local court records. Many Africanist historians have used similar local-level colonial materials in their research, but no one has used this northern Malian material until now. The novelty of the argument that I offer here is in large part the result of the new sources that I have been able to consult.

My reliance on written sources, especially on Arabic written sources, means that this book gives prominence of place to a particular kind of historical voice drawn from the circles of literate, Muslim scholars. I do not argue that these writers were wholly representative of the wider societies of the Sahel; indeed, Muslim intellectuals often saw themselves as distinct from the people around them. But it is important to emphasize that the racial ideas that were developed by Muslim intellectuals in the Sahel were the organic product of the wider social, political, and cultural context of that region. They were certainly not a quasi-colonial imposition of an Islamic framework upon otherwise non-Muslim Africans. There have been indigenous Muslims in the Sahel for more than a thousand years; the intellectual history of the Sahel is, first and foremost, the product of local historical dynamics in that region.

Early on in my research, I realized that relying exclusively on sources that gave access to the views of literate Muslims needed to be balanced by other voices. For this reason I learned to speak Songhay, the most important language spoken by the traditionally sedentary people of the Niger Bend. In this way, I hoped to be able to do oral research with those who were not literate in Arabic and who were labeled as blacks in manuscript sources that I had consulted. I targeted three clusters of Songhay villages for oral research (in the Serere region along the Niger east of Timbuktu, in the Kissou north of Diré, and in the Lake Faguibine basin). I cite about a dozen interviews in this book, but except for Chapter 7, they do not figure very prominently in the sources I use. Nonetheless, I consider my investment in the Songhay language, and the time and effort expended on oral sources, to have been a very valuable part of the research that I carried out. I was exposed to a set of moral arguments and idioms about land, resources, social hierarchy, and racial difference that have been very influential on the way I have read my written sources. Although there are different levels of sophistication in the ideas of the people I spoke with in my time in the Niger Bend, it became clear to me that a dichotomy between literate Muslim scholarly voices and those of the illiterate had been misconceived. I learned that many of the ideas and arguments that I encountered in written form had an oral life in the stories and debates of a wider range of people.

Much of the best research on low-status people in the Sahel has been based on ethnographic or other oral methodologies necessary to elicit the stories of the socially marginal. Throughout the book, I rely on much of this literature for the arguments that I make. But by focusing on written sources that permit analysis of the intellectual history of genealogy, slavery, and racial difference, I believe that this book is able to show the ways that these ideas developed and changed in the Sahel over a longer period of time (four centuries) than most oral methodologies permit. My approach allows me to demonstrate that the primary dynamic in the development of racial ideas in the Sahel was not the colonial construction of knowledge or the introduction of modern European ideas into an African milieu where they had hitherto been foreign. Instead, racial ideas were an integral part of the intellectual tradition of the Sahel for many centuries before the arrival of Europeans. This book will reveal the cultural and intellectual logics of race in the Sahel, and it will demonstrate the historical durability of racial arguments there. Above all, it will reveal some of the ways that Africans have used racial language and argument to shape their own social and political milieu.

PART ONE

RACE ALONG THE DESERT EDGE, C. 1600–1900

PRELUDE

A central argument of this book is that contemporary Sahelian constructions of race owe a great deal to ideas that were developed in the region before the arrival of European colonial forces at the end of the nineteenth century. The two chapters in Part One are about the intellectual history of race in Muslim West Africa before European occupation.

The principal geographical focus of this book is the West African Sahel, a band of arid subdesert land along the southern edge of the Sahara Desert stretching from the Atlantic coast in Mauritania and Senegal in the west to the vicinity of Lake Chad in the east. The use of the name "Sahel" to refer to this region is an academic and geopolitical convention today, but it stems from a colonial misnomer and European misunderstanding of western African uses of the Arabic word for "shore" (sāḥil), which properly refers to the northwestern edge of the Sahara.[1] Because my goal in this book is to provide a history of how people in the West African Sahel came to distinguish between themselves along racial lines, I intentionally avoid geographical terms that suggest, however unintentionally, that there is a natural racial geography in West Africa. Historians sometimes refer to a region that they call the (Western or Central) "Sudan," which is a broad term for the area north of the West African forest zone and south of the Sahara. The word Sudan, however, is a racial label meaning blacks in Arabic, and for this reason I prefer not to use it. Likewise, scholars use

[1] Ghislaine Lydon, *On Trans-Saharan Trails: Islamic Law, Trade Networks, and Cross-Cultural Exchange in Nineteenth-Century Western Africa* (New York: Cambridge University Press, 2009), 29–30.

the term "southern Sahara" to indicate the parts of the Sahel where Arabs and Tuareg are predominant, suggesting important distinctions between this area and sub-Saharan Africa where blacks are the majority of the population. These names are part of what needs to be historicized; the term Sahel carries no such racial baggage.

The Sahel is a transitional zone between the true desert to the north and the more thickly wooded savannah and forests to the south. Its characteristic vegetation includes dryland grasses, acacia-type thorn trees, and doum palms. Over many centuries, agriculture has been practiced along the floodplains of the major watercourses such as the Lake Chad basin and the Senegal and Niger rivers; specialized fishers have exploited the large bodies of water; and pastoralists have raised sheep, goats, cattle, and camels.[2] The Sahel was the historical gateway to West Africa from across the Sahara Desert to the north, the site of West Africa's great medieval empires and commercial towns, and the place where Islam was first adopted more than a thousand years ago.

All students of African history will be aware that the Sahara Desert has expanded and contracted significantly over the last 10,000 years; what is perhaps less well know is the extent to which these movements have been felt in more recent historical times.[3] The earliest written accounts of the region produced by North African and Middle Eastern geographers and historians date back approximately a thousand years, when the Sahara was considerably smaller than it is today. Many of the earliest political and commercial centers associated with the medieval empires of Ghana, Kanem, Mali, Songhay, and Bornu were situated in areas that received more rainfall at that time than they do today. The increased aridity and the concomitant southern movement of the desert edge had economic, social, and political implications across the subregion. Pastoralist groups grew in power vis-à-vis agriculturalists, and from approximately the end of the sixteenth century, large political formations disappeared in the Sahel. Further to the south, new states formed again in the eighteenth and nineteenth centuries, first along the Middle Niger River in the case of Ségou, and on the basis of reformist Islamic ideologies used as organizing political programs by a number of Fulbe-led states in the Futa Toro region of the Senegal River valley, in

[2] Timothy Insoll, *The Archaeology of Islam in Sub-Saharan Africa* (Cambridge: Cambridge University Press, 2003), 208–9.

[3] Sharon E. Nicholson, "The Methodology of Historical Climate Reconstruction and its Application to Africa," *JAH* 20, no. 1 (1979): 31–49.

Hausaland in present-day northern Nigeria, and in the Masina region of the inland delta of the Niger valley.

The research for this book was carried out in an important part of the Sahel called the Niger Bend. This term refers to a stretch of the Niger River in present-day Mali that runs northeast into the high Sahel for several hundred kilometers before turning south and eventually draining into the Atlantic Ocean. It is the annual floodwaters of the Niger River that have made the Niger Bend so historically important for agricultural and pastoral economies, especially in the context of an expanding Sahara. Although not quite as dramatic as the contrast in Egypt and northern Sudan between the rich river valley of the Nile and the completely arid desert surroundings, the contrast in the Niger Bend between well-watered floodplain and arid hinterland is striking. Like the Nile valley, the Niger Bend has hosted dichotomous social formations of sedentary riverine farmers and seminomadic pastoralists, living together in sometimes symbiotic relations, but very often also in conflict over access to the river and its resources.

Using economic and linguistic criteria, there are four main groupings of people in the Niger Bend: the traditionally pastoralist Tuareg (language: Tamashek), Arabs (language: Hassaniyya Arabic), and Fulbe (language: Fulfulde) on the one hand, and the agriculturalist Songhay (language: Koyra Chiini/Koroboro Senni) on the other. Because slavery was so significant in all the societies of the Niger Bend, it makes little sense to equate linguistic grouping with ethnic or racial distinctions. Instead, we must begin by thinking of ethnic and racial labels as social status markers within linguistically defined groups. As we will see, nobles in each of these language groupings came to think of themselves as non-black, distinct from their black slaves and other people of lower social status.

There were two main towns in the Niger Bend: Timbuktu in the west and Gao in the east. Both played important roles as commercial entrepôts linking the Saharan and trans-Saharan trade with the Niger valley and beyond in West Africa. Timbuktu was also an important hub in the production and dissemination of Islamic learning and knowledge beginning as early as the fourteenth century. The commercial and scholarly elite in these and other towns created the space necessary to negotiate the cultural and linguistic differences between traders from North Africa on the one hand and those from sub-Saharan West Africa on the other. The traces of the literate culture of trade and Islamic scholarship provide the richest sources for reconstructing the history of this region. These Muslim scholars and merchants were sometimes known in medieval description as "Takrūrī," a term drawn from the name "Takrūr," which was used as a broad geographical reference for the West African Sahel.[4] Connected to North Africa and the larger Islamic world in an intellectual sense as the bearers and local producers of Islamic knowledge, Takruri scholars and merchants in the Sahel saw themselves as part of a larger, cosmopolitan Muslim world.

It was the local gloss given to certain Islamic ideas, especially the distinction between believer and unbeliever, and the importance of notions of lineage that formed the basis of the particular Sahelian construction of race. That racial ideas would be developed in this region where the phenotypic differences between people were often pronounced, and where the practice of slavery was widespread and exclusively borne by people defined as black, is perhaps not surprising. It is important to understand from the outset, however, that although racial labels might correlate with observable differences of skin color, they often did not. This is because ideas about race came to adhere to notions of lineage and descent that did not necessarily correspond to observable – or "present" – skin color. In other words, race functioned as a kind of local ethnography that was especially useful in negotiating the diversity of the Sahel, and in "fixing" status distinctions and networks based on them that were essential to the commercial and intellectual traffic across this region.

The Niger Bend was the heartland of a large medieval state that historians refer to as the Songhay Empire. Political centralization in the Niger Bend dates back to the ninth century when there is evidence of state formation in the area of Kukiya (Bentia) and Gao. According to recent archaeological evidence, the trans-Saharan trade to the Niger Bend had become

[4] John Hunwick, *Timbuktu and the Songhay Empire: Al-Sa'di's Ta'rikh al-sudan down to 1613 and Other Contemporary Documents* (Leiden: Brill, 1999), 53ff; R.S. O'Fahey, John Hunwick, and Dierk Lange, "Two Glosses concerning Bilād al-Sūdān on a manuscript of al-Nuwayrī's *Nihāyat al-arab*," *SA* 13 (2002): 95; J. Spencer Trimingham, *A History of Islam in West Africa* (London: Oxford University Press, 1962), 41–2; Umar al-Naqar, "Takrur: The History of a Name," *JAH* 10, no. 3 (1969): 365–74. John Hunwick, "Notes on a Late Fifteenth-Century Document Concerning 'al-Takrūr'," in *African Perspectives*, ed. Christopher Allen and R.W. Johnson (Cambridge: Cambridge University Press, 1970), 10; Ghislaine Lydon, "Inkwells of the Sahara: Reflections on the Production of Islamic Knowledge in Bilad Shinqit," in *The Transmission of Learning in Islamic Africa*, ed. Scott Reese (Leiden: Brill, 2004), 42–3; Hélène Claudot-Hawad, "Identité et altérité d'un point de vue touareg. Eléments pour un débat," in *Touaregs et autres Sahariens entre plusieurs mondes. Définitions et redéfinitions de soi et des autres. Les Cahiers de l'IREMAM 7–8*, ed. Claudot-Hawad (Aix-en-Provence: CNRS, 1996), 14.

well developed as early as the eighth century.[5] Gao is mentioned as an important trade center by the ninth-century Arabic chronicler al-Yaʿqūbī (d. 897),[6] and there is archaeological and epigraphic evidence of a Muslim presence in Gao by the eleventh century.[7] Independent Songhay-speaking rulers who controlled the eastern Niger Bend were defeated and incorporated into the Mali Empire by the fourteenth century, if not earlier. However, by the end of the fourteenth century, a Songhay-speaking dynasty based at Gao had won its independence from Mali, and in 1433, the Mali Empire lost control of the town of Timbuktu in the western Niger Bend. The creation of the Songhay Empire was the work of Sunni ʿAli Beer (r. 1464–1492) who conquered Timbuktu in 1468, and Askia al-Hajj Muhammad Ture (r. 1493–1529) who founded a new dynasty, went on the pilgrimage to Mecca, and represents a much more explicitly Islamic direction in Songhay politics. In 1591, a Moroccan army sent across the Sahara defeated the forces of Songhay in a battle near the town of Tondibi, north of Gao.

Although the Moroccan conquerors were not large in number, they were able to establish a smaller successor state to the Songhay Empire, which historians refer to as the "Arma Pashalik."[8] Within several decades of the conquest of the Niger Bend, this state had become more or less independent of Moroccan control, and the social and political elite descended from the Moroccan conquerors – the Arma – had become Songhay-speakers. However, the Arma Pashalik never rivaled the Songhay Empire in terms of scale or power. It suffered from internal divisions and competed with rival Tuareg, Arab, and Fulbe groups for regional hegemony.

The most dramatic political development in the Sahel after the Moroccan invasion of the Niger Bend was the rise of Fulbe Muslim reformist movements beginning in the eighteenth century. The Fulbe were traditionally pastoralist peoples who had spread all across the Sahel. In the seventeenth-century chronicles that recount the history of the Niger Bend, the Fulbe are described as indifferent to religion (Islam) and inclined

[5] Sam Nixon, "Excavating Essouk-Tadmakka (Mali): New Archaeological Investigations of Early Islamic Trans-Saharan Trade," *Azania* 44, no. 2 (2009): 247.

[6] John Hunwick, *Sharīʿa in Songhay: The Replies of al-Maghīlī to the Questions of Askia al-Ḥājj Muḥammad* (Oxford: Oxford University Press, 1985), 7–10.

[7] Insoll, *Archaeology*, 232–7; P.F. de Moraes Farias, *Arabic Medieval Inscriptions from the Republic of Mali: Epigraphy, Chronicles, and Songhay-Tuāreg History* (Oxford: Oxford University Press, 2003), cli–clii.

[8] "Arma" is the local name for the descendants of the Moroccan conquerors. It is derived from the Arabic word "rumāʾ," which means "riflemen," and which was the term used to describe the Moroccan soldiers.

to raid agricultural land and centers of settlement.[9] Whether this was fair or not for the Fulbe of the Niger Bend, other Fulbe groups in the Senegal River valley had embraced Islam much earlier and begun to make it a part of Fulbe political culture. By the eighteenth century, Fulbe Muslim identity was increasingly instrumental in conflicts with non-Fulbe states. Beginning in the Futa Jallon highlands of modern Guinea, Fulbe leaders in that region were able to use an ideology of Muslim reform to mobilize large numbers of followers in a jihad that succeeded in creating a new Fulbe state that aspired to follow Islamic models. Successful jihads followed in the Senegal River valley in the late eighteenth century, in the Hausaland region of modern northern Nigeria and southern Niger in the early nineteenth century, and in the Masina region of the Middle Niger in modern Mali beginning in 1815. The Hausaland jihad was the most significant of these movements. It was led by a Muslim scholar named Usman dan Fodio (d. 1817), together with his brother Abdullahi dan Fodio (d. 1829), and Usman dan Fodio's son and successor Muhammad Bello (d. 1837). These three men were both political leaders and sophisticated intellectuals. They created a new state called the Sokoto Caliphate that survived until the British conquest in 1903.

The success of the Hausaland jihad inspired Fulbe reformers in the Masina region of the Middle Niger valley. Fulbe forces led by a Muslim scholar named Amadu Lobbo (d. 1845) defeated the army of the state of Ségou in 1818 and created what they called the Hamdullahi Caliphate, named after the new capital city that they built in 1821. It was this state that definitively defeated a much weakened Arma Pashalik in Timbuktu in 1833. Alliances between the Hamdullahi Caliphate and Arab and Tuareg groups controlled the western Niger Bend until the invasion in the 1860s from another group of Fulbe reformers from the Senegal River valley, called the Futanke. These Fulbe were led by another Muslim scholar named al-Ḥājj ʿUmar Tal (d. 1864). For the next three decades, the Niger Bend was a site of repeated conflict between allies and opponents of the Futanke. Timbuktu was first occupied by French forces in 1893.

The two chapters in Part One offer a history of the development of racial ideas in the Sahel between the seventeenth and nineteenth centuries. Chapter 1 focuses on the intellectual antecedents of race in the wider Islamic Middle East and North Africa; it seeks to explain how Sahelian intellectuals used this material to reconfigure the place and origin for

[9] David Robinson, *The Holy War of Umar Tal: The Western Sudan in the Mid-Nineteenth Century* (Oxford: Clarendon Press, 1985), 47.

local Arabic- and Berber-speaking peoples in ways that rendered them a part of the wider "white," Arab, and Islamic world, but more importantly, distinct from their "black" neighbors. Versions of these genealogical connections were subsequently drawn on by Fulbe intellectuals and others in the Sahel who sought prestigious origins. Our access to this process of racial construction comes in the form of the histories and genealogies that Sahelian writers produced, connecting their peoples to important figures from Arab Islamic history in North Africa, and rewriting the history of relations between local blacks and nonblacks in West Africa that gave their ancestors important roles in bringing Islam to the region. Although the ideas of race developed along the desert edge were color-coded (white, red, black), they were not based primarily on observable skin color but instead on arguments about Arab and Islamic lineage.

Chapter 2 seeks to explain, in light of the analysis made in Chapter 1, the ways in which the idea of blackness was instrumentalized in the Sahel. As in Chapter 1, I rely largely on local Arabic writings produced by Arabophone scholars based in the Sahel. The main sources used are collections of legal opinions that played an important part in defining the parameters of correct Islamic practice across the region. I focus on the ways that a set of legal ideas was produced to define collective groups according to a single juridical status. Definitions of status were made to have implications for the legitimacy of property and the possibility of juridical freedom for the people labeled by these categories. The focus of my interest in this chapter is on following the different ways that the term "blacks" appears in these legal sources, and the legal implications for property, questions of freedom, clientship, and enslavement. The chapter looks at the different sites where arguments about blackness arose and discusses a series of contestations over what meanings blackness produced in specific contexts.

1

Making Race in the Sahel, c. 1600–1900

IBN BATTUTA IN THE NIGER BEND

When the medieval Moroccan traveler Ibn Baṭṭūṭa (d. 1368) visited the West African Sahel in 1352 and 1353, he brought with him a North African conception of racial difference that appears to have been unfamiliar to the people with whom he interacted. In the written narrative of his travels, Ibn Battuta repeatedly distinguished between three principal types of people found in the area: Berbers, blacks, and whites. It is clear that those he identified as whites included only people like himself: Arab expatriates from North Africa or the Middle East who resided in the commercial towns along the Sahel, most of whom were merchants. With one exception, color terminology was not used to identify or describe the Berber-speaking peoples from the Sahel who are mentioned in his narrative, such as the Massūfa of Walata and Timbuktu or the Bardāma and Hakkār[1] of the southern and central Sahara.[2] For Ibn Battuta, the use of the term "whites" implied a set of Arab Muslim cultural practices that his local Berber-speaking hosts, although Muslims, did not share. He was so scandalized by the freedom Massūfa Berber women appeared to enjoy in their social interactions with men, and by their matrilineal system of

[1] Presumably, these are the ancestors of the Ahaggar Tuareg of southern Algeria.

[2] The exception is in a description of the women of a Tuareg group called the Bardāma: "Their women are the most perfect of women in beauty and the most comely in figure, in addition to being pure white and fat" (*Ibn Battuta in Black Africa*, ed. and trans. Said Hamdan and Noel King [London: Collings, 1975], 56). The Arabic is "maʿ al-bayāḍ al-nāṣiʿ" (Ibn Baṭṭūṭa, *Riḥlat Ibn Baṭṭūṭa* [Cairo: Sharikat al-aʿlānāt al-sharqiyya, 1966], 208).

descent, that he compared local Berber speakers to non-Muslims he had encountered in South Asia.[3]

The use of color terminology in marking human difference was not uncommon in medieval North Africa and the Middle East.[4] What Ibn Battuta meant when he used color categories to distinguish between the people he met in West Africa was a set of differences that we might recognize as primarily cultural. Despite descriptions of physical similarities between Berbers and those Ibn Battuta labeled, variously, as whites, Arabs, Moroccans, and so on, the Berbers could not be included among the whites because of their distance from, and foreignness to, the normative cultural practices of the Arab Muslim world, at least as these were understood by Ibn Battuta. Since we only have Ibn Battuta's account to guide us, it cannot be determined with any confidence how people in the Sahel thought of themselves. However, those that Ibn Battuta identified as Berbers and blacks do not appear to have identified themselves with North African or Middle Eastern ancestors. Furthermore, there is no indication of enmity between Ibn Battuta's Berber hosts and local representatives of the Mali Empire, which was the dominant political force in the region, and whom Ibn Battuta identified as blacks.

The world described by Ibn Battuta changed considerably in the centuries that followed his visit. By the seventeenth century, when local written histories were first composed by members of Sahelian societies themselves, many of the descendants of the Berber-speaking peoples encountered by Ibn Battuta had developed a much more racialized idea of themselves as whites. They had adopted some of the trappings of the wider Arab Muslim culture, including wider use of the Arabic language and Arab genealogies traced through patrilineal systems of descent. The Arabization of formerly Berber-speaking people was certainly never complete, and most Arabized groups continued to recognize Berber elements of their background and culture. Perhaps half of the original Berber-speaking population of the Sahel in the fourteenth century had become Arabic-speaking by the end of the eighteenth century. Some part of this change was caused by a series of in-migrations by Arabic-speakers, often represented as conquests in indigenous Sahelian historical traditions. However, the numbers of migrants were never very

[3] *Ibn Battuta in Black Africa*, 28.

[4] For a broad overview, see Bernard Lewis, *Race and Color in Islam* (New York: Harper & Row, 1971); Lewis, *Race and Slavery in the Middle East: an historical enquiry* (New York: Oxford University Press, 1992).

large. The fourteenth-century North African historian Ibn Khaldūn (d. 1406) wrote that in his day there were only 200 individuals among the Banū Maʿqil, the purported vanguard of the Arab invasion of the southwestern Sahara.[5] So the process of Arabization was less an invasion than a realignment of language, cultural practice, and genealogy. Most of these Arabized Berbers lived in the western parts of the region, in what is today Mauritania. They spoke a dialect of Arabic known as Hassaniyya; they are often called "Moors." Most of those who continued to speak Berber languages came to be known by the ethnic label "Tuareg." Although Hassaniyya Arabic speakers and Tuareg share many of the same territories, the Tuareg have traditionally occupied the eastern parts of the region, in what are today northern Mali and Niger, as well as southern Algeria and southwestern Libya. Both Arab and Tuareg populations came to see themselves as distinct and superior to the neighboring desert-edge black populations with whom they interacted.

TOWARD A LOGIC OF RACE ALONG THE DESERT EDGE

That people along the Sahel would employ vocabularies of color to describe themselves and others should, at one level, not be especially surprising. There are clear and easily perceivable phenotypic differences between many Arabophone and Berberophone peoples on the one hand and those commonly identified as sub-Saharan Africans on the other. There are, of course, many exceptions. Certainly, for the outsider, it is often very unclear without other clues, such as clothing, personal names, or language, what the correspondence is between the various racial categories employed by Sahelian people and the actual color of their skin. Nonetheless, it is important to acknowledge that somatic differences along the Sahel are a reality and that these differences have played a role in the development of notions of racial difference.

However, objective physical differences between the different peoples of the desert edge were not a natural prerequisite for the development of racial ideas, nor did they determine the historical emergence of ideologies of race. Racial thinking is not the same as perceptions of difference; it privileges certain types of human difference (often arbitrarily) and

[5] The passage is quoted in J.F.P. Hopkins and N. Levtzion, *Corpus of Early Arabic Sources for West African History* (New York: Cambridge University Press, 1981), 324. This is cited in Raymond Taylor, "Of Disciples and Sultans: Power, Authority and Society in the Nineteenth-Century Mauritanian Gebla" (Ph.D. Diss., University of Illinois at Urbana-Champaign, 1996), 23.

ascribes to them meanings which are objectively false. Racial ideology thereby loses its relationship to what can be thought of as objectively true: namely, that there are real differences between human beings.[6] The issue of race in the Sahel is a historical problem that revolves around how ideas about human difference, whatever their objective validity, were codified in socially significant ways. The interesting question then is not the perception of difference per se, but the ways in which difference was rationalized into larger ideologies that organized social and political distinctions.

James Webb has offered one explanation for the development of racial ideas along the Sahel. He argued that progressive desiccation after the sixteenth century allowed Arabo-Berber pastoralists to attain increasingly dominant position vis-à-vis black agricultural peoples in areas along the southward-moving frontier of the desert. Increasing aridity gave pastoral groups a number of tactical advantages in competition for control over resources with sedentary communities, whose inhabitants were forced to either migrate further to the south or enter into subordinate relationships with pastoral overlords. Webb argued that as these southern Saharan groups came to dominate the desert edge and the sedentary black African peoples who made up the majority of the local population, new ideologies of social organization and racial difference were developed as corollaries to the changing political circumstances. With their increased power vis-à-vis agriculturalists, Arabic- and Berber-speaking pastoralists began to use race as a more explicitly ideological justification of their position of dominance.[7]

Webb's work provides a largely convincing account of the social, economic, and ecological factors that led to the increasing importance of racial ideas in the Sahel, but he does not explore the cultural and ideological tools that were used in constructing them. This is the task of this book. However, uncovering the intellectual history of these shifts is quite difficult for a number of reasons. Foremost among them is the fact that our access to this dimension of the past is largely limited by extant written sources. A bigger problem is that ideas about racial difference were embedded in a wider set of ideas about authority, social order, and religion; explicit statements about the meaning of racial difference are rare.

[6] See Peter Robb, "Introduction: South Asia and the Concept of Race," in *The Concept of Race in South Asia*, ed. Robb (Delhi: Oxford University Press, 1995), 1–76.

[7] James Webb, *Desert Frontier: Ecological and Economic Change along the Western Sahel, 1600–1850* (Madison, WI: University of Wisconsin Press, 1995).

The arguments that I will make on the basis of this evidence are therefore subject to a number of caveats. By seeking to uncover and explain the historical development of racialized thinking in the Sahel, I am not arguing that this was the only, or even the most important, aspect of local worldviews in this area. I employ the term "identity" infrequently and with great caution in this chapter because although racial arguments were constructed by reference to lineage and genealogy, and thereby imply belonging to these units, they are also highly abstract in the form that they come down to us. Racial arguments became important components in the ideological ordering of relations between Arabic- and Berber-speaking groups on the one hand and sub-Saharan people on the other. Ideas about race surely developed, as Webb suggested, as a means of legitimizing the new power of ascendant groups along the desert edge. But it is not at all clear, that racial markers became primary elements of the self-identity of people in this region. Instead, racial difference operated at a level of abstraction that ordered, explained, and legitimized domination and enslavement of people defined as black. As such, the important distinction is between blacks and nonblacks.[8] There were multiple ways to argue for nonblackness. It was not the particular content of a "white" identity that was most important, but instead the assurance of not being counted among the blacks. Even so, this did not mean that racial labels ordered all social or political space, or that they went uncontested. Some arguments and rebuttals of racial labels are discussed in Chapter 2.

How then did notions of racial difference become important components of the political and cultural vernaculars of the people of the Sahel? The argument that I will make here is that this process involved two fundamental intellectual moves. First, ideas about white Arab Islamic culture that originated in the Islamic Middle East and North Africa were made part of the Sahelian cultural world by a reconfiguration of local genealogies connecting local Arabic- and Berber-speaking groups with important Arab Islamic historical figures in North Africa and the Arabian Peninsula. Second, local Arabo-Berber intellectuals rewrote the history of relations between their ancestors and black Africans in ways

[8] In a slightly different context, P.F. de Moraes Farias has argued that terms like "zanj" became abstract markers of African "barbarism" unattached to any specific African people ("Models of the World and Categorical Models: The 'Enslaveble Barbarian' as a Mobile Classificatory Label," in *Slaves and Slavery in Muslim Africa: Islam and the Ideology of Enslavement*, ed. John Ralph Willis (London: Frank Cass, 1985), I: 27–46.

that made them the bearers of Islamic orthodoxy and the holders of religious authority in the Sahelian region. As such, the introduction of Islam into the region was claimed by these Arabic- and Berber-speaking groups, and this underlay contemporary assertions of authority in religious matters. The timing of these shifts is difficult to pinpoint, above all because they were part of longer processes of cultural change in the Sahel. The work of H.T. Norris and Abdel Wedoud ould Cheikh, among others, has made clear how scholars in the Sahel reworked lineages using names taken directly from classical Arabic literature as part of a process of Arabization.[9] This was a complex process that was ongoing over many centuries, but it attained a special importance with the ascendance of the power of particular pastoralist groups during the seventeenth century and afterward. As such, it corresponds roughly with Webb's periodization of ecological change.

According to many indigenous historical traditions, the seventeenth century marks a watershed in the history of the Sahel. It was at this time that the foundations were laid for the social and cultural structures of the region that are familiar today, especially in relations between so-called clerical- and warrior-status groups so typical of Sahelian societies and so prominent in the ethnographic literature on the region. In effect, the subsequent dominance of so-called warrior-status groups over clerical ones is explained in many local historical traditions with reference to definitive and transformative conquest by (usually) Arab outsiders over indigenous (usually) Berber groups, whose members then took up religious specializations because they were no longer able to carry arms and act as warriors. In this sense, the Arabization in the Sahel is represented as an imposition by conquering outsiders over defeated local populations. The legacy of these conquests is continually reproduced in a set of ordered and hierarchical occupational specializations carried by the descendants of these earlier combatants. Most of the local histories that report in-migrations of subsequently dominant groups locate these events in the seventeenth century. The so-called War of Shur Bubba, which occurred in the 1670s in southwestern Mauritania and which I will discuss in more detail later, is the best known example, although there are many others all along

[9] The most important works are H.T. Norris, *The Arab Conquest of the Western Sahara. Studies of the Historical Events, Religious Beliefs and Social Customs Which Made the Remotest Sahara a Part of the Arab World* (London: Longman, 1986); Abdel Wedoud ould Cheikh, "Nomadisme, Islam et pouvoir politique dans la société maure pré-coloniale" (Ph.D. Diss., Université Paris V, 1985).

the Sahel from the Atlantic Ocean to the region around Lake Chad.[10] As an idealized representation of Sahelian society, these foundation stories served to justify the social hierarchy found in the region. But they also can be read as representations of an ideal racial order because they establish a relationship between important Sahelian pastoralists and those defined as blacks.[11]

Race in the Sahel is an outgrowth of the increasing importance attributed to ideas about lineage connecting people living in this region with important historical figures from Arab Islamic history. There was a widespread reconfiguration of genealogies by Sahelian intellectuals that served to justify noble social status by reference to foreign origins. The models were metropolitan to a large extent (patrilineal, Arab, white), but in function and in practice, they often acted to invert earlier Arab ideas about the branches of the human family – inherited from pre-Islamic times – that connected human difference to environment and/or the lineages that originated with the sons of Noah. Many early Arab writers assigned Hamitic origins (from Noah's son Ham) to the inhabitants of the Sahel, as well as to the Berbers of North Africa more generally.[12] Berbers and blacks alike were considered to be the sons of Ham. They suffered equally from the curse of perpetual servitude to the descendants of Noah's other sons because of Noah's curse on Ham's son Canaan.

Among the consequences of the larger process of Arabization that occurred in the Sahel were a repudiation of this idea, at least as a basis for noble Sahelian genealogy, and a claim that Arab-ness rendered noble Sahelians genuinely Semitic. Once claims to Arab-ness were established, noble Sahelians could then play on another trope connected to ideas of race from the early Islamic centuries: the superiority of "true" Arabs over non-Arab Muslim clients (Ar. muwālī) in matters of social privilege and religion. The Arab traveler and geographer Ibn Ḥawqal (d. 988) could write in the tenth century that whites who lived in the hot climate of Africa for seven generations became black and that the inhabitants of the

[10] For a discussion of these foundation stories, see C.C. Stewart, "Southern Saharan Scholarship and the Bilad al-Sudan," *JAH* 17 (1976): 73–93; H. T. Norris, "Znaga Islam during the Seventeenth and Eighteenth Centuries," *BSOAS* 32 (1969): 496–536; Norris, *Arab Conquest*.

[11] These are idealized representations of social hierarchy, and, as such, they fail to account for the actual historical dynamism and social mobility that occurred in the southern Sahara since the seventeenth century. See Timothy Cleaveland, *Becoming Walāta: A History of Saharan Social Formation and Transformation* (Portsmouth, NH: Heinemann, 2002), 3–36.

[12] H.T. Norris, *The Berber in Arabic Literature* (Beirut: Librairie du Liban, 1982), 34.

Sahel were the sons of Ham through their mothers.[13] When ideas about race were developed in the Sahel, local intellectuals insisted that patrilineal relationships to Arab ancestors, regardless of their current skin color, rendered them white.

It is possible that racial discourses have a much longer history in the Sahel than we have evidence for. Hints of an earlier significance for race can be found in North African histories of the Berber-led Almoravid movement that conquered much of North Africa and Muslim Spain from its Saharan homeland in the eleventh century. The nature of the relationship between the Ṣanhāja Berbers in the Sahara, among whom the Almoravid movement arose, and the various Sahelian peoples with whom they were in frequent contact, has been an issue of historiographical debate.[14] North African chroniclers such as Ibn Abī Zarʿ (d. 1315) described a relationship between the Sanhaja Berbers and the blacks, especially the kingdom of ancient Ghana, in ways that project an idea of perpetual Sanhaja hatred and domination over blacks. Ibn Abi Zarʿ described the Sanhaja as:

> A people who do not know ploughing, sowing, or produce; their property consists only of camels and they live on flesh and milk. One of them may pass his life without eating bread unless merchants happen to pass through their country and give them some bread or flour as a gift. Most of them are orthodox Muslims and wage Holy War upon the Sudan [blacks]. Their first king in the desert was TYWLWThĀN b. Tīklān al-Ṣanhājī al-Lamtūnī, king of the whole desert. More than twenty kings of the Sudan were in subjection to him and paid the poll tax (jizya) to him.[15]

This Sanhaja king, we are told, ruled an area so large that it took three months to cross it in any direction. His rule lasted for a period of eighty

[13] Ibn Ḥawqal, "Ṣurat al-Arḍ," in *Bibliotheca Geographorum Arabicorum*, ed. J.H. Kramers (Leiden: Brill, 1938–39), II: 105. Cited and translated in Hopkins and Levtzion, *Corpus*, 50–1.

[14] The debate has focused on whether the Almoravids conquered ancient Ghana, as medieval North African historians such as Ibn Abī Zarʿ and Ibn Khaldun suggested in their writings. David Conrad and Humphrey Fisher have argued that there was no Almoravid conquest of ancient Ghana and that instead of a hostile relationship between the Sanhaja and the blacks, there was widespread cooperation and peaceful coexistence produced in part by links of shared Islamic profession and practice. See Conrad and Fisher, "The Conquest That Never Was: Ghana and the Almoravids, 1076. I. The External Arabic Sources," *HA* 9 (1982): 44. Sheryl L. Burkhalter was skeptical of Conrad and Fisher's arguments and suggested that there was reason to believe that there was conflict between the Almoravids and ancient Ghana. See Burkhalter, "Listening for Silences in Almoravid History: Another Reading of 'The Conquest that Never Was,'" *HA* 19 (1992): 103–31.

[15] Hopkins and Levtzion, *Corpus*, 236.

years, ending only with his death in 837. As fantastic as this appears, it marks an important trope of Berber domination and authority over blacks on the basis of their adherence to Islamic orthodoxy. In all likelihood, Almoravid discourse about their Saharan past was part of an ex post facto ideology worked out in North Africa after attaining power, or one developed by later historians, rather than a product of the contemporary intellectual environment in the Sahel itself.[16] Nonetheless, it contributed to the kinds of textual historical material produced by North African authors that would later be incorporated into Sahelian writings about their own past.

Another possible source of earlier racial discourse is the old and widespread myth of Yemeni Arab (Himyarite) origins held by so many Sahelian peoples.[17] These Himyarite myths suggest that the Berbers were the descendents of the pre-Islamic South Arabian kings of Himyar who crossed into Africa. Ibn Khaldun gives a good summary of these ideas in his discussion of the errors made by historians at the beginning of the "Muqaddina":

> The history of the Tubbaʿs, the kings of the Yemen and the Arabian Peninsula, as it is generally transmitted, is another example of silly statements by historians. It is said that from their home in the Yemen, (the Tubbaʿs) used to raid Ifrīqiyah and the Berbers of the Maghrib. Afrīqus b. Qays b. Ṣayfī, one of their great early kings who lived in the time of Moses or somewhat earlier, is said to have raided Ifrīqiyah. He caused a great slaughter among the Berbers ... When he left the Maghrib, he is said to have concentrated some Himyar tribes there. They remained there and mixed with the native population. Their (descendents) are the Ṣinhājah and the Kutāmah. This led aṭ-Ṭabarī, al-Jurjānī, al-Masʿūdī, Ibn al-Kalbī, and al-Bayhaqī to make the statement that the Ṣinhājah and the Kutāmah belong to the Ḥimyar.[18]

According to Ibn Khaldun, these stories are false: "All this information is remote from the truth. It is rooted in baseless and erroneous assumptions. It is more like the fiction of storytellers. The realm of the Tubbaʿs was restricted to the Arabian peninsula."[19] The important issue at stake in these Himyarite stories is precisely the ability of certain Berber

[16] Whether or not Conrad and Fisher's suggestion that the Almoravid conquest of Ancient Ghana never occurred is correct is one thing. That later historians wrote about it in contemporary North African racial terms is more certain ("Conquest," 45.)

[17] H. T. Norris, *Saharan Saga and Myth* (London: Oxford University Press, 1972), 57.

[18] Ibn Khaldun, *The Muqaddimah: An Introduction to History*, trans. Franz Rosenthal (Princeton, NJ: Princeton University Press, 1967), I: 21–2.

[19] Ibid., I: 23.

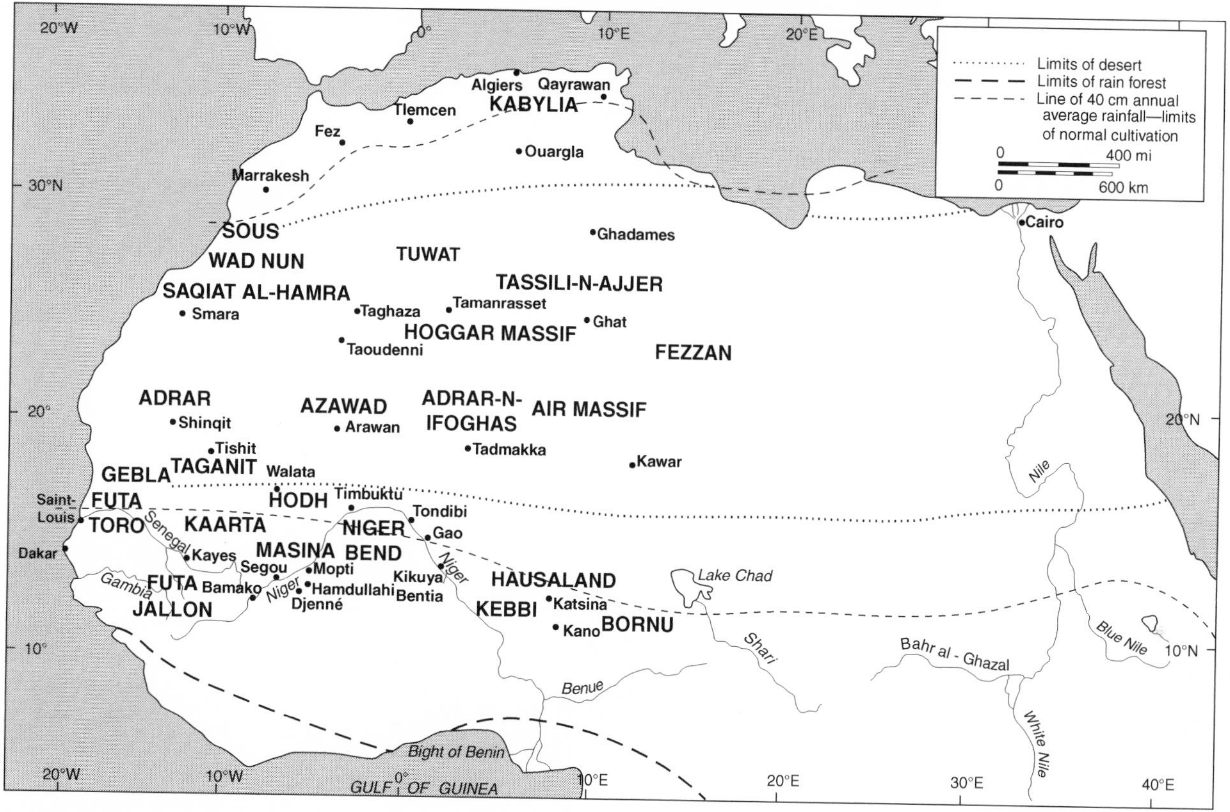

MAP 1. North and West Africa.

intellectuals to claim Semitic origins back to Noah's son Shem, rather than accept that they are sons of Ham.

In both of these possible antecedents of racial ideas in the Sahel, our access is limited by the existence and availability of historical sources. Because written sources produced in the Sahel itself are quite scarce before the seventeenth century, the likelihood of being able to push back much beyond this time seems slight. From the seventeenth century, we are on much more solid ground. I use the seventeenth century as a threshold in my analysis of the development of racial discourses in the Sahel. I first consider the intellectual foundations of race by examining the most significant sets of ideas about the subject that circulated in the region before the seventeenth century. Then I analyze the ways in which these ideas came to be associated with constructions of lineage, and with Islamic authority, beginning in the seventeenth century.

INTELLECTUAL FOUNDATIONS OF RACE

The larger history of ideas about race in the Islamic Middle East is beyond the scope of this book. What I hope to do in this section is to outline some of the most influential concepts concerning this subject that would have circulated among intellectuals in the Sahel. It is important to point out that although most metropolitan writers in Arabic held generally negative attitudes about blacks in particular, and toward most non-Arabs more generally, many also singled out individuals or groups who were exceptions to their larger derogatory evaluations. It was widely reported that the Prophet Muhammad had said to his followers: "Look after the Blacks, for among them are three of the lords of Paradise, Luqmān the Sage, Najāshī and Bilāl the muezzin."[20] The attribution of such a statement to the Prophet suggests a counterdiscourse on race that was available to Muslim writers from the very beginnings of Islamic literature. Indeed, according to the Qur'an, piety overrides any racial or ethnic quality.[21] In

[20] Luqmān is generally considered by Muslim writers to have been an Ethiopian or Nubian slave who was proverbially wise. Najāshī was the Ethiopian king of Aksum also known as Aṣḥama who gave shelter to the early Muslims fleeing Arabia. Bilāl was a freedman of Ethiopian descent who became the first muezzin (caller to prayer) in Islam. The quote is cited in the questions sent to Aḥmad Bāba of Timbuktu by al-Jirārī, *Mi'rāj al-Ṣu'ūd: Aḥmad Bābā's Replies on Slavery*, ed. and trans. John Hunwick and Fatima Harrak (Rabat: Université Mohammed V-Souissi, 2000), 17.

[21] See, for example, Surat al-Ḥujurāt (Qur'an 49:13) "O Mankind, We created you from a single (pair) of a male and a female, and made you into nations and tribes, that ye may know each other. Verily, the most honored of you in the sight of God is the most righteous of you."

the more detailed geographical and travel writings, piety and adherence to Islam by blacks or other non-Arabs often renders them exceptions to larger negative attitudes. In the hands of some writers, racial difference appears to hold little or no importance to understanding faraway peoples.[22] There were also, as I will discuss later in this chapter, writers who refuted some of the more general derogatory view of blacks.

Arab writers inherited two principal ideas about race from pre-Islamic Mediterranean sources: an environmental theory about human difference and the biblical stories about Noah's sons Shem, Japheth, and Ham. The intellectual debt that Arab writers had to earlier thinkers was often quite explicit. Al-Masʿūdī (d. 956), for example, writing in the tenth century, quoted the second-century Greek physician Galen on the inferior physical qualities of blacks, saying that "merriment dominates the black man because of his defective brain, whence also the weakness of his intelligence."[23] Arab writers generally reproduced the classical Mediterranean-centered theory of geography that divided the world into seven distinct regions, or climes, of which the medial fourth zone that coincided with the Mediterranean region was thought to be temperate and ideal for the development of human beings and civilization. The extreme cold and oppressive heat in northern and southern regions were blamed for the deficiencies of Europeans and Africans, respectively.[24] According to the fourteenth-century Syrian geographer al-Dimashqī (d. 1327), drawing extensively on earlier writers:

> The equatorial region is inhabited by communities of blacks who are to be numbered among the savages and beasts. Their complexions and hair are burnt and they are physically and morally deviant. Their brains almost boil from the sun's excessive heat.... The human being who dwells there is a crude fellow, with a very black complexion, and burnt hair, unruly, with stinking sweat, and an abnormal constitution, most closely resembling in his moral qualities a savage, or animals.[25]

[22] This is the impression I have from reading the highly empirical writing of the Andalusian geographer al-Bakrī, "Kitāb al-masālik wa-'l-mamālik," in *Description de l'Afrique septentrionale*, ed. and trans. Baron William MacGuckin de Slane (Paris: Librairie d'Amérique et d'Orient Adrien-Maisonneuve, 1965). A translated excerpt is in Levtzion and Hopkins, *Corpus*, 63–87.

[23] From al-Masʿūdī's "Murūj al-dhahab;" quoted in Lewis, *Race and Color*, 34.

[24] This theory can be traced back to ancient Greece, in particular to the text written by (pseudo) Hippocrates called "Airs, Waters, Places." A useful recent discussion of these ideas in the ancient Mediterranean is in Benjamin Isaac, *The Invention of Racism in Classical Antiquity* (Princeton, NJ: Princeton University Press, 2004), 55–168.

[25] Shams al-Dīn Muḥammad b. Abī Ṭālib al-Dimashqī, *Nukhbat al-dahr fī ʿajāʾib al-barr wa-ʾl-baḥr*, ed. A. Mehren (Leipzig: Harassowitz, 1923), 15–17; translated by John

Many other examples of such attitudes toward black Africans from medieval Arabic literature and geography could be marshaled. However, this environmental theory also was applied to other people who lived in climates similar to that of Africa; the inhabitants of South India and Indonesia found themselves identified alongside black Africans in much of this literature. Over time, more information was gathered on sub-Saharan Africa, and as a consequence, writers such as al-Bakrī (d. 1094), al-Idrīsī (d. 1154), Ibn Battuta, and most importantly Ibn Khaldun were able to add considerable detail to Arab knowledge about the "bilād al-sūdān," or the "land of the blacks." As more was learned about the continent, writers began to use different terms to describe black Africans from various regions. The four main regional groupings that developed were the Zanj for people from the East African coast, the Ḥabasha for Ethiopians, the Nūba for Nilotic groups, and the Sūdān for those in the Sahel west of the Nile Basin. The term "sudan" remained the generic label applied to sub-Saharan Africans, although it was also used in some cases to include non-Africans of dark complexion.[26]

An alternate theory explaining racial difference was drawn from the biblical story of Noah's curse on Ham's son Canaan. The story of Ham is, in obvious ways, an ex post facto popular religious justification for the widespread enslavement of black Africans, and it seems to have attained considerable popular acceptance.[27] The story is not found in the Qur'an, and many later writers did not accept it, in large part because it appeared

Hunwick in *West Africa, Islam, and the Arab World* (Princeton, NJ: Markus Wiener, 2006), 81. A slightly different translation is in Levtzion and Hopkins, *Corpus*, 205.

[26] For example, in Jāḥiẓ's (c. 776–869) "Boast of the Blacks Over the Whites" ("Fakhr al-sūdān ʿalā al-bīḍān"), he includes among the Blacks the inhabitants of India, Southeast Asia, and China (Lewis, *Race and Color*, 16–17). It is also important to note that the four broad regional terms used to label Africans were expanded on in works of greater detail on particular regions. Arab geographers divided the people of the East African region into more groups than just the zanj. See J. Spencer Trimingham, "The Arab Geographers and the East African Coast," in *East Africa and the Orient: Cultural Synthesis in Pre-Colonial Times*, ed. H. Neville Chittick and Robert Rotberg (New York: Africana Pub., 1975), 115–46; L.-Marcel Devic, *Le pays des Zendjs ou la côte orientale d'Afrique au Moyen-âge* (Amsterdam: Oriental Press, 1975).

[27] David Goldenberg has recently deconstructed the ancient biblical, rabbinic, and early Christian references to the story of Noah's curse on Ham's son Canaan. He shows how Noah's curse came to be applied to Black Africans. Goldenberg is much less convincing, in my view, when he argues that the racialization of this story occurred with the expansion of African slavery in the early Islamic world (*The Curse of Ham: Race and Slavery in Early Judaism, Christianity, and Islam* [Princeton, NJ: Princeton University Press, 2003], 170–4).

to contradict the climatic theory of racial difference. Nonetheless, there is a hadith in which the Prophet Muhammad is reported to have said that the Arabs are the descendants of Shem, the Europeans the descendants of Japheth, and the descendants of Ham include the black Africans, the Coptic Egyptians, and the Berbers.[28] An early Arab account of this story comes from Ibn Quṭayba (d. 889):

> Wahb b. Munabbih said that Ḥām b. Nūḥ was a white man having a beautiful face and form. But Allah changed his color and the color of his descendants because of his father's curse. Ham went off, followed by his children. They settled on the shore of the sea, and Allah increased them. They are the Sūdān. Their food was fish, which used to stick to their teeth. So they sharpened their teeth until they became like needles.[29] Some of Ḥām's descendants settled in the west. Ḥām begot Kūsh b. Ḥām Kanʿān b. Ḥām and Fūṭ b. Ḥām Fūṭ traveled and settled in the land of Hind and Sind, and the people there are his descendants. The descendants of Kūsh and Kanʿān are the races of the Sūdān: the Nūba, the Zanj, the Qazan [?], the Zaghāwa, the Ḥabasha, the Qibṭ [Copts] and the Barbar [Berbers].[30]

One could cite other versions of the story of Ham in Arabic literature that trace the origins of black Africans and the Berbers in slightly different ways, but the important point is that the two peoples were considered by many to be, at the very least, genealogical cousins by those who invoked the Hamitic theory.

In an important sense, these genealogical myths are foundational to the subsequent development of ideas about race and ethnicity in the Maghrib and the Sahara. From a very early date, Berber scholars attempted to refute the idea that they were descendants of Ham. A number of alternatives were proposed, including the idea that the Berbers were of Canaanite origin and descended from the giant Goliath, or that they were the descendants of purported pre-Islamic Yemeni (Himyarite) colonists in North Africa discussed earlier.[31] Confronted with subjugation by the ethnically conscious Arab-Islamic conquerors of the Maghrib, many Berbers found themselves in the subordinate position of clients (Ar. muwālī) in the hegemonic Arab Muslim community. The desire to adopt Arab culture, to convert to Islam, and to be attached to Arab tribal affiliations must have been great. The growing familiarity of Muslim Berber scholars with

[28] This is according to ʿAbd al-Raḥmān al-Suyūṭī, *Rafʿ shaʾn al-ḥubshān*, ed. Ṣafwān Dāwudī and Ḥassan ʿUbajī (Jedda: Dār al-qiblah li-ʾl-thaqāfa al-islāmiyya, 1991), 33.

[29] This was a common description of the coastal zanj in East Africa.

[30] In Levtzion and Hopkins, *Corpus*, 15.

[31] Norris, *Berber*, 33–9.

Arabic literature allowed for reworkings of indigenous cultural material that aligned the Berbers with more prestigious ancestors.[32]

It is difficult to pinpoint with any precision the chronology of the absorption of these ideas by the people living in the Sahel. Norris has argued that the mythology developed by Saharan people about heroic Himyarite ancestors and their adventures incorporates aspects of the romance traditions associated with Alexander the Great.[33] It may be that the advent of Islam and the Arab conquest only precipitated a configuration of new names and exploits into a much older tradition. It seems more likely, however, that these older ideas came to the Berbers through Arab writers who incorporated them into their works. One thing clearly changed with Arabic literary models: the shift to more strictly patrilineal models of descent. The Berbers traditionally traced their genealogies in matrilineal ways, but in the hands of Arab or Arabized writers, this tended to disappear or at least be complemented by patrilineal lineages connected to Arab ancestors.[34]

Before the process of Arabization began in the Sahel – perhaps as early as the fourteenth century – the impact of these changes to the north was less important. As mentioned earlier, when Ibn Battuta visited Walata in the fourteenth century, he remarked disapprovingly on the social freedom of Berber-speaking women, indicating perhaps that older Berber matrilineal structures were still in force.[35] Even the Sanhaja Berbers, who were the first Saharans to enter onto the stage of world history with the Almoravid conquest of Morocco and Spain in the eleventh century, constructed a patrilineally descended heroic past in the Sahara only after they had established themselves in North Africa. That this past needed to be invented once in North Africa is understandable enough, but back in the Sahara and Sahel, Berber-speakers continued to follow older ways of understanding themselves and their past for many centuries to come.[36]

The two writers who had probably the greatest influence on later Sahelian ideas about race were Ibn Khaldun and ʿAbd al-Raḥmān al-Suyūṭī

[32] Maya Shatzmiller, *The Berbers and the Islamic State: The Marīnid Experience in Pre-Protectorate Morocco* (Princeton, NJ: Marcus Wiener, 2000), 17–27; Abdelmajid Hannoum, *Colonial Histories, Post-Colonial Memories: The Legend of the Kahina, A North African Heroine* (Portsmouth, NH: Heinemenn, 2001), 1–28.

[33] Norris, *Saharan Saga*, 31.

[34] Norris, *Berber*, 40–3.

[35] *Ibn Battuta in Black Africa*, 28.

[36] Norris, *Saharan Saga*, 28–9.

(d. 1505). Ibn Khaldun was influential in a number of ways.[37] His history of the Berbers ("Kitāb al-ʿIbar") was probably the most widely read text on North African history, and it provided later Sahelian writers with much of the historical and genealogical material they would need to construct "improved" lineages for themselves.[38] Ralph Austen and Jan Jansen have argued that it was from Ibn Khaldun's text that Mande-speaking griots and specialists in oral dynastic histories in Sahelian West Africa obtained much of their information on the Mali Empire.[39]

Ibn Khaldun was somewhat inconsistent on the issue of race, but insofar as he had a larger argument to make, he suggested that adherence to Islam redeemed all other differences. In the "Muqaddima," Ibn Khaldun argued against the notion that blackness is related to descent from Ham:

> Some genealogists who had no knowledge of the true nature of beings imagined that the Blacks are the descendants of Ham, the son of Noah, and that they were characterized by black color as a result of a curse put upon him by his father, which manifested itself in Ham's color and the slavery that God inflicted upon his descendants.... The curse of Noah upon his son is there in the Torah. No reference is made there to blackness. His curse was simply that Ham's descendants should be the slaves of his brothers' descendants. To attribute the blackness of the Sudan to Ham, shows disregard for the nature of heat and cold and the influence they exert upon the air and upon the creatures that come into being in it.[40]

For Ibn Khaldun, the explanation of racial difference lay in the Mediterranean-centered theory of climes:

> As for the climes which are remote from the temperate regions, such as the First and the Second, and the Sixth and the Seventh, their inhabitants are very far from being temperate in all their features. For their buildings are of mud and reeds and their food is sorghum and herbs, and their clothes are of the leaves of trees with which they cover themselves, or skins. Most of them are devoid of clothing. The fruits and relishes of their country are of strange and abnormal form. Their transactions are not conducted with the two noble metals but with

[37] I know of two texts in Timbuktu that are devoted explicitly to providing useful excerpts from Ibn Khaldun's history. They were both written by Muḥammad b. Aḥmad b. Muḥammad b. Ḥabbata al-Ghallāwī (IHERIAB mss. 639, 4609).

[38] This was true even if the constructions made by Sahelian scholars were at odds with Ibn Khaldun's views (Norris, *Arab Conquest*, 13–14). This argument is also made by Taylor, "Of Disciples," 23.

[39] Ralph Austen and Jan Jansen, "History, Oral Transmission, and Structure in Ibn Khaldun's Chronology of Mali Rulers," *HA* 23 (1996): 17–28.

[40] Ibn Khaldūn, *Muqaddimah*, 169–70. Cited in Hunwick, *West Africa, Islam*, 80. It should be noted that elsewhere, Ibn Khaldun seems to concur with the idea of Hamitic descent.

copper or iron or skins to which they assign a value for their dealings. Their manners, therefore, are close to those of dumb animals, so that it is related of many of the Sudan, the people of the First Clime, that they live in caves and in the jungle and eat herbs, and that they have the habits of beasts, not those of men, and eat each other.[41]

In this description, Ibn Khaldun differed little from many writers who preceded him. Consistent with the theory of climes, northern Europeans were marked out for equal approbation. But Ibn Khaldun was also acquainted with the fact that there were people in sub-Saharan Africa who did not fit his description of barbarism. He had had close contacts with the Malian ruler Mansa Musa during the latter's fourteenth-century pilgrimage to Mecca, and he was well aware of past polities, such as ancient Ghana, that were described in positive terms by writers such as al-Bakri. Since the first descriptions of Ethiopia, whose king al-Najashi had played an important role in helping the early Muslims, geographers in the Muslim world were faced with a similar challenge to the theory of climes. Ibn Khaldun attempted to solve this problem by arguing that there were differences between the savages of the furthest reaches of the First Clime and the more advanced blacks who lived in closer proximity to the temperate zones in the Second Clime:

On account of their distance from temperate regions, the characteristics of their constitutions and manners are close to the characteristics of dumb animals and they are proportionately far from humanity. The features of their religion are the same; they are not acquainted with prophethood and do not submit to any revealed law except for such of them as are near to regions of temperateness, which is uncommon.[42]

But whereas writers such as al-Dimashqi had attributed the lack of revealed religion in the black regions to the very climatic factors that produced their purported barbarism, Ibn Khaldun argued that this barbarism was redeemable through the adoption of a revealed religion, as had happened in a number of cases in Africa. As such, Ibn Khaldun suggested that the real touchstone of civilization was not genealogy or climate, but religion.[43]

The influence of the famous Egyptian scholar al-Suyuti on the Muslims of the Sahel was also important, although for different reasons. He carried out a correspondence with scholars in the region from his home in

[41] In Levtzion and Hopkins, *Corpus*, 321.
[42] Ibid., 321.
[43] Hunwick, *West Africa, Islam*, 80.

Cairo.[44] Al-Suyuti's significance as an authority in the Islamic sciences is widely acknowledged in many Sahelian sources, and his views represented a flexible and liberal concession to local customs that stands in juxtaposition to the more legalistic and intolerant approach of the other major intellectual influence on West African Islam, Muḥammad b. ʿAbd al-Karīm al-Maghīlī (d. 1504), who came from Tlemcen in modern-day Algeria.[45] The more "liberal" perspective of al-Suyuti manifested itself in a treatise he wrote in defense of black people called "Raising the status of the Ethiopians" ("Rafʿ sha'n al-ḥubshān") and in an abridged version of this work entitled "The Flowers of the throne concerning information about the Ethiopians" ("Azhār al-ʿurūsh fī akhbār al-ḥubūsh").[46] The principal contribution of these works was their attempt to demonstrate that blacks had a number of virtues. Al-Suyuti based much of his text on a similar book written by Ibn al-Jawzi (d. c. 1200), entitled "The Illumination of the darkness on the merits of the blacks and the Ethiopians" ("Tanwīr al-ghabash fī faḍl al-sūdān wa-'l-ḥabash").[47] In this work, Ibn al-Jawzī praised the blacks for their physical strength, bravery, generosity, good manners, harmlessness, cheerfulness, sweetness of breath, easiness of expression, and fluency.[48] Al-Suyuti's "Raising the status" repeats much of Ibn al-Jawzi's text and explains the origins

[44] On this correspondence, see E. M. Sartain, "Jalal ad-Din As-Suyuti's Relations with the People of Takrur," *Journal of Semitic Studies* 16, no. 2 (1971): 193–8; Sartain, *Jalāl al-dīn al-Suyūṭī: Biography and Background* (Cambridge: Cambridge University Press, 1975), 50–1; Norris, *The Tuaregs: Their Islamic Legacy and Its Diffusion in the Sahel* (Warminster: Aris & Phillips, 1975), 45–7; Ould Cheikh, *Eléments d'histoire de la Mauritanie* (Nouakchott: Institut mauritanien de recherche scientifique, 1988), 23–39.

[45] Norris, *Arab Conquest*, 122–3; Hunwick, *Sharīʿa in Songhay: The Replies of al-Maghīlī to the Questions of Askia al-Ḥājj Muḥammad* (Oxford: Oxford University Press, 1985), 43.

[46] For a modern publication of "Raising the status," see note 28. The abridgement has also been published: *Azhār al-ʿurūsh fī akhbār al-ḥubūsh*, ed. ʿAbd Allāh ʿĪsā al-Ghazālī (Kuwait: Markaz al-makhṭūṭāt wa-'l-turāth wa-'l-wathā'iq, 1995). Al-Suyūṭī also wrote several other works on related subjects, such as the good qualities of slave girls, poems and sayings in praise of blacks, etc. On these different works by al-Suyūṭī, see Saud H. al-Khathlan, "A Critical Edition of Kitāb Rafʿ Sha'n al-Ḥubshān by Jalāl al-dīn al-Suyūṭī" (Ph.D. diss., University of St. Andrews, 1983), 14–17, 26, 33–4.

[47] Published as Abū al-Faraj ʿAbd al-Raḥmān b. al-Jawzī, *Tanwīr al-ghabash fī faḍl al-sūdān wa-'l-ḥabash*, ed. Marzūq ʿAlī Ibrāhīm (Riyad: Dār al-sharīf, 1998).

[48] Akbar Muhammad, "The Image of Africans in Arabic Literature: Some Unpublished Manuscripts," in *Slaves and Slavery in Muslim Africa: Islam and the Ideology of Enslavement*, ed. John Ralph Willis (London: Clarendon, 1985), I: 55. See also Imran Hamza Alawiye, "Ibn al-Jawzī's Apologia on Behalf of the Black People and their Status in Islam: A Critical Edition and Translation of Kitāb Tanwīr al-Ghabash fī Faḍl al-Sūdān wa-'l-Ḥabash" (Ph.D. diss., University of London, 1985).

of the blacks by laying out a series of hadiths that demonstrate their genealogy through Ham, although denying that their color is the result of a curse by Noah.[49] There are a number of works of a similar nature that purport to defend the blacks against their detractors. Al-Suyuti's text is not especially original or outstanding in the context of this larger literature, but because of his reputation, the text was widely read and certainly influential.[50]

The importance of Ibn Khaldun and al-Suyuti to the development of racial thinking in the Sahel is evident in a remarkable text written in 1615 by the celebrated Timbuktu jurist Aḥmad Bābā (d. 1627) on the qualities of black people in the context of slavery. Ahmad Baba had been taken into forcible exile in Marrakesh after the successful Moroccan invasion of the Niger Bend beginning in 1591.[51] In North Africa between 1593 and 1608, he found himself confronted with a much more racialized discourse – equating blackness with slavery – than he was evidently accustomed to in Timbuktu. This seems to have played a role in pushing him to write an extended rebuttal of what he considered to be the false ideas held by North Africans about black people in the Sahel. He entitled his text the "The ladder of ascent towards grasping the law concerning transported blacks" ("Mirʿāj al-ṣuʿūd ilā nayl ḥukm majlūb al-sūd"). A debate had apparently arisen in sixteenth-century North Africa about whether all black Africans were by definition non-Muslims, and therefore, whether they had permanent slave status regardless of later conversions to, or professions of, Islam. The issue was provoked by the concerns of apparently pious Muslims over whether it was legitimate to buy slaves imported from sub-Saharan Africa who claimed to be Muslims.[52] In response to a series of questions sent to him, Ahmad Baba,

49 Al-Suyūṭī, *Rafʿ*, 37–49, 207–11; al-Suyūṭī, *Azhār*, 19–22.

50 I am not aware of any extant manuscript copies of this text in West Africa, although it was quoted in the writings of some Sahelian writers such as Ahmad Baba. On the large number of copies of the manuscript extant in libraries around the Middle East, see al-Khathlan, "A Critical Edition," 44.

51 On the life of Ahmad Baba, see Mahmoud Zouber, *Ahmad Baba de Tombouctou (1556–1627): sa vie et son œuvre* (Paris: G.-P. Maisonneuve et Larose, 1977).

52 The issue would become even more controversial when in 1699, the Moroccan Sultan Mawlay Ismaʿil ordered the enslavement of the entire free Black population of Morocco in order to incorporate them into the royal army. See Chouki El Hamel, "'Race', Slavery and Islam in Maghribi Mediterranean Thought: The Question of the Haratin in Morocco," *Journal of North African Studies* 7, no. 3 (2002): 29–52; Hunwick, "Islamic Law and Polemics Over Race and Slavery in North and West Africa (16th–19th century)," in *Slavery in the Islamic Middle East*, ed. Shaun E. Marmon (Princeton, NJ: Marcus Wiener, 1999), 52–9; Allan Meyers, "Class, Ethnicity, and Slavery: The Origins of the Moroccan

who was of Sanhaja Berber origin,[53] refuted the equation of blackness with slavery by what amounted to a rejection of North African ideas about race. For Ahmad Baba, enslavement was only justified by nonbelief in Islam, and this applied to all people, black and white:

> You know that the cause of enslavement is unbelief, and that the unbelievers of the Sūdān are like any other unbelievers in this regard – Jews, Christians, Persians, Berbers or others whose persistence in unbelief rather than Islam has been established.... This is proof that there is no difference between any unbelievers in this regard. Whoever is enslaved in a state of unbelief may rightly be owned, whoever he is, as opposed to those of all groups who converted to Islam of their own free will, such as the people of Bornu, Kano, Songhay, Katsina, Gobir and Mali and some of [the people of] Zakzak. They are free Muslims who may not be enslaved under any circumstances.[54]

The argument that adherence to Islam trumps race as a factor in enslavement according to Islamic law is very well established. The issue that concerned Ahmad Baba's questioners was whether there were legitimate Muslims among the blacks in sub-Saharan Africa. One of the ways in which this could be known, according to the questioner, was according to the history of Muslim conquest of the blacks and whether the blacks who claimed to be Muslims had in fact converted to Islam by force. The questioner suggested that if the ancestors of the blacks who claim to be Muslim in the present had in fact been conquered in holy war, then they could still be legitimately enslaved. I will have more to say about the premise of the question in Chapter 2. But in his response, Ahmad Baba relied on historical arguments about the spread of Islam in Africa and the historical strength of certain Muslim states there such as ancient Ghana, the Mali Empire, and the Songhay Empire. To support his case, he quoted some of the most prominent Arab historians, such al-Bakri, al-Idrisi, and Ibn Khaldun.[55] Ahmad Baba did not deny that there were unbelievers in Africa who could rightfully be enslaved; rather, he sought to demonstrate that some Africans had adopted Islam voluntarily

ʿabīd," *IJAHS* 10 (1977): 427–42; Meyers, "Slave Soldiers and State Politics in Early ʿAlawī Morocco, 1668–1727," *IJAHS* 16 (1983): 39–48.

[53] In more recent texts from northern Mali, he is referred to by the nisba given to him during his stay in North Africa – al-Sūdānī – which of course refers to the place of his origin but which also carries the racial identifier of blackness. His full name is: Aḥmad Bābā b. Aḥmad b. Aḥmad b. ʿUmar b. Muḥammad ʿAqīt.

[54] Aḥmad Bābā, *Miʿrāj al-Ṣuʿūd*, 27.

[55] Aḥmad Bābā, *Miʿrāj al-Ṣuʿūd*, 24–6. This is noted by John Ralph Willis, "Islamic Africa: Reflections on the Servile Estate," *Studia Islamica* 52 (1980): 195–6.

and that there had long been Muslim states in Africa that raided other Africans who were non-Muslims. The dynamic of Islam in Africa was therefore an internal one.

On the question of race itself, Ahmad Baba discussed the Hamitic origins of the blacks as it was laid out in al-Suyuti and Ibn al-Jawzi, both of whom he quoted. He seemed noncommittal about the question of the Hamitic origins of the blacks, but he did reject the story of Noah's curse of Ham's son Canaan. Instead, he supported Ibn al-Jawzi's position that the story was incorrect, although he later suggested that perhaps the curse on Ham's son was effective on most of Ham's descendants, but not all of them.[56] He quoted a hadith from the Prophet Muhammad cited by al-Suyuti in the "Raising the status" as the authoritative reason for racial difference: "Adam was created from a handful [of earth] which [God] took from all parts of the world. Hence his offspring turned out according to the earth [they were made from]; some came out red, others white, others black, some were easy going, others downcast, some were evil and others good."[57] Ahmad Baba then cited Ibn Khaldun's environmental theory of racial difference. None of this seemed to be especially important to Ahmad Baba because his position was, following Ibn Khaldun, that the only important difference between human beings is religious. Since Islam is open to all people and has adherents among all peoples, racial difference should play no role in distinguishing between those who are virtuous and those who are not.

It is, however, interesting that the first explicit discussion of race by a Sahelian writer was provoked by his exposure to North Africa. Ahmad Baba's essential argument is that the North Africans just do not understand West Africa and they make serious mistakes regarding who can and cannot be legitimately enslaved. For someone such as Ahmad Baba, the abiding divide between people in West Africa was not their race but their qualities as free Muslims or nonbelievers. This argument would remain influential in the Sahel.[58] I will return to the reception of Ahmad Baba's text in Chapter 2. It was cited in another text written in the nineteenth century by a writer from Timbuktu, who wrote a very similar work on the relationship between race and slavery as he had encountered it in North Africa.[59]

[56] Aḥmad Bābā, *Miʿrāj al-Ṣuʿūd*, 35.

[57] Ibid., 32.

[58] Jennifer Lofkrantz, "Ransoming Policies and Practices in the Western and Central Bilād al-sūdūn, c. 1800–1910" (Ph.D. diss., York University, 2008), 39.

[59] Muḥammad al-Sanūsī b. Ibrāhīm al-Jārimī, "Tanbīh ahl al-tughyān ʿalā ḥurriyyat al-sūdān" (IHERIAB ms. 1575). See Hunwick's discussion of these texts in "Islamic Law," 62.

The rejection of a link between race and Islam foreshadowed an important objection to the changes that would occur in Sahelian thinking about race after the seventeenth century.

CONSTRUCTIONS OF AUTHORITY, CONSTRUCTIONS OF RACE

Ahmad Baba lived in a period of great change in the Sahel. The Moroccan invasion of the Niger Bend and the destruction of the Songhay Empire beginning in 1591 marked the start of a wider shift in political relations along the desert edge. At the height of its power, Songhay authority had extended well into the Sahara, as far as Taghaza and Agades, from where it forced many Berber-speaking pastoralists into tributary relationships. By the seventeenth century, the loci of power had begun to shift toward the pastoralists, who were increasingly able to impose themselves on sedentary populations.[60] Similar developments occurred in other areas of the Sahel, such as the Senegal valley, where pressures and interventions from Hassaniyya Arabic-speakers to the north in Mauritania undermined existing Fulbe political structures.[61] But if there was a shift at this time in the relative balance of power between communities based in the northern Sahel and those located further to the south, there were also significant upheavals within Sahelian pastoralist groups themselves that resulted in realignments of political power and status. These developments, which appear to have reached a climax in the second half of the seventeenth century, played an important role in subsequent ideological constructions of social relations within the Sahel and in defining a set of idealized relations with people defined as blacks.[62]

All across the Sahel, local traditions speak of important events that established the dominance of particular groups. In the southwestern Mauritanian region of the Gebla, a conflict in the 1670s, known as

[60] On the historical details of this shift in power in the Niger Bend after the Moroccan invasion, see Michel Abitbol, *Tombouctou et les Arma. De la conquête marocaine du Soudan nigérien en 1591 à l'hégémonie de l'empire peul du Maçina en 1853* (Paris: G.P. Maisonneuve et Larose, 1979); Elizabeth Hodgkin, "Social and Political Relations on the Niger Bend in the Seventeenth Century" (Ph.D. diss., University of Birmingham, 1987).

[61] David Robinson, *Chiefs and Clerics: Abdul Bokar Kan and Futa Toro, 1853–1891* (Oxford: Clarendon, 1975), 10–12.

[62] P.F. de Moraes Farias has argued that the seventeenth century marked the beginning of the historigraphical tradition in the Sahel, in response to the Moroccan invasion ("Intellectual Innovation and Reinvention of the Sahel: the Seventeenth-century Timbuktu Chronicles," in *The Meanings of Timbuktu*, ed. Shamil Jeppie and Souleymane Bachir Diagne [Cape Town: HSRC Press, 2008], 97).

Shur Bubba, is said to have marked the definitive conquest of Berber-speaking lineages by ḥassānī Arab groups. As a result of this defeat, the conquered lineages foreswore military activities and assumed the subordinate social role as Islamic religious specialists. As such, the hierarchical distinction between warrior- (HAr. ḥassān) and clerical-status (HAr. zwāyā) groups was formalized. In other parts of the Sahel, similar stories tell of the emergence of subsequently dominant groups among the Tuareg in approximately the same period. In the Aïr Massif, the arrival of the Kel Ewey and their displacement of the previously established Kel Gress and Kel Ferwan occurred in the second half of the seventeenth century. Likewise, the Iwellemmedan confederacy, the Kel Entsar, and the Kunta appear to have achieved their political importance at about this time.[63] Scholars have debated the degree of importance to attribute to these occurrences in the establishment of Sahelian social structures.[64] Certainly, the local representations of these events simplify more complex processes of migration and political change that must have occurred over longer periods of time. Also, the dichotomy established between so-called warrior- and clerical-status groups and their respective social roles does not fully reflect actual social practice or the historical reality that the status of particular groups sometimes changed over time.[65]

[63] Stewart, "Southern Saharan," 77.

[64] Colonial writers such as Paul Marty saw in the events of Shur Bubba a culmination of an ethnic conflict between indigenous Berber-speaking groups and hassani Arabs, which resulted in Arab hegemony (*Etudes sur l'Islam et les tribus maures, les Brakna* [Paris: E. Leroux, 1921]). Charles Stewart argued that the story of Shur Bubba was a foundation myth that provided a social charter for the complementary occupational and status distinction between warriors and clerical-status groups that came to underlie the segmentary nature of Sahelian societies. In Stewart's view, similar developments occurred all across the Sahel in the second half of the seventeenth century, all of which constituted a larger Sahelian world whose religious specialists would play an important role in spreading a particular kind of Islamic practice throughout West Africa ("Southern Saharan"). Others, such as Abdel Wedoud ould Cheikh and Pierre Bonte, have played down the importance of the seventeenth century as formative in the constitution of segmentary society and bīḍān identity. See Ould Cheikh, *Eléments*, 63–7; Ould Cheikh, "Nomadisme," 830–982; Bonte, "Tribus, fractions, et état: Les conflits de succession dans l'émirat de l'Adrar," *CEA* 22–4 (1987–88): 489–516. Webb sees the seventeenth century as a period when an increase in frontier violence along the desert edge produced articulations of black-white identity, of which the Wars of Shur Bubba are but the best known example (*Desert Frontier*, 33–4). Timothy Cleaveland highlights the history of social mobility that often lies beneath the apparently fixed categories of warrior and cleric (*Becoming Walāta*, 3–36).

[65] Stewart, "Southern Saharan," 78–81.

I do not argue that the seventeenth century marks a radical break in Sahelian history or that the social and cultural formations that appear to have been formalized at this time were not continuous with what was already there. From at least the time of the Almoravids to the Imagsharen hegemony in the Niger Bend in the fifteenth century, the Kel Essuk in the Adrar-n-Ifoghas, and the Tuareg groups in the Aïr Massif, there are recognizable antecedents to more recent social configurations. The process of social and cultural change in the Sahel was unquestionably a gradual one; it is equally clear, however, that a complex process of what, for lack of a better term, we may call "Arabization" was occurring. This process was subject to wide variation. In the western regions of the Sahel, Arabic was increasingly adopted as a language of daily social intercourse by formerly Berber-speaking populations. This did not occur to nearly the same extent in eastern areas where Tuareg groups predominated. However, the Arab influence should not be judged solely by the criteria of adoption of the Arabic language. The importance that the "social charters" of the seventeenth century assign to specialization in Islamic religious knowledge, and to the so-called clerical-status groups or lineages (the Tuareg equivalent to "zwaya" is "inesleman"), suggest that Islam itself was becoming a more important component in Sahelian life.[66] By entering ever more fully into the world of Arab Islamic culture, and by constructing and elaborating on genealogical connections to important Arab Islamic ancestors, the elite stratum in Sahelian pastoralist societies increasingly defined itself as part of one world and distinct from another.

In the fourteenth century, the Arab geographer al-ʿUmarī reported that in the land of the blacks, there were three independent white Muslim kings who were Berbers. He was referring to the sultan of Aïr, the sultan of Tādmakka in the Adrar-n-Ifoghas, and a third sultan whose identity is unclear.[67] By the end of the seventeenth century, local writers in these areas located the "land of the blacks" significantly further to the south. Whereas Ahmad Baba sought to delink race and adherence to Islam when addressing a North African (or at least Saharan) audience, later writers

[66] The dearth of local written sources, other than those that are epigraphic, before the seventeenth century, makes it extremely difficult to trace developments before this time. Certainly, sites of Islamic specialization existed before the seventeenth century. Timbuktu was well known for its scholars, the most notable of which were Ahmad Baba and Muhammad Baghayogho (d. 1523–24). For the earlier impact of trans-Saharan connections, see P.F. de Moraes Farias, *Arabic Medieval Inscriptions from the Republic of Mali: Epigraphy, Chronicles, and Songhay-Tuāreg History* (Oxford: Oxford University Press, 2003), cxvi.

[67] In Levtzion and Hopkins, *Corpus*, 274.

in the Sahel would do their utmost to ensure that religious authority was entangled with lineage. Whiteness was therefore not really about the skin color or physical characteristics of those who invoked this label, although it did sometimes manifest itself in this way in descriptions of founding figures;[68] rather, it lay in the accepted genealogical connection to important people in the historical and religious pantheon of Arab Islam. Blackness, by contrast, was defined most fundamentally by the lack of such connections. In many Arabic documents written in the Sahel, the label "blacks" (sudan) appears as the opposite of the word for "Muslims."[69]

Sahelian written literature on local history and genealogy is characterized by extremely obvious borrowings from important works on these same themes produced in the wider metropolitan Arab world. Certainly, much of the reason for this lies in the form of such literature, which placed a high premium on acknowledged and accurate quotations from accepted authorities. Writers such as Ibn Khaldun were often quoted directly by Sahelian writers on issues such as the Berber populations that lived in the area in medieval times. Likewise, there are locally written manuscripts that detail the Hamitic origins of the blacks and Berbers.[70] The important function of this borrowing, whether acknowledged or not, is that it allowed Sahelian intellectuals to insert their more local historical or genealogical material into a larger, existing structure or narrative that was part of the Arab Muslim world. Although almost impossible to prove definitively, it seems likely that the fairly widespread production of written Arabic texts in the Sahel was itself the product of the larger process I have been discussing, whereby local intellectuals,

68 See, for example, Wālid b. Khālunā's description of Nāṣir al-Dīn as white-skinned, small, with curly hair, and a nonprotruding nose; "Amr al-wālī Nāṣir al-dīn," in *Chroniques de la Mauritanie sénégalaise. Nacer Eddine*, ed. and trans. Ismaël Hamet (Paris: E. Leroux, 1911), 165 (page 8 in the Arabic).

69 Raymond Taylor, "Of Disciples," 4. Nineteenth-century Wolof ruler of Kajoor in the 1860s referred to non-Muslim Sereer as "black savages who are our subjects" (James Searing, "Conversion to Islam: Military Recruitment and Generational Conflict in a Sereer-Safen Village (Bandia), 1920–1938," *JAH* 44, no. 1 [2003]: 76).

70 See, for example, an undated manuscript entitled "Ansāb al-ʿarab," written by somebody named Muḥammad b. ʿAbd Allāh (IHERIAB ms. 1557), in which the origins of the Berbers, Copts, and blacks from Ham are laid out. I make no claim to be able to offer any quantitative evidence for the number of manuscripts that make reference to writers such as Ibn Khaldun. In addition to the manuscripts cited in note 38, there is another one devoted entirely to extracts from Ibn Khaldun and others on the origins of the Blacks (IHERIAB ms. 8625). Unfortunately, this is also an undated text, and the first page is badly damaged.

at least, increasingly identified with Arab Muslim culture. In any case, almost all of the extant written material produced by Sahelian intellectuals was produced after the seventeenth century. Where earlier material has been discovered, the overlay of external motifs and sources is less significant.[71]

The genealogical claims made by virtually every significant Arabic- or Berber-speaking "noble" group in the Sahel invoke an Arab Muslim origin. The relative strengths of different genealogical claims vary significantly in ways that suggest historical competition over power and status among different groups, which has continued down to the present day in some cases.[72] Broadly speaking, most Arabophone warrior (hassan) lineages trace their descent to Jaʿfar b. Abī Ṭālib (brother of ʿAlī and cousin of the Prophet Muhammad)[73] through a branch of the Banū Hilāl, the principal Arab Bedouin groups that migrated into North Africa in the eleventh century. In particular, these groups claim a common ancestor in Ḥassān, who was a member of a subgroup of the Banu Hilal called the Banu Maʿqil, members of which had penetrated into northern Mauritania by the fourteenth century.[74] Whatever may be the complex history of the migration of Arab groups into the southwestern Sahara and their ability to attract and assimilate clients, local historical traditions represent the emergence of Arab hassan hegemony as a result of invasions and decisive military victories.[75] It is important to note that the model of hassani descent was also taken up, at least in part, by some dominant Tuareg groups that assumed the same role as the warrior lineages in Arabophone areas. The Iwellemmedan noble lineages, for example, claim that their founding figure, Muhammad Wa-n-Ara, was a hassani Arab born in southern Mauritania in the middle of the sixteenth century. He later came to the Adrar-n-Ifoghas and offered his military services to the chief of the Tuareg of Tadmakkat. As a reward for his services, he married

[71] Thomas Whitcomb, "New Evidence on the Origins of the Kunta – I," *BSOAS* 38, no. 1 (1975), 108.

[72] Ould Cheikh, "La Tribu comme volonté et comme représentation: Le Facteur religieux dans l'organisation d'une tribu maure, Les Awlād Abyayri," in *Al-Ansāb: La Quête des Origines. Anthropologie historique de la société tribale arabe*, ed. Pierre Bonte, Edouard Conte, Constant Hamès, Ould Cheikh (Paris: Editions de la Maison des sciences de l'homme, 1991), 230.

[73] Ould Cheikh, "Nomadisme," 198–9.

[74] Ould Cheikh, "Nomadisme," 202; Norris, *Arab Conquest*, 26–7.

[75] In addition to the War of Shur Bubba, Mauritanian historical traditions speak of decisive Arab impositions of tribute on existing Berberophone populations in the fourteenth and fifteenth centuries. See Norris, *Arab Conquest*, 33–5.

the daughter of this chief. It is from this line that some Iwellemmedan claims to Arab origin arise.[76]

The genealogical claims made by many clerical zwaya- and inesleman-status groups are premised on a different kind of authority. Unlike their warrior cousins, clerical groups could not rely on the same narratives of conquest to establish their historical position. Instead, they generally established links to a "saintly" ancestor and thereby connect themselves to the "unseen" power of religious knowledge. Because these groups were, at least in theory, specialized in the practice of the Islamic religious sciences, it is not surprising that they would structure their descent from renowned religious figures. But the authority that these groups claim was derived both from a mastery of the Islamic religious sciences and from a privileged position allowing special knowledge of God, what is called "walāya" in Arabic, a term usually translated as "saintliness" or "nearness to God." It is very common in the local histories of these groups to find references to the important "awliyāʾ" (Ar. sing. "walī"), or "saints," who constitute the local ancestors from whom authority is at least partly derived. One of the best-known examples of this sort of genealogy comes from the Tashumsha, the clerical group whose defeat in Shur Bubba confirmed their zwaya status. The Tashumsha attached themselves historically to Nāṣir al-Dīn, the religious leader who launched this war in the first place and was ultimately killed by his hassani Arab enemies. But the Tashumsha also claimed descent from Abū Bakr, the companion of the Prophet Muhammad and the first caliph.[77]

Similarly, the people of Arawan in the Azawad (several hundred kilometers north of Timbuktu) traced their decent to a religious figure named Ahmad ag Adda (d. 1635) and several companions, who founded the desert town of Arawan in the late sixteenth century as a religious sanctuary. According to local traditions, Ahmad ag Adda, who was a member of the clerical Kel Essuk of the Adrar-n-Ifoghas, came to the area where he would establish Arawan after his original home in the

[76] Norris, *Arab Conquest*, 106–8. There are a number of traditions among the Iwellemmedan concerning Arab Muslim origins. Some of these seem to have more in common with zwaya/inesleman traditions than with the Arab hassani lineage discussed here. Some of these different traditions are laid out in A. Richer, *Les Oulliminden. Les Touareg du Niger (Région de Tombouctou-Gao)* (Paris: E. Larose, 1924), 49–56; Charles Grémont, "Les Touareg Iwellemmedan (1647–1898): Un ensemble politique de la Boucle du Niger" (Ph.d. diss., Université Paris I, 2007).

[77] Shaykh Sīdi Muḥammad b. Aḥmad b. Sulaymān, "Letter to Commandant of Trarza, A.M. Théveniaut," in *Chroniques de la Mauritanie sénégalaise. Nacer Eddine*, ed. and trans. Ismaël Hamet (Paris: E. Leroux, 1911), 158.

Adrar-n-Ifoghas had been destroyed by Songhay rulers. Ahmad ag Adda and his companions "became famous for jurisprudence and for their sanctity and faith. They enjoyed a status of inviolability (Ar. ḥurma) throughout all the land. People began to bestow alms upon them and to seek their Baraka (blessing), from them and from their descendants until today."[78] Among the pieces of evidence recounted in local histories demonstrating his status as a "saint" is an episode in which he and a slave were imprisoned by the Moroccan conqueror of Songhay, Jawadir. Despite being placed in irons, Ahmad ag Adda was able to miraculously free himself and his slave at the appointed moment for prayers. When asked to explain how he was able to accomplish this feat, he responded simply in a manner befitting a saint: "With the permission of God."[79] But if the people of Arawan, and those related to them, such as the Kel Entsar,[80] base their authority on their connection to Ahmad ag Adda and his descendants, they also claim a prestigious Sherifian genealogy through ʿUqba b. Nāfiʿ (d. 683), the Arab Muslim conqueror of North Africa, to ʿAli b. Abi Talib.[81]

The importance of both a prestigious Arab Muslim genealogy and local ancestors recognized as saints in constructions of authority among clerical groups is perhaps best illustrated by the case of the Kunta, an important Arabophone zwaya lineage based in the Azawad in the eighteenth and nineteenth centuries, and perhaps the most prolific of any group in producing written materials. The Kunta gained prominence in the Azawad during the lifetime of Sīdi al-Mukhtār al-Kuntī (d. 1811) and his son, Sīdi Muḥammad b. Sīdi al-Mukhtār al-Kuntī (d. 1826). Under the leadership of these two men, the lineage built an important commercial network connecting the Sahel with Saharan entrepôts such as Tuwat.[82] However, the Kunta are better known for

[78] This passage is repeated in a number of manuscript histories of Arawan. The passage is translated in Norris, *Arab Conquest*, 82.

[79] From a manuscript by an unknown author entitled "Taʾrīkh ahl agād w'-arawān wa-karāmāt baʿḍ awliyāʾ-him" (IHERIAB ms. 9197).

[80] As is obvious from their name, the Kel Entsar claim descent from the Anṣār of Madina and trace their migration into North Africa, the central Sahara, and finally to the Niger Bend. However, they also claim that their lineage connects to Ahmad ag Adda because of a marriage between his mother and a Kel Entsar man named Ifna. As such, the Kel Entsar are able to claim a genealogy that ties them to the Anṣār and to a local Saharan saint. See Norris, *Arab Conquest*, 83.

[81] No author, "Khabar al-sūq" (IHERIAB ms. 4604).

[82] J. Genevière, "Les Kounta et leurs activités commerciales," *Bulletin de l'IFAN* 12 (1950): 1111–27. See also E. Ann McDougall, "The Ijil Salt Industry: Its role in the pre-

their role as Islamic scholars and saints, attracting clients and novices, or "talāmīdh," from across Muslim West Africa.[83] The Kunta claim a role of prominence in the Sahel that goes back many centuries. Like the Kel Essuk, the Kunta trace their descent from ʿUqba b. Nafiʿ. They say that they formed originally in Qayrawan (in Tunisia), where they say, wrongly, that ʿUqba is buried.[84] Sidi Muhammad describes the Kunta origins as follows:

> The Kunta, according to the unanimous agreement of the principal historians, originated in Qayrawan; and there is found the tomb of their ancestor, the most ancient in Islam, ʿUqba al-Mustajāb, son of Nāfiʿ, to whom God granted victory over the region of Ifriqiya as far as Ghana and Berki al-Ghamād, called in our time Bu Rigrig. [ʿUqba] left his son al-ʿAqib in Sīra[85], today called Walata; and his grave is in the courtyard of the mosque that he built there. ʿUqba made other expeditions with those who returned with him, devastating the regions of Takrūr, and he took its cities and its villages, one after the other, until he reached the district of Bawwar, inhabited at that time by the Awrabiyūn.[86] He besieged them for a month and then a mighty slaughter occurred between them in which many of his soldiers were martyred.[87]

According to Sidi al-Mukhtar al-Kunti in his "Blessings in the faith of the People of the Sunna" ("Kitāb al-minna fī iʿtiqād ahl al-sunna"), the Kunta

colonial economy of the Western Sudan" (Ph.D. diss., University of Birmingham, 1980), 93–8.

83 One of the best known novices was the Mauritanian al-Shaykh Sidiyya b. al-Mukhtār b. al-Hayba, who spent sixteen years at the Kunta zwaya in the Azawad. On Sidi al-Mukhtar al-Kunti's life see Stewart, *Islam and Social Order in Mauritania* (Oxford: Clarendon, 1973), 34; Yahya ould el-Bara, "The Life of Shaykh Sidi al-Mukhtar al-Kunti" in *The Meanings of Timbuktu*, ed. Samil Jeppie and Souleymane Bachir Diagne (Cape Town: HSRC Press, 2008), 198; ALA IV 68–94. For his son Sidi Muhammad, see ALA IV 94–115; MLG 1: 256–68.

84 Charles-André Julien, *History of North Africa: Tunisia, Algeria, Morocco, from the Arab Conquest to 1830*, trans. John Petrie (London: Praeger, 1970), 11.

85 A mistake in the text. The former name for Walata is Bīru.

86 The Awraba were a Berber group in the northern Maghrib. The site of Bawwar is unknown. It may be a confusion with "Kawār" (Kaouar) in the central Sahara where ʿUqba b. Nāfiʿ is said to have gone on a punitive expedition. Batran thinks that B-W-R should read Būra or Būda, which he equates with Tahuda in Tuwat. See Aziz A. Batran, *The Qadiryya Brotherhood in West Africa and the Western Sahara: The Life and Times of Shaykh al-Mukhtar al-Kunti, 1729–1811* (Rabat: Université Mohammed V-Souissi, 2001), 10. However, since it is mentioned after Takrūr, one assumes that the author intends to suggest that Bawwar and the Awraba were in the southwestern Sahara or Sahel. See Thomas Whitcomb "The Origins and Emergence of the Tribe of Kunta: A Contribution to the History of the Western Sahara between the Almoravid Period and the Seventeenth Century" (Ph.D. diss., University of London, 1978), 58–9.

87 Sīdi Muḥammad b. Sīdī al-Mukhtār al-Kuntī, "al-Risāla al-Ghallāwiyya," in Whitcomb, "Origins," English translation, 44, Arabic text, 305; a similar passage is in Sīdi

maintained their genealogical purity from the time of ʿUqba until the time of Sīdi Aḥmad al-Bakkaʾī Bū Damʿ al-Kuntī (d. 1515) by a practice of killing off all children except for one, who was chosen by the father as his successor:

> Amongst their traditions that are reported to have passed down from father to son is that in the event that one of them became father of several children, he educated and trained them. When he felt his end approaching, he chose from amongst them the one who was noteworthy for his virtues and ability and was thus worthy to succeed him, endowed him and expressed the wish that God take the souls of others.[88]

This story is clearly a genealogical trick to project directly backward to ʿUqba and avoid the necessity of filling in the lineages that would have been produced by different branches of the family.[89] When Sidi Ahmad al-Bakkaʾi Bu Damʿ abolished this custom, the Kunta entered the scene of Sahelian history at Walata and produced their first local saint. In one example, Sidi Ahmad saved Walata from wild lions by a miracle. Sidi Ahmad also established a religious school in Walata and began to attract students. Apparently, he encouraged the education of women but insisted on the separation of the sexes. He lectured to his female students from behind a curtain. He exhorted the women to observe "hijāb" (Ar. covering themselves for reasons of modesty), thereby emphasizing his Arab identity in criticizing what can only be interpreted as older Berber norms of free mixing of the sexes reported on so disapprovingly by Ibn Battuta. Sidi Ahmad's reputation for piety and miracles is said to have grown in the Sahel, and when he died in 1515, he was buried on the bank of a seasonal stream near Walata. It was as caretaker of this tomb that Sidi al-Mukhtar al-Kunti began his religious career two hundred and fifty years later.[90]

The connection to ʿUqba b. Nafiʿ made by the Kunta and others, including the Iwellemmedan Tuareg and the Fulbe,[91] is interesting because it illustrates a larger pattern in Sahelian local histories about the structure of relations with people defined as blacks. ʿUqba b. Nafiʿ was the Arab Islamic conqueror of North Africa and the founder of the new Muslim

Muḥammad b. Sīdī al-Mukhtār al-Kuntī, *Kitāb al-ṭarāʾif wa-ʾl-talāʾid*, ed. Abadine ould Baba Ahmed (Nouakchott: al-Maʿhad al-mūrītānī li-ʾl-baḥth al-ʿilmī, 1994), II: 11.

88 Cited in Batran, *Qadiryya*, 21–2.

89 There are other Kunta texts that provide details on other branches of the family. See Whitcomb, "Origins," 56

90 On the Kunta in Walata, see Cleaveland, *Becoming Walāta*, 147–53.

91 For Iwellemmedan traditions connecting them to ʿUqba, see Richer, *Oulliminden*, 49–56. On the Fulbe see two anonymous texts: "Tarjama fī aṣl al-fullāniyīn" (IHERIAB ms. 43), "Masʾila taʾrīkhiyya" (IHERIAB ms. 97), and David Robinson, *The Holy War of Umar Tal: The Western Sudan in the Mid-Nineteenth Century* (Oxford: Clarendon, 1985), 83.

capital at Qayrawan in 670. According to the accounts of Arab historians written centuries later, his campaigns against the Berbers took him all the way to the Sous in southern Morocco, where he reached the shore of the Atlantic Ocean. He was killed in 683 in an ambush laid by a combined force of Byzantines and Berbers.[92] Although ʿUqba's campaigns were concentrated along the North African littoral, he did make one punitive excursion into the interior of the Fezzan (in southern Libya), apparently reaching the oasis of Kawar (Kaouar in modern Niger), from which he took a number of slaves.[93] Elizabeth Savage has argued that the slaves taken by ʿUqba on this expedition were likely Saharan Berbers rather than blacks because the chronicles make no mention of their ethnic or racial identity. Furthermore, black slaves did not appear in North African slave markets until the end of the seventh century.[94] Nonetheless, in the Kunta account of ʿUqba's campaigns, the claim is made that the jihad reached all the way across the desert to the land of Takrur. They say that ʿUqba and his forces penetrated deep into the land of the blacks and reached a place where no animal could survive the heat of the sun.[95] The idea that ʿUqba waged jihad against the blacks is widely believed by many people in the Sahel, and there are some parts of the eleventh- and twelfth-century texts of al-Bakri and al-Idrisi that might have led to such a construction.[96] A second expedition under the command of a grandson of ʿUqba named Ḥabīb b. Abī ʿUbayda to the Moroccan Sous and the land of the blacks is mentioned in Arab historical sources and also claimed by the Kunta.[97]

The historical likelihood of such military expeditions against the blacks in these early centuries is remote because the means of getting an army across the Sahara were not available. However, by connecting

[92] Julien, *History*, 7–11.

[93] Ibn ʿAbd al-Ḥakam (d. 871) provides an account of this in his "Futūḥ miṣr;" translated in Levtzion and Hopkins, *Corpus*, 12–13.

[94] Elizabeth Savage, *A Gateway to Hell, A Gateway to Paradise: The North African Response to the Arab Conquest* (Princeton, NJ: Darwin Press, 1997), 73–5; Savage, "Berbers and Blacks: Ibadi Slave Traffic in Eighth-Century North Africa," *JAH* 33, no. 3 (1992): 351–68. For other views about this expedition and its connection to sub-Saharan Africa, see Tadeusz Lewicki, *Arabic External Sources for the History of the South of the Sahara* (London: Curzon Press, 1974), 19–20; Knut Vikør, "The Early History of the Kawār Oasis: A Southern Border of the Maghrib or a Northern Border of the Sudan?" *The Maghreb Review* 12 (1987): 78–83.

[95] Batran, *Qadiryya*, 11.

[96] Ibid., 13.

[97] Ibid., 13. This is mentioned in Ibn ʿAbd al-Ḥakam's "Futūḥ miṣr," translated in Levtzion and Hopkins, *Corpus*, 13.

themselves to historical characters, such as ʿUqba, who brought Islam to Africa, groups like the Kunta were able to make the argument that they, too, were the bearers of Islam. North African historians and chroniclers had used the story of ʿUqba to elaborate the beginnings of the relationship between Arab Muslims and the Berbers. In effect, the Kunta picked up on this tradition and extended it to include the blacks. As such, the Kunta were able to situate themselves as the first to bring Islam to West Africa and the first to wage jihad against local black African infidels. Others who sought a similar mantle of Islamic authority over blacks attached themselves to the same genealogy. In Muhammad Bello's (d. 1837) extensive history of the Sokoto jihad in Hausaland at the beginning of the nineteenth century, entitled "The wages of the fortunate in the history of the land of Takrur" ("Infāq al-Maysūr fī taʾrīkh bilād al-takrūr"), he explains the historical relationship between blacks and the coming of Islam to West Africa.[98] Like the Kunta, he claimed that the Fulbe were the descendants of the original Arab Muslim conqueror of North Africa ʿUqba b. Nafiʿ.[99]

The story of ʿUqba's conquests of the blacks is only one example of Kunta claims to have always been at the vanguard of Islam in the Sahel. They also wove themselves into other histories of past relations between important Arab Muslims and local blacks. In the "The uncommon qualities and wonders" ("Kitāb al-Ṭarāʾif wa-ʾl-talāʾid"), Sidi Muhammad al-Kunti narrates a story about a meeting that took place in West Africa between Sīdī ʿUmar al-Shaykh al-Kuntī (d. 1552/3) and al-Maghili, the highly influential fifteenth-century Muslim scholar from North Africa who spent time in West Africa. During this meeting, it was reported that al-Maghili was highly impressed with the Kunta shaykh's vast knowledge of the Islamic sciences. The two became friends, and the Kunta shaykh was trained by al-Maghili in esoteric science (Ar. ʿilm al-bāṭin). At some point, the two men went on the pilgrimage to Mecca and stopped along the way in Egypt, where they met with al-Suyuti. The Egyptian was impressed with al-Maghili's vast knowledge and accorded him preeminence for his mastery of Islamic sciences and for his sanctity. Later, al-Maghili and the Kunta shaykh returned home to West Africa and became involved in a well-known historical relationship that connected al-Maghili with the king of the Songhay Empire Askia Muhammad and with the town of Katsina in

[98] Muḥammad Bello, *Infāq al-Maysūr fī taʾrīkh bilād al-takrūr*, ed. Haija al-Shādhilī (Rabat: Université Muhammad V-Souissi, 1996), 48.
[99] Robinson, *Holy War*, 83.

Hausaland. There was a disagreement between Askia Muhammad and al-Maghili over the death of one of al-Maghili's sons in Tuwat at the hands of the local population. The Songhay king refused to send an expedition to punish the entire town, so al-Maghili left Gao (the Songhay capital) and went to Katsina where he offered his religious services to the ruler there. Such was the wrath of al-Maghili at Askai Muhammad's behavior that he cursed the entire Songhay kingdom: "His city of Gao is a ruin-field; the state of Songhay is lost and has perished. We have transferred its structure to Katsina and the latter will be the capital [of Takrur] until the command of Allah comes. Then Tuwat will be smitten and He will ruin that town and He will wipe out its people and it is now as good as ruined."[100] When al-Maghili was about to die, he assembled the people who were around him and told them that anyone who desired his blessings should seek it from the Kunta Shaykh, Sidi ʿUmar.[101]

This story is clearly fictional. There is no external evidence to corroborate any meeting between al-Suyuti and al-Maghili. The apparent failure of the Songhay ruler to act against the people of Tuwat after the death of al-Maghili's son is contradicted by other evidence that suggests that all people from Tuwat in the Songhay Empire were arrested after news of this event reached Gao. Above all, the dates do not match.[102] However, like the story of ʿUqba, the connection to al-Maghili acts to legitimize Kunta claims to Islamic authority in West Africa. Having taken up the mantle of al-Maghili's spiritual power, the Kunta can claim their rightful role as masters in the tutelage of the blacks in matters of Islam. In effect, these stories act to structure an unequal relationship between the Kunta as the bearers of Islam, and the blacks who have always been, at best, the recipients of Islamic counsel, and at worst, non-Muslims who are the legitimate target of jihad and God's wrath.

CONCLUSION

The Kunta were not alone among clerical-status groups in weaving themselves into narratives of power and domination over people defined as blacks. The main protagonists in the War of Shur Bubba, the Tashumsha, made explicit the connection between their founding saint, Nasir al-Din, and the jihad he waged against blacks defined as infidels in the Senegal

[100] This passage is translated by Norris, *Arab Conquest*, 240.
[101] Ibid., 227–41.
[102] On these and other inconsistencies, see Hunwick, *Sharīʿa*, 42–4.

River valley.[103] Likewise, the founding figure of Arawan, Ahmad ag Adda, was given a role in the Moroccan invasion of Songhay in 1591. After being imprisoned by the Moroccans, it will be recalled that Ahmad ag Adda escaped from his chains. This so impressed the Moroccan expeditionary leader Jawadir that he bowed before the authority of this saint and, according to this tradition, would only attack the (Songhay) blacks with Ahmad ag Adda's permission, which he granted.[104]

Race was by no means the only – or even the most important – aspect of these constructions of authority. But ideas about racial difference are clearly part of the intellectual tapestry of the Sahel after the seventeenth century. What has been presented here is an analysis of an important strand of an intellectual development centered in Sahelian clerical lineages whereby authority was constructed, and transferred, by means of genealogical connections over time. As I have shown, these lines were simultaneously religious, ethno-linguistic, and racial.

There is a significant difference between ideas about color and those about race. The position that the Kunta sought to occupy in the Sahel required that they be at the head of a religious network that included people from across the area, including blacks. But the Kunta, like other Sahelian groups, also recognized internal color differences. In the "Ghallāwī epistle" ("al-Risāla al-Ghallāwiyya"), Sidi Muhammad explained a split that had occurred within the ranks of the Kunta during the seventeenth century because of a war that broke out between the "white" Awlād Mallūk and the "blacks" (Ar. al-kuḥl).[105] The term used to describe "noble" black members of the Kunta is "kuhl," rather than "sudan," which was reserved for blacks who could not claim Arab genealogy. It is the label sudan that carried the set of assumptions connected to ideas of racial difference. At root, the ubiquity of this term highlights the process whereby social status differences between nobles and non-nobles in the Sahel were racialized.

The idea of race that appears in the Arabic-language literature of the Sahel is therefore closely correlated with the idea of lineage. The absence of genealogical connections to Arab Muslim ancestors was what rendered

103 The history of this jihad is fairly well known. The details of the attack on the Blacks can be found in a local Arabic document published and translated in Hamet, *Chroniques*, 175–8.

104 This passages is from an undated anonymous document entitled "Ta'rīkh Arawān" (IHERIAB ms. 8905), f.2.

105 Sīdi Muḥammad b. Sīdi al-Mukhtār al-Kuntī, "al-Risāla al-Ghallāwiyya," in Whitcomb, "Origins," 314.

one black. Since blacks (sudan), purportedly, did not have the lineal connection to important bearers of Islam in the Sahel, they were put in the position, ideologically, of permanent tutelage or clientage to groups like the Kunta. Like the early non-Arab Muslims of the first centuries of Islamic history in the North African, blacks along the desert edge were assigned the position of clients in the constructions of authority made by scholarly Arab Muslim elites. Arabic-speaking free blacks (kuhl) among the Kunta did not find themselves defined in this way.

2

Reading the Blackness of the Sudan, c. 1600–1900

A SERVILE ESTATE?

As politically ascendant pastoralist intellectuals in the Sahel redefined themselves as distinct from those they called blacks, they also devoted attention to fixing the social and political meanings of blackness into a coherent ideological form. To do this, Sahelian intellectuals had to do more than reimagine the histories of the arrival of the first Muslims in the Sahel; they also needed to develop a set of particular interpretations of Islamic law that would juridically define blacks as people with meaningful legal disabilities. This chapter focuses on the ways that collective heritable social status was defined in the legal literature of the Sahel, and how blackness was made into a marker of permanent de jure inferiority. I will focus largely on several important collections of legal opinions written in the seventeenth and eighteenth centuries. By examining particular legal opinions, I will uncover some of the specific contexts in which racial claims were made and the concrete ends that these arguments aimed at achieving.

Blackness gained legal meaning in the seventeenth and eighteenth centuries in the Sahel. By the beginning of the nineteenth century, Muslim scholars in the region had accumulated a set of theoretical legal tools that could be used to render blacks as inferior to nonblacks. The importance of these developments is evident in the case of the forgery of the "Ta'rīkh al-fattāsh," an important seventeenth-century chronicle of the history of the Niger Bend.[1] A skilled nineteenth-century scholar loyal to Amadu

[1] The full title is "Ta'rīkh al-fattāsh fī akhbār al-buldān wa-'l-juyūsh wa-akābir al-nās" ("The history of the researcher into the events of the countries, the armies, and the notables of the people"). There are three possible authors: Maḥmūd Ka'ti (1468–1552/53),

Lobbo, the founder of the reformist Islamic state called the Hamdullahi Caliphate, inserted racial categories into the original chronicle to mark off permanent servile status for groups of people defined as black slaves.[2] By doing this, the scholar provided Amadu Lobbo with the justification for arguments he made about his authority over the people of the Niger Bend. The forged "Ta'rikh al-fattash" shows us some of the important work that the theorization of collective racial categories could perform by the nineteenth century.

Modern scholars had been suspicious about the authenticity of parts of the "Ta'rikh al-fattash" since it was first edited and translated into French in 1913.[3] Unlike the other great seventeenth-century chronicle of the Niger Bend, the "Ta'rīkh al-sūdān" ("The history of the blacks"), which had been published and translated into French in 1900,[4] there were significant problems in determining an authoritative version of the "Ta'rikh al-fattash." From the number of discrepancies in the three partial manuscript versions available to the editors, it was clear from its original publication that there had been some adulteration of the original text. The clues were quite obvious. In some manuscript versions, it was predicted that the last of the twelve caliphs of Islam foretold by the Prophet Muhammad would be a man named Ahmad, from the Sangare (Fulbe) people, in the region of Masina in the Middle Niger. Amadu Lobbo had had this "prophesy" inserted into the chronicles as part of his efforts to establish his authority.

If the prediction about Amadu Lobbo becoming the twelfth caliph was the most obvious forgery, a number of other counterfeits have also

Maḥmūd Ka'ti b. al-Ḥājj al-Mutawakkil Ka'ti (d. 1593), or Ibn al-Mukhtār Gombele. See Mahmoud Kâti ben El-Hâdj El-Motaouakkel Kâti, *Tarikh El-Fettach ou Chronique du Chercheur pour server à l'historie des villes, des armées et des principaux personages du Tekrour*. ed. and trans. O. Houdas and M. Delafosse (Paris: Adrien-Maisonneuve, 1964 [1913]), xvii–xix; John Hunwick, "Studies in the Ta'rīkh al-Fattāsh. (1) Its Authors and Textual History," *RBCAS* 5 (1969): 57–65; Nehemia Levtzion, "A Seventeenth-Century Chronicle by Ibn al-Mukhtār: A Critical Study of Ta'rīkh al-Fattāsh," *BSOAS* 34, no. 3 (1971): 579.

2 The suspected forger was Amadu Lobbo's chief counselor, Alfa Nouhoun Tayrou (Alfa Nūh b. al-Ṭāhir). He had studied with both Sidi al-Mukhtar al-Kunti in the Azawad, and Usman dan Fodio in Hausaland. See Robinson, *Holy War*, 81; Amadou Hampâté Bâ and Jacques Daget, *L'Empire peul du Macina* (1818–1853) (Paris: Mouton, 1962), 114n.

3 The editors of the "Ta'rikh al-fattash," O. Houdras and M. Delafosse, noted this in their introduction. An early skeptic was Joseph Brun, "Notes sur le Tarikh-el-Fattach," *Anthropos* 9 (1914): 590–6.

4 Written by 'Abd al-Raḥmān al-Sa'dī (1594–c. 1655/56), published as Abderrahman ben Abdallah ben 'Imran ben 'Amir Es-Sa'di, *Tarikh es-Soudan*, trans. O. Houdas (Paris: Adrien-Maisonneuve, 1964 [1900]).

been uncovered. Nehemia Levtzion demonstrated that the parts of the "Ta'rikh al-fattash" that discuss slave castes were part of the nineteenth-century material added to the text. In these passages, permanent servile status is accorded to people described as blacks, using the Arabic term "zanj."[5] The forged text says that the Songhay ruler Askia Muhammad inherited twenty-four servile castes from his predecessor Sunni Bāru (r. 1492–1493), the son of Sunni ʿAli Beer: "God bequeathed to the aforementioned Askia al-Hajj Muhammad all the land of Sunni Baru, which extended from Kanta to Sibiridougou,[6] and he found in his possession that day twenty-four tribes (qabīla) of slaves belonging to him, not free people enslaved."[7] The text names and discusses twelve of these groups of slaves, including the traditions of their origin and the annual levies that they were expected to pay to the state.[8]

The (Pseudo) "Ta'rikh al-fattash" also claims that the legal status of these slave groups was confirmed by both al-Maghili and al-Suyuti. While on his pilgrimage to Mecca, the chronicle tells us, Askia Muhammad stopped to see al-Suyuti in Cairo and asked him about a number of issues, including the legal status of these slave groups: "He asked [al-Suyuti] about the matter of the twenty-four tribes which he found in the possession of Sunni Baru, and which he had inherited from his ancestors." After describing these groups of slaves, al-Suyuti is reported to have responded: "Half of them can permissibly belong to you. It is better to renounce the other half because there is some doubt about them."[9] Al-Suyuti then went on to list the slave groups that belonged to Askia Muhammad. Among these

[5] This term would have been familiar to a scholar such as Alfa Nouhoun Tayrou from Arabic historical and geographical literature; al-Ṭabarī (d. 923) gave a detailed history if the famous zanj slave revolt in southern Iraq in the ninth century (*The History of al-Ṭabarī. Vol 36. The Revolt of the Zanj*, trans. David Waines [Albany: SUNY Press, 1992]), and it was the common word used in Arabic geographical writings to describe blacks along the East African coast. See Devic, L.-Marcel, *Le pays des Zendjs ou la côte orientale d'Afrique au Moyen-âge* (Amsterdam: Oriental Press, 1975).

[6] According to John Hunwick, Kanta probably refers to the old kingdom of Kebbi that would have been located at the same latitude as modern Say in Niger, and Sibiridougou is near modern Ségou ("Some Notes on the Term 'Zanj' and Its Derivatives in a West African Chronicle," *RBCAD* 4 [1968]: 43).

[7] The last part is: "qabīla ariqqāʾ lahu aḥrār usturiqqū." Kâti, *Tarikh El-Fettach*, 55 (Arabic text); John Hunwick, *Timbuktu and the Songhay Empire: Al-Saʿdī's Taʾrīkh al-sūdān Down to 1613 and Other Contemporary Documents* (Leiden: Brill, 1999), xxxi.

[8] Hunwick, "Some Notes on the Term 'Zanj'," 43. These passages in the (Pseudo) "Ta'rikh al-fattash" have been taken at face value by some modern historians. For example, Sékéné Mody Cissoko, *Tombouctou et l'empire Songhay* (Paris: L'Harmattan, 1996 [1975]), 169–70.

[9] Kâti, *Tarikh El-Fettach*, 14 (Arabic text).

were a number of occupational groups – what Tal Tamari calls endogamous castes[10] – including blacksmiths, leatherworkers, and praise singers, as well as the Sorko, who were the boatmen and fishers of the Niger Bend, and a group called the "ar-bi," which means "blacks" in Songhay.[11] Elsewhere in the (Pseudo) "Ta'rikh al-fattash" there are a number of references to gifts made of blacks (zanj) to Muslim scholars and descendants of the Prophet by Songhay rulers.[12]

There is a discussion in the original seventeenth-century "Ta'rikh al-fattash" of agricultural slave villages in the Songhay Empire and occupational groups of blacksmiths and praise singers, but it is only in the nineteenth-century forgery that these groups are described as servile and as the property of the ruler.[13] The other seventeenth-century chronicle, the "Ta'rikh al-sudan," makes no mention of these people as slaves either. Levtzion argued that the purposes of the forgery of the (Pseudo) "Ta'rikh al-fattash" were to legitimize the rule of Amadu Lobbo as distinct from the authority claimed by the Fulbe rulers of the Sokoto Caliphate. The value of the passages on the zanj slave castes was that they buttressed Amadu Lobbo's claims to control these people who lived along the Middle Niger and Niger Bend. In one of Amadu Lobbo's letters, he gave permission to enslave certain zanj, and he quotes the "Ta'rikh al-fattash" as his authority for this action.[14]

The importance of the racial argument made in the forgery of the "Ta'rikh al-fattash" has been missed by historians. John Hunwick, for example, argued that the passages about the zanj slave castes reflect a much older reality of statecraft in the Sahel that predates the writing of the original chronicles in the seventeenth century. Hunwick even proposed that the parts on the zanj had actually been removed after the initial composition of the "Ta'rikh al-fattash" because certain people who were descended from these slave castes had became prominent in Songhay society after the Moroccan invasion. As such, these descriptions would have been offensive or embarrassing to them. Hunwick argued that the servile castes "had traditionally been part of the inherited property of the rulers of Mali and Songhay. As claimant to the headship of the

[10] Tal Tamari, *Les castes de l'Afrique occidentale. artisans et musiciens endogames* (Nanterre: Société d'ethnologie, 1997), 10–14.

[11] Kâti, *Tarikh El-Fettach*, 14 (Arabic text).

[12] These are listed in Hunwick, "Some Notes on the Term 'Zanj'," 41–51; Levtzion, "Seventeenth-century chronicle," 592–3.

[13] Levtzion, "Seventeenth-century chronicle," 589.

[14] Ibid., 589.

Muslim community in the area [Amadu Lobbo] would naturally hope to claim such ancient rights for himself."[15]

To buttress his argument, Hunwick made an especially expansive reading of one of al-Maghili's replies to Askia Muhammad, which were written at the end of the fifteenth century.[16] In this text, Askia Muhammad asked for al-Maghili's expert advice as a scholar of Islamic law on a number of issues of statecraft in the Songhay Empire. In his sixth question, Askia Muhammad asked: "Some of them have among them slaves who are neither sold nor given away. These people say they are slaves of the sultanate to be inherited by whoever inherits it from the deceased ... So [in such cases] should all their wealth be assigned to the Public Treasury or not?"[17] The question appears to refer to a group of slaves like those mentioned in the (Pseudo) "Ta'rikh al-fattash," who cannot be sold or given away but who are in a perpetual state of servitude. They are also slaves of the state ("ʿabīd al-sulṭana"). In al-Maghili's brief response, he said that:

> As for the aforementioned slaves and their like, they are like an endowment (ḥubus) from the days of the forebears who set them aside to aid the sultan, so they should remain like that. It is not for the Commander of the Muslims to take them and place them in the Public Treasury except those whose origin is ascertained to be seizure by force or the like. Those for whom that is not established are an endowment for [the benefit of] those to whom they belong according to their customs.[18]

Hunwick read this passage as evidence that servile castes of slaves had belonged to rulers of Sahelian states for many centuries. Al-Maghili's argument that these slaves are analogous to pious endowments which are made in perpetuity suggests an Islamic legal argument available to rulers such as Askia Muhammad to justify their authority over servile groups. But nowhere in al-Maghili's replies, or in other legal sources before the eighteenth century, do we find the invocation of racial labels used to mark collective groups of slaves. The use of racial labels in the nineteenth-century forgery of the "Taʿrikh al-fattash" suggests that something had indeed changed since the original composition of this chronicle.

[15] Hunwick, "Some Notes on the Term 'Zanj'," 42.

[16] Muḥammad b. ʿAbd al-Karīm al-Maghīlī, "Ajwibat al-Maghīlī ʿan asʾilat al-amīr al-Ḥājj Muḥammad Askiyā." See Hunwick suggests that this text was written in or slightly later than 1498. Hunwick, *Sharīʿa in Songhay: The Replies of al-Maghīlī to the Questions of Askia al-Ḥājj Muḥammad* (Oxford: Oxford University Press, 1985), 41.

[17] Hunwick, *Sharīʿa*, 86.

[18] Ibid., 88.

Using the Arabic term "zanj," or the Songhay words "ar-bi," now demarcated permanent servility.[19] These racial words are only found in the nineteenth-century forgery of the (Pseudo) "Ta'rikh al-fattash" and in other nineteenth-century sources from the Sahel. P.F. de Moraes Farias has argued that the more general Arabic term for blacks (sudan) was sometimes used in the "Ta'rikh al-sudan" and "Ta'rikh al-fattash" to valorize the old Songhay elite in its struggles with new Arma rulers during the seventeenth century.[20] This may help explain why the term zanj and ar-bi were coined as alternatives. Their use was quite deliberate; they strengthened the arguments made by Amadu Lobbo about his own authority and control over different peoples in the Niger Bend.

Understanding how the concept of blackness gained instrumental value by the nineteenth century requires an excavation of the intellectual developments within the field of Islamic legal literature of the Sahel in the seventeenth and eighteenth centuries. Racial ideas about blacks gained theoretical legal justification in this period, defining whole groups of people as permanently servile on the basis of genealogical arguments. Blackness came to define servile status.

COLLECTIVE JURIDICAL STATUS AND UNLAWFUL PROPERTY

One of the peculiar historical features of the pastoralist societies of the Sahel was the existence of status categories distinguishing noble lineages as either warrior or clerical. We have already seen some of the ways that local histories represent this distinction as a kind of social charter, whereby defeated groups definitively foreswore military action and devoted themselves hitherto to the role of religious specialists. Although this was an ideal representation of social structure often belied by the historical vagaries of life in the Sahel, it did nonetheless mean that the vast majority of scholarly production was undertaken by members of clerical lineages. One of the consequences of this was that clerical scholars developed interpretations of Islamic law that were prejudicial to members of warrior lineages and beneficial to themselves. It was also a means of fixing collective juridical status in ways that could be applied more widely to blacks. As with so many other developments, it was during the

[19] P.F. de Moraes Farias, "Intellectual Innovation and Reinvention of the Sahel: The Seventeenth-century Timbuktu Chronicles," in *The Meanings of Timbuktu*, ed. Shamil Jeppie and Souleymane Bachir Diagne (Cape Town: HSRC Press, 2008), 104.

[20] John Hunwick, "Back to West African Zanj Again: A Document of Sale from Timbuktu," *SA* 7 (1996): 53–60.

seventeenth century that this doctrine was defined. The key figure in elaborating these ideas was the Shinqiti jurist Muḥammad b. al-Mukhtār b. al-Aʿmash (d. 1695–96), known in Timbuktu as Ibn al-Aʿmash.[21]

The means by which Ibn al-Aʿmash created legal liabilities for people that collectively belonged to warrior lineages was based on the issue of illegal ownership of property.[22] In the Maliki legal school, property acquired as a result of an unlawful act, such as theft, or taking of interest, is itself unlawful. Likewise, property acquired as compensation for employment by a state could be considered unlawful because of the illicit means that states often used to acquire wealth. From a strictly legal standpoint, almost all states in the Muslim world after the Prophet Muhammad and his immediate successors were considered defective in terms of full adherence to Islamic law. As early as the tenth century, the Maliki school had coined the term "mustaghraq al-dhimma" for a person whose property was derived from an illegal source. What this meant originally was that the property of a mustaghraq al-dhimma was defective in some way either because its origins were unlawful or because the legally acquired parts of the property would be theoretically consumed by the claims for compensation made by injured parties against the illegally acquired part. As such, the mustaghraq al-dhimma is someone whose "dhimma" – his legal property or assets – is considered to be already "consumed" (istighrāq).[23]

In Ibn al-Aʿmash's important collection of legal opinions, he defines the category of person whose property is by definition unlawful:

> The mustaghraq al-dhimma is he whose entire property has been consumed by claims, whether the goods belong rightfully to God Almighty in the case of zakāt, penance, redemption, or denial [of God], or whether they originate from the rights of man in the case of illegal seizure, theft, adultery, or breach of faith. He

[21] He is also known in Mauritania as Bilaʿmish. See Ghislaine Lydon, *On Trans-Saharan Trails: Islamic Law, Trade Networks, and Cross-Cultural Exchange in Nineteenth-Century Western Africa* (New York: Cambridge University Press, 2009), 303. For a brief biography, see MLG 1: 53–6. I use the name known in Timbuktu because that is where my copies of these manuscripts come from, and because it was in this form that these ideas were influential in the Niger Bend. I have relied extensively for my knowledge of the collections of legal opinions found in Timbuktu on an unpublished work written by the Timbuktu scholar Maḥmūd b. Muḥammad Dadab, known as Ḥammū al-Arawānī al-Tinbuktī, entitled "Kashf al-ḥāʾil fī ʾl-taʿrīf bi-kutub al-fatāwā wa-ʾl-nawāzil." My copy was given to me by the author.

[22] This discussion draws extensively on Rainer Osswald, "Inequality in Islamic Law," in *Law and the Islamic World Past and Present*, ed. Christopher Toll and Jakob Skovgaard-Petersen (Copenhagen: Royal Danish Academy of Sciences and Letters, 1995), 97–104.

[23] Osswald, "Inequality," 98.

thus becomes one whose assets (dhimma) are consumed and who in principle no longer has any property, but rather everything that he has is the property of others.[24]

The analogy often made in discussion of this category of person is with the highly indebted or bankrupt individual who is not allowed to dispose of his property without the consent of his creditors.[25]

The legal designation of certain individuals as mustaghraq al-dhimma did lead in some cases to the confiscation of property.[26] It is not clear, however, that this device had an appreciable impact on statecraft in the medieval Maghrib where these ideas were developed. Its effects were mostly felt in terms of personal piety. If the property of the mustaghraq al-dhimma was illegal, the implication was that it would be morally wrong to carry out business with, or even accept gifts from, such a person. These ideas were one basis of the objection sometimes made by pious scholars across the Muslim world in refusing to accept state-sponsored judgeships, or gifts from people whose morality was doubtful. Opinions differed of course on how strictly such principles should be applied. Large numbers of people in any society would theoretically fall under this legal designation; in practice, interactions with merchants who employed forms of legal fictions in their affairs or people who depended in some way on government employment could hardly be avoided completely. According to less strict views of this issue, in order to remain clean, one merely avoided accepting goods that could be directly identified as having been unlawfully obtained.[27]

In North Africa, the individual designation of mustaghraq al-dhimma had also been applied to collective groups that were considered to be predatory and beyond the pale of settled civilization. As such, the nomadic

[24] Ibn al-Aʿmash al-ʿAlawī, "Sabab al-faraj al-bashsh bi-jamʿ wa-tartīb nawāzil Ibn al-Aʿmash," compiled by Aḥmad Bul-ʿArāf (IHERIAB ms. 2750), # 245, f. 232. Osswald quotes a very similar passage, "Inequality," 98–9n.

[25] Osswald, "Inequality," 99n. The Maliki source often cited as an authority on this issue is the Andalusian jurist Ibn Rushd (d. 1276) who makes this case. See *Fatāwā Ibn Rushd*, ed. al-Mukhtār al-Ṭāhir al-Talīlī (Beirut: Dār al-gharb al-islāmī, 1987), 636–7. This is how Ibn al-Aʿmash's student Muḥammad b. Abī Bakr b. al-Hāshimī al-Ghallāwī (d. 1687), known as Ibn Hāshim al-Ghallāwī, defines the limitations of the mustaghraq al-dhimma to freely dispose of his property ("Nawāzil Ibn Hāshim al-Ghallāwī" [IHERIAB ms. 497], # 149, f.165); MLG 1: 47–8.

[26] David Powers, *Law, Society, and Culture in the Maghrib, 1300–1500* (Cambridge: Cambridge University Press, 2002), 26.

[27] One could not make such distinctions as easily when it came to money because the origins of particular coins cannot be distinguished from the origins of others (Osswald, "Inequality," 99).

Sanhaja in the southern and western Sahara, and the Arab Bedouins of the Banu Hilal invasion that began in the eleventh century, were collectively designated as mustaghraq al-dhimma because of the perception that they depended largely on raiding and theft for their livelihood.[28] When the term was taken up by Ibn al-Aʿmash in the seventeenth century, it was applied on this basis as a collective designation for all members of similar sets of people. From Ibn al-Aʿmash's perspective this meant the warrior lineages whose lifestyle depended on raiding and theft. The designation of warrior lineages as mustaghraq al-dhimma was Ibn al-Aʿmash's way of constructing a fixed juridical category for people that he otherwise described as "raiders," "thieves," "Bedouin," and so forth. They were people who did not live, he asserted, by the precepts of Islamic law. The designation as mustaghraq al-dhimma meant that they could not, by definition, possess legal property.

Ibn al-Aʿmash's arguments had a variety of implications for the relations between different groups in the Sahel and for the role clerical groups might play. In one case in Ibn al-Aʿmash's collection of legal opinions, a questioner asked how jurists should rule in a case in which each of the claimants is defined as mustaghraq al-dhimma. Ibn al-Aʿmash's response was that the legal disability of the mustaghraq al-dhimma makes it impossible to render any legitimate decision on behalf of either party:

> If those bringing the case come, we cannot be permitted to rule between them because of their lack of obedience to the sharīʿa. The designation of the claimant and the one against whom the claim is made can not be decided even when they bring their case according to the rules of evidence in the shariʿa. It is incumbent upon the honorable arbiter to make no ruling on principle. If he is compelled to make a ruling between them, then they must enforce it themselves and it cannot be considered a shariʿa ruling but rather, a ruling of political exigency.[29]

Such opinions were a way for clerical jurists such as Ibn al-Aʿmash to render warrior lineages completely outside of the realm of the legitimate Muslim social intercourse.

In theory, the only way a mustaghraq al-dhimma could overcome his condition was by repenting and returning his unlawful property to either its rightful owners, if these could be identified, or by giving it to the needy as alms. Because Ibn al-Aʿmash argued that all members of clerical lineages were by definition needy and thereby entitled to these alms,

[28] Ibid., 100n.

[29] Ibn al-Aʿmash, "Sabab al-faraj al-bashsh," # 245, f. 232.

the illegal property held by warrior lineages rightfully belonged to members of clerical lineages. Since there was no way of enforcing this opinion in the state-less conditions of the Sahel, members of clerical lineages were accorded wide license to confiscate warrior property, even by theft. Full repentance by "warriors" would mean, in theory, giving over all of their property to a clerical lineage and agreeing to live under clerical authority.

The definition of all members of clerical lineages as poor, and thereby as legitimate beneficiaries of alms, seemed to solve the problem of how a pious person might deal with the nonpious, and how members of clerical-status lineages should deal with those who belonged to warrior-status groups. There were a number of scholars in the Sahel who rejected this argument. The original problem remains: If the source of property held by the mustaghraq al-dhimma was unlawful by definition, then property acquired from such a person should also be illegitimate. This question appeared in Ibn al-Aʿmash's collection in response to a dissenting legal opinion issued by one of his former students who lived in Walata, Muḥammad b. Abī Bakr b. al-Hāshimī al-Ghallāwī (d. 1687),[30] known in Timbuktu as Ibn Hāshim al-Ghallāwī. He is quoted as saying: "Business relations with the mustaghraq al-dhimma it is not permitted under any circumstances, and indeed, that part of their property that was purchased from the mustaghraq al-dhimma is to be confiscated [from the buyer] without compensation."[31] In a long opinion, Ibn Hashim al-Ghallawi held to the stricter Maliki view found in the discussion of the individual designation of a mustaghraq al-dhimma in the legal opinions collected by the Andalusian jurist Ibn Rushd I (d. 1276) and the Moroccan al-Wansharīsī (d. 1508).[32] He argued that such illegal property obtained from a mustaghraq al-dhimma should be turned over to the public treasury of the Muslims.[33] The scholars of the Kunta shared this view and

[30] A biographical notice on his life is found in ʿAbd Allāh b. Abī Bakr b. ʿAlī al-Bartīlī, "Fatḥ al-shukūr fī maʿrifat aʿyān ʿulamāʾ al-takrūr," translated by Chouki el Hamel, *La vie intellectuelle islamique dans le Sahel Ouest-Africain (XVIè-XIXè siècles). Une étude sociale de l'enseignment islamique en Mauritanie et au Nord du Mali (XVIè-XIXè siècles) et traduction annotée de Fath ash-shakūr d'al-Bartīlī al-Walātī (mort en 1805)* (Paris: L'Harmattan, 2002), 286–8; MLG 1: 47–8.

[31] Ibn al-Aʿmash, "Sabab al-faraj al-bashsh," # 247, f. 233.

[32] I have already cited Ibn Rushd; Aḥmad b. Yaḥyā al-Wansharīsī's famous collection, is called *al-Miʿyār al-muʿrib wa-al-jāmiʿ al-maghrib ʿan fatāwā ahl Ifrīqīya wa-ʾl-Andalūs wa-ʾl-Maghrib* (Rabat: Wizārat al-awqāf wa-ʾl-shuʾūn al-islāmiyya li-ʾl-mamlaka al-maghribiyya, 1981).

[33] "Nawāzil Ibn Hāshim al-Ghallāwī," #149, f.167.

rejected the idea that the status of mustaghraq al-dhimma rendered property licit to appropriate.[34]

Ibn al-Aʿmash argued that this was incorrect on several grounds. First, he quoted two verses from the Qurʾan to the effect that such a condition would create an undue burden for the pious: "God wills that you shall have ease, and does not will you to suffer hardship;"[35] and "God does not want to impose any hardship on you."[36] He then argued that Ibn Hashim al-Ghallawi's opinion was erroneous because the mustaghraq al-dhimma:

> Does not own property. If what they possess is taken away from them by any means, and if he is capable of taking some of their property in any way, whether by force or clandestinely, even if he must do so by stealing, even if [the property] is bequeathed as an income for the poor and suffering, even if it is in the form of deposits that are not returned to them ... all of this is legitimate according to the doctrine of necessity (ḍurūra) according to the texts of the scholars.[37]

The doctrine of necessity permits the breaking of shariʿa stipulations in cases of dire need, for example, eating carrion in cases of starvation. Its use to legitimize the confiscation of warrior property could hardly go unchallenged,[38] but the designation of mustaghraq al-dhimma served as an important template for how to legitimately interact with those who were defined as outside the bounds of correct Islamic practice.

How widely known such theoretical configurations were outside of elite scholarly circles is not clear. Members of warrior-status lineages were generally illiterate. As such, even the surviving letters written by leaders of warrior-status lineages were mostly dictated to scribes (from clerical-status groups), who transformed speech into written Arabic form.[39] In addition to the shariʿa principles that the scholars sought to impose as the basis regulating social conduct, pastoralist groups relied on orally transmitted customary law (Ar. ʿurf) to regulate their affairs. The idea of authority among warrior groups was expressed using the language of

[34] Shaykh Bāy al-Kuntī, "Nawāzil Shaykh Bāy" (IHERIAB ms.121), #530, f.586.

[35] Qurʾan, 2:185.

[36] Qurʾan, 5:6.

[37] Ibn al-Aʿmash, "Sabab al-faraj al-bashsh," # 248, f. 235–6.

[38] According to Rainer Osswald, it became the dominant view in Sahelian scholarly circles ("Inequality," 102n). This does not appear to be accurate judging from the scholars that I have surveyed.

[39] Raymond Taylor, "Of Disciples and Sultans: Power, Authority and Society in the Nineteenth-Century Mauritanian Gebla" (Ph.D. Diss., University of Illinois at Urbana-Champaign, 1996), 321.

protection and collective solidarity. The tribute that was levied from subordinates was referred to as "ḥurma" ("inviolable") by members of Arab warrior lineages. They also claimed the right to one third of water from wells maintained by clerical-status lineages, and hospitality any time they visited members of clerical-status groups while travelling.[40] But members of warrior-status lineages were also bound by codes of conduct, notions of honor, and expectations that they would be solicitous for the well-being of those who had paid tribute.[41] Their idea about the legitimacy of the property that they controlled was therefore very different from the arguments made by Ibn al-Aʿmash.

KINDS OF BLACKS

The discussion of the category of mustaghraq al-dhimma helps us understand the conceptual framework used by Sahelian scholars to deal with the vexing issue of interactions with those defined as blacks. The term "blacks" (sudan) appears in a number of different ways in the legal literature produced in the Sahel. Often, "the blacks," or alternatively, "the land of the blacks," are mere descriptive terms referring to people and places to the south of the Sahara. So for example, in Ibn Hashim al-Ghallawi's collection of legal opinions that I referred to in the discussion of the mustaghraq al-dhimma, there is a question that invokes the term blacks in a spatial or geographic sense: "A man transported salt from Tishit to Walata in open country, and when he approached Walata he turned away from it inexcusably and brought the salt to the blacks (sudan)."[42] The legal issue in this case concerned the liability of a caravanner, who was likely a slave or freed slave,[43] for the proceeds of the salt that he has been charged with transporting and selling. The legal status of the blacks had no bearing on the case.

But the label "blacks" could indicate differences in legal status, usually associated with the extent to which particular blacks could be considered proper Muslims. Just as there was disagreement over whether the designation mustaghraq al-dhimma could be made to apply to a collective group rather than just particular individuals on the basis of illicitly acquired property, tension existed as well over whether the term blacks

40 H.T. Norris, *Shinqiti Folk Literature and Song* (Oxford: Clarendon, 1968), 17, 29.

41 Taylor, "Of Disciples," 152.

42 "Nawāzil Ibn Hāshim al-Ghallāwī," #165, f. 206.

43 Ghislaine Lydon, "Islamic Legal Culture and Slave-Ownership Contests in Nineteenth-Century Sahara," *IJAHS* 40, no. 3 (2007): 415.

could be made to represent a collective legal status category inferior to free Muslims. As the discussion in Chapter 1 demonstrated, there was considerable contestation over the extent to which defining blacks as a collective class according to historical, genealogical, and political antecedents could be overcome by individual behavior. In the case of the blacks, there is a consistent tension between the meanings that are made to adhere to the abstract category of blacks as unbelievers – or as Muslims who continue to carry the stain of original unbelief – on the one hand and the reality of particular individuals who might be Muslims equal to anyone else in their practice and piety on the other hand. It is precisely this tension between a set of highly abstract assumptions and more concrete realities that animates most of the cases in which the status of blacks is invoked.

In Chapter 1, I discussed at some length the treatise written by the Timbuktu scholar Ahmad Baba on the relationship between blackness and slavery. I focused mostly on Ahmad Baba's discussion of race and his contention that there were many Muslims among the blacks who could not rightfully be enslaved. But the question that provoked Ahmad Baba to write this text was more than just an ethnographic enquiry into the religious status of different peoples in West Africa. The man who sent the question was from the Saharan oasis complex of Tuwat in present-day Algeria, and his name was Saʿīd b. Ibrāhīm al-Jirārī. Nothing more is known about him. What he wanted to learn in the questions that he sent to Ahmad Baba was whether there were among the blacks certain groups that could be collectively defined as slaves as a result of an original conquest by Muslims: "[I]t is known that, according to the shariʿa, the reason why it is allowed to own [others] is [their] unbelief. Thus, whoever purchases an unbeliever is allowed to own him … Conversion to Islam subsequent to the existence of the aforementioned condition has no effect on continued ownership." In other words, individual slaves who convert to Islam after their enslavement do not thereby gain their freedom, but remain in the state of slavery. Al-Jirari wanted to apply the same logic used in the individual case of the slave who converts to Islam to whole groups of blacks: "Were those lands which we mentioned, and other similar lands of the Muslims of the blacks, conquered and [their people] enslaved in a state of unbelief, while their conversion occurred subsequently – hence there is no harm [in owning them] – or not?" Relying on the same kinds of arguments that were discussed in Chapter 1 about ʿUqba b. Nafiʿ's purported conquest of the land of the blacks, al-Jirari hoped to assign to blacks – even those who were Muslims – the status of the Muslim slave who had converted after his enslavement and hence remains in servitude: "One of the qadis of the blacks reported that the imam who conquered them whilst they were unbelievers chose to spare them as slaves, since he had the choice, or because he did not consider the five well-known options, and that they still remained in a state of slavery, and whenever the sultan needs any of them he brings in as many as he wants. Is this true or not?"[44]

The question of a reserve pool of blacks, whose forefathers had been conquered in an original jihad launched against the blacks by Muslim conquerors, does not fit with conventional understandings of Islamic law. Enslavement is one of five choices available to the Muslim conqueror of non-Muslims.[45] As such, the slave is a captive, and he or she is allotted to individual participants in the conflict as booty. The slave becomes property defined by law in an individual relationship with the master(s) from that point forward.[46] From a legal standpoint, there should be no justification for a collective category of slaves, and certainly not for areas of West Africa where whole groups of people live, generation after generation, in a permanent status of enslaveability as a result of some original Muslim conquest. Yet this is clearly what al-Jirari was pushing at in his questions to Ahmad Baba: "Explain to us the realities of these lands, for you are better informed about them and are more knowledgeable about their state – may your reward from God be copious. Was their land taken by force, or through agreement, or what? At what time did Islam reach them? During the time of the Companions or later?"[47] Ahmad Baba refuted the premise of the question, saying that he knew nothing of an imam sparing the blacks for later enslavement: "[The imam's] statement is very close to being devoid of truth. If you investigate now, you will not find anyone who will confirm the truth of what he said. What is based upon what he says, therefore, is not to be given consideration."[48]

[44] *Miʿrāj al-Ṣuʿūd: Aḥmad Bābā's Replies on Slavery*, ed. and trans. John Hunwick and Fatima Harrak (Rabat: Université Mohammed V-Souissi, 2000), 13–14.

[45] The other choices are killing them, letting them go free, making them pay a ransom, and making them pay the jizya poll tax that permits them to keep their religion. This is drawn from a passage of Khalīl b. Isḥāq al-Jundī's "al-Mukhtaṣar" translated in Hunwick and Eve Troutt Powell, *The African Diaspora in the Mediterranean Lands of Islam* (Princeton, NJ: Marcus Wiener, 2002), 23. Also cited in *Miʿrāj al-Ṣuʿūd*, 14n.

[46] *Miʿrāj al-Ṣuʿūd*, 14n.

[47] Ibid., 14.

[48] Ibid., 24.

What is at stake here is the collective category of blacks who hold the juridical status of people already enslaved de jure, if not de facto, regardless of current religious profession or practice. It is clear that this was not just an issue in North Africa because it appears in many Sahelian collections of legal opinions. For example, in the compilation of legal opinions authored by the well-known scholar from the Taganit region of Mauritania, Sīdi ʿAbd Allāh b. al-Ḥājj Ibrāhīm al-ʿAlawī (d. 1818),[49] he discussed the appropriate way to address claims made by a slave that he/she is a wrongly captured free Muslim and thereby should be set free: "It is incumbent on she who claims to be free to provide the evidence unless the claim of freedom is made during the time of purchase, and her place of origin [is a place of] Islam, in which case her claims to be free are to be believed."[50] This was accepted more or less universally by scholars in West Africa. Sidi ʿAbd Allah then sited a ruling of positive law (farʿ) attributed to the North Africa Maliki scholar Ibn Farḥūn (d. 1397):[51]

> Those who claim the freedom of origin, whether as a child or an adult, are to be accepted based on their origin among free people. If on the contrary they first appear already as property [i.e. slaves] because they were captured due to their condition as unbelievers, or if their origin as non-captives cannot be demonstrated, then [their being held as] property is permitted. She would claim freedom based on origin. For this reason, she can only demonstrate that she is a person of free origins by bringing evidence because otherwise, it is known that she will lie about it.[52]

The distinction made here centers on who holds the burden of proof. Sidi ʿAbd Allah tells us that in the case of a newly enslaved person being sold shortly after her capture, her claims to be from free Muslim people are to be believed unless someone else can bring evidence to the contrary. Conversely, for slaves who claim to have been free Muslims before their enslavement, but who have already been held in the state of slavery for

[49] Sīdi ʿAbd Allāh b. al-Ḥājj Ibrāhīm al-ʿAlawī is very well known in West African Muslim circles. A number of his works gained wide circulation. See Mohamed El Mokhtar ould Bah, *La littérature juridique et l'évolution du Malikisme en Mauritanie* (Tunis: Université de Tunis, 1981), 187–8. For a brief biography, see el Hamel, *La vie intellectuelle*, 367–69. Also, see Aḥmad al-Amīn al-Shinqīṭī, *al-Wasīṭ fī tarājim udabāʾ Shinqīṭ* (Cairo: Maktaba al-khānijī, 1989), 37–40; MLG 1: 194–202.

[50] Sīdi ʿAbd Allāh b. al-Ḥājj Ibrāhīm al-ʿAlawī, "Nawāzil al-ʿAlawī," (IHERIAB ms. 490), #335, f. 193.

[51] Ibrāhīm b. ʿAlī b. Muḥammad b. Farḥūn al-Yaʿmarī al-Andalusī, known as Ibn Farḥūn, *al-Dībāj al-mudhahhab fī aʿyān ʿulamāʾ al-madhhab* (Cairo: Dār al-turāth li-ʾl-tabʿ wa-ʾl-nashr, 1932/3).

[52] Sīdi ʿAbd Allāh b. al-Ḥājj Ibrāhīm al-ʿAlawī, "Nawāzil al-ʿAlawī," #335, f. 193.

some time, the burden of proof rests with them to demonstrate the truth of their claim. There is even a didactic verse to this effect, cited by the Azawad Kunta scholar Shaykh Bāy al-Kuntī (d. 1929):[53]

> Most slaves hide their religion
> Those from the land of the blacks who state it are free.[54]

It was in reference to the issue of the different types of blacks, and the legitimacy of enslavement of blacks who held a status as free Muslims, that Ahmad Baba's "The ladder of ascent" appears to have been best known among subsequent generations of Muslim intellectuals in the Sahel. I believe that one reason for this was that defining collective juridical status for different kinds of blacks was especially important to these scholars. One example of an extensive citation of Ahmad Baba's arguments is in Shaykh Bay al-Kunti's treatment of this question, in which he listed some of the authorities mentioned in Ahmad Baba's text, before citing other Sahelian scholars who agree with the opinion:

> In the rulings of positive law on this problem of the recently purchased slave who comes from a land in which there are many sales of free people, it is similar to the majority of the blacks about whom the erudite Ahmad Baba asserted authoritatively, following his father Sīdi Maḥmūd[55] and the jurisconsult Makhlūfi al-Balbālī[56] and others, that their freedom is proven as soon as they make the claim. It is also accepted by al-Sharīf Ḥamā Allah[57] and his maternal uncle Ahmad b. al-Imām.[58]

Shaykh Bay then quoted a passage in which Ahmad Baba cited al-Balbālī (d. after 1533–1534):

> Then Ahmad Baba said [quoting al-Balbālī]: "Whoever is known to be from those lands which are known for their Islam, and states that he is from those lands, should be let go and adjudged to be free, as ruled the jurists of al-Andalus like Ibn ʿAttāb[59] and others. They were only opposed by Ibn Lubābā[60] who said ...

[53] ALA IV, 136.

[54] "Jull al-ariqqāʾ al-dīn asarrū / Min bilad al-sūdān ḥurr[un] dhakarū." Shaykh Bāy al-Kuntī, "Nawāzil Shaykh Bāy" (IHERIAB ms.121), #500, f. 556.

[55] Sīdi Maḥmūd b. ʿUmar b. Muḥammad Aqīt al-Ṣanhājī (d. 1548), see Hunwick, *Timbuktu and the Songhay Empire*, 53–5.

[56] Al-Makhlūf b. ʿAlī b. Ṣāliḥ al-Balbālī (d. after 1533/34), see ALA II, 25.

[57] A scholar from Tīshīt, al-Sharīf Muḥammadnā Ḥamā Allāh b. Aḥmad b. al-Imām Aḥmad al-Ḥasanī (d. 1755), known as al-Sharīf Ḥamā Allāh in Timbuktu; MLG 1: 102–3.

[58] "Nawāzil Shaykh Bāy" (IHERIAB ms. 121), #500, f. 555.

[59] The Cordovan jurist Muhammad b. ʿAttāb b. Muḥsin (993–1069). Manuela Marin, "Law and Piety: A Cordovan Fatwā," *Bulletin of the British Society for Middle Eastern Studies* 17, no. 2 (1990): 132; Kahhala 3: 479–80.

[60] The Cordovan jurist Muhammad b. ʿUmar b. Lubāba (d. 926).

'Whoever seeks salvation for himself should not purchase any of them except when [they] give the name of [their] country, and it is apparent whether he is from a country of Islam or a country of unbelievers.'[61]

Ibn Lubaba's (d. 926) objection is an injunction to be especially prudent in purchasing slaves.

The eighteenth-century jurist from Tishit, al-Sharīf Muḥammadnā Ḥamā Allāh b. Aḥmad b. al-Imām Aḥmad al-Ḥasanī (d. 1755), known as al-Sharīf Ḥamā Allāh in Timbuktu,[62] provides a very good window into how those blacks that Ahmad Baba identified as free Muslims would come to have their status questioned in subsequent centuries. There are a number of examples in his collection of legal opinions that suggest the collective status of blacks was a significant issue. Let me begin with a question repeated in different compilations that appears to center on blacks who are not full Muslims, perhaps because of syncretism with other religious beliefs and practices, or because they are new adepts to Islam:[63]

The question: Is buying permitted when purchasing someone from among the blacks who denies the truth of the resurrection, although [Islam] has taken root to some extent and he has decided that God is He who created him, and that God is One, and perhaps that the action of some things are related, although he does not pray according to the conditions of the prayer, and he only fasts a little bit during Ramadan, but he does not refuse [Islamic practices] other than fasting?

The response: The denier of the truth of the resurrection is an unbeliever and thus, he is the one who attributes the action to something other than God. With his denial of the truth of the resurrection, he can not escape from the status of an unbeliever by his article of faith that God is One ... Buying and owning he who acts like the Bambara is permitted.[64]

Such an opinion obviously opens up an avenue for abuse based on an enslaver's judgment of defective Islamic beliefs or practices among his victims.

In much of the legal literature produced in what is today western Mauritania, the ethnonym Bambara represented a category of blacks

61 "Nawāzil Shaykh Bāy" (IHERIAB ms. 121), #500, f. 556; Aḥmad Bābā, *Miʿrāj al-Ṣuʿūd*, 28–9.

62 See note 57.

63 In addition to the original collection from which the following text is drawn, it is also in the collection put together by Muḥammad Yaḥya b. Salīm al-Walātī, "Ikhtiṣār nawāzil al-aʿlām li-Ibn Salīm" (IHERIAB ms. 3445), f. 7.

64 Al-Sharīf Ḥamā Allah (al-Sharīf Abī ʿAbd Allāh Muḥammadnā Ḥamā b. Aḥmad b. al-Imām Aḥmad al-Ḥasanī), "Nawāzil al-Sharīf Muḥammadnā Ḥamā Allāh" (IHERIAB ms. 146), f. 5–6.

who were considered to be unbelievers. Indeed, many Bamana-speakers were non-Muslims at this time. But the question addressed to al-Sharif Hama Allah is not about the Bambara; it is clearly about a group about whom the claim to free Muslim status might reasonably apply. The questioner's fear is precisely that of al-Jirari, Ahmad Baba's questioner from Tuwat, who worried that he would be committing a sin by purchasing a black slave who claimed to be a free Muslim. The means that al-Sharif Hama Allah used to get around the injunction that free Muslims among the blacks cannot be enslaved was to insist on a theological litmus test of the depth and theological correctness of black Muslim belief. This led al-Sharif Hama Allah to a justification of the enslavement of this suspect black Muslim on didactic grounds:

> [The enslaved person] is forced to take the assurance from us concerning the truth of the resurrection, and he does not enter Islam except by it. He is forced [to accept it] by threats and beatings just as Abū ʾl-Mawda said: "He is compelled by threats and beatings." If he is from among the blacks ruled (maḥkūm) by Islam, then he is compelled to Islam by [the threat of] death [in an original conquest]. If he repents, then the Muslim is not permitted to own him unless by previous authority which requires that his owner freely disposed of him in a sale, etc., by the generally known types of regulations for slaves. The exception is if he is ruled to be an enemy (qitl) according to apostasy, which, God forbid, we should contemplate.[65]

Here is a clear case whereby Ahmad Baba's confessional ethnography was challenged according to a stricter definition of who counts juridically as a Muslim. The importance of this intellectual move is obvious; it renders people theoretically immune from enslavement into legitimate targets – collectively – for slave raiding and the slave trade. It also relies on al-Jirari's argument about the existence of a collective category of blacks, "ruled by Islam," who are latent slaves according to an original Muslim conquest in which the unbelievers were spared death.

A concrete example of how even black Muslim practice was made dependent on a kind of clientship with better, more authoritative Muslims, comes from another legal opinion issued by al-Sharif Hama Allah. Unlike the case discussed above focused on belief, this case centered on ritual practice:

> The question: Is it permitted to emulate (iqtidāʾ) a black imam in prayer when he significantly mispronounces the letters of the Qurʾan? Are they permitted to recite the Qurʾan with their mispronunciations or not?

65 "Nawāzil al-Sharīf Muḥammadnā Ḥamā Allāh," f. 6.

> The response: If the mispronunciation of the letters of the Qur'an is caused by an incapacity to do what is correct in its recitation, or because of a shortage of time, or because of a lack of someone to teach him whose instruction he will accept, then in truth, the person who prays behind him should not emulate him but instead be raised higher than him ... If he should not accept instruction, then his prayer and the prayer of the person who emulates him is correct only to the extent that he recites correctly when he is not prevented from correct recitation by the incapacity of his tongue. [In cases of incapacity] he is rewarded, if God Almighty wills it, according to his intention and not according to his tongue. As for he who is capable of reciting correctly because he has accepted instruction, and it is possible because there is sufficient time, and someone is present to instruct him, but he still did not learn it correctly, then his prayer and the prayer of those who emulate him are invalid because it is ruled to be his intention to mispronounce the words, as is well known.[66]

This is not an issue invented in West Africa – it has a long pedigree in Maliki legal sources generally – but the work that it does in the context of blacks, and the question of the validity of their potential status as free Muslims, is to significantly restrict the membership of such a juridical group. If an imam recites prayers incorrectly, and he fails to meet the conditions outlined earlier, then all who follow him in prayer (i.e., all Muslims in a particular community) have their prayers rendered invalid. As such, their status as free Muslims can no longer be sustained.[67]

SOURCES OF PROPERTY AMONG THE BLACKS

Just as the device of the mustaghraq al-dhimma defined an inferior juridical status for members of warrior lineages in the Sahel, it also played a role in setting the juridical status of blacks. In theory, blacks could themselves be defined as mustaghraq al-dhimma, but they rarely were. This is because there was an important difference between blacks and nonblacks in terms of their potential enslaveability. In the intellectual environment of the Sahel, and in the concrete reality of life there, it was blacks who were vulnerable to enslavement, whether as a latent possibility, a present form of domination, or as a past mark of original unbelief carried forward by means of lineage. Purported black shortcomings in religion

[66] "Nawāzil al-Sharīf Muḥammadnā Ḥamā Allāh," f. 18.

[67] Amadu Bamba (1853–1927), founder of the Mouride Sufi order in Senegal, wrote a preface to one of his books in which he made explicit reference to this set of ideas: "Do not let my condition as a black man mislead you about the virtue of this work" (Cheikh Anta Babou, *Fighting the Greater Jihad: Amadu Bamba and the Founding of the Muridiyya of Senegal, 1853–1913* [Athens, OH: Ohio University Press, 2007], 62).

justified enslavement, a fate borne in practice by very few nonblack members of warrior-status lineages.

In the commercial culture in which Sahelian Muslims were very active, little serious objection could be raised to the origins of items of trade among non-Muslims. These were problems as old as the legal schools themselves. Very briefly, the man after whom the Maliki school is named, Mālik b. Anas (d. 796), had advised that Muslims should avoid trading with non-Muslims in the "land of war" (dār al-ḥarb).[68] Ibn Abī Zayd (d. 966), whose legal manual the "Risāla" is foundational to the Maliki school, wrote that: "Commerce to the land of the enemies or the land of the blacks is not recommended (makrūh)."[69] One way around such recommendations was the doctrine of necessity. Ghislaine Lydon has presented a concrete case from the first half of the nineteenth century dealing with this form of justification for trading with people defined as unbelievers. One of Amadu Lobbo's military generals in the agriculturally important region of Kaarta intercepted a caravan from the Mauritanian town of Tishit, claiming that it was operating in the "land of war" and trading with unbelievers, where Amadu Lobbo's army was waging jihad. In response, a scholar from Tishit wrote to Amadu Lobbo in an effort to free the caravan by arguing that because no grain was produced in Tishit, trade with the unbelievers was a matter of necessity for them.[70]

In the sources that I have consulted for this chapter, the issue of the provenance of property among the blacks appears in a slightly different form, focused on concerns about items whose ritual purity is unknown. So for example, the question arose about whether it was permissible to eat meat from animals slaughtered by slaves, considering that the extent of the slaves' own Islamic practice and their knowledge of the correct ritual means of slaughtering an animal might be doubtful.[71] I will discuss the issue of the relationship between slaves, blackness, and Muslim practice in Chapter 6. Here I only want to point out that insofar as the ritual correctness of blacks' practice of Islam was often considered potentially suspect (theoretically, as we will see, the slaves of Muslims should also be Muslims), questions arose as to whether objects of ritual importance were rendered impure by their contacts with these blacks.

68 Majid Khadduri, "International Law," in *Law in the Middle East. Vol. 1. Origin and Development of Islamic Law*, ed. Khadduri and Herbert J. Liebesny (Washington, DC: The Middle East Institute, 1955), 317.

69 This line is quoted in "Nawāzil al-Sharīf Muḥammadnā Ḥamā Allāh," f. 27.

70 Lydon, *On Trans-Saharan Trails*, 115–16.

71 "Nawāzil al-Sharīf Muḥammadnā Ḥamā Allāh," f. 24.

The best example that I know of this kind of problem is a case found in Shaykh Bay al-Kunti's collection of legal opinions.[72] The issue concerns an animal hide used as a prayer mat – the most common form of prayer mat in this region even today. The problem was that the hide came from the land of the blacks. As such, the questioner asks, can it be ritually pure and therefore useable as a prayer mat? Shaykh Bay's response begins as follows: "As for praying on hides that come from the region (jiha) of the blacks, where they do not pray and where they are not mindful about forbidden things, the question concerns the tanning of the skin, which is an easy matter if the general public affects the purity of the tanning of the hide."[73] Since Shaykh Bay had decided that the issue of concern regarding ritual purity was whether the hide was tanned, he then made the analogy with several of the Prophet Muhammad's hadiths related to leather from unknown or impure sources:

> If it was not tanned, then the fact is that it was not a Muslim hide. This matter is easy and therefore there can be no ignorance about it. Al-Tirmidhī[74] and others have related that al-Najashi [the Christian king of Ethiopia] presented the Prophet, may God bless him and grant him peace, with a pairs of abraded (sāḥij) black shoes and that he wore them. He then performed ablutions and wiped them. Ibn al-ʿArabi[75] and after him al-Hāfiz al-ʿIrāqī[76] suggested that this was before his conversion to Islam although several others decided that it was shortly after his conversion to Islam. In any case, most of the people in his country were polytheists and people of the book [i.e. Christians and Jews] who followed the practice of treating skins by flaying and tanning.[77]

The argument here, and in a subsequent hadith that Shaykh Bay cites about a gift of leather shoes to the Prophet, is clear: If the Prophet Muhammad accepted leather goods of unknown or non-Muslim provenance, it must be permissible for Sahelian Muslims to use prayer skins from the land of the blacks.

[72] These opinions were written in the late nineteenth and early twentieth centuries. They do, however, engage with earlier Sahelian jurists.

[73] "Nawāzil Shaykh Bāy" (IHERIAB ms.118), #169, f. 215.

[74] This is a reference to the great hadith collector Abū ʿĪsā Muḥammad b. ʿĪsā b. Sawra al-Tirmidhī (d. 892) and his text, "al-Jāmiʿ al-Ṣaḥīḥ." It is published as *Sunan al-Tirmidhī wa-huwa al-Jāmiʿ al-ṣaḥīḥ*. 5 vols. ed. ʿAbd al-Wahhāb ʿAbd al-Laṭīf, ʿAbd al-Raḥmān Muḥammad ʿUthmān (Madina: al-Maktaba al-salafiyya, 1965–1967).

[75] This is Ibn al-ʿArabī, the hadith scholar from Seville, whose full name is Muḥammad b. ʿAbd Allāh al-Maʿāfirī (1076–1148). The published version of his commentary on al-Tirmidhī is *ʿĀriḍat al-aḥwadhī bi-sharḥ Ṣaḥīḥ al-Tirmidhī*. 14 vols. ed. Jamāl Marʿshalī (Beirut: Dār al-kutub al-ʿilmiyya, 1997).

[76] ʿAbd al-Raḥīm b. al-Ḥusayn al-ʿIrāqī (d. 1404). GAL I 359, SI 612.

[77] "Nawāzil Shaykh Bāy" (IHERIAB ms.118), #169, f. 215–16.

However Shaykh Bay found that the real issue was not with the ritual purity of the skins, but with the way that they were acquired. As such, the issue of illegally acquired property reasserts itself:

> If the aspect of their question is whether the item was plundered, and indeed it was surely acquired as a result of a raid or act of theft, then it is the product of bad conduct. [The logic of this objection] is one of the errors that are made using reprehensible fastidiousness in purchasing things which no one can follow unless he wants to hurt himself. He demands more of himself than God demands of him.[78]

Shaykh Bay then launched into a long discussion of the different opinions over the degree of fastidiousness one should apply with regards to the source of property. He points out that property acquired by warriors in conflict with unbelievers has an impure source, but it is nonetheless licit as booty. He says that in some sense, all property is the product of the earth and hence ritually impure. To exaggerate one's piety on the grounds of an item's provenance is pedantic and delusional, and impossible were it to be followed through to its logical conclusions. He quotes al-Ghazālī (d. 1111) as saying: "He who thinks that he is more pious than them, and that he understood when they did not understand, is obsessed with deceitful and erroneous delusions (muwaswas)." He then says: "The person obsessed with delusions finds the whole world to be forbidden." At the same time, however, it would also be an error to pay no attention to the source of property, and what is known to be acceptable and forbidden: "There are those who do not distinguish between different kinds of property, and this is the source of religious innovation (bidʿa) and error." Ultimately, Shaykh Bay argued for a middle position between complete disregard for sources and exaggerated fastidiousness. His discussion of the provenance of property, initiated as it was by a question about hides taken from the land of the blacks, suggests that the main issue was not the nature of the item itself, the rules of which were well known, but the way in which it was acquired, by whom, and from whom. In an important sense, Shaykh Bay's logic runs completely counter to the logic of Ibn al-Aʿmash and the illegality of property among those designated as mustaghraq al-dhimma.[79]

Several opinions issued by al-Sharif Hama Allah confirm that it was the juridical status of the people involved in transactions of property

[78] "Nawāzil Shaykh Bāy" (IHERIAB ms.118), #169, f. 216.
[79] Ibid.

that was important. The first case involves a a band of robbers who stole property from blacks and then fled. The stolen property did not belong to the blacks who were only looking after it, which probably means that it consisted of grazing animals, although the text does not say this. Someone wounded the horses of the plunderers. The text is not clear about who this was. It may be that it was one of the blacks who injured them, but it seems more likely that the text should be read in a way that suggests that the unnamed owners of the property being looked after by the blacks were the ones responsible for hurting the horses. If so, these were almost certainly the patrons of the blacks mentioned in the question. It is not stated what kind of status these blacks carried, but it becomes clear in the answer that they are to be understood as blacks "ruled by Islam." The question is as follows: "About a band (qawm) that plundered some blacks of property that did not belong to them. They fled in the wake of the plunderers until they [?] injured some of their horses. What is the ruling about those who injured the horses? Does liability fall upon them or the plunderers?"[80]

In al-Sharif Hama Allah's answer, the issue of liability for the injured horses depends entirely on the juridical status of the plunderers (and not the fact that they are, in this case, thieves!). Three classes of juridical status are invoked, namely unbelievers (glossed here as Bambara), "iniquitous transgressors" who are mustaghraq al-dhimma (by which he means warriors-status groups), and those who are not mustaghraq al-dhimma (but who are Muslims). The answer is somewhat confusing because the legal destination of the property – the injured horses – depends on the status of the plunderers who own them:

> The response: The plunderers are the injured party in terms of their horses. If [the plunderers] are Bambara, then the horse is considered booty and belongs to those who wounded it. If they are iniquitous transgressors (al-fasaqa al-ẓalama) and if they were mustaghraq al-dhimma, then it belongs to whoever among them wounded the horse, according to the amount of his loss (taʿab) in what was taken from their possessions. He takes it and the rest is for the poor because it belongs to the public treasury of the Muslims. If they are not mustaghraq al-dhimma, then [the wounded horse] replaces his plundered property according to the amount of that property, and the rest of it is for the owners of the horse if [the person plundered] is entitled to less of their property according to an amount of his property which they plundered.[81]

[80] "Nawāzil al-Sharīf Muḥammadnā Ḥamā Allāh," f. 57.
[81] Ibid.

What this opinion shows is that the property of both unbelievers and mustaghraq al-dhimma can be deemed illegitimate and taken from them in full by Muslims. The difference between the two lies in the ways in which the property is apportioned. The property of the unbelievers can be taken in whole by the fighter who captures it according to the rules of war. However, the property of the mustaghraq al-dhimma that can be taken by the individual who captures it is, in this case, limited by the mustaghraq al-dhimma's liability on the individual property plundered. Because of his status as a mustaghraq al-dhimma, he loses all his property. But the part beyond the individual liability for the specific act of plunder is assigned to the treasury of all the Muslims, and therefore to the needy and the poor. This is because of the illegality of all mustaghraq al-dhimma property in principle. In the third category of status mentioned here, in which the plunderers are Muslims but not mustaghraq al-dhimma, the stolen property is a liability that can be paid by the requisite part of the injured horse. But because of his status as a free Muslim, the plunderer is able to keep the part of the horse not required to cover the liability of the goods he previously stole. It is only the part of his property acquired in the act of theft that is illegal, not the whole of his property as in the case of the mustaghraq al-dhimma.

The impact of these three categories of property on blacks is clearer in a second case, which involves taking grain from fields abandoned by their owners:

> Question: About the agricultural fields of the blacks and the Bambara. If they flee from [their fields] and leave them in ruin, fearful of riflemen etc., is it permitted for us to take [the crops] or not?
>
> The response: If the field belongs to the Bambara then it is permitted for us to take [the crops] because they are unbelievers in the land of war. However, it is not [considered] booty but instead a tax for the lack of agreement about it, as if it were hidden property. If it belongs to those blacks who are ruled over by Islam, it is judged to be what is in "al-Jawāhir" by Ibn Shās,[82] the text of which is precisely as follows: "The property was not presented to him as inviolable (maʿṣūm). Is it for its finder because it is ruled to be already used up (mustahlak), or for its owner? There is a disagreement therefore about what is left to rot in the sea or on land, which its owner is incapable of using."[83]

This is the end of the opinion, and as such, not very satisfying in addressing the last question. But on the issue of the blacks, it identifies two

[82] This is the Egyptian Mālikī scholar ʿAbd Allāh b. Muḥammad Shās (d. 1219), author of "al-Jawāhir al-thamīna fī madhhab ʿālim al-madīna" (Kahhala 2:303).

[83] "Nawāzil al-Sharīf Muḥammadnā Ḥamā Allāh," f. 69.

principal juridical-status markers, namely unbelievers who are often glossed as "Bambara" and blacks "ruled by Islam." As we have seen, there is little theoretical difficulty in establishing the rules of property for those defined according to the juridical status of unbelievers. The more difficult issue is the blacks "ruled by Islam" because, as I discussed earlier, they are not fully accorded the juridical status of free Muslims. The passage from Ibn Shas does not resolve the issue, except to say that there are those who consider the crops to be a used-up resource that can be taken by anyone. This short opinion does not resolve the question of legitimacy of property taken from blacks who are "ruled by Islam."

The issue is perhaps more approachable in a third case, this one concerned with a person charged with retrieving plundered slaves:

> The question: About a man who confronted some warriors (muḥāribīn) demanding the return of slaves whom they had taken from some clerics. He came to them after they had already sold [the slaves] to some blacks, over whom two Arabs[84] from the warriors were established as rulers. In the meantime, the two Arabs sheltered [the slaves] until they went off to the blacks... [The two Arabs] then took those who were free among [the blacks] and they were prevented from returning home unless the slaves who had been sold to them were sent back in exchange ... So [the blacks] sent four of the slaves back to them. They gave [the blacks] some cows, sheep, and donkeys in place of those [slaves] in the original sale, and they sent them back their free people except for one free woman whom they held back in [the place of] one of the sold slaves. So [the blacks] turned all of [the slaves] over to the two Arabs, and they turned them over to the man, and [in exchange, the man] turned over to them some of the cows, sheep and donkeys that had been taken. He brought the rest and turned them over to those who had been sent to bring back one of the slaves on behalf of their masters (mawālī).[85]

The legal issue for the person who asked the question is about his reward for having arranged the return of these slaves. What is interesting for our concerns, though, is the status of the blacks to whom the slaves were originally sold, and from whom they were demanded back. These are the same category of blacks "ruled by Islam" that we have encountered already, but here there is added detail about a group that I have glossed as "two Arabs" who are charged by a warrior lineage with overseeing the

[84] In the copy of the text that I have used from Timbuktu, what I have translated as "two Arabs" is actually written "ʿurafāʾ" which could mean "deputies." Another copy of this text held at the Institut Mauritanien de Recherche Scientifique (IMRS) in Nouakchott, Mauritania, has the word "ʿarabān" (two Arabs) instead of "ʿurafāʾ" (deputies). Either word might be correct, although neither is especially clear. I thank Ghislaine Lydon for this information.

[85] "Nawāzil al-Sharīf Muḥammadnā Ḥamā Allāh," f. 57–8.

blacks. As such, these blacks "ruled by Islam" are represented as vassals of Arabophone groups.

The ambiguity of the status of the blacks is highlighted in this case by the incident that is related in the question. When the two Arabs attempted to retrieve the slaves who had been sold to the blacks, they took some of these blacks "ruled by Islam" hostage as a guarantee. Whereas this is not represented in legal terms, whether as licit or otherwise, it seems clear that blacks "ruled by Islam" was a status that carried with it a particular vulnerability to enslavement because at the root of the category was the idea that these blacks had already been conquered by Muslims and were a latent reserve pool of potential slaves when the moment arose. It is difficult to imagine a similar tactic being used and reported on almost in passing if the people from whom slaves had to be retrieved were Sahelian whites.

Although the primary issue of concern for the questioner is the share for the man who retrieved the slaves, he also asks about the status of the free black woman who continued to be held by the two Arabs, and whether it was permissible to put the free black hostages to work as slaves for their captors' benefit during the period of imprisonment. Both questions push at the heart of the status of people considered to be blacks "ruled by Islam." After dealing with the issue of compensation for the man who retrieved the slaves, al-Sharif Hama Allah turned to the issue of appropriate compensation for the blacks in return for the slaves. The complexity of the answer is the result of the issue of juridical status and the concomitant differences of property associated with these categories:

> The amount of cows, sheep and donkeys brought in return for the person [i.e. slave] whom the blacks had sold is decided according to the amount that the blacks would need for their purchase price if they were Muslim blacks who were not mustaghraq al-dhimma. If they were only Muslims because they were mustaghraq al-dhimma, then [their compensation] belongs to the public treasury of the Muslims, and it should not be held by the masters of the sold slaves, just as the text on this confirms. If they are blacks who are governed because they are unbelievers, then [their compensation] is also for the public treasury because it is incumbent on the warriors who sheltered [the slave] to donate him. The warriors should donate [the slave] because that is what was required by their liability (dhimma) in terms of the slaves whom they sold who are mustaghraq al-dhimma. The mustaghraq al-dhimma are not possessed alone by the owner of the sold property according to the price paid for him, but instead he belongs to the public treasury.[86]

[86] "Nawāzil al-Sharīf Muḥammadnā Ḥamā Allāh," f. 58.

As we have seen now in many examples, the property of the mustaghraq al-dhimma is considered illicit, and since slaves are considered property, there can be no compensation for property that is illegally held. More interestingly, though, is that al-Sharif Hama Allah outlines different status categories for blacks that are parallel to status categories for non-blacks. Those he identifies as Muslim blacks who are not mustaghraq al-dhimma are accorded the same property rights as other free Muslims. This is a theoretical set of possibilities. We already know from the question that these particular blacks are vassals of warrior lineages, and as such, they are mustaghraq al-dhimma. This has an impact on the question about the status of the free black woman kept as a slave and not returned to her people: "As for freedom: if she is from the blacks ruled over because of unbelief, then she is a female slave who belongs to the warriors responsible for her. And the property of the warriors belongs to the public treasury because they are mustaghraq al-dhimma. Unless she is from the Muslim blacks, freedom is not possible for anyone in her position and she is considered to be property."[87] Since we already know that the blacks in this case are vassals of those defined as mustaghraq al-dhimma, it seems likely that al-Sharif Hama Allah's intention here is to suggest that the free black woman taken hostage should be considered a slave a priori. A similar attitude appears in the historical traditions of certain Tuareg groups in the Aïr Massif in Niger. Ghoubeïd Alojaly reported on a seventeenth-century tradition in which all enslaved blacks, regardless of whether they claimed to be Muslim or not, became slaves because they were black.[88] Al-Sharif Hama Allah is not quite so direct but his legal opinion amounts to much the same thing.

COMMERCIAL AND POLITICAL RELATIONS WITH THE BLACKS

More than perhaps any other factor, trade relations across the West African subregion brought different kinds of people together. It was one thing to define different categories of blacks according to juridical status and property, quite another to manage commercial activities in areas controlled by black states, even those led by non-Muslims. Unsurprisingly given the fact that trade was a principal economic activity of Arabic-speaking clerical groups in the Sahel, the legal opinions of scholars from

[87] "Nawāzil al-Sharīf Muḥammadnā Ḥamā Allāh," f. 58.

[88] Ghoubeïd Alojaly, *Histoire des Kel-Denneg avant l'arrivé des Français*. ed. Karl-G. Prasse (Copenhagen: Akademisk Forlag, 1975), 22. I thank Benedetta Rossi for this reference.

these groups were quite pragmatic. One of the devices used to organize trade with the largely non-Muslim Bambara was a pact that permitted free movement of Muslim and non-Muslim merchants.[89] A significant impediment to trade with people defined as non-Muslims, or as suspect Muslims, was the actions of nineteenth-century militant Muslim reformists such as the aforementioned Fulbe forces of Amadu Lobbo who held up a Tishit caravan in Kaarta.[90] The two cases that I will present here will add to this literature by revealing some of the issues that arose out of commercial relationships with those defined as blacks, and by demonstrating some of the legal logic used to justify them. The first addresses relations with non-Muslim "Bambara," the second with the Fulbe reformist state in Masina.

The first case was provoked by a question about proper relations with the Bambara:

> The question: About the ruling on the Bambara, and those who buy things from properties of the Muslims from them: Are they to be considered people of war (ahl ḥarb) or people with whom one can make pacts ('ahd)? Or are they [to be considered] just like all thieves? What is the ruling concerning dealings with them because of necessity? What about their neighbors, and their commissions, and the conclusion of contracts between us and them in cases of corrupted sales, and the stealing of deposits and the like? ... What about the acceptance of their presents and their alms and [the animals] that they slaughter for their idols, and their prohibited games ...[91]

The two issues that have been the focus of this chapter appear in this question: collective juridical status and its relation to property. Since we know that the term Bambara is used in al-Sharif Hama Allah's collection to refer to unbelievers, their property, deposits, and so on can in principle be seized as booty. In practice, however, such behavior would render commercial relations very difficult for Sahelian merchants. The key new piece of information here is the idea of a pact between the Muslims and the Bambara. The authority used to declare that a pact can supersede the juridical status such people would otherwise be subject to is

[89] On the structure of trading relations between Arabic-speaking traders and the Middle Niger region, see Richard Roberts, *Warriors, Merchants, and Slaves: The State and the Economy in the Middle Niger Valley, 1700–1914* (Stanford, CA: Stanford University Press, 1987), 48–9; E. Ann McDougall, "The Ijil Salt Industry: Its role in the pre-colonial economy of the Western Sudan" (Ph.D. diss., University of Birmingham, 1980), 243–62.

[90] Lydon, *On Trans-Saharan Trails*, 114.

[91] "Nawāzil al-Sharīf Muḥammadnā Ḥamā Allāh," f. 25.

from the Walata jurist al-Ḥājj al-Ḥasan b. Āghbudī al-Zaydī (d. 1711).[92] According to the response:

> The Bambara are warriors just as it says in the opinion issued by the greatest of our shaykhs, the jurist al-Hajj al-Hasan, who said that: "The fact that they are warriors is obvious to he who knows the truth about pacts and their rules. How do we say that in the pacts that permit us to buy their children, we can forbid them to buy from us when the pact between us is proven to be valid? If merchants from the people of war come to us, and we make a pact with them in their country so that we will not kill them or release them, then they will sell us their children. Their purchases are not denied to them because of [the status] assigned to their minors (ṣighār) from the pact that [is concluded] by their adults (kibār)." The end of the quotation.
>
> [al-Hajj al-Hasan said]: "Instead of conducting the business between us when we enter their country for [the purposes of] commerce, when they likewise enter some of our countries under our protection, the purchase from the warrior is nothing more than this, following his statement about it. As for he who attacks us, and we have no pact with him in our country, do not trust any of them, neither their fathers or their sons, nor their women or their mothers of children. Their attack on the warriors in our country is not done on the basis of their pact..."[93]

These long quotations make it clear that slavery was a key issue in the rationalization of these political relationships. If the people of the "land of war" will sell their own people, there is no need to launch military action against them whether they are warriors or not. But this also suggests that the legal status of the "minors" as slaves should not determine the status of all "Bambara."

However, al-Sharif Hama Allah goes on to outline the rules of comportment with such people, and in particular the rules of residence:

> As for their neighbors who live with them in their land, this is forbidden according to the statement of the Prophet, may God bless him and grant him peace: "I am not responsible for any Muslim who resides among the polytheists."[94] According to Abū ʾl-Qāsim al-Burzulī[95] and others, whoever is forbidden to us in our oath swearing is inviolable when he has not been vanquished. Ibn al-ʿArabi [said] that "God forbade in principle that Muslims reside among the polytheists whom he decreed

[92] Born 1654/55, died 1711 (Maḥmūd b. Muḥammad Dadab, "Kashf al-ḥāʾil fī ʾl-taʿrīf bi-kutub al-fatāwā wa-ʾl-nawāzil," 30; El Hamel, *La Vie intellectuelle*, 252–3; MLG 1: 63–4).

[93] "Nawāzil al-Sharīf Muḥammadnā Ḥamā Allāh," f. 25.

[94] *Sunan Abū Dāwūd*, Book 14, #2630.

[95] Aḥmad b. Muḥammad b. Muʿtall al-Burzulī (d. 1438), *Fatāwā al-Burzulī: Jāmiʿ masāʾil al-aḥkām mimmā nazala min al-qaḍāyā bi-ʾl-muftīn wa-ʾl-ḥukkām*, 7 vol. ed. Muḥammad al-Ḥabīb Hīla (Beirut: Dār al-gharb al-islāmī, 2002); GAL II, 247, SII, 347–8; Hunwick, *Sharīʿa*, 88n.

should follow the Prophet, may God bless him and grant him peace, in Madina. So when God conquered Mecca abolishing the [requirement for] the hijra,[96] it remained forbidden to reside amongst the polytheists."[97]

According to this logic, dealings with the Bambara were also forbidden. Al-Sharif Hama Allah quotes the Maghrib scholar ʿAbd al-Raḥmān al-Akhḍarī (d. 1585)[98] as saying the social intercourse with an iniquitous person (fāsiq) is only allowed because of necessity. Further support for this view is drawn from Ibn al-Aʿmash.[99]

The second case that I will discuss is more complicated because it involves relations with the reformist Muslim Fulbe of Masina, defined in this text as a state ruled by blacks. The text is preserved in Tishit, in Mauritania,[100] and it is based on a question sent by a certain Aḥmad b. Ḥama Allāh to al-Shaykh Sīdi al-Mukhtār al-Ṣaghīr al-Kuntī (d. 1847),[101] who became head of the Kunta-Mukhtāriyya order after the death of his father in 1826.[102] The Kunta enjoyed broadly good relations with Amadu Lobbo in Masina; Alfa Nouhoun Tayrou, the suspected forger of the "Ta'rikh al-fattash" and close councilor of Amadu Lobbo, spent twenty years with the Kunta in the Azawad as a student.[103] So we would expect that the author's Kunta identity would influence the fatwa that he issued, which is certainly sympathetic to Amadu Lobbo's claims. The document is undated, but the details in it suggest that the fatwa was probably issued after Sidi al-Mukhtar al-Saghir became head of the Kunta-Mukhtariyya in 1826, and before the death of Amadu Lobbo in 1845.

The question in this case is one of allegiance (bayʿa) to the Hamdullahi Caliphate headed by Amadu Lobbo in Masina. An act of allegiance would have been theoretically necessary for Arabophone merchants wanting to

96 Because Mecca had been controlled by polytheists, Muslims were forced to emigrate to Madina.

97 "Nawāzil al-Sharīf Muḥammadnā Ḥamā Allāh," f. 26.

98 ʿAbd al-Raḥmān b. Muḥammad al-Ṣaghīr al-Akhḍārī al-Bunṭyūsī al-Mālikī (d. 1585). Presumably he quotes the very well-known didactic text, "Mukhtaṣar fī 'l-ʿibādāt ʿalā madhhab al-imām Mālik" (GAL S II 705).

99 "Nawāzil al-Sharīf Muḥammadnā Ḥamā Allāh," f. 26.

100 I am indebted to Ghislaine Lydon for sharing this document with me. It is from a private library in Tishit, Mauritania. I will refer to the document as "Lydon ms. Tishit"

101 Aziz A. Batran, *The Qadiryya Brotherhood in West Africa and the Western Sahara: The Life and Times of Shaykh al-Mukhtar al-Kunti, 1729–1811* (Rabat: Université Mohammed V-Souissi, 2001), 134; ALA IV, 115–18; MLG 1: 245–6.

102 Ghislaine Lydon discusses a similar document by Sīdi Muḥammad al-Kuntī (d. 1826) (Lydon, *On Trans-Saharan Trails*, 309).

103 C.C. Stewart "Frontier Disputes and Problems of Legitimization: Sokoto-Masina Relations, 1817–1837," *JAH* 17, no. 4 (1976): 500; Bâ and Daget, *L'Empire peul*, 114n.

conduct business there if the Hamdullahi Caliphate was recognized as a proper Islamic state. Such an act of allegiance carried with it a set of obligations to that state in terms of taxes, rules of property, and so on, which would not be the case in polities for which this status of Islamic legitimacy did not apply. The question is as follows:

> We ask you to please open your heart and allow us to acquire the brilliance that comes from your light, by explaining for us the state (ḥāl) of the Fulbe in general, and specifically in the case of Amadu Lobbo and his people, and all the rest of his emirs. [Please] explain and distinguish first of all between their authority (amr) and its foundation, its instruments, its current form, and its meaning. What results from this according to the exigencies of discernment (firāsa) and the evidence of the states (aḥwāl)?
>
> Is it required of everyone to swear allegiance to them if they are not already under allegiance to another power? Or is it not required initially but only after the required conditions are fulfilled? Or, are [the Fulbe] like all of the rest of the vanquished (al-mutaghallibīn) who are to be dealt with, as the poet said: "Their house remains their house, and their land remains their land?" In this case, one does not pay zakat to them voluntarily, nor does one divide up the payment [of zakat], nor does one cooperate voluntarily with what they do, even when presented in logical order, because of our uncertainty about their authority.
>
> We have not heard that either you or Shaykh Sidi Muhammad have sworn allegiance to them, nor that you have ordered the people to swear allegiance to them and cooperate with them. What, in the eminence of your knowledge about the requirements of cooperation pursuant to uprightness and God-fearing is incumbent upon us? What do you know about someone who has recently died while not under allegiance. Did he die in a state of ignorance (jāhiliyya)? What about those who have left this lax (sāʾiba) land but have been unable to reach a place in which they can swear allegiance? Is this close enough to the newly-arrived inhabitant in a country of which the rulings of the emir of the Muslims is analogous, or is it necessary to swear allegiance personally or in writing or to swear before witnesses?
>
> Should one refuse to have anything to do with this lax country and abstain from appointing an imam with a confirmed consensus?[104]

The stakes in this set of questions are quite significant because it represents a set of claims that Sahelian merchants were unaccustomed to in their interactions with political entities in the "land of the blacks." That there would be material consequences for allegiance to Hamdullahi seems to be a motivating factor in the question. Above all, other sources indicate that Hamdullahi was seeking to control access by Sahelian merchants to the important agricultural region of Kaarta because of ongoing

[104] Lydon ms. Tishit., f. 1–2.

military activities that they were involved in there.[105] The claims made on behalf of the Islamic credentials of Amadu Lobbo's state were also contested in the subregion in the first decades of its existence.[106]

There is not a single mention in the question of the term blacks, although it does come up in the response. Yet, at the heart of the question is a racial argument. The passage that suggests that Hamdullahi's legitimacy as a Muslim polity depends on the state of the Fulbe, and whether they are to be considered juridically as among the "rest of the vanquished." We now know what such phrases allude to, and the theoretical consequences for the Fulbe should their status be established as blacks "ruled by Islam." If this could be demonstrated, then there would be no question of allegiance to Hamdullahi or to any Fulbe, regardless of current Muslim practice. This is the argument being put forward by the questioner.

As the discussion of Ahmad Baba's "The ladder of ascent" demonstrated, racial arguments made in questions sent to scholars could – and did – sometimes provoke explicitly nonracial responses. We know from Ghislaine Lydon's work that there are other cases of more explicit racial questions posed in the same region by traders connected to Tishit. In an undated, but slightly earlier, fatwa issued in response to this kind of question, Sidi Muhammad b. Sidi al-Mukhtar al-Kunti wrote: "the political allegiance of blacks is just like the political allegiance of whites. If it is done well, it is binding, like all transactions [between Muslims]. But it is considered a reprehensible act (makrūh) if it is done under compulsion. So one must act according to what most protects the faith and the universe."[107] Thus, an explicitly nonracial argument was offered to a question posed on the basis of racial difference between blacks and whites.

The fatwa under discussion here is another example. In Sidi al-Mukhtar al-Saghir's response, he began by pointing out the hypocrisy of his questioners, since they are entirely comfortable making political arrangements with non-Muslims such as the "Bambara":

What confuses us about the authority of the Fulbe [is that] some who come from your side say that you prefer the Tuareg warriors over them, while [at the same time] you do not like to fight the Bambara warriors who are infidels. We have

[105] This was discussed earlier, in reference to Lydon, *On Trans-Saharan Trails*, 114; See also John Hanson, *Migration, Jihad, and Muslim Authority in West Africa* (Bloomington, IN: Indiana University Press, 1996), 23–5.

[106] On the competing claims of Hamdullahi and Sokoto see Stewart, "Frontier Disputes," 497–514.

[107] Quoted by Lydon, *On Trans-Saharan Trails*, 309.

> learned that indeed, praise be to God, you are very discerning! Our wish is that we also might be so discerning day and night about following these errors in courage and restraint, for it is only by the nobility of your knowledge that the people of our land acknowledge them because of commerce with the country of the Bambara, which is under the authority of the people of Ségou.[108]

The problem, it seems, is that Sahelian merchants were willing to deal with unbelievers in Kaarta, from where they purchased much of the grain consumed in places such as Tishit, but they were unwilling to make allegiance to the Fulbe at Hamdullahi. Sidi al-Mukhtar al-Saghir explained that the levels of insecurity in Kaarta meant that Sahelian merchants were forced to enter commercial partnerships with merchants in Kaarta, to live among the non-Muslim blacks for reasons of safety, and to otherwise ignore the directives that we have already discussed about how to conduct business in the land of the blacks. Sidi al-Mukhtar al-Saghir extended the nonracial argument rendered by Sidi Muhammad, mentioned earlier, and wrote:

> There is no impediment for them [to make the pledge of allegiance] or to settle in Kāla and live together with the blacks. If they settle with [the blacks] in Kaarta, the insecurity of the road is a deterrent to the possibility of friendship with them... Islam should be extended so that one people are connected with another. They will then pass from one authority to another that they consent to, just like we have advised.[109]

The benefit, according to Sidi al-Mukhtar al-Saghir, of pledging allegiance to the Fulbe of Amadu Lobbo is that such actions will potentially lead to a wider dispersion of Islam among the blacks. This is a comprehensive rejection of the racial argument put forward by the questioner.

CONCLUSION

The racial arguments discussed in this chapter were discursive interventions, claims made in hopes of justifying other real-world objectives. They were never final or permanent, and they cannot be said to represent the condition of a particular place or people. Ideas about race did not exist as some kind of ahistorical discursive denigration of blacks, or of blackness; instead, racial ideas had to be inhabited, used, and reproduced. They were always, by definition, dialogical. And as such, they very often provoked nonracial arguments in response. I have traced some of the ways in which specific racial arguments were made in collections of legal

[108] Lydon ms. Tishit, f. 2.
[109] Lydon ms. Tishit, f. 2–3.

opinions produced by Arabophone scholars between the seventeenth and nineteenth centuries. I will return to these sources in the chapter devoted to slavery, where some of the problems that were discussed here will be developed further. I want to conclude by indicating that the meanings and arguments associated with blackness spread more widely than might be assumed from my reliance on a particular subset of legal collections from the desert edge of present-day Mali and Mauritania.

We have already seen that the nineteenth-century forger of the "Ta'rikh al-fattash" inserted the racial terms "zanj" and "ar-bi" into that chronicle as a means of legitimizing arguments made on behalf of Amadu Lobbo that he should rightfully control certain groups of so-called slaves. These were arguments made on behalf of a state that understood itself to be Muslim, and whose founder and leader claimed to have been predicted by the great Egyptian scholar al-Suyuti as a true successor (caliph) to the original seat of Islamic authority. Amadu Lobbo's right to control those he labeled "blacks" was inherited, according to the (Pseudo) "Ta'rikh al-fattash," from the Muslim authority vested in Askia Muhammad of the Songhay Empire. For the Fulbe leaders of the Hamdullahi Caliphate, the racial labels "zanj" and "ar-bi" were ways of claiming authority over the category of blacks "ruled by Islam" that is found in the legal literature of the Sahel. It was a claim to a particular kind of Muslim authority that blacks could not achieve.

There is a similar racial dynamic in the writings of the Fulbe founders of the Sokoto Caliphate. I have already discussed the reception of Ahmad Baba's "The ladder of ascent" by Sahelian intellectuals and how it focused primarily on the question of enslavement of free Muslims among the blacks. However, by the nineteenth century, Fulbe writers such as Usman dan Fodio had come to reject the list of those blacks whom Ahmad Baba considered to be free Muslims. In his "Evidence for the duty of emigration" ("Bayān wujūb al-hijra") written in 1806 to justify the jihad he had launched against Hausa rulers in 1804, Usman dan Fodio argued that Ahmad Baba had been wrong about the Hausa being among the free Muslims:[110]

> Another class is those lands where Islam predominated and unbelief is rare such as Borno, Kano, Katsina, Songhay and Mali according to the examples given by Ahmad Baba in the aforementioned book. These, too, are lands of unbelief without any doubt, since the spread of Islam there is [only] among the masses but as for their sultans, they are unbelievers ... even though they profess Islam. [That is] because they are polytheists, turning [people] from the path of God and raising

[110] *Miʿrāj al-Ṣuʿūd*, 7.

the banner of the kingdom of this world above the banner of Islam – and that is all unbelief according to the consensus of the scholars.[111]

Usman dan Fodio needed to define his Hausa opponents as non-Muslims to justify the jihad he had proclaimed against them. He did not deny that there were true Muslims among the blacks, but because "the status of a land is that of its ruler,"[112] all people under the authority of these non-Muslim rulers were obliged to emigrate or be subject to legitimate military attack. But Usman dan Fodio went even further in arguing that there were no parts of the land of the blacks that should be considered part of the land of Islam: "I have read in the writings of a certain scholar [a statement] which reports that there are absolutely no lands of Islam in the land of the blacks."[113] Such a designation of status rendered all blacks not already "ruled by Islam" into legitimate targets of enslavement.

In the extensive academic literature on the Sokoto Caliphate and its founders, these criticisms of local practice of Islam among black (Hausa) rulers are well known.[114] All too often, however, the reformers' descriptions of black (Hausa) Islamic laxity are taken at face value. What I think should be clear by now is that the use of the term blacks is quite intentional in this literature because it conveyed a set of meanings that invoked a range of socially inferior status positions for the people who would become the targets of the jihad. As this chapter has demonstrated, there was nothing natural in the opposition between blacks and nonblacks; such distinctions were loaded with social and political meaning. If the Arabic-speaking scholars in the Sahel made a dichotomy in their writings between themselves and the blacks by the pairing "the whites and the blacks" ("al-bīḍān wa-ʾl-sūdān"), Fulbe scholars arrived at a similar distinction between "the Fulbe and the blacks" ("al-fulān wa-ʾl-sūdān") that did the exactly the same thing.

The extent of the intertextuality across Arabic writings in West Africa is beyond the scope of this book. It is clear from even the briefest look at this literature, however, that Fulbe writers constructed a social and political world in Hausaland that they aimed to transform by deploying racial labels and arguments that marked off blackness. The leaders of the Sokoto

111 Usman dan Fodio, *Bayān wujūb al-hijra ʿalā ʾl-ʿibād*, ed. and trans. F.H. El Masri (Khartoum: Khartoum University Press, 1978), 50.
112 Ibid., 50.
113 Ibid., 51.
114 See, for example, the exchange of letters between Muhammad Bello and al-Kanemi, leader of Bornu, in Thomas Hodgkin, *Nigerian Perspectives. An Historical Anthology*, (Oxford, Oxford University Press, 1975, 2nd ed.), 261–7.

jihad often used the term blacks as their word for Hausa speakers.[115] For example, Muhammad Bello introduced the main character in one of his histories of the jihad entitled "The presentation of the discourse concerning what happened between us and ʿAbd al-Salām" ("Sard al-kalām fīmā jarā baina-nā wa-baina ʿAbd al-Salām") as follows: "ʿAbd al-Salām is a man from the blacks (ahl al-sudan), from the clan of Arewa."[116] Further in the text, he says: "This is what happened between us and the blacks .... Many of the blacks who were with us, both Muslims and 'ahl al-dhimma,'[117] withdrew when they saw our weakness."[118] In Muḥammad Bello's extensive history entitled "The wages of the fortunate in the history of the land of Takrur" ("Infāq al-Maysūr fī taʾrīkh bilād al-takrūr"), he explained the historical relationship between blacks and the coming of Islam to West Africa in terms of an original Muslim conquest.[119] I do not want to suggest that the uses of racial labels in this literature was not responsive to the social and political dynamics found in Hausaland, which were different than those elsewhere in the Sahel. It is striking, however, how much Fulbe writers borrowed from earlier Sahelian writers, and I think we need to understand that this was itself a rhetorical strategy useful in their mobilization efforts. Usman dan Fodio even invoked and described the juridical category of mustaghraq al-dhimma in his "Light of the brothers" ("Sirāj al-ikhwān"),[120] which suggests to me that the purchase of the complex set of ideas bound up with the blackness of the sudan was much wider than has been hitherto understood.

[115] I do not want to be overly categorical here because I have not made a full survey of this literature. Muhammad Bello certainly uses the term consistently. See Rainer Osswald, *Das Sokoto-Kalifat und Seine Ethnischen Grundlagen. Eine Untersuchung Zum Aufstand des ʿAbd as-Salām* (Beirut: Franz Steiner Verlag, 1986), 87–8. Usman dan Fodio sometimes uses the term "ahl Ḥawsa." For example, his "Nūr al-albāb," ed. I.A. Ogunbiyi, "Nūr al-albāb: The Litmus-Test of Pure Islam as Interpreted by Shaikh ʿUthmān b. Fūdī," *RBCAD* 18/19 (1990–1991): 7.

[116] Muḥammad Bello, "Sard al-kalām fīmā jarā baina-nā wa-baina ʿAbd al-Salām," ed. and trans. Rainer Osswald, *Das Sokoto-Kalifat und Seine Ethnischen Grundlagen. Eine Untersuchung Zum Aufstand des ʿAbd as-Salām* (Beirut: Franz Steiner Verlag, 1986), 37.

[117] Literally "people of protection," although this appears to be a term analogous to the "blacks ruled by Islam" found in the Sahelian literature.

[118] Muḥammad Bello, "Sard al-kalām," 38, 40.

[119] Muḥammad Bello, *Infāq al-Maysūr fī taʿrīkh bilād al-takrūr*, ed. Haija al-Shādhilī (Rabat: Université Muhammad V-Souissi, 1996), 48.

[120] ʿUthmān b. Fūdī, "Sirāj al-ikhwān," ed. Ulrich Rebstock, *Die Lampe der Brüder (Sirāǧ al-iḫwān) von ʿUṯmān b. Fūdī. Reform und Ǧihād im Sūdān* (Walldorf-Hessen: Verlag für Orientkunde, 1985), 18–19.

PART TWO

RACE AND THE COLONIAL ENCOUNTER, C. 1830–1936

PRELUDE

Most of the Sahel was colonized by France. The process of French conquest and consolidation began in the middle decades of the nineteenth century with expansion up the Senegal River. It did not end until the 1920s, when French forces finally established control over the remotest corners of the Sahara Desert. The French military campaigns that led to the conquest of the territory that would be called Soudan Français, and that would become the postcolonial country of Mali, began in 1879 from bases in Senegal. For the next twenty years, French officers led battalions of African soldiers in the slow conquest of the new colony, which only gained a separate administrative structure in 1891. By the time that the original capital located at the Senegal River town of Kayes had been moved to Bamako on the Niger River in 1899, French rule was well established in the southern parts of the territory. Beginning in the late 1880s, attention turned to the as yet unconquered Niger Bend, and in particular the famous town of Timbuktu. After a few years of delay while French forces consolidated their control over southern and western Soudan, the first French military forces arrived in the town of Timbuktu in December 1893.

Colonial forces spent much of the next decade attempting to win the acceptance and recognition by the seminomadic pastoralist populations of the Niger Bend to the fact of French rule. They saw the Tuareg as their principal antagonists, and a number of military campaigns were launched against Tuareg groups over the first two decades of the French occupation. The Saharan and Sahelian territories were of little economic value to France, yet they were among the most difficult areas to control. Dissidents and rebels were able to use the harsh environment of the Sahara Desert as a refuge from French control and as a base from which they periodically launched raids on French-controlled territory. These Saharan incursions were only ended definitively in 1934, when a joint French and Spanish force occupied the town of Smara in the Saqiat al-Hamra region of the western Sahara. Nonetheless, French colonial authority in the Niger Bend itself was relatively well established by the middle of the first decade of the twentieth century.

Race was an important tool of French colonial rule. Part Two of this book explores the relationship between ideas about race that were articulated in the francophone world during the nineteenth century and the application and reconfiguration of these ideas, first in Algeria after 1830, and then in the Sahel at the end of the century. The two chapters in this section focus on the history of French notions about race and the way that these ideas shaped the colonial encounter that occurred in the Niger Bend, and the way that political leaders in the Niger Bend used their conceptions of race as a way of winning advantage with the new French forces. It demonstrates that in the colonial encounter that occurred in the Niger Bend, both sides – French and African – brought with them ideas about race that affected the nature of colonial rule. I argue that for both French officers and local people, ideas about racial difference were meaningful and useful in negotiating the new political context of colonial rule. The form and content of French and Sahelian notions about race differed; despite this, the idiom of race was something that both sides thought they shared in common.

In Chapter 3, I briefly trace the history of French ideas about race in the nineteenth century and the ways that these ideas were put into practice in Algeria and then in the Sahara Desert in relation to the Tuareg. It is impossible to understand the politics of race that organized the exercise of French colonial power in the Niger Bend without reference to the development of the racial regime in Algeria. I argue that a popular French idea of the Tuareg was already formed by the 1870s on the basis of a variety of encounters and exchanges between French people and the Tuareg in the central Sahara Desert. The French image had both a positive and a negative side to it; the Tuareg could be represented as honor-bound, almost feudal knights, or as untamed and vicious marauders. In either case, the Tuareg were thought to be racially distinct from Arabs and blacks, and possibly even the racial cousins of Europeans as the descendants of a classical, originally European, Atlantic race. These ideas about the Tuareg shaped the colonial encounter that occurred in the

Niger Bend in the 1890s and helped organize the way that French colonial officials approached the Tuareg in this region.

In Chapter 4, I explore the confrontation between the nascent French colonial state and the Tuareg and Arab confederacies that dominated the Niger Bend at the end of the nineteenth century. It was principally the Tuareg who fought against the French during the initial years of conquest, and it was these same groups that would always pose a very real potential threat to the colonial position. This chapter discusses the military strategies, negotiations, and alliances formed by the new colonial regime in the Niger Bend in regards to different pastoralist groupings. I trace the most important conflicts between French forces and particular pastoralist groups, as well as the alliances and accommodations made by Arabophone groups with the French. The chapter demonstrates that the particular shape that the colonial state took in the Niger Bend was the result of a set of relationships and negotiations between French and pastoralist leaders in the early decades of the colonial presence. Race was an important political idiom used by both sides.

3

Meeting the Tuareg

> Theoretically speaking, racism is a philosophy of history or, more accurately, a historiography which makes history the consequence of a hidden secret revealed to men about their own nature and their own birth. It is a philosophy which makes visible the invisible cause of the fate of societies and peoples; not to know that cause is seen as evidence of degeneracy or of the historical power of the evil.
>
> Etienne Balibar[1]

PREFIGURING RACIAL ENCOUNTERS

In the account of a reconnaissance trip made from the Atlantic coast of West Africa at Dahomey to the Niger River in 1896, Georges Toutée narrates his first encounter with the Tuareg:

> For the last three days, my trip has taken on a new interest; we are surrounded by white faces, fine figures, worried looks, numerous demonstrations of friendship, and rare but certain signs of hatred and treachery.... Are these Tuareg, who have given us such a good welcome, enemies or friends? I don't know anything anymore, but they are whites.[2]

This passage captures remarkably well the expressed sentiments of so many French military officers upon meeting the pastoralist, seminomadic

[1] Etienne Balibar, "Racism and Nationalism," in *Race, Nation, Class: Ambiguous Identities*, ed. Balibar and Immanuel Wallerstein (New York: Verso, 1991), 55.

[2] Georges Joseph Toutée, *Dahomé, Niger, Touareg. Récit de voyage* (Paris, 1897), 280; cited in Paul Pandolfi, "La construction du mythe touareg. Quelques remarques et hypothèses," *Ethnologies comparées* 7 (2004): 6.

Tuareg people of the West African Sahel at the end of the nineteenth century. Again and again in published narratives, and in official and private correspondence, the Tuareg make an ambiguous entrance on the stage of colonial encounter as, on the one hand, wild and dangerous "tribes" of nomadic warriors who threaten the nascent colonial enterprise, and on the other hand, as racially white, lightly touched by Islam, suggesting a capacity for civilization certainly not shared by their black neighbors. The consistency of French writing about the Tuareg suggests that the colonial encounter was in an important sense *already* imagined before it occurred, already structured into the outlines of a colonial vulgate that reduced the social and political complexities of the Sahel into a series of dichotomous and mutually exclusive groupings, namely nomad and sedentary, master and slave, black and white.

The echoes of other imperial adventures (and misadventures) are obvious, although in the history of European colonial expansion, I cannot think of a people other than the Tuareg from whom so much was expected on the basis of so little actual exposure and experience. There were important consequences of French hopes for the Tuareg in terms of shaping the structure of the colonial regime that was constructed in the Niger Bend, and in opening up the space for many Tuareg themselves to play the French-assigned role of the "nomad" in order to maximize the relatively privileged position they were allotted in the ethno-racial hierarchy of colonized people. My purpose in this chapter is to explore the genealogy of the French racial ideas that informed the colonial encounter. Race fed into a larger myth about the Tuareg, even before French forces set foot in the lands where the Tuareg people lived.

Much of the historical literature concerning the emergence of European racial ideas has focused on early-modern encounters with non-Europeans, and especially on encounters with Africans. There is a whole literature on the racial construction of blacks that dates back to the earliest European travelers' accounts of Africa.[3] It is blacks who were made to represent the furthest extent of difference, the most primitive end of most racial hierarchies. Kim Hall has made much of the

[3] For the French case, see William Cohen, *The French Encounter with Africans: White Responses to Blacks, 1530–1880* (Bloomington, IN: Indiana University Press, 1980); William Schneider, *An Empire for the Masses: The French Popular Image of Africa, 1870–1900* (Westport, CT: Greenwood, 1982); Dana Hale, *Races on Display: French Representations of Colonized Peoples, 1886–1940* (Bloomington, IN: Indiana University Press, 2008).

early-modern literary uses of black imagery as precursors to European colonial expansion.

> The use of Africa and blackness as signs of disorder is the first step in preparing for Europe's ordering and later exploitation of Africa's human and natural resources. In the ordering of such strange variety, there lies power as well as wealth. At first only a culminating sign of physical oddity and natural disorderliness, blackness begins to represent the destructive potential of strangeness, disorder, and variety, particularly when intertwined with the familiar, and familiarly threatening, unruliness of gender.[4]

These ideas about blacks and blackness were vitally important to the development of Euro-American racial projects, but we need to be careful to avoid teleology. Critics have argued that Kim Hall's focus on the imagery of color misrepresents a more complex history of racial ideas in early-modern Europe. Roxann Wheeler, for example, suggests that in eighteenth-century England, racial ideology "forms mainly around English responses to certain customs, dress, religion, and especially trading – in short, around a concept of civility."[5] The focus on the negative imagery of blackness may act to conceal the multiple ways in which racial difference can be constructed.

In this chapter, I trace some of the important steps that contributed to French imaginings of the Tuareg as a proximate race closer to Europeans than either Arabs or blacks. I will have little to say about the development of French ideas about people defined as black. This subject has been treated by others and does not need to be rehearsed here. As important as ideas about blackness were in structuring French colonial power, it was often the issue of how to understand and manage groups thought to occupy medial positions in the larger racial hierarchy that posed the bigger problem. It was with these "higher order" colonized groups that the French administration sought "natural" alliances. The problem of race faced by French officers and administrators in the Niger Bend and across the Sahel more broadly was not about blacks, but about how to deal with Arabic- and Berber-speaking peoples whom Europeans identified as white. Encounters with Arabs and Tuareg did not lead to a colonial discourse of alterity, but instead to efforts at intellectual excavation and recovery of the natural (racial) ties of affection that would/should bind them to France.

[4] Kim F. Hall, *Things of Darkness: Economies of Race and Gender in Early Modern England* (Ithaca, NY: Cornell University Press, 1996), 28.

[5] Roxann Wheeler, *The Complexion of Race: Categories of Difference in Eighteenth-Century British Culture* (Philadelphia: University of Pennsylvania Press, 2000), 92.

THE IDEA OF "RACE" IN FRANCE

The word race entered into the French language in the late fifteenth century. As elsewhere in Europe, the first meanings attributed to this word concerned the qualities of breeding animals. In sixteenth-century usage, the term had expanded to include people who were thought to possess valuable inherited qualities, such as royal families and others in the nobility. In these early uses, the term was closely associated with the idea of lineage, designating a family line.[6] The biological continuity that was thought to adhere to a race through the course of generations sustained the integrity of noble lineages and the social order. It contributed a political rationalization of status, providing a natural foundation for the hierarchy of virtues, aptitudes, and temperaments that found its highest form in upper social groups.[7]

The literature concerning the non-western peoples encountered by European travelers rarely employed the term race in its descriptions before the late eighteenth century. Insofar as explanations were offered on the physical and moral differences between Europeans and others, climate was seen as the primary variable. Montesquieu, for example, writing in the middle of the eighteenth century, made the argument that national character and forms of government were shaped by environmental influences. Referring to Africa, he stated that "countries where excess of heat enervates the body, and renders men so slothful and dispirited that nothing but the fear of chastisement can oblige them to perform any laborious duty: slavery is there more reconcilable to reason."[8] As is well known, Montesquieu and other Enlightenment thinkers in France opposed the Atlantic slave system. However, the environmental theory of African inferiority, and the consequent "natural" state of slavery in Africa, allowed advocates to argue that the institution of New World slavery acted to raise the status of blacks, to educate them, and to lift them out of the debased condition in which they lived in Africa.[9]

[6] Pierre H. Boulle, "François Bernier and the Origins of the Modern Concept of Race," in *The Color of Liberty: Histories of Race in France*, ed. Sue Peabody and Tyler Stovall (Durham, NC: Duke University Press, 2003), 12; Michael Banton, *Racial Theories* (Cambridge: Cambridge University Press, 1987), 1–27.

[7] Claude Blanckaert, "On the Origins of French Ethnology: William Edwards and the Doctrine of Race," in *Bones, Bodies, Behavior: Essays on Biological Anthropology*, ed. George W. Stocking, Jr. (Madison, WI: University of Wisconsin Press, 1988), 25.

[8] Cited in Banton, *Racial Theories*, 8.

[9] Cohen, *French Encounter*, 145–7.

In the nineteenth century, the term race was used by liberal historians in France, such as Augustin Thierry (1795–1856), as a polemical weapon against royalist opponents. Thierry argued that the Franks (nobles) and the Gauls (commoners) were distinct races with discrete origins that had retained their identity through time and maintained their salient characteristics and their purity. Contrary to the environmental arguments about human difference made by writers in the eighteenth century, Thierry wrote that "new physiological investigations, together with a deeper look at the great events which have changed the social conditions of various nations, prove that the physical and moral constitution of various peoples depends much more on their heritage and the primitive race to which they belong than on climatic influence under which they have fallen by chance."[10] The criteria used by nineteenth-century historians and philologists to distinguish different races seem, from our perspective, to be largely cultural. Ernest Renan (1823–1892), for example, cited five distinguishing factors that determined race: language, literature, history, religion, and law. However, such differences were often understood as immutable.[11]

The fields of ethnography and anthropology were created in France during the nineteenth century as a means of better understanding the racial dynamic in human history. When William Edwards (1777–1842) founded the Paris Ethnology Society in 1839, its stated purpose was to identify the principal elements that distinguished human races by studying the physical organization, the intellectual and moral character, the languages, and historical traditions of various peoples.[12] Edwards argued that racial types were permanent because even in cases of racial mixing between closely related peoples, one of them – usually the stronger – would predominate in the population. Where small groups of conquerors had arrived in certain places, they had been swamped by the larger indigenous population, and consequently, the indigenous racial type had

[10] Augustin Thierry, *Dix ans d'études historiques* (Paris, 1834), 191; Cited in Blanckaert, "On the Origins," 26. Thierry's idea of history as fundamentally a struggle of races drew on the ideas of the German historian Barthold Niebuhr (1776–1831) who claimed to have uncovered what he called the "temper and character" of the Romans. Niebuhr's approach to history emphasized matters of blood and race. See Ivan Hannaford, *Race: The History of an Idea in the West* (Baltimore: Johns Hopkins University Press, 1996), 237–40.

[11] Patricia M.E. Lorcin, *Imperial Identities: Stereotyping, Prejudice and Race in Colonial Algeria* (New York: I.B. Tauris, 1999), 281.

[12] Cohen, *French Encounter*, 218–19.

remained predominant.[13] When the Paris Anthropological Society was founded in 1859 by Paul Broca (1824–1880), its objectives were similarly racial, aiming at a comprehensive *anthropologie* that would study both physiological and cultural dimensions of different people.[14] These ideas were popularized by the illiberal polemicist Arthur de Gobineau in his "Essay on the inequality of human races," which was published in 1853–1855. In it, he claimed that all human history could be understood using the "master-key" of race.[15]

ARABS AND BERBERS

Ideas about race were widely used in nineteenth-century French efforts to understand the peoples of Africa. Military doctors were especially important in carrying racial ideas to the colonies and using them in their empirical investigations of indigenous populations.[16] The French experience in Algeria was formative. It was here that the French constructed a colonial vulgate that would organize their thinking about, and administration of, North Africa.[17] This laid the basis for the ideas that organized colonial conquest in the Sahel. The distinction made between Arab and Berber was especially important in Algeria, where French sympathy for the Berbers – and their antipathy for the Arabs – was justified according to racial arguments. The construction of what has been called a "Kabyle myth" of Berber superiority, and consequent susceptibility to the influences of French civilization, was largely based on an application of racial theory and the assertion that the North African Berbers were

[13] Martin Staum, "Paris Ethnology and the Perfectibility of 'Races'," *Canadian Journal of History* 35 (2000): 223.

[14] Emmanuelle Sibeud, *Une science imperial pour l'Afrique? La construction des saviors africanistes en France, 1878–1930* (Paris: Editions de l'EHESS, 2002), 35–7.

[15] Arthur de Gobineau, *The Inequality of Human Races* (New York: Howard Fertig, 1999), ix.

[16] Richard Fogarty and Michael A. Osborne, "Constructions and Functions of Race in French Military Medicine, 1830–1920," in *The Color of Liberty: Histories of Race in France*, ed. Sue Peabody and Tyler Stovall (Durham, NC: Duke University Press, 2003), 206–36.

[17] Edmund Burke III has described its broad outlines as follows: "These assumptions included the anarchic state of precolonial society, the essentially negative and obscurantist role of Islam in North African society, the innate fanaticism of Islam, and the divisions of the society into dichotomous and mutually exclusive groupings: Arab and Berber, nomad and sedentary, rural and urban" ("The Sociology of Islam: The French Tradition," in *Islamic Studies: A Tradition and Its Problems*, ed. Malcolm Kerr [Malibu, CA: Undena Publications, 1980], 77).

relatively closer racially to Europeans than were the Arabs. The myth supported a colonial ideology that was triangular rather than binary. The privileged position of the Kabyles in this construction was only tenable as long as it stood in relation to Arabs. When the French began to penetrate southward into the Sahara Desert, where they would encounter the Berber-speaking Tuareg, similar arguments for racial proximity helped in constructing what Paul Pandolfi has called a "Tuareg myth."[18] On the southern side of the Sahara Desert, blacks stood in for the Algerian Arabs as the racially inferior part of the indigenous population.

The French conquest of Algeria began in 1830. Initial resistance was led by ʿAbd al-Qādir al-Jazāʾirī (1808–1883), who used the idiom of jihad to rally Algerian opposition to the French presence in a fifteen-year war that ended in 1847. He used a variety of tactics, both military and political, taking advantage of the terrain of the Algerian Tell and Petit Sahara to launch raids and to carry out strategic retreats. French officials defined the Arabs of the Algerian plains as nomads, as erratic and unreliable people who resorted to innumerable ruses and who were susceptible to uncontrolled fanaticism when confronted by the French. For Thomas-Robert Bugeaud, the French governor who led the military campaign against ʿAbd al-Qadir, these Arabs would always be elusive, difficult to control, and a potential danger. Their nomadic social organization and their religion necessitated a continual use of force to maintain colonial control and served as a justification for the scorched-earth policy used against them.[19] In the early decades of colonial occupation in Algeria, colonial officials represented the Arab nomads as incorrigible and impervious to the influence of French civilization.[20]

When the Berber-speaking Kabyles were conquered in 1857, a very different image was produced. The Kabyles were sedentary, and their resistance appeared to be justified in certain French circles as a defense of their land and homes. The Kabyles used the mountainous geography of their region to wage a very different kind of military defense against French forces than the tactical retreats that the largely Arab forces of ʿAbd al-Qadir employed, preferring to defend difficult terrain rather than flee. French officers were struck by the fact that Kabyle women participated in the fighting, urging their men-folk to battle. Unlike the nomadic Arabs, the Kabyles appeared to be similar in some ways to European

[18] This point will be developed later in the chapter. See Pandolfi, "Construction," 4.
[19] Lorcin, *Imperial Identities*, 32.
[20] Ibid., 38.

peasants. After the conquest had been completed, the Kabyles, as sedentary peoples, were seen to be more industrious and susceptible to the civilizing influence of Europeans than the Arabs ever would be.[21]

French sympathy for the Kabyles is evident in works written even before the completion of the conquest of Kabylia. For example, in 1845, the French military physician Eugène Bodichon published a work setting out his views on the situation in Algeria called "Considérations sur l'Algérie." In the chapter on the indigenous population, Bodichon argued that the Kabyles and Arabs constituted distinct and pure racial types. The Arabs were a race whose moral and intellectual traits had altered little over time; the Arab face and the general demeanor of the Arab body revealed the existence of brutal instincts. They were naturally pillagers and thieves. The lack of cross-breeding with other races meant that their love of thieving and raping had developed and been passed down over generations. The Arab race also possessed two other hereditary characteristics, overexcitability and unreliability, which were only reinforced by the nomadic tribal form of social organization natural to the Arabs. The Kabyles, on the other hand, were a race whose anatomical features correlated with honor, honesty, and integrity unknown among African nations. The Kabyles as a race were predisposed to understand and adopt European civilization. As agriculturalists, they did not disdain work. They had a community spirit and a marked aptitude for mechanical arts. In short, they were a race capable of advanced civilization.[22]

Central to the idea of a dichotomy between Arabs and Berbers was the notion of racial conflict. The distinguishing features of the Kabyles had been forged in conflict with invaders, among whom the most important had been the Phoenicians, Greeks, Vandals, Romans, Arabs, and Turks. The Berbers, it was argued, were the descendants of the original indigenous population of North Africa. They were seen as being innately patriotic and xenophobic, characterized by a stubborn resistance to any unifying religious or political system.[23] When Adolphe Hanoteau (1814–1897) published his "La Kabylie et les Coutumes Kabyles" in 1872–1873, he drew attention to the persistent way in which the Berber race had preserved its physiognomy, its language, its individuality and its independence despite all the invasions it had been subjected to. Hanoteau

[21] Ibid., 35–40.

[22] Eugène Bodichon, *Considérations sur l'Algérie* (Paris, 1845); Lorcin, *Imperial Identities*, 122–7.

[23] Lorcin, *Imperial Identities*, 127.

believed that miscegenation had been a major feature of Kabyle society over the centuries. He thought that miscegenation had been regenerative for the Kabyles, raising the level of their civilization, and ultimately, it was hoped, Kabyle society would therefore be more receptive to French influence.[24]

There were attempts to carry out strictly anatomical studies of the indigenous populations of Algeria in the hope of arriving at precise scientific racial types for the Arab and the Berber. Paul Topinard (1830–1911) claimed to have specified certain physical types in Algeria, and that a typical physiological Kabyle was distinct from a similarly typical Arab:[25]

> The Kabyle has a fixed abode. His communal administration is highly liberal. He is active, hardworking, honest, dignified, open-minded, honest and good humored. He has elevated sentiments of equality, honor, human dignity and justice. He is courageous and attacks his enemy frontally. The exact opposite of the points enumerated in the summary correspond to the physiological type of the Arab.[26]

The precise physical distinctions between Arab and Berber remained elusive, and Topinard was forced in the end to admit that the Berbers and Arabs could not be considered as pure races.[27] Yet, in an anthropological project in which physical and moral qualities were inextricably linked, his concept of racial typology continued to be used as the framework for understanding populations in Algeria.

One popular idea in nineteenth-century France that has not altogether disappeared even today is that of the so-called blond Berbers. The apparent existence of blond-haired Berbers in North Africa led many writers, both popular and academic, to propose that the Berbers were originally Europeans. Some went as far as to suggest that the Berbers were descended from Noah's son Japheth, like the races of Europe.[28] However, most stuck

[24] Adolphe Hanoteau and Aristide Letourneux, *La Kabylie et les Coutumes Kabyles* (Paris, 1872–1873); Lorcin, *Imperial Identities*, 137–40; Philippe Lucas and Jean-Claude Vatin, *L'Algérie des anthropologues* (Paris: François Maspéro, 1975), 17.

[25] He distinguished five principal types of indigenous Algerians: two Arab types, two Berber types, and a fifth type that was Arab and Kabyle at the same time. See Gilles Boetsch and Jean-Noël Ferrie, "Le Paradigme berbère: approche de la logique classificatoire des anthropologues français du XIXe siècle," *Bulletin et Mémoires de la Société d'Anthropologie de Paris*, nouvelle série 1, no. 3–4 (1989): 264.

[26] Paul Topinard, *Eléments d'Anthropologie Générale* (Paris, 1885), 190; Cited in Lorcin, *Imperial Identities*, 157.

[27] Ibid., 257–8.

[28] Louis Rimm, "Essai d'études linguistiques et ethnologiques sur les origines berbères," *Revue Africaine* 33 (1889): 121; Cited in Lorcin, *Imperial Identities*, 142.

to a more secular line of argument. When Topinard carried out anthropological research on this question in 1870, he concluded that there were in fact no blond Berbers.[29] Those who argued against the theory of Berber origins in northern Europe suggested that they were in fact the original indigenous population of North Africa. Connections were therefore sought with North African peoples mentioned in classical sources.[30] Jean Périer published a comprehensive account of the available sources on the origins of the Berbers in the Paris Anthropological Society's journal in 1873, and this became one of the most authoritative references on the subject.[31] Périer argued that the Berbers were not European, but originally members of the "Atlantic race" whose ancestral home was in the Atlas Mountains. At some point, the branches of this race had separated, and Périer thought that the Kabyles were the descendants of the ancient Libyans, the people of the North African littoral in classical sources, whereas the Tuareg were descended from the Getules, another branch of the Atlantic race whose home territory in antiquity was the mountains of the interior. For Périer, the Tuareg and the Kabyles had become distinct races at some unknown time, and it was only with the entrance of the Arabs into North Africa that they had acquired the name "Berbers." Périer argued that there was no such thing as a "Berber" in terms of ethno-genealogy. It was only possible for Périer (and others) to maintain such a racial schema by a kind of mystification of genealogy that would render coherent the connections over these great periods of time. As he wrote elsewhere:

> One must acknowledge the proper faculties that are transmitted from age to age, and which constitute the fundamental differences that one observes between the human stocks and races. Neither climates, nor foods, nor manner of living, as far as we are able to tell, have been able to endow these natural groups with the characteristics of the type that distinguishes them, and that we can say are invariable. The forms of government and the political and civil laws depend less on climate and environmental factors than on the physiological constitution of those who compose a nation.[32]

[29] Boetsch and Ferrie, "Le Paradigme berbère," 263. The theory of the blond Berbers was not definitively rejected by scholars until much more recently. See H. H. Kidder, C. S. Coon and L. C. Briggs, "Contribution à l'anthropologie des Kabyles," *L'anthropologie* 59, no. 1 (1955): 62–79.

[30] Lorcin, *Imperial Identities*, 150–1.

[31] J.-A.-N. Périer, "Des races dites berbères et de leur ethnogénie," *Mémoires de la Société d'anthropologie de Paris 1*, 2nd série (1873): 1–54; On the influence of this work, see Lorcin, *Imperial Identities*, 128.

[32] J.-A.-N. Périer, "De l'influence des milieux sur la constitution des races humaines et particulièrement sur les mœurs," *Mémoires de la Société d'anthropologie de Paris 1*, 2nd série (1873): 200.

The hold that the idea of race had on French writers interested in Algeria was so strong that it could be made to work *in spite of* all evidence to the contrary that there were significant physiological differences between Berber- and Arabic-speakers. There was no contradiction between the idea of racial unity and the diversity of physical types.[33] When the French military pushed south into the Algerian Sahara, the encounter with the Tuareg provided a new site for racial imagining.

ENCOUNTERING THE TUAREG, IMAGINING THE TUAREG

One of the most complicated issues in the development of French ideas about the Tuareg is the ways in which the idea of the desert shaped the representations of its inhabitants. This was true of Algeria as much as later French colonial territories that included the Sahel. European cultures have had a complicated relationship with the idea of the desert. Since at least the Middle Ages, the desert has carried with it two fundamental notions. On the one hand, the desert was equivalent to the wilderness – that inhospitable place of extreme climate and savage, even monstrous, inhabitants. On the other hand, the desert had always been a mythical site where isolation from civilization could be found, and where corporeal appetites could be slain.[34] In important ways, this duality in European ideas about the desert was subjected to a process of secularization after the eighteenth century and instead of a site of religious mysticism, the desert came to represent either a place where the regime and values of modern European civilization did not apply, or a social *tabula rasa* where utopian projects of social reengineering could occur. For nineteenth-century modernist-positivists such as the Saint-Simonians, the desert was seen as a site that could act as a laboratory for their projects of development and human improvement.[35] Even in the early decades of the colonial occupation in Algeria, many Saint-Simonians were inclined to

[33] Boetsch and Ferrie, "Le Paradigme berbère," 265–7.

[34] Danielle Lecoq, "Place et fonction du désert dans la représentation du monde au Moyen Age," *Revue des Sciences humaines* 258 (2000): 15–16. See also Jacques Moulin, "Le Désert en chemin de littérature," in *Sociétés sahariennes entre mythe et développement. Les Cahiers d'URBAMA* no. 12, ed. Jacques Fontaine (Tours: Université François-Rabelais, 1996): 133–51.

[35] On Saint-Simonian views of the desert, see Philippe Régnier, "Le Mythe oriental des Saint-Simoniens," in *Les Saint-Simoniens et l'Orient: ver la Modernité*, ed. Magali Morsy (Aix-en-Provence: Edisud, 1989), 29–52; Régnier, "Les Saint-Simoniens au désert: désir d'aridité et quête d'un espace prophétique au lendemain de 1830," *Revue des Sciences humaines* 258 (2000): 247–65; Dominique Casajus, *Henri Duveyrier: Un saint-simonien au désert* (Paris: Ibis Press, 2007).

view the Arab nomads in a more positive, if certainly romantic, light than the military officers in the colonial administration. People such as Ismayl Urbain (1816–1884), Barthelémy-Prosper "Père" Enfantin (1796–1864), and Ernest Carette (1809–1890), among others, argued that the Sahara and the nomads who live there could become an integral part of the project of French colonial development and civilization.[36] However, the Saint-Simonians were in agreement with the broad consensus that they would do so only after they had ceased to be nomads.

Those who lived in the desert – the nomads – would always be seen as dangerous because they represented the opposite of civilized life. In most European accounts of the deserts of the Near East produced before the eighteenth century – mostly in accounts of trips to the Holy Land – the Bedouin Arabs stood in for the desert nomad more generally. They were portrayed in starkly negative terms as thieves and bandits, as cruel and uncultured fanatics. In short, they were the ultimate barbarians who wreaked havoc on urban or settled populations, as well as on desert travelers. Sarga Moussa has argued that from the eighteenth century, one can detect in European travel literature to the Near East an increasing romanticization of the figure of the nomad as a kind of "savage gentleman" who is represented as hospitable, honor-bound, and patriarchal. This idea of the nomad that developed in the second half of the eighteenth century was not that of someone living in a state of nature, excluded from all sociability; rather, the nomad was seen as someone at an earlier stage of civilization, perhaps feudal in the European medieval sense, perhaps patriarchal like the biblical Hebrews.[37]

The early image of the Tuareg nomad was similar in some ways to that of the Arab. In the traveler accounts of the Sahara written during the nineteenth century, the Tuareg are represented as extremely dangerous pillagers who attacked caravans. René Caillié described the Tuareg whom he met on his voyage down the Niger to Timbuktu and across the desert to Morocco as "pillagers and vagabonds," people who terrorized both the blacks of the Niger Valley and the Arab-led caravans in the Sahara and Sahel.[38]

[36] Philippe Régnier, "Le Mythe oriental des Saint-Simoniens," 29–52; "Les Saint-Simoniens au désert," 247–65. Part of this discussion is based on Benjamin Brower, *A Desert Named Peace: The Violence of France's Empire in the Algerian Sahara, 1844–1902* (New York: Columbia University Press, 2009), 61–74.

[37] Sarga Moussa, "Une peur vaincue: L'émergence du mythe bédouin chez les voyageurs français du XVIIIe siècle," in *La Peur au XVIIIe Siècle. Discours, représentations, pratiques*, ed. Jacques Berchtold and Michel Porret (Geneva: Droz, 1994), 206–7.

[38] René Caillié, *Journal d'un voyage à Temboctou et à Jenné* (Paris, 1830), 2: 281–2, 287–9, 360–1.

The first detailed description of the Tuareg of the Hoggar Massif was Eugène Daumas' fictional narrative of a trip across the Sahara published in 1848 and based on information he obtained from Saharan merchants in Algiers. In this work, the Tuareg are presented in contrasting ways; denounced as "nomad pillagers" and "pirates" of the desert who "live only on the goods of others," they are "savages without divine or human laws." However, for all of this, the Tuareg are also described as "a vigorous race, with energy and a staunch sobriety," and as audacious and brave warriors.[39]

The German traveler Hienrich Barth provided the most detailed account of the Tuareg to date in his account of his travels first published in 1854, extracts of which were translated into French by Victor Malte-Brun in 1856.[40] Barth outlined his theory on the origins of the indigenous Berber population of the Sahara as follows:

> All the original population of North Africa appears to have been a race of the Semitic stock, but who, by intermarriage with tribes which came from Egypt, or by way of it, had received a certain admixture. The consequence was that several distinct tribes were produced, designated by the ancients as Libyans, Moors, Numidians, Libyphoenicians, Getulians, and others, and traced by the native historians to two different families, the Beranes and the Abtar, who, however, diverge from one common source, Mazigh or Madaghs. This native widespread African race, either from the name of their supposed ancestor, Ber, which we recognize in the name Afer, or in consequence of the Roman term *barbari*, has been generally called Berber, and in some regions Shawi and Shelluh. The general character and language of these people seem to have been the same, while the complexion alone was the distinguishing point of difference.[41]

Barth's descriptions of the Saharan Tuareg were more sober than some writers, but his own experience as a traveler confirmed for him their propensity for banditry in attacking Saharan caravans. What is more interesting in Barth's account of the Tuareg is the importance he places on racial mixing. As we have seen, Barth argued that the Berbers were the

[39] Eugène Daumas, *Le Grand Désert. Itinéraire d'une caravane du Sahara au pays des Nègres, Royaume de Haoussa* (Paris, 1869 [1848]); see Jean-Robert Henry, "Les Touaregs des Français," in *Touaregs et autres Sahariens entre plusieurs mondes. Les Cahiers de l'IREMAM* 7–8, ed. Hélène Claudot-Hawad (Aix-en-Provence: CNRS, 1996): 254.

[40] The first publication was undertaken using Barth's materials sent back to Tripoli before he had completed his journey. See A Petermann, *An account of the progress of the expedition to Central Africa: performed by order of Her Majesty's Foreign Office, under Messrs Richardson, Barth, Overweg & Vogel, in the years 1850, 1851, 1852, and 1853* (London, 1854). The French translation is of this work is Victor Adolfe Malte-Brun, *Résumé historique de la grande exploration de l'Afrique centrale faite de 1850 à 1855 par J. Richardson, H. Barth, A. Overweg* (Paris, 1856).

[41] Barth, *Travels and Discoveries in North and Central Africa* (New York, 1859.), 1: 195.

indigenous population of North Africa. To the south of the original Berber areas was the Sahara, where the original population consisted of so-called Ethiopian races. Only in the eleventh century, according to Barth, following Ibn Khaldun, were the Berbers forced to retreat southward into the more arid regions of the Sahara by migrant Arab populations.

Barth identified the racial composition of the Saharan Berber populations as a mix between the original Berbers and the Saharan Ethiopian races. The results of this mixture were characterized in a couple of different ways. In the case of the Tuareg groups known as the Kel Ajjer, who live in the region around Ghat (in southwestern Libya), Barth suggested that the ruling class (imoshagh) was relatively whiter and quite small in numbers. The great majority of the population, however, consisted of what Barth called a subject or "degraded tribe" known as the imghad, and these vassal groups were more racially mixed, and therefore more black: "I formerly considered [the imghad] to be a gentile name, but I found afterward that it is a general epithet used by all the different tribes of the Imoshagh to denote degraded tribes." Barth wrote that the social status of imghad referred to those who were servile, which was contrasted to the term imoshagh, which he defined as free people: "The Imghad of the Azkar [Kel Ajjer] differ a great deal from the ruling tribe, particularly the women; for while the Imoshagh are tolerably fair, a great many of the former are almost black, but nevertheless well made, and not only without negro features, but generally with a very regular physiognomy, while the women, at least in their forms, approach more to the type of the negro races."[42]

Barth also stressed the mixed origins of the Tuareg Kel Ewey further to the south in the Aïr Massif (in northern Niger): "I have already observed that the Berbers, in conquering this country from the negro, or I should say the sub-Libyan race (the Leucaethiopes of the ancients), did not entirely destroy the latter, but rather intermingled with them by intermarriage with the females, thereby modifying the original type of the race, and blending the severe and austere manners and the fine figure of the Berber with the cheerful and playful character and darker color of the African."[43] According to Barth, "the consequence of this covenant has been an entire mixture between the Berber conquerors and the female part of the former [black] population, changing the original Berber character entirely, as well in manners and language as in features and complexion."

[42] Ibid., 1: 202.
[43] Ibid., 1: 279.

As a consequence, the Kel Ewey "are regarded with a sort of contempt by the purer Berber tribes, who call them slaves (ikelan)."[44] For Barth, the mixture with the indigenous black population was not necessarily a negative thing. The Kel Ewey, he wrote, "are greatly civilized by the influence of the black population, nevertheless they are still 'half demons,' while the thoroughbred and freeborn Amoshagh … is regarded by all the neighboring tribes, Arabs as well as Africans, as a real demon ('jin')."[45]

The French traveler Pierre Trémaux, who traveled in North Africa and up the Nile to Sudan between 1847 and 1854, claimed to have met Berbers from both sides of the Sahara. He noted that those from the southern side of the desert were black, whereas those to the north were white. Trémaux explained this difference according to climatic influences rather than racial mixing or migration, which he thought had played little role: "The Arab and Berber peoples who live in Soudan were transformed [into blacks] in proportion to the amount of time that they spent there."[46] Trémaux explained that the blacks, like all people, were the descendants of an original white race. He thought that the populations of the Saharan oases and the Tuareg were the descendants of a mix of Egyptians and Ethiopians. Forced to flee from Egypt by the Arab invasions, the Berbers found in the Sahara a population that was, by origin, white (the Leucaethiopes mentioned by Barth drawing on classical sources). However, these white Ethiopians were already so black and so deformed by their exposure to the Saharan environment that the Berbers refused to see in them the brothers that they were. Because of this, those who did not escape were reduced into slavery. According to Trémaux, the slaves in the Saharan oases were of the same origin, not sub-Saharan Africans but white Ethiopians who had degenerated because of the hot sun.[47] Interestingly, Trémaux thought that both the Tuareg and the Songhay of the Niger Bend were Berbers.[48]

HENRI DUVEYRIER'S "TOUAREGS DU NORD"

The key date for the crystallization of French ideas about the Tuareg was 1864, the year that Henri Duveyrier's book, "Les Touaregs du Nord," was published. Duveyrier had traveled for more than two years (1859–1861)

[44] Ibid., 1: 280–1.
[45] Ibid., 1: 392.
[46] Pierre Trémaux, *Origines et transformation de l'homme et des autres êtres* (Paris, 1865), 85; Cited in Boetsch and Ferrie, "Le Paradigme berbère," 266n.
[47] Boetsch and Ferrie, "Le Paradigme berbère," 266n.
[48] Pierre Trémaux, *Le Soudan* (Paris, 1870), 341–42.

in the Sahara, including a seven-month stay among the Tuareg Kel Ajjer in the Fezzan (in southern Libya). While only a teenager, Duveyrier spent a year under Heinrich Barth's tutelage in London preparing for his voyage, and then he continued his preparation in Paris with the assistance of Renan.[49] With the appearance of this book, a number of stereotypes that would remain fundamental to French constructions of the Tuareg were first articulated. While it is certainly true that there was an evolution in this image over time in response to different historical contexts and according to the political positioning of subsequent authors, the essential features of a Tuareg myth were already in place. The main elements of this construction included the idea that the Tuareg were strange and mysterious, that they were Berbers of the white race, that they were nomads and warriors, that their practice and belief in Islam were superficial, and that their women played a primordial and unusually important role in their society.[50]

Duveyrier's portrait of the Tuareg was almost entirely sympathetic, yet the positive attributes that he assigned to them were always, in some way, meant to be contrasted with his equally negative view of the Arabs. For example, in his discussion of the role of Tuareg women, he wrote:

> If there is a point by which Tuareg society differs from Arab society, it is by the contrast between the elevated position occupied by the woman compared to the state of inferiority of the Arab woman. Among the Tuareg, the woman is equal to the man; in certain contexts she is even superior. The girl receives an education; the young woman gives her own hand in marriage, and paternal authority only intervenes to prevent bad alliances. In marriage, she manages her personal fortune without ever being forced to contribute to the expenses of the household.... The children belong more to her than to her husband because it is her blood and not that of her spouse that confers on them the rank they will take in society, in the tribe, and in the family.... Free in her actions, she goes where she wants without having to account to anyone for her behavior as long as her duties to her spouse and as mother of the family are not neglected.[51]

Duveyrier contrasted the practice of monogamy found among the Tuareg with what he considered to be the degrading and powerless position of Arab women in polygamous family structures. He also contrasted

[49] Michael Heffernan, "The Limits of Utopia: Henri Duveyrier and the Exploration of the Sahara in the Nineteenth Century," *Geographical Journal* 155, no. 3 (1989): 344; Dominique Casajus, "Henri Duveyrier et le désert des Saint-Simoniens," *Ethnologies comparées* 7 (2004): 3; Emmanuelle Mambré, "Les Touaregs du Nord d'Henri Duveyrier. Eléments d'une controverse," in *Le Politique dans l'historie touarègue. Les Cahiers de l'IREMAM* 4, ed. Hélène Claudot-Hawad (Aix-en-Provence: Edisud, 1993): 19–23.

[50] Pandolfi, "Construction," 3. See also Brower, *Desert*, 230–4.

[51] Henri Duveyrier, *Les Touareg du Nord. Exploration du Sahara* (Nendeln: Kraus Reprint, 1973 [1864]), 339.

very unfavorably the character of Tuareg and Arab religious specialists, people we have called clerics and that he calls "marabouts." Somehow, Duveyrier believed that the relatively weak hold that he thought Islam had over the Tuareg made Tuareg clerics more enlightened than their Arab counterparts. He reported that, "unlike Arab marabouts who wait for their clients at home, Tuareg marabouts, for the little influence that they are able to exercise over their fellows, are obliged, like missionaries, to go wherever their intervention is necessary."[52] The Tuareg were Muslims, but only the clerics and a few others among them who were pious even practiced Islamic rituals. Duveyrier blamed this on the difficulty of the environment in which they lived, and on their poverty. But again, whereas their neglect for the form of religion was well known, Duveyrier claimed that their inward morality in following the core principles of Islam was far greater than the Arabs. For Duveyrier, this was explained largely by the traces of Christianity that he detected everywhere: in their use of the motif of the cross, in their monogamy, their respect for women, their horror at theft, at lying, and in their propensity for keeping their word:[53]

> In Tuareg society, the role of the marabout and that of the woman seems rather to follow from Christian civilization more than Muslim institutions. Should we see in these two exceptions a residue of a former tradition? We remind ourselves that the Tuareg carries this name for having long resisted and refused Islamization.[54] Among them, there were prolonged struggles between an older faith and the new religion. But, whatever may have been the causes of the Tuareg resistance to Islamization, it is without doubt that their exceptional society, in the midst of such elements of destruction, was maintained, such that we find it, by the woman and the marabout. Isn't French civilization, of which we are rightly proud, also the work of the Christian woman and the enlightened bishops of the Middle Ages?[55]

[52] Ibid., 333.

[53] Ibid., 414.

[54] The name "Tuareg" is supposed by some, including many Tuareg themselves, to come from the Arabic word "tārik" (pl. tawārik), which means "abandoner, leaver" (of God). The idea behind this is that the Tuareg were considered by the Arabs to have left religion because of their outright refusal of Islam or their slowness in accepting it. The Tuareg themselves do not use this name to refer to themselves, preferring to use the name for "nobles" (Ta. "imohagh" in the case of the Kel Ajjer as Duveyrier describes here) (*Touareg du Nord*, 317), or in more recent times with the emergence of a larger "modern" sense of ethnicity, Kel Tamāhaq, for "people of the Tamāhaq language" (among the Kel Ajjer). There are significant dialectical variations in different Tuareg areas, and consequently, in Mali for example, the Tuareg there refer to themselves today as Kel Tamashek.

[55] Duveyrier, *Touareg du Nord*, 341.

Like the Kabyles, the Tuareg would have found themselves very much at home in medieval Languedoc.[56]

Duveyrier was not a racial theorist. However, he did provide the outline of a racial typology of the Tuareg that his more sophisticated readers expected. Like Barth, Duveyrier remarked on the fact that the nobles among the Kel Ajjer were lighter skinned than their vassals (imghad). He reported that the nobles made it a point of honor to abstain from any sexual union with their inferiors, thereby safeguarding their racial purity: "Preserved since their arrival at the center of the Sahara from any invasion: from the north, by the defensive zone of the dunes of the Erg; from the south, by the barrier that their brothers of the Aïr and the Aouelimmiden [Iwellemmedan] provide against the reaction of the black race against the white race, the Tuareg of the North seem to represent, to the highest degree, the primitive type of the Berber race, if this type can be found in all purity."[57] Duveyrier then described the physical character of the noble Tuareg. They were tall, thin, dry, and nervous. They had white skin in infancy, but exposure to the sun gave them a tanned color as they grew older:

> Their figure is that of the Caucasian type: oval face, elongated among some, round among others; large forehead, black eyes, small nose, protruding cheekbones, medium-sized mouth, fine lips, beautiful white teeth when they have not decayed because of the use of natron, black and thin beard, sleek black hair. Some have blue eyes, but this exception is met infrequently.[58]

The moral character of the Tuareg, essential to nineteenth-century French ideas of race, was also described by Duveyrier in exceptionally glowing terms. Among the qualities of the Tuareg were their bravery, their chivalry in defending their guests and clients, their patience, their generosity, industriousness, and love of independence. Another virtue was their honesty:

> The fidelity of promises, of treaties, is pushed so far by the Tuareg that it is difficult to obtain engagements from them, and dangerous to take them because

[56] The motif of an archaic residue of Christianity among the Tuareg remained a very popular idea. Among the more far-fetched explanations offered for this was that they were the descendants of Saint Louis' failed Eighth Crusade: "What of the unlikely case that after the abandonment of the Eighth Crusade, right after the death of Saint Louis, the knights consumed by this thirst for adventure which animated the greater part of them, were trapped in the desert." (Marie-Anne de Bovet, *Le désert apprivoisé. randonnées au Sahara* [Paris: Editions Argo, 1933], 195.); Cited in Pandolfi, "La construction du mythe touareg," 6n.

[57] Duveyrier, *Les Touareg du Nord*, 381.

[58] Ibid., 382.

if they have misgivings about reneging on their word, they insist on a rigorous fulfillment of the promises which they do make. It is a maxim among the Tuareg, in the matter of a contract, to only commit oneself for half of what one can do, so as not to expose oneself to the accusation of infidelity. Like all other Muslims, they subordinate their exactitude to the will of God, but they do not speculate on this reserve.[59]

Duveyrier was only twenty-four years old when his book was published.[60] The work was extremely well received and it was awarded the coveted gold medal by the Paris Geographical Society.[61] However, the highly sympathetic portrait of the Tuareg presented by Duveyrier was subjected to significant challenges in the decades that followed by a series of misadventures in the Sahara experienced by European explorers. In 1869, a Dutch woman named Alexine Tinné was assassinated in the Fezzan by someone from the same Kel Ajjer Tuareg group that had hosted Duveyrier. In 1874, Norbert Dournaux-Dupéré was killed on the road to Ghat. Most spectacularly, an official French mission sent into the Sahara to survey a possible route for a trans-Saharan railroad under the leadership of Colonel Flatters was massacred by the Tuareg Kel Ahaggar in the vicinity of the town of Tamanrasset in 1881. These events, and in particular the massacre of the Flatters mission, horrified French public opinion and delayed the advance of the French into the Sahara by twenty years. They also created a terrible image for the Tuareg, very different from that put forward by Duveyrier.[62] Some in the metropolitan press even accused Duveyrier of being indirectly responsible for the massacre of the Flatters mission because he had painted a totally misleading portrait of these "barbaric" Tuareg, and because he had been involved in the planning for the mission.[63] Duveyrier defended himself, first blaming members of the Sanūsiyya brotherhood for these killings[64] and then blaming the manner in which European travelers and the Mission Flatters had

59 Ibid., 384.

60 Duveyrier fell seriously ill toward the end of his Saharan trip, rendering him mentally enfeebled for a time. It is unlikely that he was the sole author of *Les Touareg du Nord*. See George Trumbull, *An Empire of Facts: Colonial Power, Cultural Knowledge, and Islam in Algeria, 1870–1914* (New York: Cambridge University Press, 2009), 61–3; Jean-Louis Triaud, *La Légende noire de la Sanūsiyya: une confrérie musulmane saharienne sous le regard français (1840–1930) (Paris: Editions de la Maisons des sciences de l'homme, 1995)*, 1: 106–10; Casajus, *Henri Duveyrier*, 105–27.

61 Heffernan, "Limits of Utopia," 345.

62 Henry, "Touaregs des Français," 258 ; André Bourgeot, *Les Sociétés touerègues. Nomadisme, identité, résistance* (Paris: Karthala, 1995), 312 ; Casajus, *Henri Duveryrier*, 210–14.

63 Bourgeot, *Sociétés touerègues*, 348.

64 Triaud, *Légende noire*, 1: 312–13.

undertaken their voyages into the Sahara – not as part of a peaceful and fraternal enterprise that he had imagined, but as the vanguard of an army of invasion.[65] The error of the European explorers after him had been to treat the Tuareg as if they were Arabs, using a show of force at the initial encounter rather than friendship. In an article written after the death of Alexine Tinné in 1869, Duveyrier elaborated on this point:

> It is essential to establish a distinction, as necessary as it is subtle, between the Arabs and the Tuareg. In confusing the two races, one falls into an error bigger than if one wanted to unite together the Arab race and the Israelite race, thus treating each of them as a homogeneous mass. The Arabs, like the Israelites, belong indisputably to the Semitic race; the Tuareg, with all the Berbers, although neighbors of this human family, are distinguished from it, however, by language, by laws, by character and national spirit that is specific to them, so that one places them in a separate family from the ancient Egyptians. The preponderant place occupied by the woman in Berber society, the line of transmission of power passing from chief to eldest son of his eldest sister, the fidelity of the given word, etc., are as much fundamental points of demarcation.[66]

Duveyrier's sadness at the direction of French policy in the Sahara, and at the accusations of barbarity thrown at the Tuareg, contributed to his eventual suicide. However, his portrait of the Tuareg remained the essential point of reference for subsequent authors, even if he was sometimes accused of being overly generous in his description of the Tuareg moral character.[67]

The French conquest and occupation of Timbuktu in 1893–1894 ushered in a period of sporadic military engagements with Tuareg groups in the circum-Sahara that lasted until the end of the First World War. The victories over these "ferocious" Tuareg warriors were celebrated in the popular French press.[68] However, even in this period of confrontation, many French writers imagined the Tuareg in highly romantic ways. For example, Emile Masqueray, writing in 1890 from Algeria, described the Tuareg as members of a lost European civilization: "They are barbarians, but barbarians from our race with all the instincts, all the passions, and all the intelligence of our ancestors. Their nomadic customs are those of

[65] Casajus, "Henri Duveyrier," 10.

[66] Quoted in Casajus, "Henri Duveyrier," 8.

[67] Many examples could be cited. However, one can see Duveyrier's influence especially well in Bissuel's book based on information obtained from Tuareg prisoners in the 1880s (Le Capitaine H. Bissuel, *Les Touaregs de l'Ouest* [Algers, 1888]). For an example of a largely positive evaluation of his work, although critical of its treatment of the Tuareg character, see Augustin Bernard and N. Lacroix, *La Pénétration saharienne (1830–1906)* (Algers: Imprimerie algérienne, 1906), 48–9.

[68] Schneider, *Empire*, 113–17.

the Gauls who took Rome."[69] Such representations fit well with the larger theme that most often saw in the Tuareg the errant knights of medieval Europe. Even when in conflict with the French, the Tuareg, like the Kabyles before them, were accorded a certain amount of respect for their fierce determination to maintain their independence, and for their obvious bravery and steadfastness. When the Lieutenant de vaisseau Hourst published his book in 1898, detailing his encounters with the Tuareg of the Niger Valley in 1895–1896, he noted that, "if one reflects on the bravery of the Tuareg, if one underlines the great difficulty that our troops had in crossing the region in which they live, one will recognize that it is far from being a negligible quality and that the effective conquest of their land cost us dearly."[70]

CONCLUSION

In Hourst's account, the Tuareg are represented in much the same way as in Duveyrier's work. Although Hourst did acknowledge a number of what he called defects in their character, he presented a largely positive picture and concurred with Duveyrier's much criticized contention that the Tuareg were men of their word and utterly averse to theft.[71] By the time people like Hourst and Toutée arrived in the Sahel, they thought that they already knew the Tuareg whom they would encounter there. The fixity of these ideas owes much to their foundation in racial theory. Despite, or perhaps because of, twenty years of conflict between various Tuareg forces and the colonial army between initial conquest and the end of the First World War, the French officers who served along the desert edge were sure that the Tuareg were natural friends of French civilization (even if the Tuareg themselves seemed not to know it yet).

There is a larger argument in Hourst's work about the nature of the colonial regime that was being established in the Niger Bend as he wrote. He was very optimistic about the productive input that he believed the Tuareg nomads could make to the colonial economy. The imperviousness of the Tuareg myth for French colonial officials was such that they often worried about the consequences of their relationship with the Tuareg. Colonial officers feared that the very qualities in the Tuareg that they so admired would be seriously threatened by Tuareg contact with modern

[69] Cited in Henry, "Touaregs des Français," 260.

[70] Le Lieutenant de vaisseau Hourst, *La Mission Hourst sur le Niger et au pays des Touaregs* (Paris, 1898), 200.

[71] Ibid., 202.

European civilization. Duveyrier and many other French military writers on the Tuareg expressed regret and nostalgia for the Faustian bargain that their interactions with the Tuareg represented. Hourst envisioned an optimistic, even utopian, future: "The [Tuareg] race will be civilized; its defects, which all stem from violence, will disappear. Modern society will have conquered a new terrain in Africa." But at the same time, Hourst was worried:

> And yet an idea comes to me: for the Tuareg, will it be good? When I imagine their wandering life, free of any hindrance, their world in which courage is the first among virtues, in which the people are nearly equal, I ask myself if they are not happier than us.... Savage customs, but at least they have heroic and proud sentiments. What will the Tuareg gain from their transformation? The sons of those of today will be citizens. Nothing will be remembered of them any more as the former knights of the desert. They will not go to war anymore, on raids against neighboring tribes, they will not pillage again. But perhaps also, in a stock market which will replace the tent of the amenokal, they will attempt to launch dubious ventures, problematic mines. What will they be then? Thieves? Decidedly, I prefer my pillagers: the Imochar who is free, free like the lion.[72]

Much would change in the way that French colonial officials understood the Tuareg over the decades of colonial occupation, but this sentiment, like so much of the Tuareg myth, remained deeply embedded in French thinking. In 1993, a former French colonial administrator named Phillipe Loiseau, who served in the Niger Bend during the dying days of colonial rule in the 1950s, wrote:

> The administrators who served in the countries of the Sahel where nomads and sedentary people lived together, had, more or less, a marked preference for nomad society.... We were attracted by the prestige of the desert, and by a society whose somewhat feudal nature played on our minds and our sensibility. We were seduced and attracted by a living society that we helped to destroy. Objectively, we were accomplices in this phenomenon, despite the fact that subjectively, we wanted to conserve and defend this culture and society that has disappeared.[73]

The Tuareg, however, were neither brought into existence by French discovery, nor destroyed by the experience of colonialism. The conceits of the colonial project only give up their ghosts with great difficulty.

[72] Hourst, *Mission Hourst*, 235–6; quoted in Pandolfi, "Construction," 8–9.

[73] Philippe Loiseau, "L'administration et les rapports nomades/sédentaires," in *Nomades et commandants. Administration et sociétés nomades dans l'ancienne A.O.F.*, ed. Edmund Bernus, Pierre Boilley, Jean Clauzel, and Jean-Louis Triaud (Paris: Karthala, 1993), 164. Cited by Martin Klein, "Slavery and French Rule in the Sahara," *Slavery and Abolition* 19, no. 2 (1998): 86.

4

Colonial Conquest and Statecraft in the Niger Bend, c. 1893–1936

A TUAREG MENACE?

In West Africa, the colonial encounter with the Tuareg began in the 1890s. It involved a series of battles, military reconnaissance missions, and meetings that all had the intention of forcing different Tuareg groups to submit to the new reality of French authority over the Niger Bend and the southern and central Sahara. Because a bifurcated French image of the Tuareg had already been created and popularized by the 1870s – one which ranged from the admirable errant knights of the desert on the one hand to the wild and dangerous marauders on the other hand – French officers approached the Niger Bend with hope tempered by trepidation. Those involved in reconnaissance missions, such as Georges Toutée or the Lieutenant de vaisseau Hourst, tended to be more hopeful about the possibilities of French-Tuareg understanding. Those engaged directly in fighting the Tuareg were more likely to emphasize what they thought of as the wild and natural predilection to violence that could be identified in the Tuareg character. Louis Frèrejean, a junior officer who participated in the conquest of Timbuktu, wrote in his journal that the French mission was justified squarely in terms of eliminating the Tuareg menace: "[W]e must remove from Timbuktu the brutal domination of the Tuareg, who are the tyrannical, bullying and extortionist masters of the inhabitants, living on the backs of their clients." Frèrejean imagined the Tuareg as marauders, explaining that, "a Tuareg on his horse, meeting someone from Timbuktu, simply leans over and plucks off the clothes, blankets or bags of provisions that he is carrying without a word of protest from the victim. The Tuareg is a perpetual menace to the desert-edge regions that he terrorizes. Therefore, we have decided to end this state of affairs."[1] Such sentiments appear to be very far removed from the portrait of the Tuareg created by Henri Duveyrier.

In the first decades of colonial occupation in the Niger Bend, the image of the Tuareg as untrustworthy, inveterate rebels fills the pages of French correspondence. As French officials struggled to impose their rule over this difficult region, those whom the French called "nomads" proved to be especially frustrating to deal with. To the French, they were proud, haughty, and honor-bound, threatening constantly to rebel and throw off the Christian yoke. These disparaging descriptions of the Tuareg served the purposes of a Tuareg myth in ways that are not at first obvious. Like the Kabyles in Algeria, Tuareg resistance ultimately generated French respect. Those in the French military could not help but admire the vociferousness of the Tuareg groups that had fought them. By granting a certain amount of esteem to their defeated enemy, the cultural and institutional value of the actions French military officers took in defeating them were elevated in importance.[2] Likewise, the social hierarchy and highly developed culture of honor so important in desert-edge society could not help but impress those Frenchmen whose own set of values, so central to institutions such as the French military and the nascent colonial service, were in many respects quite similar. If the Tuareg were wild and dangerous, they were not debased or degenerate, perhaps not even entirely inferior. Compared to the blacks of sub-Saharan Africa, the Tuareg appeared remarkably akin to the French themselves. Seen from the perspective of a mature colony in the early 1930s, the Governor General of French West Africa described the initial Tuareg resistance to French conquest as heroic:

> This date [16 December 1893] marks the beginning of the struggles which we had to undertake against the Tuareg, who had unrelentingly oppressed the sedentary populations of this region. They fought us for supremacy with a rare tenacity and during these years they kept coming back at us endlessly, never letting their previous defeats discourage them. Their extreme mobility, their perfect knowledge of the country, their utter disregard for death, made them formidable adversaries upon whom we inflicted many cruel losses.[3]

[1] Louis Frèrejean, *Objectif … Tombouctou. Combats contre les Toucouleurs et les Touareg* (Paris: L'Harmattan, 1996), 219–20.

[2] André Bourgeot, *Les Sociétés touarègues. Nomadisme, identité, résistances* (Paris: Karthala, 1995), 312.

[3] Gouverneur-Général de l'Afrique Occidentale Française, *Le Soudan* (Paris: Société d'Editions géographiques, maritimes et coloniales, 1931), 9.

In this chapter, I present the story of colonial conquest and statecraft in the Niger Bend. Unlike other parts of French colonial Africa, or most other parts of Soudan Français, the establishment of more or less full French control took forty years to complete. As such, more than half the colonial history of the Niger Bend involved attempts to suppress open revolts or challenges to colonial control by rebels or raiders based in the Sahara Desert. The history of these challenges and the steps taken by French officials to manage the issues that arose from them were the most important factor in the kind of colonial political economy that was put in place in the region. I trace the history of the local politics of the uneven process of colonial state-building and consolidation under French rule. The colonial state that was constructed in the Niger Bend was fundamentally reactive, consistently arriving at ad hoc policies to meet the continual challenges presented by this difficult region. This occurred, of course, in the context of the larger French colonial project across West Africa, which limited the range of possibilities for local French officials. It is important, however, to understand how much the local French administration was also the recipient of advice on statecraft from indigenous allies and the extent to which French officials often molded their policies to meet the demands of those whom they perceived to be their friends.

The French regime in the Niger Bend was fundamentally structured along lines of racial difference. This is very clear in the colonial records left behind by this state. There was, of course, a wider French policy in West Africa of identifying and incorporating local authority figures into the colonial administration. In 1909, William Ponty, the Governor General of French West Africa, coined the phrase "la politique des races" for the model of colonial rule that he supported, which would privilege "tribal" or "racial" units as the basic organizing principle of African administration.[4] This certainly was applied in the Niger Bend, although here, a race policy was perhaps less novel than in some other parts of West Africa. Previous chapters have demonstrated that in their different ways, both French and Sahelian intellectuals already imagined a world in which race was an important organizing principle. The relative weight that I give here to local political leaders in the Niger

[4] Andrew Hubbell, "Patronage and Predation: A Social History of Colonial Chieftaincies in a Chiefless Region – Souroudougou (Burkina Faso), 1850–1946" (Ph.D. diss., Stanford University, 1997), 53–4; Alice Conklin, *A Mission to Civilize: The Republican Idea of Empire in France and West Africa, 1895–1930* (Stanford, CA: Stanford University Press, 1997), 110.

Bend in the forging of colonial structures demonstrates, I think, the extent to which the colonial political economy must be understood as both a local and colonial construction. It was certainly not exclusively an imposition from above that failed to take account of local interests and ideas.

COLONIAL CONQUEST IN THE NIGER BEND

The French colonial encounter with the Tuareg of the Niger Bend began in tragedy and farce. Reaching Timbuktu had been a goal of Europeans since at least the first maritime expeditions of the Portuguese along the African coast, and certainly after the publication of Leo Africanus' "History and Description of Africa" in the sixteenth century, which had described the wealth and marvels of the fabled city. In the nineteenth century, four European travelers reached Timbuktu (René Caillié, Hienrich Barth, A. Gordon Laing, and Oskar Lenz).[5] Although the descriptions of the town published by these nineteenth-century travelers were disappointing, Timbuktu retained a reputation as an important commercial entrepôt connecting the interior of West Africa with the trans-Saharan trade. One of the principal objectives of the French expansion up the Senegal valley in the 1850s and 1860s was the extension of their commercial network as far as Timbuktu, which they hoped would make the city a sort of lynchpin between French possessions in North and West Africa.[6] After the French had established a base on the Niger River at Bamako in 1883, they immediately set their sights on Timbuktu. A gunboat called the *Niger* was assembled and sent downriver in 1885. Under Lieutenant Davoust, the boat reached as far as Diafarabé in the Masina but was unable to obtain any local assistance needed to proceed to Timbuktu, so it returned to Bamako. In 1887, a second mission with the *Niger*, now accompanied by a second boat called the *Mage*, named after the officer who was sent to the Niger valley in the 1860s to prepare the way for

[5] I have already discussed Caillié and Barth. Laing was killed after his return from the city in 1826. For his published writings from this expedition, see *Missions to the Niger*, ed. E. W. Bovill and Frederich Hornemann (Cambridge: Hakluyt Society, 1964); For Oskar Lenz, see *Timbuktu: Reise durch Marokko, die Sahara und den Sudan, ausgeführt im Afrikanischen Gesellschaft in Deutchland in den Jahren 1879 und 1880* (Leipzig, 1884); translated into French by Pierre Lehautcourt as *Timbouctou, voyage au Maroc, au Sahara et au Soudan* (Paris, 1886–1887).

[6] A.S. Kanya-Forstner, *The Conquest of the Western Sudan: A Study in French Military Imperialism* (London: Cambridge University Press, 1969), 27.

eventual French occupation,[7] succeeded in reaching Korioumé, the river port of Timbuktu. The commander of this mission, Lieutenant Caron, had been given the task of signing treaties of friendship with Tijani Tal, leader of the Tukolor forces in the Masina, and with the so-called Grand Council of Timbuktu. He was successful in neither of these tasks. The notables of Timbuktu refused to meet with him, and he was forced to return to Bamako without disembarking.[8]

By 1890, the French had managed to obtain the recognition, more or less, of the other European powers for the inclusion of the Niger Bend within the French sphere of influence. After a series of successful military campaigns between 1890 and 1893 against Tukolor forces in Kaarta, at Ségou, and in the Masina, and also against Samori's forces on the Upper Niger, the French again turned their attention to Timbuktu. One of the principal complexities of the French conquest of the territory that they would call Soudan Français was the frequent conflict between French military officers on the ground, who consistently pushed to extend the area controlled by France, and their political masters in Saint-Louis and Paris who insisted on a less expansionist policy. Louis Archinard was the major figure in leading the French military campaigns in the late 1880s and early 1890s, but his consistent disobedience of orders from his political superiors, as well as the high costs of his expansionist campaigns, resulted in his dismissal as military commander in 1893, when a civilian governor was appointed to administer Soudan.

The new military chief in the territory, Etienne Bonnier, was one of Archinard's protégés, and he followed in his patron's footsteps by putting in motion a plan to capture Timbuktu before the arrival of the civilian governor. Against his orders, Bonnier initiated a two-pronged plan of attack to capture and occupy the town. He sent a column led by Joseph Joffre to march overland from Ségou to Timbuktu, while he headed a second column himself, which approached on river barges. Bonnier's forces arrived in Timbuktu on January 10, 1894. Ironically, Bonnier claimed that his actions were necessitated by the disobedience of another officer, named Boiteux, who had stolen a march on Bonnier and taken a flotilla under his command based at Mopti down river to Timbuktu. Upon

[7] On Mage's time on the Upper Niger, see his memoirs, E. Mage, *Voyage dans le Soudan occidental* (Paris, 1868).

[8] Kanya-Forstner, *Conquest*, 151; Daniel Grevoz, *Les Canonnières de Tombouctou. Les Français à la conquête de la cité mythique (1870–1894)* (Paris: L'Harmattan, 1992), 74–95.

reaching Timbuktu in December 1893, Boiteux ran into trouble and lost a European officer who was killed in a skirmish with local Tuareg. Bonnier argued that his expedition to Timbuktu was a rescue mission.[9]

After only a couple of days in Timbuktu, Bonnier set out westward with half his forces toward Goundam to await the arrival of Joffre's column and to scout the route. On the night of January 15, 1894, Bonnier's sleeping men were attacked at a site called Takoumbao near the village of Dongoï (located between Timbuktu and Goundam). Local Tengeregif and Kel Entsar Tuareg forces had followed the column and at four o'clock in the morning charged the bivouac with foot soldiers and cavalry. The death toll was devastating for the French; Bonnier and ten of his European officers (of a total of twelve) were killed. Other victims included the African interpreter, two European non-commissioned officers (of nine), and sixty-eight African troops (of two hundred and four). It proved to be the worst military defeat suffered by the French in the whole period of conquest in Soudan.[10] The Tuareg forces lost more than fifty men.[11] Apparently, Bonnier had failed to defend the bivouac properly to counter Tuareg military tactics. A subsequent commander of Timbuktu wrote to Bonnier's brother in 1896 to explain that Bonnier had had no way of knowing, based on his previous experiences fighting against Samori's forces in the southern part of Soudan, what he was up against in the Tuareg: "We would certainly have been protected if he had known the tactics of the Tuareg at that time … by a double row of thick, well-spaced, spiny bushes." The Tacoumbao disaster taught French forces to defend against "the tactics of the Tuareg, which they have tried against us again at Farash and at Bankoré four months ago, and which consist of rushing en masse towards the enemy after having approached stealthily as close as possible."[12]

News of the massacre of Bonnier's forces reverberated in France and provoked further hostility between the French military officers in Soudan

9 Boiteux was later disciplined by the French military and he eventually committed suicide in France. Bonnier's brother detailed the relationship between Bonnier and Boiteux in an effort to redeem his late brother's name. See G. Bonnier, *L'Occupation de Tombouctou* (Paris: Editions du monde moderne, 1926), 55.

10 Kanya-Forstner, *Conquest*, 217–21.

11 Bonnier, *Occupation*, 61.

12 Letter from Commandant Réjou to G. Bonnier, January 5, 1896, Timbuktu; printed in Bonnier, *Occupation*, 224. For Réjou's account of his time in Timbuktu, see his memoir "Huit mois à Tombouctou et dans la région Nord," *Le Tour du Monde, Nouvelle Sér.* 4 (1898): 409–32.

and the civilian authorities.[13] In the six months that Joffre remained in Timbuktu as commander of the French forces there, he repeatedly disobeyed orders by launching punitive expeditions against local Tuareg groups, including members of the Tengeregif and Kel Entsar who had attacked Bonnier's column, but also against others in the area who had had nothing to do with the affair, including members of the Kel Temulayt and the Irreganatan confederacies.[14] In March 1894, a force led by Joffre entered the Kissou region southwest of Timbuktu in search of the Tengeregif. On March 23, 1894, at a site called Dahouré, near the Niger River town of Diré, French forces attacked a large group of Tengeregif, massacring 120 of them including their chief, a number of prominent leaders, and taking almost 1,300 goats, cattle, and camels.[15] In another sortie made by forces based at the French post at Goundam in June 1894, a group of Kel Entsar was attacked north of Goundam between the hills and Lake Fati; twenty-seven Tuareg whom the French reports identified as "whites" were killed, and 1,200 animals were captured.[16] Such actions were designed to terrorize the local population so as to force both sedentary and pastoral communities to submit to French power.

Faced with an enemy that employed guerrilla tactics of ambush and disruption of supply lines, French forces indiscriminately attacked any Tuareg group that they encountered during the first years of their colonial occupation. Crops were destroyed, slaves taken, and villages or pastoral camps thought to be dependent on Tuareg groups were burned. Those Tuareg captured by French forces, especially those described as belonging to the "type sémitique," were often accused of spying and executed. One such case was mentioned by Louis Frèrejean, the same junior officer quoted earlier in the chapter, who participated in Joffre's initial march to Timbuktu. Frèrejean described a Tuareg prisoner as "one of these sinister pirates of the desert, a man about forty years old,

[13] Jacques Hureiki, "La version touarègue de la bataille de Taqinbawt (Tacoubao) (15 janvier 1894)," *Journal des Africanistes* 73 (2003): 127–36; William Schneider, *An Empire for the Masses: The French Popular Image of Africa, 1870–1900* (Westport, CT: Greenwood, 1982), 113–17.

[14] For Joffre's account of these missions, see General Joffre, *My March to Timbuctoo*, trans. Ernest Dimnet (New York: Berger-Levrault, 1915), 149–63.

[15] A. Hacquard, *Monographie de Tombouctou* (Paris: Société des études colonials et maritimes, 1900), 79–80.

[16] "Rapport du Capitaine Gérard, Commandant le détachement, sur une opération militaire dirigée le 9 juin 1894 contre un partie de Kel Antessar qui était venu piller le village de Ougoukoré." Poste de Goundam, 1894 (ANM FA 1E-40).

small, dry, with brilliant eyes, a Semitic profile, a face burned by the sun." Despite protesting his innocence, the prisoner was tied up and "during the rest of the day, his brown and poorly shaved skull heated up under the sun while in a drawling and guttural voice, he invoked Allah." Having no desire to continue to hold this prisoner on their march, the French officer ordered him executed: "Before the column set out, a soldier received the order to kill the captured Tuareg with a rifle shot; and in the abandoned camp, his dead body remained stretched out near the stake to which he was still attached."[17] In another case in 1895, French forces displayed the severed heads of two Tuareg men in the market of the village of Tassakant in order to demonstrate to the local sedentary population that it was the French, not the Tuareg, who were now the dominant force in the area.[18]

Many other examples of French brutality toward the Tuareg could be cited, and indeed, the ubiquity of violence was hardly remarkable in the context of colonial Africa. However, the nature of the violence in the Niger Bend and the way that its French authors intended it was somewhat peculiar to the desert-edge setting and to the indigenous population encountered there. For the first French officers, the Tuareg were more than an enemy that stood in the way of successful colonial occupation; they were also an opportunity to acquire a distinguished military record that could lead to recognition and promotions of rank. The institutional value of military service in the Niger Bend, and to some extent in the circum-Sahara as a whole, lay in the ferocity and ultimately – although this was only admitted in moments of reflection or years later – the honor of the enemy to be defeated. The most spectacular example was Joffre himself, who won the Legion of Honor for his actions in the Niger Bend and who was feted as a hero and promoted to the rank of lieutenant colonel when he returned to France.[19] He eventually reached the very top of the French military hierarchy in 1916 when he was appointed marshal of the entire French army.[20]

The French presence in the Niger Bend was initially limited to a garrison at Timbuktu, with military posts at the river ports of Korioumé and Kabara to protect communications and supply lines on the Niger River.

[17] Frèrejean, *Objectif*, 244.
[18] Hacquard, *Monographie*, 86–7.
[19] Barnett Singer and John Langdon, *Cultured Force: Makers and Defenders of the French Colonial Empire* (Madison, WI: University of Wisconsin Press, 2004), 144.
[20] Ibid., 148.

Another post was established at Goundam, in order to have soldiers in the proximity of the Tengeregif and Kel Entsar.[21] To achieve the desired domination over the various pastoral groups, more posts were needed. In 1895, a new post and administrative district was created at Soumpi to the west of the town of Niafounké. In 1896, a post that would later become an administrative "cercle" was established at Ras-el-Ma on the western edge of Lake Faguibine. The creation of these new positions, and the military missions launched from them, succeeded in generating the formal submission of some Tuareg groups active in the areas west of Timbuktu by 1896. In that year, the governor of Soudan, Colonel L.E. Trentinian, paid a visit to the Niger Bend. At Timbuktu, he had a meeting with Sobbo ag Fondogomo,[22] who had recently assumed the leadership of the Tengeregif after the massacre at Dahouré. Sobbo was still a young man, and he had participated in the combat at Takoumbao in 1894 that had resulted in the death of Bonnier. During this encounter with Trentinian, a treaty was agreed on March 1, 1896, in which Sobbo formally acknowledged French suzerainty over the region on behalf of the Tengeregif, whereas the French accepted that Sobbo would be permitted to maintain his administrative control over those subordinate groups ruled by the Tengeregif.[23] In effect, the French acknowledged Sobbo's authority and agreed not to intervene in his internal matters. The scorched-earth campaign waged by the French in the area around Lake Faguibine eventually forced the submission of most of the clans of the Kel Entsar confederacy, although it was not until 1898 that the dissident Kel Entsar leader N'Gouna[24] was killed by the French. The new, more pliant leadership of the Kel Entsar was afforded a similar arrangement of noninterference in the internal affairs over those subgroups under their authority.

For all the apparent success of the French in obtaining the formal submission of Tuareg groups to the west of Timbuktu, the authority of the colonial regime remained very tenuous. With good reason, the French doubted the sincerity of those Tuareg leaders who had accepted

[21] Joffre, *My March*, 82–4.

[22] The French knew him as "Chebboun." However, he signed his name in Arabic as "Ṣubbu," and pronounced it "Sobbo." This is how he is known to many people in the Niger Bend today.

[23] Gouverneur du Soudan Français, "Arrêté No. 5," March 1, 1896 (ANM FA A9).

[24] "N'Gouna" is a nickname from childhood. His full name is Muhammad ʿAli ag Muhammad Ahmad ag Hwalan, born c. 1830, died 1898. He became leader of the Kel Entsar confederacy in 1865 and held this office when the French arrived in 1893.

the colonial presence. Among the most difficult area to control was to the east and south of Timbuktu, on the "right bank" of the Niger River (called the Gourma), which was home to Tuareg groups such as the Kel Temulayt, Irreganatan, and Igawaddaran. Their leaders wrote letters of submission to the French but refused to come in person to Timbuktu.[25]

The ambivalence of these leaders regarding the French reflected a larger set of strategic problems for Tuareg groups. Too close an association with the French would create a backlash within their own communities because there were many among the warrior-status lineages (imoshagh) who opposed any accommodation. Yet open hostility to the French could result in direct military aggression by colonial forces and a blockade of the riverine areas that they depended on economically. By biding their time, Tuareg leaders were able to assess whether the French were going to stay.[26] Further afield, the French exercised no control whatsoever over the Arabophone pastoralist groups based to the north of the river, such as the Barābīsh and Kunta. Before 1898, when the French established a post and administrative district at Bamba, several hundred kilometers to the east of Timbuktu on the Niger, and at Gao, the only means of exercising colonial authority was in periodic military missions sent from Timbuktu that, as one officer admitted in 1898, only weakened the nomads indirectly by the damages inflicted on riverine villages that provided them with grain.[27]

Those groups that remained openly hostile to the colonial presence employed tactics that were somewhat similar to those of the French. For the most part, anticolonial groups avoided direct confrontations with colonial forces and instead raided those who had submitted to the French and could therefore be considered under their protection. In effect, the conquest of the Niger Bend, and the resistance that challenged it, was

[25] An example of this is Assalmi, leader of the Irreganatan, who in 1898 refused to come to Timbuktu to meet the French commander, claiming that his health would not permit such a trip. Assalmi assured the French agent of his loyalty and even sent a couple of animals to Timbuktu as a gift to the French commander. Cercle de Tombouctou, "Rapport de Lieutenant Cauvin sur la tournée de recensement faite dans le Bingha, le Gourma et le Kissou du 3 février au 3 mars 1898," March 15, 1898 (ANM FA 1E 78–81).

[26] Hélène Claudot-Hawad, "Elite, honneur et sacrifice. La hiérarchie des savoirs et des pouvoirs dans la société touarègue précoloniale et la recomposition des rôles socio-politiques pendant la guerre anticoloniale et après la défaite," in *Elites du monde touareg et maure. Les Cahiers de l'IREMAM* 13–14, ed. Pierre Bonte and Hélène Claudot-Hawad (Aix-en-Provence: CNRS, 2000), 25.

[27] Région du Nord, "Rapport politique, 1ère semestre," July 14, 1898 (ANM FA 1E 78–81).

carried out as a series of raids and counterraids on tributary populations, punctuated by rare direct confrontations. Sedentary people and those of lower social status in pastoralist societies found themselves under pressure from both sides. Tributaries lost livestock to French and rebel forces; sedentary people had their villages burned, grain stolen, and were often themselves taken away in slavery by pastoralist raiders. I will discuss the effects of these actions on their victims in Part Three of the book.

The strategies of resistance were based on much older patterns of raiding in Tuareg and Arab society that had existed long before the arrival of Europeans on the scene. As in so many pastoralist societies worldwide, raiding played an important part in economic accumulation and in political competition among the Tuareg and Arabs before the colonial conquest.[28] Principally, raiding was a matter for members of so-called warrior-status lineages. We have seen already some of the negative evaluations of these people made by Muslim scholars who argued that the warriors' practice of raiding and their lack of respect for Islamic norms rendered their property illegal. It was also true that there were shared cultural codes that governed the behavior of members of warrior-status lineages when they participated in raids against other pastoralist groups. Anthropologists such as Hélène Claudot-Hawad tell us that the behavior of the combatants was to some extent codified, and the honor that resulted from victory was not necessarily dependant on the death of the adversary.[29] But when Tuareg and Arab groups raided outsiders, combat was often much more deadly and the pillage of material goods and slaves more common. Vassal groups paid warrior-status groups for protection. Raids against vassals under the protection of another group were a way of demonstrating the weakness of an adversary, and perhaps a means of gaining new clients.[30] It was in this sense that the raids launched against populations that had submitted to the French were forms of resistance to the colonial regime.

The history of raids launched by opponents of the French position in the Niger Bend is complicated. In the initial stages of colonial occupation, before the French had extracted the submission of pastoralist groups, raids were essentially local. However, from the very beginning, a second

[28] On the issue more generally, see A. M. Khazanov, *Nomads and the outside world*, trans. Julia Crookenden (Cambridge: Cambridge University Press, 1983), 156.

[29] Hélène Claudot-Hawad, *Les Touaregs. Portrait en fragments* (Aix-en-Provence: CNRS, 1993), 13–27.

[30] Pierre Boilley, *Les Touaregs Kel Adagh. Dépendances et révoltes du Soudan français au Mali contemporain* (Paris: Karthala, 1999), 101–2.

type of raiding made its appearance: raids launched from Saharan territories outside of colonial control against populations inside the sphere of French protection. These raids, which the French referred to as raids of "les grands nomades," targeted two main areas in the Niger Bend: Lake Faguibine to the west of Timbuktu, and the Niger valley between Bamba and Bourem to the east of Timbuktu. Each of these regions was sufficiently far away from French military forces in Timbuktu to ensure impunity, and in addition, supported significant populations from whom cereals, livestock, and people could be taken. In many cases, the raiding parties drew from central and western Saharan groups such as the Rgaybat, Shaʿāmba (Chaamba), and Kel Ahaggar, but they were often led by dissidents from the Niger Bend who allied themselves with these groups. Only in the mid 1930s were these raids finally suppressed definitively.

The French faced a number of very significant raids by outsiders allied to local rebels. In 1896, a group of Kel Ahaggar Tuareg from the Hoggar Massif in southern Algeria, together with a number of Kunta from the Azawad, launched a raid into the Niger Bend and attacked other pastoralist groups that had submitted to the French in the area around Timbuktu. Alerted by Muḥammad b. Haima, the leader of the Guwānīn, an Arabophone subgroup of the Barabish whose pastoral activities centered in the hinterland east of Timbuktu, French and allied Guwanin forces initiated a counterraid. At a site called Akenkan, the French and allied forces came upon the raiders and killed more than twenty of them. A year later, another raiding party of Kel Ahaggar and various rebels from the Niger Bend,[31] including the Kel Entsar chief N'Gouna and ʿĀbidīn al-Kuntī,[32] returned; this time they destroyed the French column sent to meet them in a battle in the Serere, a large island in the Niger River east of Timbuktu. The French survivors fled back to Timbuktu ahead of the rebels. For a moment, it looked as if Timbuktu might fall. ʿAbidin al-Kunti, the rebel leader, sent a letter to the French commander demanding that he convert to Islam or face death. However, the rebels mistook the arrival

[31] Among the groups that participated were, according to the French, the Tengaregadash, Kel Burem, Kel Essuk, Kel Tabankort, members of the Kel Entsar of the East, Igawaddaran, and the Kel Temulayt. In other words, virtually every Tuareg group in this region. Cercle de Tombouctou, "Rapport politique," 1ère semestre 1898 (ANM FA 1E 78–81).

[32] Zayn al-ʿĀbidīn b. Muḥammad b. Sīdi Muḥammad b. Sīdi al-Mukhtār al-Kuntī, born in 1848, died in 1927. He led numerous raids against French positions in the Niger Bend from areas outside of colonial control in the Tafilalt and Draa Valley in Morocco. His sons Hamā and Sīdi al-Amīn led a number of raids also. See Paul Marty, *Etudes sur l'Islam et les tribus du Soudan, vol. 1, Les Kounta de l'Est, Les Berabich, les Iguellad* (Paris: E. Leroux, 1920), 100–13.

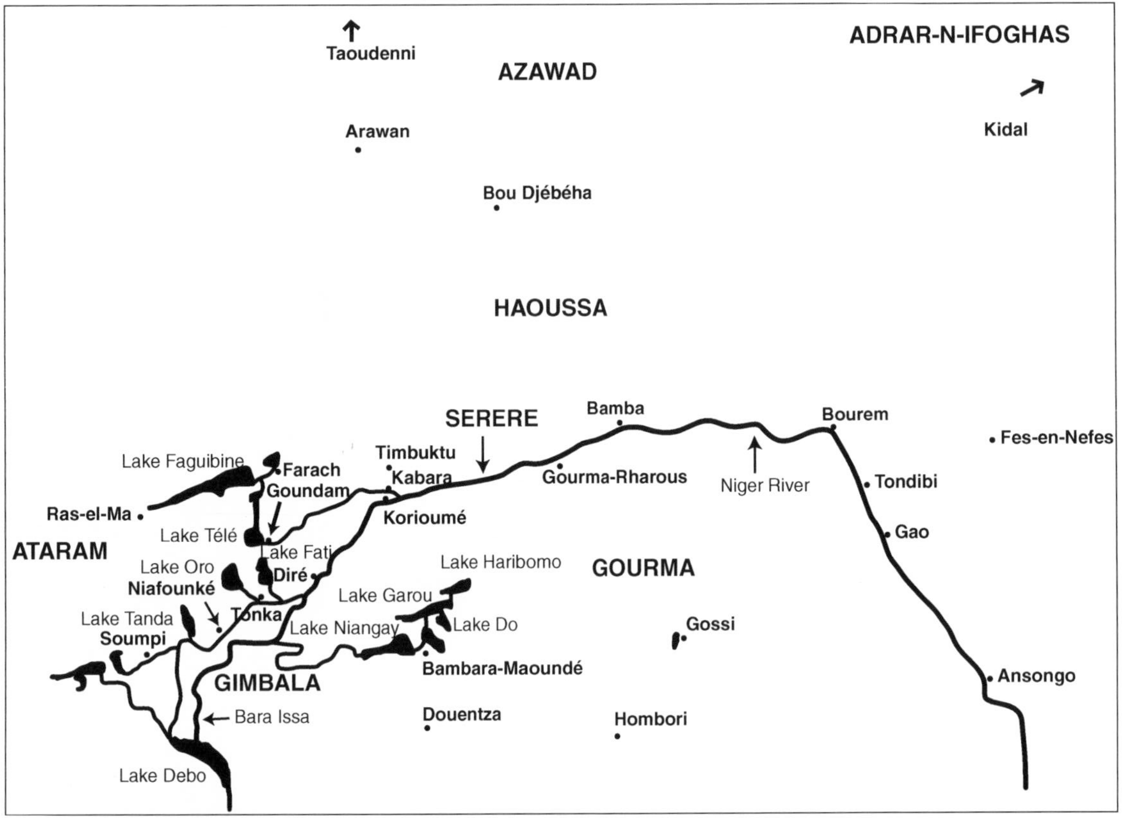

MAP 2. The Niger Bend.

of a French boat at Koriomé for military reinforcements and withdrew. When additional French troops did arrive several weeks later, a devastating mission led by a French officer named Goldshen razed the Serere. All the inhabitants of the Songhay villages of Kano and Minkiri were accused of helping the raiders and were deported from their burned villages.[33]

FRENCH-BARABISH CONFLICT, 1893–1900

These early French efforts to defeat insurgents using military means came up against certain limits of effectiveness given the relatively small number of personnel at the disposal of French commanders. The military tactics that had been employed in other parts of Soudan based on the use of foot soldiers and cavalry were ineffective against camel-mounted opponents who were able to move at twice the speed of French forces.[34] In order to extend French control over the highly dispersed Tuareg and Arab population, new camel-mounted "méhariste" colonial regiments had to be created, and alliances had to be made with at least some pastoralist leaders. Since it was the eastern Tuareg groups that seemed to pose the greatest threat to the colonial position, the French were keen to win local Arabs to their side and exploit what they perceived to be the historical enmity between Arabs and Tuareg. Despite a history of animosity toward Arab groups in North Africa, French officials were ready to follow whatever political expediency presented itself to them in the Niger Bend.

The Tuareg were much more numerous in the Niger Bend than the Arabs. A colonial estimate in 1906 of the population of the region centered in Timbuktu – the area where most Arabs lived – put the Tuareg population at 60,000 and the Arab population at 24,000.[35] Tuareg numerical superiority was even greater than this in the eastern Niger Bend. Both Arabs and Tuareg depended primarily on pastoralism. The two most important Arab groups in the Niger Bend were the Barabish, a hassani – or warrior-status – group based in the Azawad, north of Timbuktu, and the Kunta, a very prominent zwaya – or clerical-status – group that had exercised significant religious and secular authority across the Sahel in the eighteenth

[33] Hacquard, *Monographie*, 97–104.

[34] Le Capitaine Bouchez, *Guide de l'Officier méhariste au Territoire militaire du Niger* (Paris: Emile Larose, 1910), 7.

[35] Capitaine Maziller, "Etude sur les populations de la Région de Tombouctou: Situation économique et agricole, sécurité et éléments de troubles intérieurs; Rezzous venus de l'extérieur, organisation de la lutte contre eux, sûreté à organiser," 1906 (ANM FA 1D-59-11).

and nineteenth centuries. The distinctions I have made throughout this book between warrior- and clerical-status lineages should be understood primarily as an important way in which Arab and Tuareg people in the Sahel represented the social structure in their societies. It is probably true that warrior groups were more likely to resist the colonial presence, but certain clerical groups did so as well. Moreover, colonial rule provoked new configurations of interests and alliances that had little to do with the warrior/clerical distinction. In practice, clerical status had never meant a definitive renunciation of arms. The Kunta, for example, were a clerical group that had been able to convert their significant religious prestige into military power in the middle of the nineteenth century under the leadership of Aḥmad al-Bakkāy al-Kuntī (d. 1865). As we will see, the Kunta proved to be the most important Arab military ally that the French were able to enlist to their cause in the early colonial period.

To a much greater extent than the Tuareg, Arab groups based in the Niger Bend engaged in regional commerce, transporting and trading products such as salt, grain, cloth, and tobacco. The French hoped that the commercial orientation of many Arab groups would make them more amenable to friendly relations with the new colonial regime. One of the principal French justifications for their initial occupation of Timbuktu was to remove the purported negative impact of Tuareg domination on commerce. At least initially, however, the French occupation made things worse for merchants who were subject to exorbitant new taxes and frequent theft of their goods as a result of their perceived relations with the colonial state.[36] The commerce in salt, for example, ceased completely on several occasions during the 1890s because of a 50 percent tax levied on all cereals leaving the town of Timbuktu, which was the principal exchange item for salt. The Barabish, who organized the annual salt caravan known as the "azalaï" to the salt mines at Taoudenni (750 km north of Timbuktu in the Sahara), began to divert their trade away

[36] Among the principal sources of French information on the activities of dissidents were the merchants living in villages along the Niger Valley. They appear to have identified their interests with that of the colonial state to a much larger degree than with the region's pastoralist groups. This was clearly understood by the Tuareg in particular. After a "police" column attacked and imprisoned a group of Igawaddaran in the Gourma because of their refusal to pay their taxes in 1899, many other Tuareg belonging to different groups based in the Gourma came to Timbuktu to settle the private debts that they had previously refused to pay to the town's merchants. It seems that the threat of French military action in support of payment of taxes had an impact on private financial relations as well. These cases are reported on in "Rapport politique," 1ère Territoire militaire, 1ère semestre 1900 (ANM FA 1E 78–81).

from Timbuktu to areas in the Niger valley outside of French control. In response, the French attempted to mount their own salt caravan to Taoudenni in 1897 with the assistance of merchants based in Timbuktu, but this failed because of Barabish attacks. In 1898, the French were forced to revise the commercial tax structure that they had established in Timbuktu, eliminating the export tax on grain and reducing the tax on salt entering the town to one-fifteenth in kind. Negotiations with the Barabish were launched, and the azalaï did bring salt to Timbuktu in 1898.[37] However, Timbuktu was in crisis again in 1899 because of a poor harvest and disagreements with the Barabish; the French responded by again prohibiting any exportations of grain into the Azawad.[38]

The disruption of the salt trade caused economic losses for the Barabish and this enflamed already existing internal political tensions. In 1900, a majority of Barabish notables deposed their leader, Sīdi Muḥammad ould Amhammad,[39] who had resisted French entreaties, and appointed a new leader named Maḥmūd ould Daḥmān,[40] who promised to cooperate with the French and ensure the success of the azalaï in the future.[41] In return for such cooperation, the French furnished the Barabish with arms to help them defend themselves against raiders, and they sent colonial troops to accompany and protect the azalaï. In addition, they promised to dig wells in the Azawad.[42] This bought the cooperation of a majority of Barabish. However, it also made them a target for dissident raiders who repeatedly inflicted significant losses on those Barabish allied to the French state until into the 1920s.[43]

[37] Région du Nord, "Rapport politique," 1ère semestre 1898 (ANM FA 1E 78–81).

[38] Cercle de Tombouctou, "Rapport politique," November 1899 (ANM FA 1E 78–81).

[39] Sīdi Muḥammad b. Amhammad b. Aḥmad b. Abayda, born 1848. After losing his position as the head of the Barabish, Sidi Muhammad led numerous raids against Barabish clans loyal to Mahmud ould Dahman and, in 1909, retreated north into the territory outside of colonial control in southern Morocco. He launched a number of raids from the Tafilalt on groups in the Azawad. His son Khalifa also became involved in raids against the Azawad and followed his father in becoming leader of this group of dissidents. For a brief biographical sketch, see Marty, *Etudes*, 121–3.

[40] Born 1870, died 1971.

[41] 1ère Territoire militaire, "Rapport politique," May 1900 (ANM FA 1E 78–81).

[42] These actions began to turn into complaints by French officials who doubted their utility once the colonial position was more secure. See for example, Cercle de Tombouctou, "Rapport de tournée faite dans les villages du fleuve du 16 au 31 août 1919 par Capitaine Loppinot," 1919, no.15.R (ANM FA 1E 78–81).

[43] On this history of the Barabish see Rita Aouad-Badoual, "Réseaux d'échange des Maures Bérabichs de l'Azouad à l'époque coloniale," in *Touaregs et autres Saharriens entre plusieurs mondes. Les Cahiers de l'IREMAM* 7–8, ed. Hélène Claudot-Hawad (Aix-en-Provence: CNRS, 1996): 183–98.

The difficulty of the choices available to the Barabish in the first decades of colonial rule is discussed in a chronicle entitled "A Barabish history of the Azawad" ("Taʾrīkh Azawād fī ʾl-akhbār al-Barābīsh").[44] This text was written by an unknown author sympathetic to the position of Mahmud ould Dahman, perhaps based on interviews with Mahmud ould Dahman himself. The chronicle describes the arrival of the French, who are referred to as Christians (collectively as "naṣārā," individually as "rūmī"), and the failure of French-Barabish negotiations with Sidi Muhammad ould Amhammad.[45] According to the text, a pact (ʿahd) was made between the two sides, along the lines of the agreement made between Arabophone Muslim traders and non-Muslim "Bambara" in Kaarta discussed in Chapter 2. This pact between the Barabish and the French is described as an agreement of mutual security, with the condition imposed on the Barabish that they remain within French-controlled territory.[46]

Throughout the second half of the 1890s, the Barabish became involved in a number of raids and counterraids with other Sahelian and Saharan groups that, coupled with the decision to block the sale of grain into the desert, made life extremely difficult. The Barabish called 1897 "the year in which the Christians prohibited food from coming to the nomads." The chronicle, however, blames Sidi Muhammad ould Amhammad because he "had sent [the Christians] a letter in which he had spoken inappropriately about the matter of gifts (amr al-ʿaṭiya)." French officials in Timbuktu insisted that colonial sovereignty marked the end of the right of the Barabish to collect what the chronicle calls the "jizya." Theoretically, the jizya is a tax paid by non-Muslims to a Muslim sovereign, in return for his protection.[47] In this context, the jizya was a tax in kind levied by the Barabish on black sedentary farmers in Barabish-controlled villages in the Niger valley. Sidi Muhammad ould Amhammad had demanded that the French pay him

44 The full title is: "Taʾrīkh Azawād fī ʾl-akhbār al-Barābīsh wa ḥurūbi-him maʿ al-rakībāt wa-ḥajār Afūghās wa-Idnān wa-dhikr baʿḍ akābiri-him mithl Sīdī b. Muḥammad b. Amhammad wa-Muḥammad b. Amhammad wa-Maḥmūd b. Daḥmān wa-dakhūl al-nasārā fī Tinbuktū wa-ghayr dhālak" (IHERIAB ms. 279). No author is mentioned. No date of composition is given. It is a year-by-year treatment of mostly Barabish history in the nineteenth century and first half of the twentieth century. The years are named according to the events that occurred during them; they are not given numerical values.

45 According to colonial documents, the Barabish made their initial submission to Joffre almost immediately after the initial occupation of Timbuktu in February 1894. However, it was not until 1899 that peace was effectively established with the French.

46 "Taʾrīkh Azawād," f.19.

47 Hasan Khalilieh, "Amān," *Encyclopedia of Islam. Third Edition*. ed. Gudrun Krämer, Denis Matringe, John Nawas, and Everett Rowson (Leiden: Brill Online, 2009).

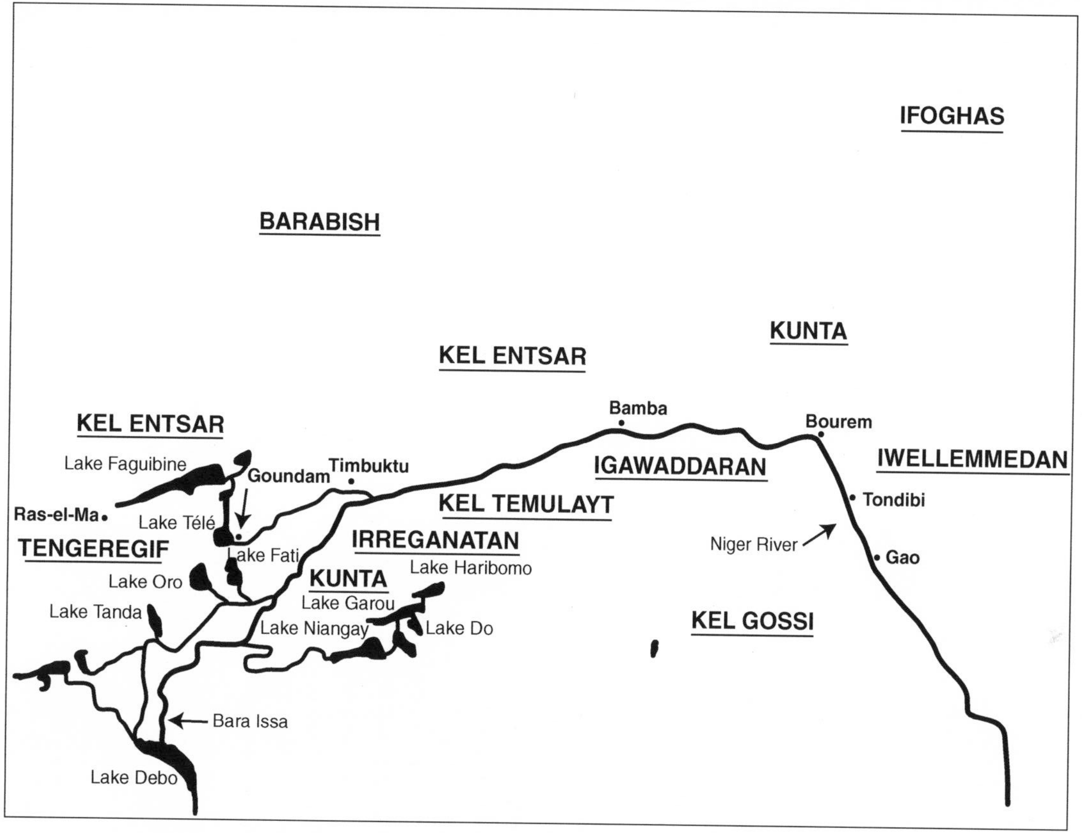

MAP 3. Major Tuareg & Arab Groups of the Niger Bend.

tribute as the Muslim sovereign in the area north of Timbuktu; whereas colonial officials sought to impose a tax which they termed "jizya" on the Barabish. Arguments between French officials and the Barabish chief over who had the right to collect the jizya were therefore disputes over who held ultimate authority in the Niger Bend. By rhetorically demanding the jizya from the French, Sidi Muhammad ould Amhammad was explicit about his view that Christian rule over Muslims was illegitimate. When the French officials prevented grain or people from moving into the desert north of Timbuktu, Sidi Muhammad ould Amhammad responded "by sending letters to the chiefs of the Tuareg, including the Igawaddaran, to N'Gouna, head of the Kel Entsar, and to ʿAbidin al-Kunti asking them to help him fight against the injustice of the Christians."[48]

But from Mahmud ould Dahman's perspective, aligning the Barabish with the most prominent anticolonial dissidents in the Niger Bend was not a wise course of action. The chronicle reports that "Mahmud ould Dahman rode towards Timbuktu when he saw the ongoing depravity in the land from the lack of food for the people. It appeared to him that because of the power of the Christians, injustice would only increase. So it seemed proper to make amends on account of the people's suffering."[49] Upon Mahmud ould Dahman's arrival in Timbuktu, and with the help of some of the town's notables, he arranged a meeting with the French commander Jean-François Arsène Klobb.[50] In the reported dialogue, Mahmud ould Dahman addressed Klobb as follows: "I came to request that you do not prohibit food from going to the people." Klobb responded, "We have only forbidden food because of the statements made in a letter by your chief Sidi Muhammad. That kind of discourse is not acceptable." Mahmud ould Dahman then claimed that the dissidents who surrounded Sidi Muhammad ould Amhammad had turned him against the French, to which the French officer said: "It is not because of you that we have prohibited food for the people." At this, the French commander agreed to end the food blockade and work with Mahmud ould Dahman, who had accepted a new pact with the colonial forces on behalf of his sublineage

48 "Taʾrīkh Azawād," f. 22.

49 Ibid., f. 22.

50 Leutenant-colonel Jean-François Arsène Klobb was appointed military commander of the Niger Bend in 1897 and was based at Timbuktu, from where he led several military missions to the east in 1897 and conquered Gao in 1898. He was killed on July 14, 1899 at Damangara, near Zinder in Niger, while trying to arrest the renegade French officer Paul Voulet. See Jean-François Arsène Klobb, *Dernier Carnet de Route* (Paris: Ernest Flammarion, 1905).

of the Barabish. The chronicle says that this was the "first difference that occurred between Mahmud and his cousin and chief Sidi Muhammad, who claimed that Mahmud opposed him in the matter of [control over] vassals (raʿiya)."[51]

The tension between the themes of Muslim sovereignty and pragmatism were rarely resolved definitively in the early colonial period. Mahmud ould Dahman's engagement with the French was a version of the argument of necessity (durura) that I discussed in Chapter 2 to permit Muslims to trade for grain with non-Muslims in Kaarta. At one point in the intermittent conflict between Barabish and French forces in 1899, the chronicle reports that a notable from Arawan named ʿArwata told a French officer: "You are ruining our camels and our kin. You have not brought improvements to our country, only war."[52] This was the predicament that led to Mahmud ould Dahman's conflict with the chief Sidi Muhammad ould Amhammad. From Mahmud ould Dahman's perspective, his actions were an attempt at saving the Barabish from a suicidal path of confrontation with the colonial state. The chronicle reports that in 1899, Mahmud ould Dahman told Sidi Muhammad ould Amhammad to "stop this [conflict] because we don't have the capacity to fight a war against the Christians."[53] Sidi Muhammad ould Amhammad's removal from his position as chief in 1900, and his replacement by Mahmud ould Dahman, is celebrated as the triumph of common sense.

Sidi Muhammad ould Amhammad's response to his removal as chief of the Barabish was to leave the Azawad and join with others who had refused to accept French authority. However, in 1906, he returned to French-controlled territory and made his formal submission to the colonial regime. The strained relations between the kin of Sidi Muhammad ould Amhammad and those of Mahmud ould Dahman led to episodes of violence between them. Eventually, the French agreed to establish two separate Barabish chiefdoms, one led by Mahmud ould Dahman and the other by Sidi Muhammad ould Amhammad. Despite this, Sidi Muhammad ould Amhammad rebelled against French authority again in 1909 and went to join other dissidents in southern Morocco. From there, he participated in a number of raids on French-controlled territory in league with western Saharan groups opposed to the French presence.[54]

51 "Taʾrīkh Azawād," f. 23.
52 Ibid., f. 24.
53 Ibid., f. 25.
54 Mansọur Ayoub, "Comte Rendu – Tournée effectuée dans la Région de Tombouctou du 16 février au 16 avril 1924," April 17, 1924 (ANM 1E-2336, Num. Sér. III).

Mahmud ould Dahman was briefly removed from his position as chief of his part of the Barabish in 1910, but in the end, the French managed to work out a political arrangement that permitted the Barabish salt caravans to function regularly with French support. At least from Mahmud ould Dahman's perspective, the French-Barabish alliance could be made to serve Barabish interests. Mahmud Dahman remained chief of his section of the Barabish throughout the entire colonial period. As an old man, he was active in the racial politics of decolonization in the 1950s. He died in 1971 at the age of 101.

THE FRENCH-KUNTA ALLIANCE

Commercial interests played a part in the important alliance established between the French and the Kunta, the other major Arabophone group in the Niger Bend. The Kunta played a significant role in the Saharan commerce that connected the Niger Bend with the Tuwat region of the Algerian Sahara, as well as the local salt trade. Unlike the Barabish, who had been held responsible for the killing of the English explorer Gordon Laing north of Timbuktu in 1826,[55] the Kunta enjoyed a very good reputation even before the colonial occupation because of the protection Ahmad al-Bakkay al-Kunti had offered to Hienrich Barth in the 1850s when he visited Timbuktu.

From the very beginning, the French understood the value that support from the Kunta might offer them. When Hourst made his voyage up the Niger in 1895–1896, he had a very friendly meeting with Kunta notables based in the Gourma (right bank of the Niger) at the village of Kagha, after which he mused about the utility of a French-Kunta alliance: "If we whites, who have force on our side, conclude an alliance with the Kunta, who would put at our service their religious influence, then their venerable power would be reborn." Hourst foresaw that the Kunta "would be our honest courtiers, working for the pacification of the country, which would bring them the benefits of peace and allow them to remain influential."[56] Indeed, the Kunta themselves saw the potential

[55] The standard story is that he was killed by Aḥmad ould Abayda, the chief of the Barabish, while being escorted from Timbuktu to Arawan. See Robert Gaffiot, *Le Major A. Gordon Laing à Tombouctou (1826)* (Dakar: Presse de l'Etat-Major, 1931). Felix Dubois made his own queries in Timbuktu and arrived at a slightly different version of events in which the killer, whom he calls Muhammad al-Bayda, was acting on the orders of Timbuktu. See *Timbuctoo the Mysterious*, trans. Diana White (New York: Negro Universities Press, 1969 [1896]), 327–9.

[56] Le Lieutenant de vaisseau Hourst, *La Mission Hourst sur le Niger et au pays des Touaregs* (Paris, 1898), 102.

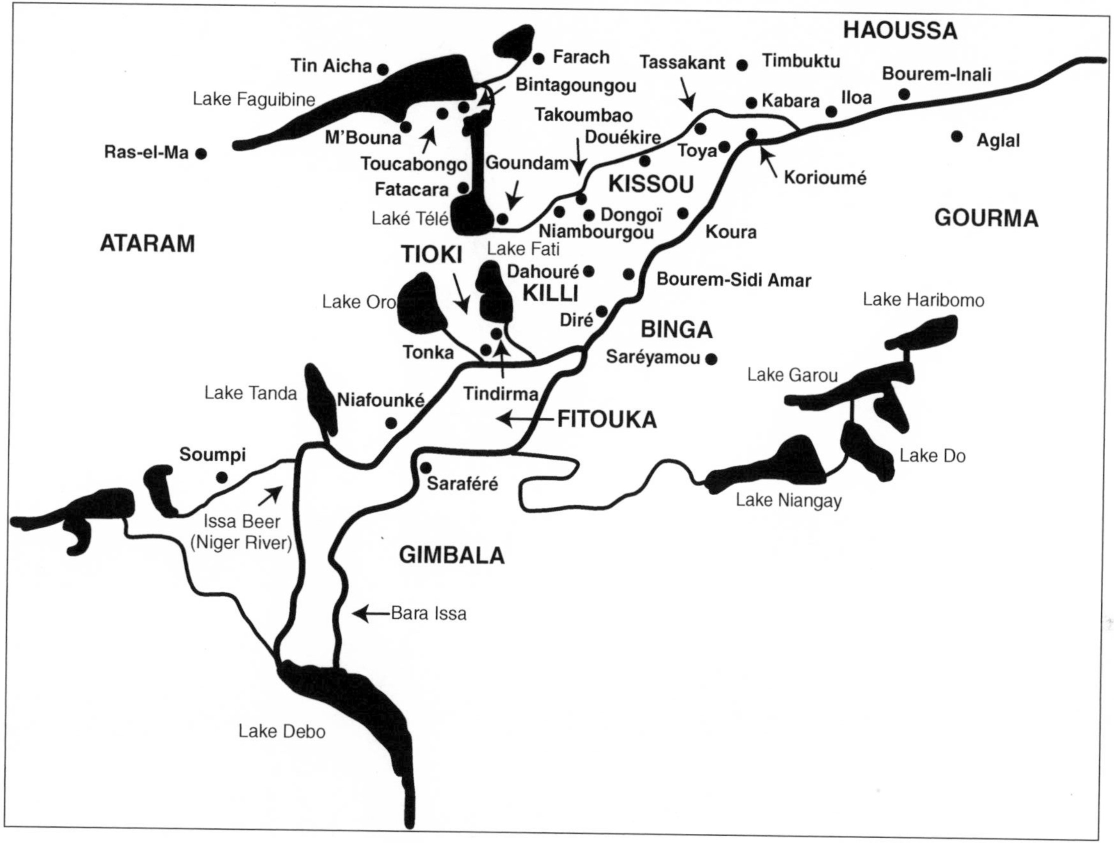

MAP 4. The Niger Valley West of Timbuktu.

benefits of a close relationship with the French because their authority in the region had significantly diminished after the death of Ahmad al-Bakkay al-Kunti in 1865.[57] In the thirty years after Ahmad al-Bakkay's death, the Tuareg confederacies of the Tengeregif and Kel Entsar had largely displaced the Kunta as significant political players in the western part of the Niger Bend. To the east, they found themselves in conflict with the Tuareg Iwellemmedan confederacy.

The Kunta were concentrated in two main areas: A small group was based in the Gourma with two tributary villages along the Niger River at Kagha, and Billasao to the east of Timbuktu. These Kunta used traditional pastures in the lacustrine area of the Gourma, especially around Lake Garou and Lake Niangay.[58] There was a much larger Kunta population based in the Haoussa (left bank) to the north of the Niger River in the area between Bourem and Bamba, and north into the Adrar-n-Ifoghas. The Kunta of the Gourma were not a sufficiently large population to offer the French much assistance in their struggles with the more numerous and powerful Tuareg confederacies of that region, such as the Irreganatan, Igawaddaran, and Kel Temulayt. However, there was great political advantage to be had for the French from an alliance with the Kunta groups north of the river.

In the early year of the colonial occupation, influential Kunta figures opposed the French presence. The most notable among them was ʿAbidin al-Kunti (mentioned earlier) who, with his sons, became the most prominent dissident against the French presence and led many raids against the Niger Bend well into the 1920s with the support of Saharan Arab groups such as the Shaʿamba and the Rgaybat.[59] Yet despite the presence of these oppositional figures, the French entered into an alliance with Kunta political leaders that became essential to the establishment of effective colonial

[57] Elias Saad, *Social History of Timbuktu: The Role of Muslim Scholars and Notables, 1400–1900* (Cambridge: Cambridge University Press, 1983), 219. This was also the French view in their first assessments of the relative power of different pastoralist groups. For example, in a study written in 1896 by an Algerian in the service of the French named Mohamed Ben Saïd, one finds the following passage: "Since around 1860, the Kunta have been losing their prestige daily and their religious influence has become less significant each day; Nonetheless, the black and nomadic populations still accord them some consideration because of the memory of their great ancestor." "Notice sur les Tribus sahariennes et les Touaregs de la Région de Tombouctou," 1896 (ANM FA 1D-59-5).

[58] This group is often referred to in colonial sources as the Kunta of the Aribinda.

[59] On ʿAbidin's career, see Rita Aouad-Badoual, "Le rôle de `Abidine el Kounti dans la résistance nomade à la conquête française de la boucle du Niger (1894–1902)," in *Le politique dans l'histoire touarègue. Les Cahiers de l'IREMAM* 3, ed. Hélène Claudot-Hawad and Dahbia Abrous (Aix-en-Provence: CNRS, 1993): 35–48.

control over the Niger Bend. French confidence in the Kunta was nearly absolute because of the perceived similarity of colonial and Kunta interests. The principal French objective in this policy was to weaken those Tuareg groups that remained hostile to the colonial presence and that had participated in and supported raids against French positions in the 1890s. For the Kunta, colonial support offered the opportunity to turn the tide against Tuareg enemies who had dramatically weakened Kunta power in the second half of the nineteenth century.

The Kunta made their formal submission to the French in 1899. Unlike so many other pastoralist leaders, the Kunta came in person to Timbuktu, ready to demonstrate the full sincerity of their desire to work with the new power. At their initial meeting, they provided the colonial officials with useful information on the various Tuareg groups in the eastern half of the Niger Bend. They agreed to send couriers from Timbuktu on behalf of the French to the Fourneau-Lamy mission in the Aïr Massif (in northern Niger). They also agreed to organize salt caravans to Timbuktu to get around the obstructions still posed by the Barabish chief Sidi Muhammad ould Amhammad at that moment. Most importantly, they offered to send their own people to fight against Tuareg groups to force them to submit to French rule.[60] In return for these demonstrations of friendship, the French began to supply the Kunta with arms and authorized a series of Kunta raids against the most powerful Tuareg warrior-status group in the eastern half of the Niger Bend, the Iwellemmedan. The colonial alliance shifted the balance of power in the eastern Niger Bend toward the Kunta.[61]

Hourst had exchanged messages with Madidou, chief of the Iwellemmedan, in Gao in 1896 and promised him that the French desired only peaceful relations.[62] In a letter written to the French authorities in Timbuktu in 1896, Madidou made clear his intentions with regards to the Europeans:

> Between you and us, there will be nothing but goodness and peace. Your merchants will come to us by land or by water and they will return assured that nobody here will molest them in any way. You will not bring any trouble to our land that will affect our traditional, civil or religious way of life. Know also that since the people that you send to us will be able to return safely, we expect your guarantee that our people going to your territory, alone or in groups, by land or

[60] Région du Nord, "Rapport politique," 2ème semestre 1899 (ANM FA 1E 78–81).

[61] Charles Grémont, "Les Touareg Iwellemmedan (1647–1898): Un ensemble politique de la Boucle du Niger" (Ph.d. diss., Université Paris 1, 2007), 404–5.

[62] Hourst, *Mission*, 164–9.

by water, will be treated likewise ... When you have made these promises that you have discussed with us, we will be brothers.[63]

I have not found the Arabic original of this letter, but even in the French translation, it is clear that Madidou was using the legal language of "amān," or "safe conduct," as a guide for relations between Muslims and non-Muslims.[64] He was, in fact, offering to the French the right to travel unmolested for commercial purposes in a Muslim land, consistent with the rules governing treaties of this kind. The term "amān," like the term "ʿahd," or "pact," which we have encountered already, appears frequently in the Arabic writings about relations with the French in the Niger Bend. It is these terms that the Barabish chief Sidi Muhammad ould Amhammad used in his letters to the French. As in the case of the Barabish chief, colonial officials found Madidou's language of safe conduct and treaties to be insulting precisely because to accept them would deny their claims to supremacy in the area. It was the French, not Arab or Tuareg leaders, who were in the position to grant safe conduct. It was the French who would collect the jizya tax, certainly not they who would pay it. Colonial officials demanded submission to their supreme authority, not a relationship between different sovereign powers. Nonetheless, in the twentieth-century Arabic-language histories of the Niger Bend such as "A Barabish history of the Azawad" discussed earlier, the terms "aman" and "ʿahd" are the terms most often used to describe the establishment of relations with the Christians, not submission.

When Madidou offered refuge to the anti-French rebel ʿAbidin al-Kunti in 1897, and a year later when certain Iwellemmedan groups participated in raids against French positions, the French authorities decided that "peaceful" penetration into the eastern part of the Niger Bend was impossible.[65] Even after having established a post at Gao in 1899, they were still unable to engineer the submission of the Iwellemmedan. After Madidou died of natural causes in 1899, some Iwellemmedan subgroups did submit to French authority, but others refused to do so and continued to resist the French presence. Once the Kunta made their submission in 1899, the French began to authorize and encourage Kunta attacks against the Iwellemmedan in the hopes of forcing them to sue for peace.

[63] A.-M.-J Richer, *Les Oulliminden. Les Touareg du Niger (Région de Tombouctou-Gao)* (Paris: E. Larose, 1924), 140.

[64] Muhammad Sani Umar, "Islamic Discourses on European Visitors to Sokoto Caliphate in the Nineteenth Century," *Studia Islamica* 95 (2002): 135–59.

[65] Richer, *Oulliminden*, 143.

The key figure in the French-Kunta alliance was Ḥammādi ould Muḥammad Bū-Addi,[66] the chief of the Kunta of the Haoussa, whom the French called "Hammoadi." He became intimately involved in negotiating the terms of the French relationship with different pastoralist groups from the moment that the French-Kunta alliance was formed in 1899. His enmity was principally directed at Tuareg warrior-status groups, the most important of which was the Iwellemmedan. He made much of the difference between warriors and clerics, reserving the term "Tuareg" exclusively for Tamashek-speaking warrior-status groups. Hammadi claimed that Tamashek-speaking clerical groups would be happy to make accommodations with the French, if only warrior pressures could be removed. So, for example, in a letter written to the French officer at the post of Tosaye (between Bamba and Bourem) in late 1899 or early 1900, Hammadi explained that Tamashek-speaking clerical-status groups, in this case the Kel Essuk, were being prevented from making peace with the French: "Concerning the camels that you demanded from the Kel Essuk, know that the [warrior-status] Tuareg are currently with them and that they would have sent the camels to you but they knew that the Tuareg would have raided them. This is the reason that they were unable to send them to you." Hammadi then added that "the Kel Essuk would like you to force the [warrior-status] Tuareg to move away from them so that they could then come and set up their camps in your vicinity, just as the Arabs have done. But, they are afraid of the Tuareg." Hammadi arranged a system of secret codes that could be used to circumvent the pressure put on politically weak groups like the Kel Essuk by warrior-status groups: "If they send you a letter carrying the sign of a five-sided star, it means that you must send troops in their direction so that they can be protected from the Tuareg [warriors]."

The aggression of French forces was criticized by Hammadi in his counsel to his new allies: "At all times when different people go to see you, or move into territory close to you, be careful that they only see goodness and clemency from you. The rest of what I want to say will be communicated [orally] by the carrier of the letter. Goodbye."[67] In another letter written at around the same time, he advised a French officer of the importance of his behavior, and of French comportment more broadly, in

[66] Ḥammād b. Muḥammad Bu-Addi b. Muḥammad al-Ṣaghīr b. Sīdi Muḥammad b. Sīdi al-Mukhtār al-Kuntī, born 1867, died 1912.

[67] The letter is a French translation. I have not been able to locate the Arabic original. There is no date on the letter, but it was translated in Timbuktu on January 27, 1900. Letter from Hammadi to the Commandant, Tosaye. No.2 (ANM FA 1E 95).

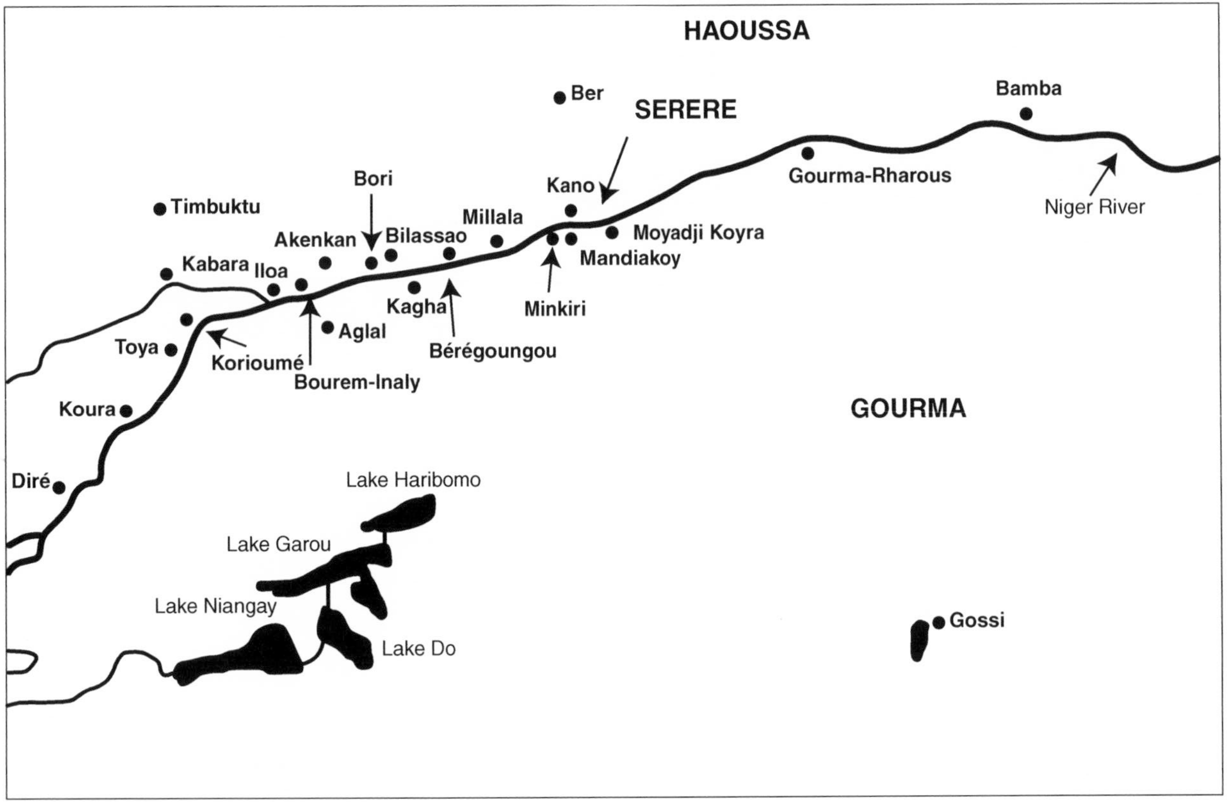

MAP 5. The Niger Valley East of Timbuktu.

winning over pastoralists to the colonial cause: "Know that your way of behaving towards the people either attracts them towards you or pushes them away from you."[68]

The extent to which allies like Hammadi actually managed the process of submission and the realignment of local politics in the conquest period is evident from the authority that French officials accorded to him. In another letter written in 1900, he made clear that he was the person orchestrating new alliances: "The commander wrote to me saying that he accords a pact of safe conduct (aman) to all the people to whom I accord a pact of safe conduct. As such, I have given my protection to the Kel Takarangat, to the Kel Tinagsan, and to all those who are dependent on them [as their vassals]." In effect, the Kunta used their alliance with the French as an opportunity to reconstitute a larger confederacy under their own control that included both Arabic- and Tamashek-speakers. Hammadi wrote, "independently of that, we have worked together with these people since the era of our ancestors until today. All the necessary information will be given to you by the letter carrier." Since French actions reflected on their Kunta allies, Hammadi was keen to ensure that his word would be respected. For example, he told the French official to "release the caravan of these people that you have arrested and do not take anything from them because it is me who told them to go to you on the basis of the trust that I have in you. They are in this way under my protection."[69]

Hammadi was unequivocal in his support for the colonial policy against the Iwellemmedan. The Kunta organized regular raids against Iwellemmedan targets, pillaging their goods and taking their slaves. Theoretically, Kunta forces required French permission to attack the Iwellemmedan, but the tone of the correspondence between Hammadi and colonial officials makes clear that the Kunta had a free hand. An idea of the Kunta perspective on their alliance with the French can be gleaned from one of Hammadi's letters written in 1902:[70]

I obeyed the order that you gave me and I would not disobey it in any way, but my submission to you and the frank affection that I have for you because of the

[68] Letter from Hammadi to the Commandant, Tosaye. No.3. Translated in Timbuktu on January 27, 1900 (ANM FA 1E 95).

[69] Letter from Hammadi to the Commandant, Tosaye. No.4. Translated in Timbuktu on January 27, 1900 (ANM FA 1E 95).

[70] This letter is a French translation made by the colonial regime of an Arabic letter that I have not been able to locate. Letter from Hammadi to the Commandant, Timbuktu, April 10, 1902 (ANM FA 1E 78–81).

fulfillment of all my expectations does not prevent me from being distressed by all that distresses you and delighted by all that delights you. I consider myself to be like yourself in the service of your government, which has been established to allow justice to reign, to make injustice disappear, and to eliminate abuses and reestablish peace after the discord that everybody considers with the repugnance that they hold for everything that is bad.

The Iwellemmedan are opposed to these principles and avoid any contact with them. You are not unaware of all the ways that they have brought us injustice, tyranny, the rape of our wives, the destruction of our goods, and trouble all over this country including scorn for the weak and violations of sacred places. It is thus that with their own hands they have caused their power to collapse, despite the extent of their empire and the supremacy that they once had in this country. They are people who have practiced injustice for a long time and all the evil that we have suffered from them has only continued since my alliance with you ... When they are forced to come under my power, I will bring them to an accord with you.

This letter is important because in it, Hammadi is very explicit in explaining both his alliance with the French and his enmity toward the Iwellemmedan in terms that evoke the Sahelian language of race as collective status and warrior impiety. Hammadi's argument is made in moral terms. The remote France is a force of justice. France's representatives in the Niger Bend, like Hammadi himself, are the agents of that justice. Such an alliance is represented here as natural.

Hammadi would argue repeatedly that the only way to bring about the submission of the Iwellemmedan was by the exercise of Kunta force against them. Any protestations of submission by the Iwellemmedan were to be regarded as insincere because, as Hammadi wrote to the French commander: "How can you hope to claim that you have become their masters without trouble or deaths of men, nor the pillage of those who were powerful and oppressors. That is not rational." As the Kunta pressed home their advantage by sending regular raids against Iwellemmedan positions, Hammadi sought to reassure the French that force was the only way to deal with Tuareg warriors such as the Iwellemmedan:

For what is the motivation that pushes them [Iwellemmedan] to employ this detour, which is to say, making this insincere request for peace? It is only the desire to defend themselves against us in case we attempt to pillage their goods. Concerning their goods, they continue to oppress and boast, counting on the return of their power. As long as they remain in such a disposition, no force will be effective against them, and we will no longer be able to live with them. In acting thusly, their goal is only to gain some time on you and on us. But this will permit you to understand their lack of sincerity and frankness.

Even if they were sincere, you would not get from them what you want as long as they remain in such a state because you inspire in them an aversion, because they lack loyalty, and because they nourish hatred against you and against us because

> you have made yourselves masters of their kingdom and because you have done bad things in killing some of them and pillaging their goods, which you know, is for them, the worst of the two. If in their offer of submission they were sincere, and they bring to you a small amount of their goods to support their new situation, the fact of our raiding them will only increase their frankness in their relations with you. They have not asked for peace because of their affection for you or in the consideration that they have for your justice and your good ways of proceeding in your relations with your subjects. They have placed themselves under your protection and authority because they do not want to struggle and suffer any further losses.

Hammadi continued his lesson in statecraft, arguing that violence was the only language that Tuareg warrior-status groups understood, and emphasizing the crucial role played by Kunta forces in the imposition of French rule across the Niger Bend:

> The proof of what I say will not escape you if you take the time to reflect upon it thoroughly because every time that one of their fellows places himself under your protection, they only do it after having had their goods pillaged and their people killed. If you take what I have told you for the words of an enemy against your enemy and if, as a consequence of the good opinion that you have for them, you think that it doesn't concern them, then look at the case of the Kel Temulayt. When we fought them and stole their goods, they came and submitted to you in the best way that you could hope for despite the tyranny that they had subjected us to, and the repugnance that you inspired in them.
>
> The Ifoghas also came and gathered around you when we subjected them to the same treatment. It was the same for the Idnan. Even the Kel Essuk, despite the fact that they are the weakest creatures that God has ever created, did not come to you except because of the fear that the Arabs would pillage them. You have experienced the same pattern before with other Tuareg groups such as the Tengeregif, the Irreganatan, the Kel Temulayt, the Imghad, the Kel Entsar, the Kel Horma and others. Even though they were all vassal groups or slaves of the Iwellemmedan, you were not able to make yourself masters over them except when you pillaged them and fought them. And despite that, they only agreed to submit after you had killed their chiefs one after the other.

The political expediency is what is most obvious in such letters. But it is important to see in the terms Hammadi used to describe the Iwellemmedan, and other Tuareg groups more generally, the old language of the difference between warrior and clerical lineages. This letter is a critique of the warriors as pillagers, as people who are ignorant of justice and the shariʿa. They respect only force, and as such, their juridical status is that of the mustaghraq al-dhimma.

The most prominent Kunta intellectual at the time of French conquest was Shaykh Bay al-Kunti, whom we have already encountered in Chapter 2. In his collection of legal opinions, he included responses to several questions specifically about the property of the Iwellemmedan. Although his opinions are undated, they almost certainly arose from the context of colonial conquest. One of them begins as follows:

> About the ruling on the nature of the property of the Iwellemmedan of our land? I have heard about their [status] as warriors because they steal the property of Muslims. Are they mustaghraq al-dhimma because of that? Is it permitted to take what they possess by force? After taking it, can it be appropriated or should it be spent on the general welfare?[71]

In Shaykh Bay's response, and in others opinions concerning the issue of the mustaghraq al-dhimma, he acknowledged that the source of their property distinguishes them from legitimate "warriors" who fight in jihad and whose booty is legal under specified conditions.[72] The Iwellemmedan, however, do not behave according to Islamic norms and should therefore be considered as mustaghraq al-dhimma, according to Shaykh Bay. As such, it is best to avoid handling property that comes from them.[73] In another opinion, he wrote:

> As for what is seized unlawfully on the part of robbers or by the poor who [have] no proof [authenticating the validity of their property], it is forbidden under [the chapter on] unlawful seizure and the slaughter of animals. This is similar to the case of the Kel Ahaggar and the Iwellemmedan, and others who resemble them, who raid from those who are not their companions. In these cases, the purchaser of that [which they have seized illegally] is [considered] a usurper like them.[74]

If Iwellemmedan property is taken, he tells the questioner, it must be turned over to the public treasury of the Muslims to be used to support the poor and needy rather than be consumed by the individual who took it: "In order to thwart your endeavor, know that he who mentions the mustaghraq [al-dhimma] is most certainly expanding the disagreement about the permissibility of taking that which he possesses, by transferring (iḥyāl) or stealing the confiscated goods so as to allow him to consume them."[75] Such a warning from Shaykh Bay certainly constrained the license of his questioner in profiting from stolen Iwellemmedan property.[76] But the status of the Iwellemmedan as mustaghraq al-dhimma was not in question, only the legitimate use of their property.

71 Shaykh Bāy al-Kuntī, "Nawāzil Shaykh Bāy" (IHERIAB ms. 124), #812, f. 27.
72 Ibid., #811, f. 27.
73 Ibid., #810, f. 26–7.
74 Shaykh Bāy al-Kuntī, "Nawāzil Shaykh Bāy" (IHERIAB ms. 119), #348, f. 390–1.
75 Shaykh Bāy al-Kuntī, "Nawāzil Shaykh Bāy" (IHERIAB ms. 124), #812, f. 27.
76 This opinion was backed up by a fatwa issued by Sīdi Muḥammad b. Sīdi al-Mukhtār al-Kuntī (d. 1826) that Shaykh Bāy cited.

THE ARAB-TUAREG WARS: KUNTA VERSUS IWELLEMMEDAN

In 1902, the Iwellemmedan confederacy made Fihrun their leader, and in 1903 he offered his formal submission to the French. However, the conflict between the Kunta and Iwellemmedan continued unabated despite French attempts to rein in their Kunta allies. French officers on the ground understood that their own weakness required the alliance with the Kunta because they were completely unable to respond effectively from their posts at Bamba and Gao to raids made into the Niger valley. However, the French worried that the Kunta had benefited too much from the alliance; their raiding activity had significantly increased the size of their herds, the number of slaves they possessed, and the pasture land they controlled. Nonetheless, the French authorized Kunta attacks on the Iwellemmedan in 1903.[77] Until 1905, the Kunta paid no taxes to the colonial state: "Our provisional allies the Kunta are the object of continual complaints on the part of the riverine population, whether for theft of goats, camels, rice, or for a refusal to pay the boatmen who transport them across the river; the Kunta appear to act just as we do and it is certain that if we levy taxes, they think that they are also owed something by the riverine population."[78] Even after Firhun's official submission to the French in 1903 on behalf of the Iwellemmedan, the Kunta-Iwellemmedan conflict continued to be played out in raids and counterraids.

A sense of the extent to which the Kunta took advantage of their relationship with the French to settle scores with the Iwellemmedan, or even just to profit from opportunities for pillage, comes from a case in 1905, two years after the full Iwellemmedan submission to French rule. The French commander of the post at Bamba was forced to launch an investigation after a Kunta raiding party attacked a camp of an Iwellemmedan subgroup, killing twenty people. The French government at Timbuktu had authorized Hammadi to form a Kunta raiding party that would search for and attack a Tuareg group called the Shamanamas that had not submitted to colonial authority.[79] Hammadi formed a war party of 300 men, of which 100 were mounted on camels, 100 on horses, and 100 traveled on foot. The men were well armed with French-supplied rifles. Hammadi did not participate himself in the war party. After several days

[77] Colonel Mangeot and Paul Marty, "Les Touareg de la boucle du Niger," *BCEHS-AOF* 3–4 (1918): 436.

[78] Cercle de Bamba, "Rapport politique," April 1902 (ANM FA 1E 21–22).

[79] There had been a number of incidents between the Kel Ahara and Kunta before this, including the killing by members of the Shamanamas, a Kel Ahara subgroup, of two Kunta in 1898. See Grémont, "Touareg Iwellemmedan," 401–5.

of marching, the party came across a camp of Kel Ahara, a fraction of the Iwellemmedan, at a waterhole called Z'Guiret, and attacked on the night of July 1, 1905. According to the Iwellemmedan version of events collected by a French officer:

> Everyone was sleeping in the camp of [the chief] Abakalib. It was around midnight when the Kunta horsemen came within about a hundred meters of the tents of the Kel Ahara. The first tent on that side belonged to the brother of Abakalib, called by some Saoua, by others Dengazouri. The Kunta arrived at a gallop and began firing on the camp without warning. Dengazouri came out of his tent armed with a spear to see what was happening and once he saw the Kunta he took flight. He was killed by a rifle shot. That was the first death. At the sound of the gunfire Abakalib and all the other Tuareg came out of their tents and froze at the sight of the Arabs. Abakalib tried to flee on a horse but it was killed by a gunshot. He was trying to mount a camel passing near him when he was overtaken by about forty Kunta horsemen who surrounded him. Abakalib cried out to them: "Mazin [the leader of the Kunta raiding party]! For the love of God, let me live." He responded: "No, not even in the name of God will I let you live. We have come here today to kill you." Abakalib then fell, riddled with bullets. They removed his possessions and amulets from his body. Everyone else in the camp took flight and the Kunta began to pillage.[80]

In addition to the 20 Kel Ahara killed in this action, the French inquiry estimated the total booty taken from the camp as follows: 65 slaves, 5 horses, 140 camels, 400 cattle, 100 donkeys, and 1,100 sheep. The booty had been divided between the members of the raiding party. The explanation for these events offered by the French inquiry was that "there exists an ancient racial hatred between the Kunta and the [Iwellemmedan]. Until the submission of the [Iwellemmedan], the Kunta were given the task of maintaining the peace and policing their territory. These operations were enormously profitable to them and the submission of the [Iwellemmedan leader] Fihrun threatens to put an end to them."[81] Given what Hammadi had written to French officials, this explanation appears more reasonable, and more locally coherent, than we might assume without this context. The idea of racial hatred was not just a French construction, even if it did not function quite as the French imagined.

Kunta-Iwellemmedan conflicts continued apace, and despite increasing French efforts to reconcile the two sides, mutual recriminations were hard to overcome. In a letter that Fihrun wrote to the French

80 Capitaine Lacroix, Commandant of the Cercle de Bamba, "Rapport sur l'enquête qu'il a conduite au sujet de l'attaque des Kel Aharas par le rezzou Kounta dirigé contre les Chamanamas," September 28, 1905, No.97 (ANM FA 1N 28).

81 Ibid.

commander at Gao in 1907, after a colonial effort at bringing the Kunta and Iwellemmedan together to settle their differences, he responded to Kunta claims that he was holding slaves who had been raided from the Kunta: "With all the lies that the Arabs have told about me, it is not possible that I could have done these things. Moreover, if you wish to listen to everything that the Arabs say, you will have to kill me."[82] Despite such rhetoric, French officials were finally able, on December 26, 1908, to convene a meeting of Kunta, Iwellemmedan, and Kel Ifoghas leaders in an attempt to put an end to hostilities and establish separate zones of pasturage for each group. Following this, in 1909, the French imposed formal conventions on the different sides that created a buffer zone between the Kunta and Iwellemmedan in the area between Tondibi and Fes-en-Nefes, and managed pasture lands in the Adrar-n-Ifoghas.[83] In the same year, the French established a post in the Adrar-n-Ifoghas at Kidal to better manage the Tuareg and Arab pastoralists in this region. Despite the convention, and the growing authority of the colonial state, Kunta-Iwellemmedan violence continued. To give but one example, an Iwellemmedan raid on the Kunta in 1911, very similar to the one described earlier, left thirteen Kunta dead.[84]

The last act of overt Tuareg resistance and rebellion against the new colonial order occurred in 1916, when Iwellemmedan rebels, under the leadership of their chief Fihrun, launched what he called a jihad against the French colonial state. Taking advantage of reduced colonial military forces because of the First World War, Fihrun and others in the region east of the Niger valley around the town of Meneka, began planning for some kind of action soon after war broke out in 1914. The extent of the original plot is unclear, but Fihrun was arrested in 1915 and sentenced to ten years in prison and twenty years in exile for anticolonial agitation. Along with five other Iwellemmedan prisoners, Fihrun was sent to serve his jail sentence at Timbuktu. However, French officials in the Niger Bend feared that the humiliation of important leaders such as Fihrun would lead to a breakdown of Tuareg authority more generally, which they relied on to govern the widely dispersed pastoralist population. As

[82] Letter from Fihrun to the Commandant, Cercle de Gao, letter arrived October 15, 1907. There is no Arabic text of this letter, only the French translation published by Richer, *Oulliminden*, 331.

[83] These conventions were published by Richer, *Oulliminden*, 323–4.

[84] Report by Capitaine Lauzanne, Commandant, le détachement de police chez les Oulliminden, to the Commandant, Cercle de Gao, December 13, 1911, No. 4A (ANM FA IN 39).

such, they decided to revise the sentence passed against Fihrun, and after the intervention of important notables such as Shaykh Bay al-Kunti, he was returned to Gao in December 1915 where he continued to be held in a colonial jail.[85] In the meantime, the French administration became fearful of a larger revolt by other Tuareg groups in the Gourma at the end of 1915.[86] They asked Fihrun to use his influence to calm tensions among these people; he complied and sent a letter saying that revolt against the French would be useless. Then, on the night of February 13, 1916, he and his fellow Iwellemmedan prisoners escaped from their confinement in Gao and headed east toward the Iwellemmedan camps. This began the so-called Iwellemmedan revolt.

In a letter later captured by the French that was written by Firhun to Musa ag Amastan, the leader of the Ahaggar Tuareg in southern Algeria, the Iwellemmedan rebel leader made an explicit appeal to jihad:

> I inform you that the only thing that caused me to go to Gao despite its impurity (najas) was to gather news of the infidels... God conquers those things that are in it. It is He who insists that the Muslims of the towns of this land agree on their word and combat all the divisions made by those who follow the orders of the infidels. This is just what is required of them in the saying of God: "Fight those unbelievers who are near to you, and let them find harshness in you, and know that God is with those who keep their duty [to Him]"[87] It is time for us to behave according to this command and turn to God in repentance ... I inform you that I am acting according to this command, and this will lead to war between me and them. I have already taken three of their notables, together with their firearms and mounts. So I follow their example. I want you to agree to do the same ...[88]

[85] Richer, *Oulliminden*, 263–72.

[86] There had been major confrontations between French forces and Tuareg warrior lineages in the Gourma in 1908, as colonial forces began to effectively impose the conditions of "la politique nomade" on the Tuareg confederacies based in the Gourma. This included prohibiting access to certain grazing lands in the Niger valley and imposing significant requisitions of animals in fines for previous refusals to obey French orders, in addition to annual taxes. The most important warrior-status group in the Gourma was the Irreganatan, and in 1907, they refused to pay any taxes to the French. A colonial military column defeated a force of an estimated 1,300 mounted Tuareg fighters on June 10, 1908 in a battle outside of the village of Baney. Forty-seven Tuareg were killed, and this effectively put an end to open hostilities between the French and the Tuareg warrior-status groups in the Gourma. The colonial estimate of the Tuareg participants who fought the French at Baney are as follows: Igawaddaran (Sakhaoui) 150 horsemen; Igawaddaran (Sakib) 200; Imededran 300; Kel Temulayt 80; Irreganatan 600. Chef de Bataillon Laverdure, Commandant, Région de Tombouctou, "Rapport sur les opérations du Gourma (rive droit) du 23 mai au 1ère juillet 1908 inclus contre les Touareg," 1908 (ANM FA IN 46).

[87] Qur'an 9:123

[88] Letter from Fihrun to Mūsā ag Amāstān, no date [1916]. This is my translation of the Arabic letter published by Richer, *Oulliminden*, 331.

Unfortunately for Fihrun, he was unable to rally the Kel Ahaggar. After several months of skirmishes, French forces marched against him and forced an engagement at Andéroumboukane on May 10, 1916, which effectively destroyed the rebel forces and left hundreds dead. Fihrun was killed a month and half later, on June 25, 1916, by a small raiding party of Kel Ahaggar Tuareg.[89] Kunta forces asked permission to join the fight against the Iwellemmedan. Although permission was granted, they were unable to participate in the battle of Andéroumboukane itself because they did not arrive in time. It is in the context of regular Kunta-Iwellemmedan conflict, and the close relationship between the Kunta and the colonial state, that we must understand the last act of rebellion of Iwellemmedan forces against the French.

DEFENDING THE SAHARAN CONFINES

One of the reasons that the colonial state in the Niger Bend did little to address these kinds of ongoing conflicts between different pastoralist groups was French weakness and limited capacity. The Kunta had made themselves indispensable to the French in their role as irregular forces that guarded the Niger Bend against rebel incursions. It was only in the early 1930s that this danger was finally ended. The last raids occurred just before Spanish authorities in the colony of Rio Oro were able to establish colonial control over the interior of the western Saharan region south of Morocco from where many of the raids against the Niger Bend were launched. The definitive end to these trans-Saharan raids came in 1934, when a combined French and Spanish force sacked the Saharan town of Smara. The continued resistance of dissidents like ʿAbidin al-Kunti and his sons, or the former Barabish chief Sidi Muhammad ould Amhammad and his sons, manifested itself mostly in raids undertaken with people drawn from the northern and central Sahara, such as the Arabophone Rgaybat and Shaʿamba, and the Tuareg Kel Ahaggar.

I have already mentioned several of the more important raids launched in the conquest period of the 1890s. Raiding parties formed in the northwestern Sahara, especially in the Saqiat al-Hamra region, and they typically set out across the desert at the end of October.[90] The constraints of the desert, and especially of the availability of water and pasturage for

[89] Richer, *Oulliminden*, 288–9, 296–7.

[90] Colonel Mangeot, "Manuel à l'usage des troupes opérant au Soudan Français et plus particulièrement en zone saharienne," *BCEHS-AOF* (1922): 599–600.

camels, limited the raiding parties to about sixty men, just as it imposed a deadline by which the raiders had to recross the desert again in a northward direction before the beginning of the hot season in mid-March. Once the raiders had crossed the desert heading south and arrived in the Sahel, they sometimes joined together to form larger groups of as many as 500 men. Usually, the men in these parties were armed with rifles, and they lived on the livestock and grains that they were able to steal. They were especially interested in capturing camels and slaves to bring back with them across the desert as booty. Their raiding targets included agricultural villages and the azalaï salt caravan from Taoudenni.[91]

Most often, the raiders sought to avoid a direct confrontation with colonial forces. As such, from the vantage point of colonial officials, defending against raiders was a difficult game of cat-and-mouse requiring good intelligence networks, local allies, and mobile forces ready to respond quickly to raids. In the early years especially, French officials lacked the means to effectively defend the territory that they claimed. Raiders could be present in the Niger Bend for weeks or even months, and this produced lots of colonial correspondence based on rumors and sporadic information. For example, a raiding party attacked the eastern Niger Bend in the winter of 1904, but French officials had difficulty trying to track it. One official at the French post in Bamba reported: "Here are the results of the interrogation that I undertook with a bellah named Kara, who was taken prisoner by the Moroccans [the name used for the raiders], but who escaped from his captivity two days ago." The official then summarized the testimony he had received: "The Moroccans are about 300 men. They are almost all armed with rifles.... They do not speak Tamashek but they have a guide who is an Idnan [a Tuareg group], who interprets for them." His informant described the party as possessing many camels but moving on foot: "They are only looking for camels and slaves. They have about 15 of the latter, of which 12 are still children." The raiders were not interested in cattle or goats because these could not be led across the desert on the return trip. Reportedly, "they do not know rice, and after having found some abandoned in [the village of] Ouagai, they tried to eat it without de-husking it." The informant escaped his captors at night because, "they sleep in a circle without a sentry or guard."[92]

91 Capitaine Mazillier, "Note sur les rezzous Marocains-Tombouctou," April 21, 1906 (ANM FA IN 16).

92 Letter from Capitaine Aymard, Commandant, Cercle de Bamba, to the Commandant, 1ère Territoire militaire, Tombouctou, November 14, 1904 (ANM FA 1E 118).

Three days later, a French officer based at Kabara, near Timbuktu, reported that the same raiders were camped on a dune near Bamba, and that they had captured as many as 500 slaves by raiding villages along the river: "From this camp, they spread out and make expeditions against riverine villages in parties of ten to twenty men. In the beginning, they present themselves as disinterested visitors looking for hospitality which is offered to them because of the fear of violence and depredations." But at dawn, "they threaten the people and inform them of their true purposes. Some villages have been surprise-attacked. Those of Abba Koyra and Moïra were raided thoroughly and their whole population taken away. Other villages have attempted to cross the river and stay on the right bank."[93] In 1904, there was relatively little that the French could do about such raids themselves. They did send a company of colonial troops mounted on camels to protect the Barabish in the Azawad, but they depended mostly on local allies such as the Kunta to track down the raiders and attack them. In the case of this raid, the Kunta chief Hammadi organized and led the pursuit. The raiders were forced to divide into smaller groups and disperse, but they were not captured or killed.[94]

The solution to the problem of Saharan raiders involved several aspects. One important principle was the French occupation of strategic wells and towns in the Sahara. Colonial posts were to be established in Arawan, Bou Djébéha, Taoudenni, Kidal, and at the site of a number of important wells. The French government in Algeria was encouraged to do the same by occupying strategic wells in the southern part of that colony. Colonial camel corps called "méharistes" were trained to operate in the desert and stationed at these sites. Such units were first organized in 1899, using camels gained in colonial raids or in payments of taxes and tribute. The soldiers were initially drawn from the same sub-Saharan groups as regular colonial troops. It was only in 1905 that a reorganized méhariste corps became relatively effective.[95] But the key strategic dimension to the French defense of the Saharan confines was the enlistment of active support by irregular forces from different Arab and Tuareg groups in the Niger Bend. Because these same groups were often victims of Saharan raids, it made sense to involve them in defense measures. The colonial officials in the Niger Bend referred to these irregular forces, which were under the

[93] Letter from Lieutenant Ferrière, Commandant, Poste de Kabara, to the Commandant, 1ère Territoire militaire, Tombouctou, November 17, 1904 (ANM FA 1E 118).

[94] Letter from Lieutenant de Barbeyrac, Commandant, Poste de Bourem, to the Commandant, Cercle de Bamba, December 11, 1904. No.95 (ANM FA 1E 188).

[95] Bouchez, *Guide*, 11–14.

command of local Arab and Tuareg leaders, as "goums," and the fighters themselves as "goumiers."[96] It was in one such "goum" mission that the Kunta leader Hammadi and many of his men, as well as a French officer named Rossi, were killed by a party of Rgaybat raiders in May 1912 at a site in the Azawad south of Taoudenni called El Gettara.[97]

Over time, colonial policy evolved somewhat on the question of Saharan defense. Significant raids continued to be launched against the Niger Bend until the end of the 1920s, but French military officers became more active and more important in directing military action. In 1920, the Governor General of French West Africa expressed his concern at the autonomy of what he called "tribal goums" and encouraged the military officials in the Niger Bend to put these irregular forces under French commanders.[98] Hammadi had been replaced as leader of the Kunta in 1911 by Alouata who had formerly been the leader of the Kunta in the Gourma. After the disaster at El Gettara, the French reorganized their desert defenses and began to incorporate more Tuareg forces into the méhariste regular units. Under Alouata's leadership, the Kunta continued to furnish significant forces for colonial purposes, but they were no longer quite as important as they once had been. As the colony's defenses became more secure, many Kunta migrated into Niger to take advantage of better pastures and to pursue their commercial activities. After the First World War, the strategic importance of the French-Kunta alliance diminished considerably. Many internal divisions within Kunta ranks led to further migrations, and this weakened the ability of Kunta leaders to extract the kind of concessions from the colonial state that Hammadi had been able to obtain.[99] The Kunta remained a significant group, but the era of a French-Arab pact against the Tuareg had passed.

In October 1923, a massive attack was launched from the Saqiat al-Hamra by mostly Rgaybat raiders led by a local dissident from the Niger Bend named Ḥammū b. Sīdi al-Mukhtār who had been promised, and later denied, the position of chief of a small Arabophone group called the Tormoz.[100]

96 Mangeot, "Manuel," 622–3.

97 Boilley, *Touaregs Kel Adagh*, 129–34.

98 Letter from the Gouverneur-Général de l'Afrique Occidentale Française, Dakar to the Lieutenant-Gouverneur du Haut-Sénégal-Niger, Koulouba, November 23, 1920, No.1021 (ANM FA 2N 76).

99 For a colonial analysis of this changes, see Cercle de Tombouctou, "Monographie du Cercle de Tombouctou," 1923, No. 13R (ANM ID-2103, Num. Sér. I).

100 Letter from Lieutenant-Gouverneur du Haut-Sénégal-Niger, Koulouba, to Gouverneur-Général de l'Afrique Occidentale Française, Dakar, No.25A, January 25, 1924 (ANM FR 2E 157).

Unlike many other raids, this group launched a direct attack on colonial forces and succeeded in destroying a French-led méhariste unit on September 29, 1923, killing fifty colonial soldiers at a site called Dayat (100 km north of Timbuktu). The raiders then attacked the villages around Lake Faguibine and took an estimated 400 people as slaves from the villages of M'Bouna and Toucabango. After the attacks on these villages, some of the raiders headed north to return home with their booty, but others remained in the areas and were attacked by French-led forces that included Kel Entsar and Barabish irregulars at the site of the present-day village of Tin Aicha on the north shore of Lake Faguibine. The French estimated that at least seventy-five raiders were killed in the attack, which also freed some of the people who had been enslaved. The survivors fled north but were not followed.[101] A decade later, colonial reports indicated that of the estimated 400 Songhay-speaking villagers captured and enslaved by this raid, only 5 had managed to return to their homes; four had returned from Mauritania and one from southern Algeria. Most of these enslaved people remained in southern Morocco, especially in the area of Wād Nūn.[102] When I visited M'Bouna in 2002, I was told that one of the last survivors of this raid, who had spent more than forty years as a slave, and then as a freed slave, in southern Morocco before managing to return home with the help of the Malian government in the 1960s, had only recently died.[103]

Saharan raids shaped the colonial approach to both Tuareg and Arab pastoralists in important ways. Once particular pastoralist groups were brought into a relationship with the colonial state, it was very much in French interests to keep their leaders happy so that they would contribute to the defense of the colony. A French report written to evaluate the causes of the 1923 raid led by Hammu b. Sidi al-Mukhtar came to the following conclusion: "Like Mauritania, the Hodh, and perhaps the Niger Territory, the Region of Timbuktu is inhabited by a population identical to that of North Africa. They have the same origin, the same customs, the same religion, the same mentality and more or less the same language." For this reason, "it makes sense for us to employ a special politics here that is different from that which is in place in entirely black colonies."[104] As we

[101] Mansour Ayoub, "Comte Rendu – Tournée effectuée dans la Région de Tombouctou du 16 février au 16 avril 1924," April 17, 1924 (ANM 1E-2336, Num. Sér. III).

[102] Letter from Commandant, Cercle de Goundam to the Gouverner, Soudan Français., March 25, 1935 (ACG); Cercle de Goundam, "Rapport Politique," 2 trimestre. July 9, 1931 (ANM FR 1E 18).

[103] Interview, Oumar Kasey, Alamir Baba, Mahamadou Sahibou, November 3, 2002, M'Bouna.

[104] Mansour Ayoub, "Comte Rendu – Tournée effectuée dans la Région de Tombouctou du 16 février au 16 avril 1924," April 17, 1924 (ANM 1E-2336, Num. Sér. III).

will see in Part Three, this translated into colonial policy that respected and enforced the existing political and social hierarchy within pastoralist societies. It also meant that the colonial state tended to favor politically important pastoralist groups in the conflicts they might have with others in the Niger Bend, notably with blacks.

CONCLUSION

Although smaller raids continued in the early 1930s, the last significant Saharan raid on the Niger Bend occurred in 1929. As the threat of outside raiders diminished in the 1930s, the French began to pay less attention to the desert and its inhabitants.[105] By the late 1930s, the colonial regime was actively disarming pastoralists in the Azawad.[106] This was part of a larger shift in colonial policy toward its Sahelian territories in general as it became clear that the early dreams of the economic potential of the region had been unrealistic and that the French preoccupation with potential pan-Islamic opposition had been greatly exaggerated.[107] The French had positioned military units in a number of posts in the Azawad to defend against raiders; they also encouraged the people who lived in the Azawad to maintain their presence there. One such place was the small hamlet of Bou Djébéha (200 km north of Timbuktu) subsidized by the French in order to ensure that the settlement remained populated. The chief of Bou Djébéha until his death in October 1936 was a man named Shaykh Zayni b. ʿAbd al-ʿAzīz al-Jubīhī, whom French officials in Timbuktu considered to be very influential among his Barabish neighbors.[108] Shaykh Zayni was a scholar who kept close relations with Kunta intellectuals such as Shaykh Bay. What interests me for the moment is not Shaykh Zayni's scholarship, but the fact that the colonial administration at Timbuktu had agreed to pay him a subsidy in foodstuffs to remain in his home.

105 The threat was still perceived to be real by local French officials in 1935. Gaston Mourgues, Commandant, Cercle de Goundam, "Desiderata exposés par Mohamed Ali à la conférence économique," No.9/C, March 23, 1935 (ACG).

106 Lieutenant-Colonel Bertrand, Commandant, Cercle de Tombouctou, "Rapport annuel 1938" (ANM FR 1E 42).

107 On these changes, see Conklin, *A Mission to Civilize*, 142–73; Finn Fuglestad, *A History of Niger, 1850–1960* (Cambridge: Cambridge University Press, 1983), 119–46; For the development of French ideas and policy regarding Islam, see Christopher Harrison, *France and Islam in West Africa, 1860–1960* (Cambridge: Cambridge University Press, 1988).

108 Lieutenant-Colonel de Perier, Commandant, Cercle de Tombouctou, "Rapport annuel 1936," January 21, 1937 (ANM FR 1E 42).

The French commander at Timbuktu visited Shaykh Zayni in Bou Djébéha in 1932 and he wrote a glowing report about this man who would have been in his late sixties at the time: "Shaykh Zayni is venerated like a saint. In all of the Azawad, his reputation for saintliness is considerable and this reputation extends even to the banks of the Niger, all the way to Hombori. His religious influence could be useful or harmful to us according to whether he is for us or against us." The commander then admitted that he was currently "firmly rallied to the French cause, because he has realized that we can be helpful to him." The strategic value of Shaykh Zayni was not only his religious influence, but his location: "He lives in Bou Djébéha with his family and his slaves (serviteurs), making a population of six men, nine women, and twenty children.... We can only hope that he will not leave this place." The commander thought that because Shaykh Zayni's ancestors were buried in the hamlet, he would remain there: "Shaykh Zayni told me that he would prefer to die of hunger in this place than leave the tombs of his grandfathers. In order to allow him to satisfy his desire, and as a consequence, turn his considerable religious influence to our advantage, it will be enough for us to provide his food supplies."[109] The governor of Soudan agreed to this proposal and set the annual subsidy for Shaykh Zayni at 560–600 francs, beginning in August 1932.[110] After receiving the first shipment of grain, Shaykh Zayni wrote a letter to the governor in Bamako thanking him: "The purpose of this letter is to inform you that your aid, your charity, and your authority (siyāsa) reached us for our use. We can therefore remain in this country after the savagery and difficulties that we have suffered. Our hearts shall not forget and we are reassured in our abodes."[111]

The value of Bou Djébéha to the French diminished as security improved in the Sahara. After Shaykh Zayni died in 1936, he was replaced as head of his small hamlet by a son named Sīdi Ibrāhīm. The death of Shaykh Zayni meant the end of the colonial subsidy to his people.[112] Sidi Ibrahim put the matter to the French commander at Timbuktu in a letter he wrote in 1937: "I am in a place where grain is rare and difficult to find. My

[109] Colonel Marmet, Commandant, Cercle de Tombouctou, "Rapport de Tournée effectuée du 1 au 20 Juin 1932 dans le Cercle de Tombouctou," 1932 (ANM FR 1E 74).

[110] Letter from the Gouverneur, Soudan Français, Koulouba, to the Commandant, Cercle de Tombouctou, No.A51; July 5, 1932 (ANM FR 1E 74).

[111] Letter from Zayni b. ʿAbd al-ʿAzīz al-Jubīhī to the Gouverneur, Soudan Français, no date [received February 1933] (ART B25).

[112] Subsidies for religious figures were ended in the year 1937. Telegram from the Gouverneur du Soudan Français to Cercle de Tombouctou, No.6975, November 28, 1936 (ART B25).

father lived here before me because of the great assistance of the state and the alms that he received from all sides." But times had changed: "As for me, I receive only a small amount of alms because the local people have stopped giving it. As for the state assistance in cereals which I am due, it has been many months and I have received nothing." If the colonial administration was unwilling to continue to subsidize the family, Sidi Ibrahim wrote, "I will be unable to support myself on my means alone. If you judge that my presence in this country is not very useful and necessary, then I ask your permission to leave and move to a country where I am able to live."[113] This neglect by the French government at Timbuktu suggests that the era of military logic in the organization of the colonial confines of the Sahara was coming to an end. Sidi Ibrahim's family did finally receive a reduced subsidy of 100 francs later that year,[114] but soon thereafter the family was forced to establish a residence in Timbuktu, and spent only part of the year in Bou Djébéha.[115]

I have traced the history of conflict and statecraft in the early colonial Niger Bend because it lay at the foundation of the racial state that French officials and Tuareg and Arab leaders constructed there. Assertions of a fundamental difference between Arabs and Tuareg, between warrior-status groups and clerics, and – although we have yet to discuss this in detail – between blacks and whites were the conceptual and political aperture used in building the colonial regime. The form that the colonial state took in the Niger Bend was the product of the struggles discussed in this chapter, and the threat posed by different pastoralist groups. We will turn in the following chapters to some of the concrete ways that race was made to work in this particular colonial configuration.

113 Letter from Sidi Ibrāhīm b. Shaykh Zayni b. ʿAbd al-ʿAzīz al-Jubīhī at Bou Djbéha to the French Commandant at Timbuktu, April 7, 1937 (ART M13).

114 Letter from Sidi Ibrahim b. Shaykh Zayni b. ʿAbd al-ʿAzīz al-Jubīhī at Bou Djbéha to the French Commandant at Timbuktu, November 14, 1937 (ART M13).

115 This is the situation that has been maintained ever since. When I visited Bou Djébéha in 2001, part of the family maintained a residence there and was restoring the family library of Arabic manuscripts, which have since been catalogued. See ʿAbd al-Qādir Mammā Haidara and Ayman Fuwād Sayyid, *al-Maktaba al-zayniyya, Būjbīha, Mālī* (London: al-Furqan, 2006).

PART THREE

THE MORALITY OF DESCENT, C. 1893–1940

PRELUDE

There were different components to the ideas about race brought to the Niger Bend by French officials working for the new colonial regime. Colonial writers were sometimes interested in physiognomic differences between the various people who lived in the region, and they generally took a dim view of the racial potential of the mass of the population, which they saw as racially degraded. However, the practical focus of French officials was on identifying those elements within different populations that were robust and noble, and therefore capable of ruling over others. Race was a way for colonial officials to judge the potential of the country and to find those who could best lead it. Over time, this would develop into a colonial idea of entire ethnic groups in racial terms.

The earliest ethnographic sketches of the Niger Bend produced in the first decade of colonial occupation juxtaposed blacks and whites, sedentary people and pastoralists. Ethnic labels were sometimes used but at least in the first few decades, there was no racial coherence to ethnic categories, because each group was composed of racially distinct social strata. In each of the main linguistically defined groupings of the Niger Bend – Tuareg, Arab, Songhay, Fulbe – French writers identified a racially superior noble class that ruled over degraded and inferior vassals and slaves. In this sense, the early French uses of race were similar to Sahelian notions based on lineage and social status, which marked social inferiority with the label of blackness.

The three chapters in Part Three of the book focus on the dialogues between the agents of the colonial state and various people in the Niger Bend vying for position in this new political configuration. A racialized social hierarchy stood at the center of these discussions, and it was accorded moral meanings by its advocates. In the chapters of Part Three, I discuss the most important arguments made in defense of social hierarchy by examining separately the discourses around the three principal status positions established under colonial rule: noble white pastoralists, black pastoralist slaves, and black sedentary farmers. Such a division does not provide a full accounting of all the social positions found in the colonial Niger Bend, but it does represent the three most meaningful categories that did the most social and political work. It was also around these categories that local and colonial arguments about the morality of descent were engaged.

Over time, French colonial officials placed more emphasis on ethnic categories, which became important tools of administrative control, often referred to as "la politique des races." This tended to produce more racially coherent ethnic categories over time. The noble Tuareg, Arabs, and Fulbe were rendered white or red; all of the Songhay plus the slaves of the Tuareg, Arabs, and Fulbe were made black. By the end of the Second World War, when a new politics of reformed colonialism and eventually decolonization arose, the polarization and simplification of racial categories into white/red versus black produced a racialization of local politics along these lines. This is the subject of Part Four. But these ethno-racial categories were not produced by colonial fiat, and they did not appear simply as the result of the instruments of colonial rule. Instead, they arose out of the arguments and accommodations of different people in the Niger Bend for position in the colonial hierarchy that French rule (re)produced.

Chapter 5 discusses a series of relationships between the colonial administration in the Niger Bend and important Tuareg chiefs over the question of social status and control over vassals. Because both French officials and local elites in the Niger Bend used the lens of race as a way of understanding social status, it is not surprising that a principal site of colonial dialogue invoking race would focus on issues of lineage and genealogy, as well as the relationship between social status and claims to authority over social inferiors. Yet despite the intentions of most French officials and many Tuareg leaders, colonial rule tended to undermine the bases for social hierarchy that colonial and noble writers found so natural. Authority was the product of particular noble genealogies and histories of previous rule. Arguments about authority differed according to warrior or clerical status, but in each case, genealogy was the essential factor that determined social position. The example of the Tengeregif chief Sobbo ag Fondogomo's career is used to illustrate these processes.

The chapter also examines a chiefdom dispute among a small clerical-status group called the Igillad.

In Chapter 6, the question of slavery and different positions of servility are examined. I argue that colonial administrators (and modern scholars) have overestimated the size of the precolonial slave population in the Niger Bend by conflating a variety of tributary and servile status positions into a single category of slaves. Colonial officials instrumentalized Sahelian arguments about black servility de jure, and created social pathways for those defined as slaves that produced a racially distinct stratum of servile people whom the French called bellah. The deployment of race as a tool of colonial rule over Arab and Tuareg societies was designed to allow masters to maintain slaves and other servile people in dependant relationships. The chapter then examines some of the ways in which slaveholders defended slavery. In particular, I focus on the issue of slavery in the Kunta scholar Shaykh Bay's large collection of legal opinions. Shaykh Bay used Islamic law to justify the morality of slavery and to reiterate the racial arguments discussed in Chapters 1 and 2 about the ultimate stain of unbelief – and hence junior status – that continues to adhere to former slaves.

Chapter 7 considers the question of the black sedentary farmers. These were people whose first language was one of several Songhay languages of the Niger Bend. I argue that the tributary structure of relations between the pastoralist Tuareg in particular and Songhay-speaking sedentary villages was dramatically changed by the colonial occupation. French rule freed the Songhay-speaking population from Tuareg domination, but it also tended to undermine the existing hierarchy within Songhay-speaking communities. Unlike in the case of the Tuareg and Arabs, the local colonial administration lost interest in the elite, racially distinct stratum of the Songhay society because it posed no threat to the colonial presence. One result of this was that the landholding systems that had supported Songhay elites were undermined by the colonial goal of increasing agricultural production. Control over land provoked conflict between pastoralists and sedentary farmers in the Niger valley, and within different Songhay communities themselves. Land was the central issue of Songhay politics throughout the colonial period, and it played itself out in a series of genealogical arguments about tenure rights. These conflicts lay behind the later arguments after the Second World War that sought to valorize the blackness of the Songhay as the autochthonous people of the Niger Bend.

5

Defending Hierarchy

Tuareg Arguments about Authority and Descent, c. 1893–1940

A RACE APART?

French officials in the Niger Bend understood the nobles in Tuareg and Arab society to be outsiders who were racially distinct from the "indigenous" black peoples of the Niger Bend. From the beginning of the colonial occupation, French writers sought racial explanations for social distinctions between nobles, vassals, and slaves. In the French productions of thumbnail histories and sociologies of the pastoralist peoples of the Niger Bend, the "nobles" were almost always described as "white," even when referring to groups such as the Kunta, who were otherwise considered to be quite dark-skinned because of their purported intermixing with their slaves.[1] We find the Arabs, or "Moors," described as "a more or less pure race." Furthermore, "the Moors have the feature of Mediterranean peoples: straight nose, thin lips, soft hair."[2] In the context of the Niger Bend, such racial description stood in (often unstated) contrast to the population defined as black.

Tuareg nobles were described in nearly the same way. It was argued that they had retained the purity of their blood, at least with respect to black, if not always Arab, admixtures. In 1923, a colonial study reported that among the Tuareg, "mulattos do not exist because the men do not recognize their bastards and the women pour such scorn on their slaves for having relations with them." The Tuareg possess "Mediterranean

[1] Paul Marty, *Etudes sur l Islam et les tribus du Soudan* (Paris: Ernest Leroux, 1920), 1:79, 142, 171.

[2] Cercle de Tombouctou, "Monographie du Cercle de Tombouctou," 1923, No. 13R (ANM ID-2103, Num. Sér. I).

features with a fine nose, thin lips, leather color, and soft hair."[3] In a book published by the colonial government about Soudan on the occasion of the colonial exposition organized in Paris in 1931,[4] Tuareg nobles are described as a race apart from their black neighbors: "Everyone who has observed the Tuareg will acknowledge their noble and majestic gait, how they hold themselves up high with great slenderness, and their long and gracious arms and legs." This book added to the catalogue of Mediterranean features by noting that the Tuareg nobles possess "thin joints and arched feet."[5]

Even though French writers did invoke physiognomic differences to mark race, they also relied on a less visible set of markers connected to what they thought of as racial character. Just as the Kabyles in nineteenth-century Algeria had been assigned a racial position closer to Europeans based on their purported attachment to the land and good treatment of women, the nobility among the Tuareg was defined in similar ways:

> One notices in the Tuareg an intelligence, pride and courage, a deep sense of hospitality, an enormous respect and real courtesy for their women. On the other hand, one must also reproach their love of pillage, greed, dishonesty and the tendency to forget their promises. If one made a summary of their good qualities and their defects, one would obtain a composite picture that would not differ very much from that offered of medieval European societies. The resemblance is even more pronounced if we consider the importance of the arts among the Berbers, who are devoted as we know to dance, music and poetry.[6]

Such descriptions comparing Tuareg nobles to medieval European knights were coupled with the idea that Tuareg society also had an equivalent of European serfs for those people who held the status of vassals. As one French official put it at the end of the nineteenth century, these vassals were "the vestiges of ancient Saharan tribes reduced, by their weakness, to become the tributaries of families or tribes less feeble."[7] The slaves, of course, were entirely recruited from subject populations defined as black.

French officials used the lens of race as a way of understanding social hierarchy in pastoralist Tuareg and Arab societies. A racially superior

[3] Ibid.

[4] Dana Hale, *Races on Display: French Representations of Colonized Peoples, 1886–1940* (Bloomington, IN: Indiana University Press, 2008), 103–4.

[5] Gouverneur-Général de l'Afrique Occidentale Française, *Le Soudan* (Paris: Société d'éditions géographiques, maritimes, et coloniales, 1931), 19.

[6] Ibid., 21–2.

[7] "Monographie du Cercle de Tombouctou" 1897 (ANM FA 1D 59–7).

noble class ruled over degraded and inferior vassals and slaves. In this sense, the early French uses of race were similar to Sahelian ideas based on lineage and social status, in which blackness was the marker of social inferiority. Race was not used as a synonym for ethnicity in the Niger Bend, at least not in the early decades of colonial rule. Racial difference was understood to cut across linguistically defined communities, even among the Songhay, whose noble stratum was initially accorded non-black status by French officials. It is not surprising, therefore, that a principal site of colonial dialogue invoking race focused on issues of lineage and genealogy, and the relationship between social status and claims to authority over social inferiors. Who had the right to rule was a racial question in the colonial Niger Bend.

I have already discussed some of the details of French policy toward the Tuareg and the Arabs, what they called their "politique nomade." Here, I will focus on the issue of who among the Tuareg had the authority to rule, and how the colonial state and important Tuareg leaders arrived at a *modus vivendi* based on colonial recognition and support for a particular kind of hierarchy in Tuareg society. Despite the intentions of most French officials and Tuareg leaders, colonial rule tended to undermine the bases for social hierarchy that colonial and noble writers found so natural. The slow establishment of a *pax gallica* over the Niger Bend made the kinds of protections offered by large confederacies less important. The abuses and corruption that flourished in the collection of taxes using an indirect system of colonial administration also undermined the legitimacy of the kinds of authority relied upon by the colonial state. As a result, Tuareg nobles found themselves in the position of having to defend their positions of authority over subordinates. To do this, they relied on arguments that were, in the intellectual context of the Niger Bend, racial in nature. Authority was the product of particular noble genealogies and histories of previous rule.

LA POLITIQUE NOMADE

Even after the initial conquest, French officials often suspected that the political arrangements they had forced on different Tuareg leaders were mere tactical maneuvers meant to win time until the moment when the colonial administration was most vulnerable and could be defeated. Firhun's rebellion in 1916 only confirmed what many had suspected, and indeed what the Kunta leader Hammadi had repeatedly told his French interlocutors. Again, in the run-up to the Second World War, French administrators in the Niger Bend sounded the alarm about potential Tuareg rebellion. In 1938, the commander at Goundam wrote that "we must consider the fact that we are in a Sahelian country, that we administer an evasive and difficult population.... We must know that in the event that the international situation drives us into conflict in Europe, we would not be surer of our populations in the [Saharan] confines than in 1914."[8]

Things looked very different from Tuareg perspectives. When Fihrun launched his rebellion against French rule in 1916, he certainly had many sympathizers among non-Iwellemmedan groups, but he received virtually no support from other areas of the Niger Bend. Part of the reason for this was that there were significant personal rivalries between different leaders and historical enmities among the various confederacies and subgroups. But the main explanation for why the leaders of all the major Tuareg groups in this area remained "loyal" to the colonial state and opposed to the rebels is found in the nature of the relationships that developed between the colonial state and Tuareg leaders. Above all, leaders of the warrior-led confederacies needed French support to defend their authority and position of privilege.

The initial impulse of French officials regarding the Tuareg was to destroy them. To take one example, the commander of the district of Timbuktu wrote in 1901 that "there is good reason at this moment to prepare for the complete destruction of the Tuareg. They produce nothing, and they are opposed to the work of the sedentary population." More than this, the Tuareg were an environmental menace: "The trees of the forests are mutilated by their axes and the rice paddies and flood lands are destroyed by their herds. The shores of the Niger that are so rich in agricultural land, and that are fertilized each year by the flood of the river, will remain unproductive as long as their right to pasturage remains in the region."[9] The pastoralists, according to this analysis, had impoverished the country and "rendered it sterile little by little."[10]

Despite such sentiments, French policy never intended to destroy the Tuareg. Once the initial conquest had been achieved, the colonial administration aimed at freeing the Songhay-speaking sedentary population of

[8] This quote is slightly paraphrased from Gaston Mourgues, Commandant, Cercle de Goundam, "Rapport sur les déclarations faites à l'Administrateur-adjoint Tanguy par Ousman ag Rhalala, marabout des Kel Antessar, contre le chef de tribu Mohamed Ali ag Attaher," No.54/C, November 17, 1938 (ACG).

[9] Cercle de Tombouctou, "Rapport politique," July 1901 (ANM FA 1E 78–81).

[10] Cercle de Tombouctou, "Rapport politique de l'année 1901" (ANM FA 1E 78–81).

FIGURE 1. "Arab" man, Timbuktu, 1940 (source: Horace Miner, *The Primitive City of Timbuctoo* [Princeton, NJ: Princeton University Press, 1953].)

the Niger valley from Tuareg domination and creating separate administrations for the sedentary agricultural and pastoralist populations. In this way, powerful Tuareg groups would be politically weakened and the development of the agricultural economy of the Niger valley could be unleashed. As the commander at Timbuktu explained, "the policy of the territory is to hold an equal balance between the sedentary population and the nomads. Shelter the sedentary villages from the exactions and depredations of the nomads, develop agriculture and livestock-raising under the aegis of tranquility, such is the goal of the commander of the district."[11]

Economic development was, however, only a secondary concern beside the larger political issue of managing the Tuareg. If colonial policy aimed at weakening the Tuareg to some extent, it did not intend to diminish them too much. As such, the colonial state authorized Tuareg groups to

[11] Ibid.

retain control over their vassal and servile populations and it attempted to manage the often-conflictual interests that farmers and pastoralists had over access to the Niger floodplain. For political reasons, the colonial state sought to manage a balance between pastoralists and sedentary people along the river.

The central tenet of colonial policy toward the Tuareg and Arabs was the concentration of political power in the hands of a few leaders who found the French presence acceptable to one extent or another. French policy identified and supported large confederations administered directly by traditional leaders themselves. Rather than attempt to weaken important chiefs by dividing up the different clans under their control, the French sought to increase their power by a system of indirect rule in which particular leaders were given colonial sanction to collect taxes, raise manpower for colonial military and labor needs, and implement various colonial policies that concerned the pastoralist population. Consequently, politics in the colonial period centered on a set of relationships between the colonial state and a handful of important pastoralist leaders.

One of the fears expressed early on by some French officials was that the noble warrior-status groups (imoshagh) among the Tuareg were relatively vulnerable to social change as a consequence of colonial occupation. For example, the commander of French forces in the Niger Bend in 1906 wrote that the warrior "off-loads everything onto his vassals and his slaves. Many among the nobles possess practically nothing themselves. The livestock are kept by the vassals ... who provide the warrior with all that he needs." According to this understanding of Tuareg society, power was based on the number of vassal clans that a warrior lineage controlled. Vassals (imghad) were free people in Tuareg societies, although they were not considered to be noble. Beneath the vassals were the "bellah," the term used by French officials to denote slaves (iklan): "The bellah, who are even more servile and carry out all the work in the camps ... are indispensible for the way of life of the warrior because, just like the women of this caste, [warriors] are unaccustomed to all manual labor." Among the biggest threats to the noble warrior-status groups, according to this colonial perspective, was the loss of their servile bellah-iklan: "We can imagine easily that the Tuareg will do everything possible to keep their bellah. Putting our ideas of equality into practice among them would ruin them completely."[12]

[12] Mazillier, Commandant, Région de Tombouctou, "Rapport sur l'attitude des Touaregs de l'Ouest et la nécessité d'une prochaine répression," No. 33C, October 25, 1906 (ANM FA 1E 78–81).

FIGURE 2. "Gaabibi" woman, Timbuktu, 1940 (source: Horace Miner, *The Primitive City of Timbuctoo* [Princeton, NJ: Princeton University Press, 1953].)

"Ideas of equality" were not high on the French agenda for the Niger Bend; instead, colonial policy aimed at bolstering warrior chiefs in return for their loyalty to the French cause. When Tuareg groups rebelled, as some Iwellemmedan did under Firhun's leadership in 1916, colonial officials in the Niger Bend often argued that such actions were the result of policies that had weakened the authority of hereditary chiefs too much. Instead, French officials made the case that "our administration among the Tuareg should consist of a large protectorate, which will rest on a traditional framework, with a single chief, who is alone responsible for dealings with us, and to whom we give an enormous authority in return for complete loyalty."[13]

Defending the authority of Tuareg chiefs was a shared objective of local French officials and Tuareg leaders themselves. The role of the

[13] This is from a French administrator named Bonamy in 1917, quoted by A.-M.-J. Richer, *Les Oulliminden. Les Touareg du Niger (Région de Tombouctou-Gao)* (Paris: E. Larose, 1924), 311.

chiefs in the collection of taxes on behalf of the colonial state served the interests of both sides. France won local political allies without having to invest in an elaborate administrative structure, and local leaders were able to use their position as a means of enrichment. Within pastoralist societies, however, there was a constant struggle between chiefs who sought to increase the number of people under their administrative control and smaller clans that sought their own independence. The colonial state played the role of arbiter in such disputes, most often siding with the important leaders, especially in the first decades of colonial occupation. In one such case in 1903, a French officer explained that "the Zimmaten tribe, who are vassals of the Tengeregif, as well as some Tormoz families, have shown a tendency to free themselves from their status as vassals." Such efforts by vassals might be justified in the eyes of some colonial officers, but larger strategic concerns made the recognition of vassal independence undesirable: "Later, when the present generation is gone, we could perhaps divide to infinity the Tuareg and Moorish clans without fear. Today, we must not broach this idea. In effect, there is a pressing need to politically and administratively group together under the authority of the most influential chiefs ... those tribes that, if isolated and left to themselves, would avoid us completely."[14]

Colonial rule did, however, usher in fundamental changes to the political structure of the Niger Bend. Gone were the underlying conditions of insecurity that had allowed warrior lineages to become the most powerful people in the Niger Bend before European conquest. To maintain a privileged position, Tuareg and Arab leaders needed European allies. Colonially sanctioned control over people was the primary means of preserving a dominant position with respect to pastoral resources. But even with the support of the colonial regime, French rule changed the underlying logic of social hierarchy. This was evident as the early as the 1920s with regard to control over rich pastures: "Before the conquest, the warriors reserved for themselves the best pastures and particularly those on the islands that the river leaves covered with burgu [a river grass]. The imghad and clerical tribes were relegated to the meager pastures of the wells of the interior." The advent of colonial control meant that "the imghad and clerics are getting richer. They aspire to take advantage of the good pastures with their former masters. But the warriors do not want to hear this talk, and they molest the imghad who venture onto the islands

[14] 1ère Territoire militaire, "Rapport politique," May 1903 (ANM FA 1E 78–81).

What does it mean to say that something is constructed?

FIGURE 3. "Tuareg in Timbuktu," 1940 (source: Horace Miner, The Primitive City of Timbuctoo [Princeton, NJ: Princeton University Press, 1953].)

and they kill their animals."[15] Violence was always a tactic in defending imoshagh power. As we will see, the colonial state was forced to invest significant effort to manage conflict over access to land between different pastoralist groups, and between pastoralists and sedentary farmers.

SOBBO AG FONDOGOMO AND IMOSHAGH ARGUMENTS

Among the most demanding and successful of all colonial-era Tuareg leaders was Sobbo ag Fondogomo, chief (Ta. amenokal) of the warrior-led Tengeregif confederacy based in the western half of the Niger Bend. Sobbo was made chief of the Tengeregif confederacy in April 1894, after his father, Muhammad ag Ayub (also known as Fondogomo), was killed by French forces at Dahouré on March 23, 1894. As the new chief of the Tengeregif, Sobbo made his official submission to French forces at Timbuktu on September 6, 1894, and two years later, a treaty was signed by the French governor of Soudan recognizing Sobbo's position

[15] Lieutenant Devouton, Chef de Subdivison nomades, Cercle de Tombouctou, "Tournée de recensement effectuée du 13 Avril au 3 Mai 1924 dans la tribu Touareg des Imidedrens," May 30, 1924 (ANM FR 1E-42).

as supreme ruler of the Tengeregif confederacy.[16] For the next fifty years until his death on November 13, 1946, he dominated local politics in the western half of the Niger Bend unlike any other person.

The Tengeregif were the most important warrior-led group in the western half of the Niger Bend. They had been an independent power since breaking away from the Tadmakkat confederacy in 1813,[17] and had played an important role in the shifting military and political alliances and conflicts that marked the region in the nineteenth century.[18] They had famously opposed the Fulbe forces led by Amadu Lobbo in the second quarter of the nineteenth century in battles at Toya and Sareyamou. At the time of the colonial conquest, they claimed sovereignty over the western half of the Niger Bend, including Timbuktu. When Sobbo was invested as the new chief of the Tengeregif in 1894, he was a young man in his twenties. His authority derived from his late father's military legacy and his own bravery in battle against Bonnier's forces at Takoumbao, where he sustained a shoulder wound. Upon assuming the leadership of the Tengeregif, Sobbo quickly sued for peace and was permitted, as I mentioned previously, to retain control over Tengeregif vassal groups. Sobbo was a popular figure among the other Tuareg groups of the Gourma, and despite his protestations of loyalty to the French, he was often suspected by the administration of preparing anticolonial rebellion. At one time or another, he was accused of hosting anticolonial fugitives and rabble-rousing clerics whom the French feared were preaching jihad against them. In 1916, as Firhun's rebellion unfolded, Sobbo was suspected of trying to reunite the former Tadmakkat Tuareg confederacy in order to launch a similar revolt among the warrior-status groups in the Gourma.[19] The French commander in the district of Goundam thought that a wider rebellion by warrior-status groups had been avoided only because the clerical-status Kel Entsar had

[16] These details can be found in Colonel Mangeot and Paul Marty, "Les Touaregs de la Boucle du Niger," *BCEHS-AOF* 2–3 (1918): 87–136, 257–88, 432–71.

[17] There are two main genealogical "branches" of Tuareg imoshagh in the Niger Bend, the Iwellemmedan and the Tadmakkat. Those considered to be part of the Tadmakkat are the Tengeregif, Kel Temulayt, Irraganaten, and Igawaddaran. The Kel Entsar trace their origin to Arab groups and consider themselves to be Igillād (Iguellad). They claim to be the descendants of the Anṣār, the "Companions" of the Prophet Muhammad in Madina. Having migrated to Morocco over several centuries, they claim that their ancestor moved south and took up residence with local Tuareg groups, married Tuareg women, and consequently, their descendants in the Azawad and Niger Bend speak Tamashek and have adopted much of the Tuareg culture of their cousins.

[18] The other major players were the Hamdullahi Caliphate based in the Masina, the Tukulor of al-Hajj ʿUmar Tal, and the Kunta.

[19] Cercle de Goundam, "Rapport politique de l'année 1916" (ANM FA 1E-40).

advised against war with the French: "As we know, it is an old custom among the warriors, who always want to make war, that the chief should go and consult the principal clerics of the religious tribes on the issue of the conflict which they are preparing for."[20]

But French officials also valued the authority that they thought Sobbo exercised among a variety of Tuareg groups in the Niger Bend. In 1901, for example, the commander at Timbuktu wrote that Sobbo "in particular is intriguing. He is intelligent and ambitious, and has an authority which extends well beyond the limits of his little Tuareg group of Tengeregif which he commands."[21] The main form of political agitation that Sobbo undertook over his long career was not, however, the stoking of anticolonial rebellion, but the defense of the status of the Tengeregif as a ruling confederacy that would retain control over as many people as possible.

The Tuareg and Arab confederacies of the colonial Niger Bend consisted of numerous subgroups of different social status, each of which had its own chief, what the French called a "chef de fraction." These "fractions," which I will call clans, were distinguished vertically according to social status. The social status of a clan was determined according to lineage. So for example, a confederacy was typically made up of dozens of clans that included some combination of warrior-status lineages (Ta. imoshagh), clerical-status lineages (Ta. ineslemen), vassal-status lineages (Ta. imghad), and servile groups. But whatever the social status of the free people in a particular clan, it almost always also included servile people who were considered to be outside of the lineal markers of descent that marked the clan as a whole. Servile groups were either organized as separate clans of pastoralists, or as dependants of free people, or as agricultural settlements called "dagas."

Usually, the chief of the entire confederacy – an office called the amenokal in Tamashek – also ruled over a clan that bore the name of the whole confederacy. So for example, in 1917, the Tengeregif confederacy ruled over by Sobbo included fourteen warrior-status clans, the largest of which was also ruled by Sobbo and bore the name of the larger confederacy. The confederacy also included two vassal-status clans (imghad). The total population of the Tengeregif confederacy was 7,267 people, of which 1,799 were free and 5,568 were slaves.[22] The confederacies of Arab and Tuareg pastoralists in the Niger Bend included different configurations of

[20] Ibid.

[21] Ecorsse, Commandant, 1ère Territoire militaire, "Rapport annuel pour l'année 1900" (ANM FA 1E 78–81).

[22] Mangeot and Marty, "Touaregs."

clans according to status and as percentages of free or slave members in the larger group. It was also not uncommon for Arabophone lineages to be attached to Tuareg confederacies, and vice versa.

In their efforts to make sense of the very complicated pastoralist milieu, the French administration spent much time collecting and drawing up genealogical tables that they thought lay at the foundation of authority in these societies. Above all, the French distinguished between confederacies that were led by warriors and those led by clerics. According to this criterion, the major confederacies in the Niger Bend were as follows:

Warrior-led confederacies:

Barabish (Arab)
Iwellemmedan (Tuareg)
Tengeregif (Tuareg)
Igawaddaran (Tuareg)
Kel Temulayt (Tuareg)
Irraganatan (Tuareg)

Clerical-led confederacies:

Kunta (Arab)
Kel Entsar (Tamashek-speaking, claim Arab descent)

There were also many other, smaller groups of less political importance to French officials, but they appeared to be much less threatening to the colonial position. Writing about these smaller independent groups in 1906, a French official claimed that "the fear of being made vassals under the authority of the more powerful chiefs keeps them apart in a much fuller submission to our orders."[23]

Sobbo was an enigma for French officials and a constant subject of internal complaints and debate in the administrative reports of the Niger Bend. As early as 1895, colonial officers were complaining that Sobbo disobeyed their orders, refused to come and see them when he was summoned, and thought he was indispensible to French rule.[24] Two decades later, with French rule well established, Sobbo appeared as almost an anachronism to some colonial writers. For example, in 1924, an inspection of the administration of the Niger Bend reported that Sobbo "is the

[23] Mazillier, Commandant, Région de Tombouctou, "Rapport sur l'attitude des Touaregs de l'Ouest et la nécessité d'une prochaine répression," No. 33C, October 25, 1906 (ANM FA 1E 78–81).

[24] Commandant, Région de Tombouctou, "Rapport politique du novembre et décembre 1895" (ANM FA 1E-78–81).

perfect representative of his race. Authoritarian, brutal, not subtle, he often invokes the advantage of his birth in his favor." Yet despite his bearing, "he is an energetic figure for a native chief. The administration evidently finds in him an uncommon auxiliary in this lord who remembers well the sovereignty that he used to exercise over this region with the help of the Iwellemmedan, his racial brothers."[25] Two years later, in 1926, the frustrated commander of the district of Goundam wrote that Sobbo "is a chief of little intelligence, and all of his prestige comes from us rather than his subjects. This is our doing. A military event that, because of a failure of precautions, turned out terribly for our troops, has given him a value for our administration as a result of what was really a massacre and not a battle." The reference to the battle at Takoumbao recurs again and again in colonial writing: "From this inexplicable consideration, [Sobbo] has used and abused us.... He has simply exploited our good will. He has always demanded and he has always received. In exchange, he always promises and always procrastinates. The least services, he only carries out after being badgered, and is continually late."[26]

As someone who would hold his position for more than fifty years, Sobbo saw many colonial administrators come and go, even though there were some French officials who stayed in the Niger Bend for more than twenty years. Sobbo insisted on being treated as at least an equal of his French interlocutors. He insisted that the French accord him the respect that someone of his standing merited. On one occasion, he refused to come and see the French commander at Goundam because he considered the honor guard sent to meet him at the outskirts of the town to be insufficient for a man of his status. A measure of his importance can perhaps be gleaned from the fact that the French official apologized and sent out a larger honor guard that made a multiple-gun salute on his next visit to Goundam. Such honors were part of the treaty between Sobbo and the French administration from the earliest days.[27] In his later correspondence with the French commanders at Goundam, the administrative area under whose authority the Tengeregif fell, he would sometimes begin his letters with "you are my sons and my chiefs,"[28] to emphasize

[25] Mansour Ayoub, "Comte Rendu – Tournée effectuée dans la Région de Tombouctou du 16 février au 16 avril 1924," April 17, 1924 (ANM 1E-2336, Num. Sér. III).

[26] Letter from the Commandant, Cercle de Goundam to the Commandant, Région de Tombouctou, July 30, 1926 (ACG).

[27] Soudan Français, "Décision," March 1, 1896 (ANM FA A9).

[28] Letter from Sobbo ag Fondogomo to the Commandant, Cercle de Goundam, July 5, 1939 (ACG).

the authority that his age and position entitled him to, and the relative youth and inexperience of many colonial officials. One thing was never in doubt: Sobbo demanded, and received, respect.

THE LIMITS OF IMOSHAGH POLITICS

The politics of the chiefs of the large pastoralist confederacies was based on maintaining the social hierarchy in the face of the new context of colonial rule, and the competition with other groups to maintain control of as many subordinate clans as possible. The logic of social status started to weaken over time as the colonial state became well established. Even though the French administration continued to work through the structure of the pastoralist confederacies, it became less concerned with supporting specifically warrior claims to continue to control recalcitrant subordinates under their authority. For example, in 1920, two imoshagh clans called the Ihimid and the Arka were transferred from the administrative control of the Tengeregif to the clerical-led Kel Entsar.[29] This outraged Sobbo who claimed authority over all warrior lineages in the western Niger Bend, as well as sovereignty more generally over the area and all of the Tuareg population including the Kel Entsar.

Part of the reason that the moral authority of chiefs was undermined was their own abuse of their position. Complaints about abuse of authority against chiefs such as Sobbo were very common. For example, the chief of the Inataben, a warrior clan that had been assigned to the Tengeregif confederacy in 1920, made a number of complaints to the local French administration about Sobbo's extortion, theft, and overtaxation. In one letter written to the colonial authorities in 1935, the clan chief Muhammad ag Jaddu claimed that, "the chief of our tribe [Sobbo] has always wanted to do bad things to us and seize our property every time he has had the chance. Therefore, in 1933, he made us pay a sum of 12,452F30." Muhammad ag Jaddu listed a number of instances of Sobbo's bad behavior as evidence of Inataben suffering: "Just recently during the census of the Tinalfarayamane, [Sobbo] took five cows from us without giving us anything in return. He also took a nice camel named Gaga for the price of 150 sheep and five head of cattle that he refuses to pay until today."[30] The

[29] The formerly Kel Entsar lineages Idnan and Inataban were joined to the Tengeregif; the formerly Tengeregif clans Arka, Taraoma, Ihimid, Abarshashod were joined to the Kel Entsar. Région de Tombouctou, "Convention," December 23, 1920 (ACG).

[30] Letter from Muhammad ag Jaddu, Chef de fraction des Inataben, to the Commandant, Cercle de Goundam, November 3, 1935 (ACG).

specificity of the accounting of misdeeds is fairly common in complaints lodged by nobles in different pastoralist confederacies. In part, this was because the noble social status of letter writers such as Muhammad ag Jaddu gave them the right to address the colonial administration.

There are far fewer letters written by people of lower social status in the first four decades of colonial rule. Local French officials often thought that the burden of taxation and labor was borne mostly by lower-status people in these confederacies. The long-serving administrator Gaston Mourgues, for example, wrote in 1933 about Sobbo's efforts to administer lower-status clans: "[Sobbo] always complains about these clans that are better able to escape from him. He reproaches them for their bad will like all the other non-noble clans." Mourgues thought that Sobbo made, "the vassal clans (imghad, clerics, bellah) support the largest part of the responsibility of the tribe, which is mainly in the form of the zakat tax."[31] For whatever reason, there were few lower-status people in the Tengeregif who made complaints against Sobbo, or whose complaints were recorded and saved.

It is not difficult to understand Sobbo's broad political strategies using the colonial records left behind by the French administration in the Niger Bend. His abiding goals were to maximize the number of people over whom he ruled, and to maintain existing social hierarchy within his confederacy and more broadly in the Niger Bend as a whole. He was not shy about these goals. In 1925, he announced to a meeting of notables organized by the local colonial administration in Goundam that slavery should be reinstituted and that more severe penalties should be put in place to regulate the relationship between slaves and masters.[32] According to the colonial officials with whom he dealt, he repeatedly demanded the return of clans that had been joined to other confederacies, and he was, to translate the French expression directly, "impervious to the progress of civilization."[33] But if the broad strokes of a proud, imperious, and conservative man can be drawn from the colonial record, penetrating Sobbo's perspective in more nuance is not as easy as it is for some other figures discussed in this book. Although he wrote letters in Arabic to the French administration, his sophistication in this language was limited. I

[31] Extract of telegram-letter from Gaston Mourgues, Commandant, Cercle de Goundam, November 12, 1933. "Dossier Chebboun" (ACG).

[32] Cercle de Goundam, "Compte Rendu du Conseil des Notables du 10 avril 1925" (ANM FR 2E-82).

[33] "Ce nomade est nettement réfractaire à toute civilisation." Cercle de Goundam, "Rapport politique, 3ème trimestre 1921," September 30, 1921 (ANM FR 1E 18).

have read dozens of his Arabic letters but most of them are little more than quick notes offering excuses for not having come to meet a colonial administrator, explaining delays in paying his taxes, or simply communicating some other matter very rapidly.[34] The same characterization applies to much of the correspondence that is only available in the French translations of his letters made by the local colonial administration in the district of Goundam. There is one exception to this. In 1924, Sobbo sent a long letter to the governor of Soudan that was written in French. Although Sobbo did not speak or write French, and there is no indication of who translated and wrote the letter, it does provide a better indication of how he represented himself politically than any other source.

The letter seeks the governor's intervention in a number of local issues, most of which are the result of rivalries between the Tengeregif and Kel Entsar confederacies over the control of vassals. The chief of the Kel Entsar in 1924 was a man named Attaher, who ruled over this confederacy between 1914 and 1926.[35] The first thing that is obvious in the letter is the distinction Sobbo makes between warrior and clerical lineages, explaining to the governor the superiority that warriors like himself have exercised over clerics such as his rivals, the Kel Entsar. He begins his letter by making clear his claim to authority over the Kel Entsar, led by Attaher:

> For a long time I have been the chief of all the Tuareg living in the Haoussa [left bank of the Niger]. I inherited the kingdom from my father and I found that the father of Attaher was a close friend of my father. As such, I treated Attaher in the same way. He followed me like a simple cleric. On the basis of this friendship, and because of me, I put forward the name of this friend to the French authorities to be the chief of the Kel Entsar, who are clerics. He was named chief by the administrator Mr. de Loppinot and this put all of the Tuareg under my rule. I always considered Attaher to be an honest man and not a traitor or a shirker. Some time later, I saw my former friend respond by making trouble between the French, the Tuareg, the natives (indigènes), and me. All of a sudden, trouble was created in the tribes (tribus).[36]

The rhetoric that Sobbo uses here indicates the extent to which his claims to authority are based on lineal arguments and on differences in status between warriors and clerics. This is the other side of the argument made

[34] Most of Sobbo's original Arabic correspondence that I was able to find was in the "archives" of the Région de Tombouctou (ART B24, M13).

[35] Al-Tahir ag al-Mahdi ag Muhammad ag Habda, b. c. 1868, died March 25, 1926.

[36] Letter from Sobbo ag Fondogomo to the Commandant, Cercle de Goundam, August 13, 1924 (ACG).

by clerical-status scholars about the mustaghraq al-dhimma.[37] For Sobbo, no clerical lineage could legitimately claim to be on the same level of political authority as a warrior-led group like the Tengeregif.

Sobbo had many complaints to make in his letter. However, the most pressing issue was the loss of vassals to the Kel Entsar. Sobbo referred to a meeting that occurred at Goundam on December 19, 1920, at which the Tengeregif lost four clans to the Kel Entsar while gaining two new ones for themselves. In his letter, Sobbo described how the dishonest maneuvers of his Kel Entsar rival Attaher led to colonial misunderstanding and to the Tengeregif loss of subjects:

> The commander asked me about what I wanted. I responded to him by saying that I wanted him to make all of the Tuareg come [to Goundam] so that they could be divided up [between us] because I see now that there exists between me and Attaher a real rivalry. In this way, if my brother Mohamed Hamed prefers Attaher, you can count him in the tolls of the latter, and if on the other hand, the brother of Attaher prefers me, he will be given to me. So the administrator made all the Tuareg come to Goundam without exception. The Tuareg were so happy to know that their chief had such a numerous following that two young men amused themselves by beating their war drums. All of a sudden Attaher left to go and see the commander and tell him that the Tuareg of Sobbo were rebelling.... When he divided up the Tuareg, [the French commander] gave me two tribes and Attaher four. This is what made me unhappy. I said to him that he should give me the same number of men as were taken from me by Attaher because my men are richer in livestock and can pay more zakat [tax].[38]

The French administration was so alarmed by the beating of the war drums that they sent a military detachment from Timbuktu to Goundam to restore order and disarm sixty of Sobbo's warriors.[39] This fiasco and the fact that the colonial administration had been manipulated by Attaher to intervene on behalf of the Kel Entsar did not go completely unnoticed by local French administrators. Sobbo's supporters in the colonial administration recognized how skillfully Attaher had played both the French and Sobbo. The commander at Timbuktu, Colonel Mangeot, reported in 1922 that between Sobbo and Attaher, "there is a hatred which will only disappear with their death. [Sobbo] has always been seen in a very bad

[37] For an account of similar warrior-status views, see Xavier Coppolani, *Rapport d'ensemble sur ma mission au Soudan Français (1ère partie: chez les Maures)* (Paris, 1899), 14–16.

[38] Letter from Sobbo ag Fondogomo to the Commandant, Cercle de Goundam, August 13, 1924 (ACG).

[39] This occurred on December 19, 1920, at the main office of the Cercle de Goundam. Le Lieutenant-Colonel Mangeot, Commandant, Région de Tombouctou, "Rapport annuel de l'année 1920," No.451/C, March 11, 1921 (ANM FR 1E-42).

light by the commanders of the district of Goundam, and treated with a mistrust that has been little disguised."[40] The result was that Sobbo continued to lose vassals to the Kel Entsar.

In his letter, Sobbo presents himself as a victim of the tricks and corrupt practices undertaken by Attaher against those he administered: "Last year, Attaher brought together the Kel Timbarak, Kel Daoukoré and the Dagakama in order to take 100 head of cattle from them on the pretext that the commander of the district had asked for it on behalf of the market of Timbuktu. Afterwards, he sent them to the Gold Coast with his Arab friend Mahmud Dahman ag Sidaa."[41] Such dishonesty was, according to Sobbo, a pattern of deceit: "He does the same thing every year.... The owners of the animals never complain because they think that it is true that the commander demanded it from them." According to Sobbo, Attaher behaved in a similarly corrupt way in regards the agricultural fields worked by the slaves of the Tuareg: "In the fields which you have distributed in your goodness among the Kel Entsar, Attaher takes them all and they are cultivated exclusively on his behalf."[42]

Finally, Sobbo made reference to his status as a warrior and that fact that it is only the French presence that permits non-warriors like Attaher and the Kel Entsar to attain an important position:

> [Attaher] also wants me to leave the country so that he could be the supreme chief. I will never do that. This is why I went to Bamako to inform myself of these things. I see also that the French only look after our interests and do not exploit us. You know Mr. Administrator that if it were not for the French, Attaher would not bother me as he does, because I would have swept him away a long time ago. This is the only objective of my letter. I believe with this, I have made myself very clear.[43]

The final appeal is made as a warrior. Unfortunately for Sobbo, the importance of warriors to the French administration decreased as the threat of Tuareg rebellion diminished over time. This undermined the value of the imoshagh politics that Sobbo played so skillfully. By the 1930s, warrior-led groups like the Tengeregif seemed an impediment to all progress in the colony, and many colonial administrators found themselves working much more closely with clerical-led groups that seemed more amenable

[40] Le Lieutenant-Colonel Mangeot, Commandant, Région de Tombouctou, "Rapport annuel de l'année 1921," No.584/C, February 18, 1922 (ANM FR 1E-42).

[41] This is Mahmud ould Dahman of the Barabish, discussed in Chapter 4.

[42] Letter from Sobbo ag Fondogomo to the Commandant, Cercle de Goundam, August 13, 1924 (ACG).

[43] Ibid.

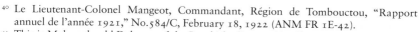

to the development, limited though it was, that the French wanted to bring to the Niger Bend.

The letter is a rare written example of what must have been a rhetorical strategy most often deployed orally and in person to French officials. His complaints consistently annoyed his French interlocutors. The commander of Timbuktu wrote after one meeting with him in 1927, "[Sobbo] came to see me in Timbuktu just after my arrival and, as is his habit, began right away with his recriminations and demands. There is nothing to hope from him; he is too old to change his way of being and the manner in which he does things." Sobbo's manner, his "arrogance, his pretentions and his demands," were to be attributed to "the defaults of the old imoshagh, defaults which tend to be exacerbated with age."[44] In 1928, Sobbo asked for permission to make the pilgrimage to Mecca and Madina, but authorization was denied.[45] For French officials, religious piety was not the province of warriors.

Toward the end of his life, Sobbo came to see some of the advantages in appearing to embrace certain French development priorities. In 1931, he asked that his son Addarib,[46] whom he had designated as his successor, be allowed to attend the French colonial exposition in Paris.[47] Local administrators in Goundam noticed the favorable impression that this trip had made on Addarib, just as it had affected Attaher's son and successor Muhammad ʿAli ag Attaher who went with him.[48] Sobbo finally died in 1946. More than anyone else, over the course of the more than

44 Telegram-letter from Carbou, Commandant, Cercle de Tombouctou to the Gouverneur, Soudan Français, 15 April 1927 (ACG).

45 Jousset, Commandant, Cercle de Goundam, "Rapport politique, 1ère trimestre 1928," March 31, 1928 (ANM FR 1E 18).

46 Addarib ag Sobbo was born in 1899. He was appointed co-administrator of the Tengeregif with his father Sobbo in 1939. On the night of July 27, 1943, he fell into his burning tent after a lightning strike caused a fire. He was left badly burned. He was moved to Goundam where he was treated by colonial medical staff, but he died of an infection on August 24, 1943 (Telegram-letter from the Commandant, Cercle de Goundam, to the Gouverneur, Soudan Français, No.38/C, October 9, 1943 [ACG]). The next co-administrator and successor was appointed in September 1943. He was a nephew of Sobbo named Muhammed Ahmad ag Salsabil. He died of pulmonary congestion on January 15, 1946 (Telegram-letter, Cercle de Goundam to the Gouverneur, Soudan Français, No.5/C, January 21, 1946 [ACG]). After him, Sobbo's son Alkissas was named successor. He was born in 1925. He became the amenokal of the Tengeregif after his father's death on November 13, 1946. He died May 12, 1951.

47 Cercle de Goundam, "Rapport politique, 4ème trimestre 1930," January 17, 1931 (ANM FR 1E 18).

48 Gaston Mourgues, Commandant, Cercle de Goundam, "Rapport politique, 4ème trimestre 1933," January 18, 1934 (ANM FR 1E 18).

fifty years that he spent as chief of the Tengeregif, his career shows the arc of possibilities and ultimate limits of imoshagh politics and dialogue with the colonial regime. As successful as Sobbo was, his stance was defensive, seeking to safeguard power and privilege that accrued to him because of his status as an important warrior chief. The power of the imoshagh had already ebbed away late in his life.

CLERICAL ARGUMENTS: THE IGILLAD

The details of Sobbo ag Fondogomo's political career are mostly accessible through the records left from his long-standing dialogue with colonial officials. The political history of the Niger Bend that can be traced from these sources is extremely important because the decisions and policies that resulted from this relationship shaped the lives of almost every person who lived under this colonial regime. It is, however, not an accurate accounting of the breadth of opinion in the Niger Bend, the range of representations of the relationship between French officials and Tuareg leaders, or the relationship between different Tuareg groups themselves. To access some of these ways of seeing that are less visible in the colonial record, I will discuss an obscure struggle between local French officials and a small Tuareg clerical group in another part of the Niger Bend, around the town of Bamba to the east of Timbuktu. Here, an almost completely inconsequential series of events in the mid-1930s, which left very little trace in the colonial archives, was recorded by an unknown author writing in Arabic. His text gives us access to a different set of ideas and arguments about authority among Tuareg nobles.

The text is entitled "The proper lineage of the emirate of the Igillād" ("Maktūb fī sha'n aṣl imārat Igillād li-Kal-Insīd al-daib kānū qātinīn bi-arḍ Bamba").[49] No date is given for the composition of the work, nor are the years given for the events discussed in the text. These I have been able to fill in using colonial sources. The document concerns the issue of authority in a small group of four clans who identified themselves as "Igillād," a name connecting them to other Igillad (or Iguellad) groups of the Niger Bend, the largest of which are the Kel Entsar, Kel Haoussa, and Cheurfig. These groups claim an Arab origin, but they underwent a historical process of Berberization and now speak Tamashek as their first language. The French sometimes called this group the "Iguellad de

[49] No author, "Maktūb fī sha'n aṣl imārat Igillād li-Kal-Insīd al-daib kānū qātinīn bi-arḍ Bamba" (IHERIAB ms. 1503).

Sahamar," after the Niger River village around which they claimed pasture rights.[50] They were divided into four lineage segments, each of which held clerical status:[51] the Kel Insīd, Ifaqqar, Kel Inalshinan, and Kel Tabhū. A colonial census in 1937 counted 1,850 people in these four groups; by 1942, the number had dropped to 1,572.[52] As such, it was neither a large nor politically important Tuareg group as far as the colonial administration was concerned. Discussing an encounter with the chief of the Ifaqqar clan in 1899, a colonial official wrote: "[T]hey are pastoralist clerics who are gentle and inoffensive, extending their peaceful honor to the extent that they are pillaged by all their neighbors, including the blacks of the villages, against which they ask to be protected."[53]

The principal drama in "The proper lineage" derives from the French appointment of a person from the Kel Tabhu as chief of the entire confederacy, rather than a person from the Kel Insid, the lineage that had held the office of chief until that point. I was able to find only the briefest reference to this event in the colonial archives. The official gazette of Soudan reported that "by the decision of the Lieutenant-Governor, on the date of April 14, 1934, the named Diambou ag Oumar is appointed chief of the Iguillads tribe (subdivision of Bourem, district of Timbuktu) as replacement for the named Oyé ag Mohamed, deceased."[54] The reasons behind this decision and the drama that they provoked are barely even hinted at in the extant colonial records. "The proper lineage," on the other hand, describes the corrupt way that this decision was made, and the steps taken by the French administrator responsible for the error to cover his mistake in order to save face. It also describes in great detail the political strategies employed by the aggrieved parties to reclaim their rightful position.

According to "The proper lineage," the first principle of exercising political authority is genealogical. The text begins with an argument

[50] Mengeot and Marty, "Touareg," 456.

[51] I have been unable to ascertain the degree of genealogical relationship between the Igillad of our text and other, better-known Igillad groups. On the history of the larger Igillad groups, see Marty, *Etudes*, 1:251–327.

[52] The colonial administrator who carried out the census thought that the reason for the decline in population had to do with low fertility among white Tuareg women because of widespread obesity and a pattern of late marriage among white Tuareg men. Jean-Jacques Villandre, Chef de Subdivision de Bourem, Cercle de Gao, "Rapport de Tournée du 17 mai au 1 juin 1942" (ANM FR IE 11).

[53] Poste de Bamba, Cercle de Tombouctou, "Rapport politique avril 1899" (AMN FA 1E 21–22).

[54] "Décision 846," *JOSF* no. 669 (April 15, 1934): 238. He is called Uwy b. Aḥmad in the Arabic text.

connecting the Igillad to the most important political bodies in the area: "Let he who comes across this document know that the original lineage (aṣl) of the chiefdom of the Igillad belongs to the Kel Insid. The chiefs of the Kel Insid are the ancestors of Uwy b. Aḥmad b. ʿAbd al-Raḥmān b. Intasubbit b. Ukā b. Iknan b. Muḥammad b. Uḥām b. Aḥmad b. al-Ṣādiq." After the explicit link is made between the right to rule and the genealogy of the deceased chief Uwy (who is called Oyé ag Mohamed in the official colonial record), the text connects the Igillad to the post-Songhay Empire state of the Arma, and to the most important warrior confederacies that dominated the eastern part of the Niger Bend: "This [genealogy] is well known by all the people of the important polities including the Arma who are the ancestors of Dūdū b. ʿAbd al-Raḥmān when they first settled in this country.[55] Then, after them, the Tadmakkat, the ancestors of Tūkha,[56] the Igawaddaran, the ancestors of al-Sakhāwī, and, after them, the Ifrans." The connection is made to all of these known historical authorities in the eastern Niger Bend because it allows the text to situate the chiefly lineage of Uwy as the recognized Igillad counterpart to this exercise of power: "Whenever the people of each one of these polities received the assurance of safe conduct (aman) from the Igillad, they obtained it from one of the afore-mentioned ancestors of Uwy. This is well known and attested to by everyone who knows about their life histories."[57] The reader is made to understand from the first sentence that there was a disagreement about which lineage among the Igillad had the right to rule over the larger, four-clan group. The argument made on behalf of the rights of the Kel Insid is historical and genealogical.

In the text, relations with the French are legitimized by claims of historical prominence. The historical encounters with French forces at the end of the nineteenth century were important elements in many local histories written in Arabic in the Niger Bend, precisely because the response to these events served to justify subsequent claims to authority. One of the most important tropes in this kind of literature is the initial act of resistance. The text claims that the Igillad were among those who had initially resisted the French invasion: "Then the French state came, which abrogated all of the existing polities but has not replaced them with any polity until today. When they seized the village which is called Bamba, the people fired upon them and then fled. Among all of those who fled was

[55] He was a Songhay-speaking "chef de canton" of Bamba, and of Arma descent. Cercle de Bamba, "Enquête sur l'Islam," 1923 (ANM FR 1D 34–2).

[56] Toha ag Ifesten, chief of the warrior-status Kel Temulayt

[57] "Asl imara," f. 1.

the tribe which is called the Igillad." They sought refuge "in the desert and at wells, and they took an oath to struggle for their faith and to never pledge allegiance to the Christians. Some of them decided to depart for the two holy cities of Mecca and Madina; others left for the region of the Ahaggar, from whom they took the guarantee of safe passage because they sought refuge from the activity of Hammadi."[58] The disorder created by colonial conquest and the invocation here of the memory of Hammadi al-Kunti's raids and actions ring true.

The practical motives ascribed to Uwy, the Igillad chief at this time, are similar to those attributed to Mahmud ould Dahman and the initial Barabish encounter with the French. Uwy put the interests of his subjects ahead of any emotional or religious imperative to fight because he understood that resistance would be futile: "When Uwy saw that the Igillad had decided to disperse, he – like his ancestors before him – felt terrible about the division of his people. They hate division because everything that results from it is harmful to the general good, even if only a little bit. But because they were the chiefs and rulers of the Igillad, they forgave their subjects just as fathers forgive their sons." Just as Mahmud ould Dahman had done, Uwy "went by himself to the Christians at Bamba. He went willingly and with no rancor because in his opinion, the Christian state was clearly superior and more powerful than all the other local polities. For this reason, he went and took the assurance of safe passage from Colonel Klobb." Klobb entered into a set of individual commitments with the Igillad chief: "Uwy promised [Klobb] that all of the Igillad would return to him. He guaranteed it. He fulfilled his promises and guarantees to [Klobb] and became proficient in the behavior of the Christians and he never betrayed them in any serious matter."[59]

According to the text, Uwy's honor in his dealings with the colonial state also applied to his honesty and incorruptibility in administering his own people: "He struggled to carry out all of the Christians' orders and to end his own peoples' prohibition on dealing with the Christians. He did not require a salary for this until he grew older and became advanced in years." After many years of service, a successor and co-administrator of the confederation was appointed, as was the custom in the colonial Niger Bend. Just as the French officials had made Sobbo ag Fondogomo designate his son Addarib as successor and co-administrator of the Tengeregif in 1939, the chief of the Igillad was made to do the same thing. The text says,

[58] Spelled Ḥammādda, presumably Hammadi al-Kunti. "Asl imara," f. 1.
[59] Ibid., f. 1.

"[Uwy] became too weak to really carry out some of the important tasks of his office so he sought out Muḥammad al-Muṣṭafā, the son of his brother Ḥammādda, as his deputy to fulfill his duties and carry out some of what he was too weak to do." However, Muhammad al-Mustafa had not yet finished his education, so while he completed his studies, each of the four clans appointed a "responsible person (ḍāmin) from each tribe, asking for help from each one until [Muhammad al-Mustafa] had finished his studies."[60] In effect, due to Uwy's advanced age and Muhammad al-Mustafa's youth, the administration of the Igillad devolved onto the four chiefs of the individual clans. Even if this was meant only as a temporary measure, it weakened the power of the office of chief of the whole confederacy.

What followed the devolution of power were accusations of corruption: "Uwy did what he was advised to do. But when Uwy took the responsible people from the tribes, they turned out to be people who wanted to remove Uwy from the office of chief. So they began to lie about him and they said: He steals from us, etc." Such accusations stung Uwy but he responded by assuring people that the French would never believe these lies: "They would not believe you because he who does not steal, cheat, and deceive when he is young and strong will not deceive or steal when he is old and weak and approaching death at any hour." Although the text tells us that the lies about him continued, it was not until Uwy's death appeared to be close at hand that the issue of succession became really important. The text says that, "at that point, the administrator Lieutenant Garinet[61] appointed one of the three responsible people whom Uwy had sent for to be the chief of the three clans." Worse than this, he appointed someone from the Kel Tabhu, the least prestigious clan of the Igillad, to the position of successor to Uwy. This was completely out of the question: "The Kel Tabhu are not among the people who can hold the office of chief. They have never before provided the chief because the office of chief of the Muslims is only a matter for people of knowledge (ahl al-ʿilm). The Kel Tabhu are not people of knowledge, nor are they people of judgment (ahl al-raʾy), nor people of justice (ahl al-ʿadl); but rather, their status is that of those who compose poetry for the tails of cows (shaʿr al-dhanab min al-baqara)."[62] Explaining how a French official could appoint a man to be chief of the Igillad from the wrong clan

[60] Ibid., f. 1–2.

[61] Lieutenant Georges Garinet, named Chef de Subdivision de Bourem, January 13, 1934. *JOSF* no. 663 (January 15, 1934): 53.

[62] "Asl imara," f. 2.

and from people completely lacking in the genealogical basis for rule is the subject of the rest of this text.

Lieutenant Garinet had apparently refused to honor Uwy's wish to appoint the young Muhammad al-Mustafa as his successor. Two months after the initial rebuff, Uwy went again to see Garinet, at the behest of the Igillad notables. Meeting him at his office at Bourem, Garinet reportedly told Uwy: "You just want to appoint a worker so that you can send him on important missions because your presence harms you and the status of your chiefdom. I don't care about this or your dismissal. I am not in a position to do this while you remain alive."[63] Such a rejection of Uwy's wishes, and the insults which were leveled at the old chief, led the notables of the Igillad to swear allegiance to Muhammad al-Mustafa themselves, independent of colonial recognition. This new state of affairs is represented as a return to the correct social and moral order:

> He who was between Timbuktu and Gao, from among the whites[64] and the blacks, bore witness to the fact that the only people from the Igillad who were not present [at the meeting] were Muhammad al-Mustafa and some of the Kel Tabhu, who deserve no attention because they do not have the right to speak politically and they do not enter into the affairs of the chiefdom because they are not people of knowledge or judgment. In the Muslim chiefdom, only people of knowledge and judgment can gather for a political meeting; no man who is not a scholar can hold a position of responsibility or power.
>
> A man does not entrust the office of chief to a non-scholar. He who is not a scholar does not act in accordance with his knowledge, and the reason for this is that the adherence to French law is only possible for he who agrees with Muslim law (qānūn). He therefore adapts it to French law even if the two do not agree in many matters. But because each one commands justice and forbids injustice, and justice is the result of knowledge whereas injustice is the result of ignorance, for this reason knowledge and justice are in accordance with the allegiance of the Igillad to Muhammad al-Mustafa.[65]

This is an appeal to natural justice, and it is done in the context of a defense of social hierarchy and the rights of particular lineages to the office of chief.

"The proper lineage" argues that other local colonial officials had recognized the importance of "knowledge" as a criterion for ruling. Once Garinet had left Bourem, his replacement, Lieutenant Jules Auban,[66] paid a

[63] Ibid., f. 3.

[64] This refers to white Tuareg and Arabs, not Europeans who are referred to as "Christians."

[65] "Asl imara," f. 4.

[66] Lieutenant Jules Auban was designated to replace Garinet on March 15, 1933 (décision No.247, February 6, 1933), Subdivision de Bourem, Cercle de Tombouctou, "Rapport politique 1ère trimestre 1933" (ANM FR IE 11).

visit to the old chief Uwy and agreed that Muhammad al-Mustafa should be appointed as successor instead of the person from the Kel Tabhu. Muhammad al-Mustafa then began to fulfill the duties of his new role as Uwy's assistant. Uwy died on January 22, 1934,[67] and Muhammad al-Mustafa informed the colonial administration at Bourem three days later. A civilian administrator named Arthur Massot[68] was at the post to receive the news, and because he had been a supporter of Muhammad al-Mustafa's position as chief-designate, he is reported to have said the following on hearing the news of Uwy's death: "He who died and left a son like you – he did not die. You were the emir during the lifetime of your father and the people of the emirate. You are his indisputable successor. But I am not today the ruler of Bourem. The period of my rule has reached its end and the one who is responsible for the affairs of Bourem since yesterday is Lieutenant Garinet."[69] The return of Garinet, who had refused to recognize Muhammad al-Mustafa's position in the first place, spelled trouble.

When Garinet arrived at Bourem to take up his post for the second time, he called a meeting to decide on the succession of the chiefdom of the Igillad. Once Muhammad al-Mustafa arrived at this meeting, he encountered "all the fools of the Igillad who were already there blocking the door."[70] There was not a single man among them who was righteous. So Muhammad al-Mustafa said to them, "What are you doing gathered here? Has something happened that has frightened you from an enemy or some sort of conflict?" The crowd responded, "No, but the Commander Lieutenant sent for us so that we could decide who would be the successor to Uwy." This news led Muhammad al-Mustafa to declare, "You and your elders would not swear allegiance to me during the lifetime of Uwy. I have worked for you in justice. I have not oppressed anyone of you and I have not stolen any money." Those gathered agreed that this was true but said that they would exercise their ability to choose who would be chief. Exacerbated, Muhammad al-Mustafa asked them, "In which law? In the law of the Muslims or in the law of the Christians?" They said that this was in the "law of the Christians." So he said to them:

> You are liars to say that the law of the Christians is not at variance with the law of the Muslims in this case. It is a man who served the French state and the

[67] "Asl imara," f. 6.

[68] Arthur Massot was moved from his post in Bourem to become the adjoint to the Commandant of the Cercle de Goundam on January 13, 1934. *JOSF* no. 663 (January 15, 1934): 53.

[69] "Asl imara," f. 6.

[70] Ibid., f. 6.

> Islamic state for a period such as that which Uwy served for the Christians and for you, O Igillad. His service for the Christians and for you was good. He was not disloyal; he did not make excuses; and he always gave the proper significance to matters good and bad. French law is not contradictory and nor is Islamic law. He had a son so he taught him and his learning was good. He disciplined him and his discipline was good; he brought him up and his behavior was good. Even when he himself was good in weakness he asked for advice from the notables, scholars and jurists from the tribes of the Igillad in appointing his successor.[71]

The indignation at this social revolution and the overturning of the moral order is laid directly at the hands of the French officer Garinet.

The crowd of electors responded to Muhammad al-Mustafa's speech: "We don't know and we don't care that… Lieutenant Garinet ruled that French and Islamic law were at variance with each other. We don't care about the two laws. It is he who sent for us to elect the person we want as chief." Muhammad al-Mustafa responded, "You lied when you claimed that the lieutenant sent for you because the lieutenant is instead accustomed to sending for notables, scholars, and jurists rather than the ignorant people, the vile (al-arādhil), and the keepers of goats. If he wanted to send for the notables to invest me with authority he would not have ordered you (to come)."[72] The problem was compounded by the African translator who worked for the colonial administration and who had apparently summoned the electors to this meeting. His name was Sotbar Mahamane, and his official title was "interprète adjoint."[73] Muhammad al-Mustafa excoriated Sotbar for not having summoned the notables of the Igillad for such an occasion. The text lists several dozen prominent nobles who were not present, but it admits that Muhammad al-Mustafa did not know whether his speech was translated by the interpreter to Garinet. The text then narrates the election of the new chief as a stunning act of perfidy on the part of the colonial official: "Lieutenant Garinet then summoned those Igillad commoners (awāmm) who were present. They were sixteen men. He asked them whom they chose to rule them. Seven of them voted for Muhammad al-Mustafa, six chose Muḥammad b. Ḥammādda, although one of the six who voted for him was the slave of a shepherd, and three voted for Janbu." Despite this result, Lieutenant Garinet said, "According to the rules of French law, the

[71] Ibid., f. 6–7.
[72] Ibid., f. 7.
[73] His name and rank in the colonial civil service appears in his appointment as Interprète adjoint, Subdivision de Bourem, Cercle de Tombouctou, *JOSF* no. 669 (April 15, 1934): 225.

chiefdom belongs to Muhammad al-Mustafa b. Hammadda. However, I am reversing this and appointing Janbu as chief over you. Do you accept this O Igillad? Those who were present from among the Kel Insid and the Ifaqqar said: No, no, no." But the electors who were present there had come more or less at random: "The only people present were travelers on business who happened to be in Bourem when the issue was brought to them unexpectedly. They were asked to grant their permission for such a move although some who were present were ignoble people from the Kel Inalshinan and the Kel Tabhu. They said: Yes, we accept the rule of Janbu." At this, Lieutenant Garinet said, "O clans of the Igillad, I appoint Janbu as your chief; and I order Muhammad al-Mustafa to serve [as chief of clan of] the Kel Insid. So they were dismissed and they left."[74] Muhammad al-Mustafa remained the "chef de fraction" of the Kel Insid. But such devious behavior by the French official is represented in this text as corrupt and almost inexplicable. It is at this local level of one particular administrator that the text offers a critique of colonial rule.

Once Janbu[75] had been appointed, the drama shifts to a new figure from among the Kel Insid named al-Shaykh Sadīdi,[76] who attempted to rectify the problem of the appointment of the wrong chief, from the wrong lineage. Shaykh Sadidi is the one person in this story who attained a wider reputation in the Niger Bend because of his work on behalf of the Tijaniyya Sufi order. Both Shaykh Sadidi and Muhammad al-Mustafa were Tijani activists, and a number of their Arabic writings on the Tijaniyya survive.[77] Not all of the four clans of the Igillad were Tijani, although this does not seem to have played a role in the political disagreements discussed in this text.[78] Shaykh Sadidi had been absent when the events that I have been

[74] "Asl imara," f. 7–8.

[75] He is called Diambou ag Oumar in French sources.

[76] He was born in approximately 1890, and he died in 1946/47.

[77] I have only located two short texts directly related to the Tijaniyya. Both are written by Muhammad al-Mustafa: "Ijāza fī 'l-ṭarīqa al-tijāniyya" (IHERIAB ms. 1832); "Maqāla fī 'l-tijāniyya" (IHERIAB ms. 2160). There is also a poem in praise of Muhammad al-Mustafa written by Shaykh Sadidi's son ʿAbd al-Raḥmān (IHERIAB ms. 3378). This same ʿAbd al-Raḥmān b. al-Shaykh Sadīdi is the likely author of the historical text I have been discussing. The colonial concern about the influence of Ibrahim Niasse arose in the late 1950s ("Atarbya. Extrait du Rapport de l'Administrateur Clauzel du 24/2/1957" [ACG]). On this issue in Sudan, see Rüdiger Seesemann, "The History of the Tijâniyya and the issue of tarbiya in Darfur (Sudan)," in *La Tijâniyya: une confrérie musulmane à la conquête de l'Afrique*, ed. Jean-Louis Triaud, David Robinson (Paris: Karthala, 2000), 393–438.

[78] Prominent religious figures in the Ifaqqar and Kel Inalshinan belonged to the Qadiriyya order. Georges Garinet, Chef de Subdivision de Bourem, Cercle de Tombouctou, "Rapport politique de l'année 1935" (ANM FR IE 11).

discussing occurred. He was sent to speak with Garinet because when "the Igillad heard about these events, they sought God's protection from the harm caused by lowering the high-ranking and raising the lowly." Shaykh Sadidi went to Bourem and met with Garinet on February 9, 1934. He told him that, "We are kinfolk of the Igillad and we will never accept the chiefdom of Janbu even if you destroy us in prison." Garinet responded, saying that, "If I knew about this from the beginning of the affair, I would not have appointed Janbu as chief over you. However, I did not know about this until I did what I did and now there is no excuse for me to revoke my decision only five days after making it."[79]

Garinet presented Shaykh Sadidi with a way out of the dilemma, and he asked for Shaykh Sadidi's support in his ruse. He said, "But you will be delighted by something because I wrote two documents, the lower one is for Janbu as chief, and the higher one is for Muhammad al-Mustafa as chief. I wrote these two documents on the day after the [appointment of] Janbu as chief so that I could reverse myself on this matter. So have a little bit of patience and come to an agreement amongst yourselves." At this, Shaykh Sadidi returned home and informed the Igillad about what had happened between him and Garinet. He asked them to agree to be patient for a little while, but they told him unequivocally that, "They do not have the power to remain patient for even one hour as long as the chiefdom is in the hands of Janbu."[80] The text then recounts several angry confrontations between Muhammad al-Mustafa and Lieutenant Garinet, and details some of the frustrations Garinet felt in attempting to collect the jizya tax from Janbu. Garinet at one point threatened to separate the four clans of the Igillad into independent political entities, each with its own chief responsible for the collection of the colonial jizya tax itself.

The colonial reports filed by Garinet do make reference to the "turbulence" and "inquietude" of the Igillad over Janbu's position as chief. He blamed Shaykh Sadidi for "using his influence on the Kel Insid and Ifaqqar of the Igillad to oppose the current chief [Janbu], whose authority is only recognized among the Kel Inalshinan and Kel Tabhu."[81] The climax of "The proper lineage" is a speech made by Muhammad al-Mustafa in which he fully confronts the French officer:

> "Listen to what I say to you Lieutenant and do with me what you want after that. You know Lieutenant that since we have kept the peace for the Christians

[79] "Asl imara," f. 9–10.
[80] Ibid., f. 9–10.
[81] Georges Garinet, Chef de Subdivision de Bourem, Cercle de Tombouctou, "Rapport politique de l'année 1935" (ANM FR IE 11).

> and taken safe passage from them and given them the jizya that we had never before seen, you have reversed our [social] statuses and made the freeman into a slave and the slave into a freeman, the noble into a commoner and the commoner into a noble, the princes into subjects and the subjects into princes, for no reason. There is no reason for us to give them the jizya when they do not leave us in the circumstances in which they found us, when the slave was a slave, the freeman a freeman, the subject a subject, the commoner a commoner, the prince a prince, the noble person noble and the base person base. So that when you needed something from them, they could ask one of the nobles and they could carry out the request if they were able. But the chiefs are now incapable of carrying out orders so the weak ones are considered to be in the right because of the incapacity of the chiefs, even though the Christians do not ask us for money which we are incapable of giving them. You, Lieutenant, have relied on the assembly of the Kel Insid and the Ifaqqar but your conduct, and that of other representatives of the French state, has weakened us in the matter of the jizya and in other similar matters that we promised to deliver to you in our pact.... The reason for your anger is our non-acceptance of Janbu as chief, which none of our forefathers appointed over us, nor anyone ever from all of the Kel Tabhu. So do what you must do but I will never agree to Janbu as chief, even if you destroy us in prison."[82]

This dramatic and frank speech angered the French officer and he threw Muhammad al-Mustafa in jail.[83] Muhammad al-Mustafa responded defiantly: "Welcome to prison and to death. I choose to die in freedom generously enjoyed rather than live watched over and numb."[84]

The solution to this problem with the Igillād was found in the person of Shaykh Sadidi. According to "The proper lineage," Garinet sought the counsel of ʿUthman ag Aldaillah, chief if the Idnan, about what he could do about this situation. ʿUthman told him to summon Shaykh Sadidi: "He is their scholar (ʿālim) and judge (qāḍī) and their most worthy person. You should do what he tells you because he is honest."[85] Once Shaykh Sadidi was summoned, Garinet said to him, "I want you to ask the Igillad to accept Janbu as chief over them for the period of one year or less. I will then dismiss him. I am afraid that if I dismiss him today, people would hear that I appointed a man as chief whom I later dismissed. That would be a humiliation." Shaykh Sadidi's responded, "Far be it for me to assume responsibility for a lie, or enumerate the

[82] "Asl imara," f. 12.

[83] Many of the details of this story were confirmed by Muhammad al-Mustafa's youngest son when I was able to interview him in 2009. But his son did not know that he had been imprisoned. Interview ʿAbd al-Rahman ag Muḥammad al-Muṣṭafā al-Igillādī, March 19, 2009, Ber.

[84] "Asl imara," f. 12.

[85] Ibid., f. 13.

merits of an affair that I know with absolute certainty will not come to pass. As for the Igillad, they are well aware of their circumstances. If you want the most suitable person for them, return the office of chief to its proper lineage in the person of Muhammad al-Mustafa." Shaykh Sadidi then offered Garinet a list of other possible candidates who could legitimately take up the office of chief of the Igillad, but he still refused to budge. The text tells us that as a result, "When they gave up all hope that the Christians would dismiss [Janbu], they dispersed man by man throughout the country. The proper organization of their confederacy was upset because they chose death over having anyone from the Kel Tabhu come to power over them."[86]

However, Shaykh Sadidi and his supporters were winning this confrontation with the local French administration. They had rendered the Igillad temporarily ungovernable. Garinet himself came to accept this and reported to his superiors in Timbuktu that a change in the chiefdom had to be made. A 1936 report announced the impending administrative action: "The uneasiness seems more and more serious in the region north of Bamba, among the Iguellad principally, than what was reported in the last bulletin. This has led the commander of the subdivision of Bourem to propose the emergency removal of the chief of the Iguillad, [Janbu] ag Oumar." The only person whom the colonial administration could envision attaining sufficient authority was Shaykh Sadidi: "His dealings have maintained enmity between the clans, but he is the only one who appears capable of reestablishing unity and peace. It is worth a try because the current situation can not continue."[87] In April 1937, Janbu was removed from his post as chief of the Igillad, and replaced by Shaykh Sadidi.[88] Problems continued, however, between partisans of the deposed chief and those of the new one. Muhammad al-Mustafa regained his position as chief of the Kel Insid, and Janbu retained his position as chief of the Kel Tabhu. When I met with one of Muhammad al-Mustafa's sons, he told me that the problems over the chieftaincy among the Igillad only ended after Janbu had died.[89]

[86] Ibid., f. 13.

[87] De Périer, Commandant, Cercle de Tombouctou, "Bulletin de renseignements, octobre 1936" (ANM FR IE 137–3).

[88] The official decision was dated April 26, 1937. *JOSF* no. 749 (May 1, 1937): 264.

[89] Interview, ʿAbd al-Raḥmān ag Muḥammad al-Muṣṭafā al-Igillādī, March 19, 2009, Ber. Janbu would have been forty-nine years old when he was deposed as chief in 1937. I do not know when he died. Georges Garinet, Chef de Subdivision de Bourem, Cercle de Tombouctou, "Rapport politique de l'année 1935" (ANM FR IE 11).

CONCLUSION

This story of the Igillad gives us access to a different way of representing the relationship between noble Tuareg lineages and the colonial state than the sources I used to discuss Sobbo ag Fondogomo's career. Yet both cases make very clear that arguments for political authority were based on genealogy and history. In Sobbo's case, the argument was the warrior's claim to be the inheritors of political domination based on past conquest; for the clerical Igillad, authority was based on differentiations of lineage according to historical retainers of knowledge. In both cases, however, there was a sense that these genealogical arguments ran up against the realities of colonial rule, which over time found less and less need to align itself so closely with particular claimants of this sort. As such, both Sobbo and the Igillad make arguments in defense of positions of privilege that they understood to be under threat.

David Robinson has devoted a book to what he terms the "paths of accommodation" with French colonial rule taken by Muslim leaders in Senegal and Mauritania. He argues that in the very hierarchical set of societies of the Sahel, Muslim leaders of important groups, whether strictly religious in orientation or not, found it useful and necessary to reach an accommodation with the French colonial state to serve their own interests, and those of their subjects, in the new colonial order. Such accommodations implied the recognition that the colonial state possessed a certain amount of legitimacy in the eyes of Sahelian Muslim leaders, and that this was an important support for colonial rule in these areas. Robinson is especially keen to stress the legitimacy that accrued to the French colonial project in Sahelian West Africa because of the purported respect for Islamic institutions and practices by French officials, especially in the domain of law and Sufism. As Robinson says: "The symbolic capital that the French developed as a regime capable of working with Muslim societies ... mitigated the need for the constant application of force."[90]

The relationships established between the nascent colonial state and important pastoralist groups in the Niger Bend can be understood in Robinson's terms. In both Sobbo's letters and in "The proper lineage," France is represented as a force for good based on its ability to create order and defend an idea of natural justice. Particular representatives of France might lie and behave in immoral ways, but the colonial project

[90] David Robinson, *Paths of Accommodation: Muslim societies and French colonial authorities in Senegal and Mauritania*, 1880–1920 (Athens, OH: Ohio University Press, 2000), 6.

is not called into question by these failings. I would add to Robinson's analysis the importance of French respect and support for genealogy. This was an especially important dimension of the establishment of colonial legitimacy among leading Tuareg and Arab groups in the Niger Bend. But as central as genealogy was at the beginning of the colonial period, and as much as French officials always showed an interest in charting genealogical tables to be sure that the leaders they recognized possessed the requisite "natural" authority to govern those over whom they ruled, the logic of genealogy became less important as the colonial state matured. Under the *pax gallica* that slowly took hold in the Niger Bend, there was much more pressure from subordinate clans to free themselves from the control of overlords. By the 1920s, this was recognized by French officials as a clear threat to the authority of chiefs such as Sobbo. It would not be until after the Second World War that large numbers of slaves from Tuareg and Arab groups began to take serious and concerted actions to free themselves from their masters in similar ways. The French state in the Niger Bend attempted to manage these challenges to the authority of its "natural" allies by siding with important chiefs and attempting to minimize the centrifugal tendencies of subordinate clans in larger pastoralist confederacies. As the case of the Igillad shows, however, they were not always very skilled in managing these issues.

What is important to understand about these defenses of social hierarchy is that the arguments deployed by Sobbo and the writer of the Igillad history in defense of positions of privilege are racial in the local context of the Niger Bend. These are arguments that assert a natural authority that draws its basis from genealogy. For both French officials and pastoralist nobles, social hierarchy had a racial basis and justification, but the stakes of these claims were greater for pastoralist elites. Racial arguments used to defend privilege became less and less effective over time as the utility to the colonial state of large, hierarchal confederacies diminished. By the onset of the Second World War, the racial right to rule had largely run its course.

6

Defending Slavery

The Moral Order of Inequality, c. 1893–1940

ENDURING SLAVERY

To many observers, the institution of slavery seemed to have remained intact in the Niger Bend throughout the colonial period and beyond. Although slavery was officially abolished in Soudan in 1908, colonial authorities did little to encourage the liberation of slaves in the northern, desert-edge parts of the territory where colonial authority was most precarious. In these areas, the colonial administration developed policies designed to ensure that slaves remained subject to their masters. Faced with a League of Nations enquiry into the question of slavery in colonial territories in the 1930s, the French regime presented the investigators with a fiction of benevolent colonial emancipation policies that concealed their reliance on slavery as the basis of both the economic and political stability of French rule in the Niger Bend and other Sahelian territories. Such was the durability of slavery that French administrators were still debating the question in the 1950s, on the eve of independence. In 1961, an English antislavery activist named Robin Maugham published a book revealing that slavery remained alive in Timbuktu when he had visited the town in 1958, and that he had been able to purchase a slave himself.[1] After independence in 1960, the first postcolonial government of Mali, led by Modibo Keita, made the elimination of slavery an important basis of its policy in the Niger Bend.

[1] Robin Maugham, *Slaves of Timbuktu* (New York: Harper, 1961). For a similar account from Mauritania, see Kélétigui Mariko, "L'attitude de l'administration face au servage," in *Nomades et commandants: Administration et sociétés nomades dans l'ancienne A.O.F.*, ed. Edmund Bernus, Pierre Boilley, Jean Clauzel, and Jean-Louis Triaud (Paris: Karthala, 1993), 199.

The persistence of slavery was the result of deliberate colonial policy in response to arguments made by slaveholders in the Niger Bend. When French rule was established, there was a brief period of perhaps a decade in which emancipation and the abolition of slavery were sometimes encouraged; thereafter, colonial officials did what they could to keep slaves attached to their masters. Access to resources and legal independence for slaves was largely denied by the colonial state. Slaves were also made to carry the greatest burden of colonial labor demands and military conscription.[2] The colonial state accepted Sahelian arguments about the morality of slavery and the importance of slaveholder custody and guidance over their slaves. For slaves of the Tuareg, Arab, and Fulbe pastoralists, race was used as a tool to define servile people as black, forever stained with the sin of original unbelief, even after having attained manumission.

The important thing to understand is that the colonial state's instrumentalization of Sahelian ideas about race increased the number of people who fell under the slave regime when compared to the nineteenth century. The apparatus of the colonial state sometimes subordinated people to its power even when the claims to their servility were only rhetorical. The apparent persistence of slavery is not then simply the legacy of some otherwise bygone precolonial era; it is also the product of the colonial history of this region. The colonial deployment of race to distinguish between noble and servile people was not novel in the Niger Bend, but making the idea of the social inferiority of blacks into an instrument of state was effectively a colonial invention. The role of the state in policing social status differences tended to reduce local variations and gradations of social hierarchy and servility. What slavery meant in different contexts, and who was, properly speaking, a slave, was flattened into a larger racial equation of blackness with slavery.[3]

This chapter examines some of the ways that slaveholders defended the institution of slavery during the first decades of colonial rule. Islamic legal principles played an important part in both the justification of

[2] A similar process occurred in Mauritania. See Urs Peter Ruf, "Ending Slavery. Hierarchy, Dependency and Gender in Central Mauritania" (Ph.D. diss., University of Bielefeld, 1998), 35–6; Benjamin Alcoque, "Embarras de l'administration coloniale: la question de l'esclavage au début du XXème siècle en Mauritanie," in *Groupes serviles au Sahara. Approche comparative à partir du cas des arabophones de Mauritanie*, ed. Mariella Villasante-de Beauvais (Paris, CNRS, 2000), 105–7.

[3] A version of this idea, substituting "caste" for my use of "race," appears in James Searing, "*God Alone Is King": Islam and Emancipation in Senegal. The Wolof Kingdons of Kajoor and Bawol, 1859–1914* (Portsmouth, NH: Heinemann, 2002), 150–1.

slavery and continuing social inequality for former slaves. Sahelian racial ideas helped make the case that the stain of slavery was effectively permanent.

THE PROBLEM OF SAHELIAN SLAVERY

As elsewhere across the African Sahel, there is a long history of slavery in the Niger Bend. For at least a thousand years, enslaved people from the region were forcibly taken into the trans-Saharan slave trade, and slavery played an important role in the internal social structure of all Sahelian societies. But for such an important and apparently ubiquitous institution, we know relatively little about the lived experience of slaves in the Niger Bend, or the extent of the slave system there. Claude Meillassoux's influential approach to African slavery, which was largely based on research carried out in the Sahel, distinguished between three types of slave labor systems found in African societies: those in which slaves were employed on plantations, working under supervision in gangs and producing marketable products; semiautonomous slave villages that had to pay a more or less fixed share of their harvest to masters; and domestic slavery in which slaves lived in their masters' households and replaced the labor of their masters' kinsmen.[4] In the Niger Bend, plantation slavery did not exist on any significant scale after the defeat of the Songhay Empire in 1591, except perhaps in the area immediately adjacent to Timbuktu.[5] Most people in the Niger Bend defined by Meillassoux as slaves lived in their master's households, or in semiautonomous villages and pastoral groups.

Almost all of the local Arabic source material specifically addressed to the issue of slavery in the Niger Bend is about domestic slaves. This includes legal opinions, manumission documents, wills, bills of sale, and correspondence. There is very little documentation about slaves living in semiautonomous groups.[6] We know already that people living in such villages were sometimes the subject of claims to service made by people

[4] Claude Meillassoux, *Anthropologie de l'esclavage: Le ventre de fer et d'argent* (Paris: Presses Universitaires de France, 1986), 117–19.

[5] Michel Abitbol, *Tombouctou et les Arma: de la conquête marocaine du Soudan nigérien en 1591 à l'hégémonie de l'Empire du Macina en 1833* (Paris: G.P. Maisonneuve et Larose, 1979), 156–7.

[6] One of the few documents that I was able to uncover directly related to this issue is a letter written in 1844 on behalf of the ruler of the Hamdullahi Caliphate, Amadu Lobbo, certifying that two men from one of these villages are to be considered free (Letter from Aḥmad b. Aḥmad b. Muḥammad b. Abī Bakr al-Māsinī, April 2, 1844 [IHERIAB, ms. 3433]).

such as Amadu Lobbo, who had them defined as blacks (zanj) in the (Pseudo) "Ta'rikh al-fattash." These same people were called "blacks ruled by Islam" in Sahelian legal literature. However, Meillassoux and others have confused claims made about the slave status of people in semiautonomous villages with the reality of the historical lives that people lived there. In cases in which there were only limited means of enforcing assertions of slave status over particular groups of people, we cannot reasonably use the terminology of slavery to describe them. To the extent that the Songhay Empire, the Hamdullahi Caliphate, or the Tuareg Iwellemmedan were able to back up their arguments with the exercise of power over these communities, the language of slavery is appropriate. But this was not the case much of the time. As we have seen, the people in these groups were vulnerable to enslavement as blacks. But most were not actually enslaved. We must be careful not to confuse argument for social fact. It is precisely this mistake that colonial officials made at the beginning of the colonial period. It was the apparatus of the colonial state that converted these claims into fixed servile status with concomitant material disadvantages.

The distinction between slaves and other servile people who were not slaves is important. This is particularly clear in the case of those communities that were under Tuareg domination. During the nineteenth century, different Tuareg groups competed for control over pastureland and Songhay-speaking sedentary villages of the Niger Bend, from which they extracted annual levies of grain and other tribute. Several Tuareg groups also settled some of their own Tamashek-speaking servile people in agricultural villages on a seasonal basis to grow cereals. Although these included slaves (Ta. iklan), the vast majority, according to Pierre Bonte, were low-status freed slaves (Ta. iderfan). The Tuareg also employed a combination of slaves, freed slaves, and other servile groups in pastoral activities.[7] All of these different statuses for Tamashek-speaking servile people were conflated under the single Songhay term "bellah." The first French colonial administrators who came to the region assumed that the bellah were the slaves of the Tuareg. These tributary communities were very vulnerable to Tuareg raids, and they were at times subject to slave raids themselves.[8] However, they were not all slaves. This is a point that

[7] Pierre Bonte, "Esclavage et relations de dépendance chez les Touareg Kel Gress," in *L'esclavage en Africque précoloniale*, ed. Claude Meillassoux (Paris: Maspéro, 1975), 49–76.

[8] Jean-Pierre Olivier de Sardan, *Quand nos pères étaient captifs. Récits paysans du Niger* (Paris: Nubia, 1976), 48. There are numerous colonial remarks to this effect. To take one

was made emphatically and repeatedly in interviews that I carried out in some of these villages. One informant described the behavior of the Tuareg toward Songhay-speaking sedentary people as follows: "When the Tuareg came, they stayed and they didn't fight against anyone. However, if they took certain people whom they used like bellah, they otherwise got along with the villagers." The same informant insisted on a kind of symbiosis between villagers and the Tuareg: "The villagers had boats and they took the Tuareg in their boats to cross the river.... The sedentary people were equal to the Tuareg. They got along with each other until the time that the Christians [French] came."[9] There is perhaps some willful forgetting in this perspective,[10] but it does suggest that although sedentary people in tributary villages were vulnerable to Tuareg demands for slaves, they did not live in what were necessarily "slave villages." In fact, informants indicated that although the Tuareg took tribute, there was also an element of exchange in which animals were given to villagers either as loans, in which case they could consume their milk, or as gifts.[11] Bonte's research on the sedentary agricultural communities of one Tuareg group, the Kel Gress, suggested a slave population in these tributary villages of only 10 percent.[12]

It has to be admitted that measuring the size of the slave population cannot be very precise. The French sent out questionnaires on the number of slaves in each administrative district in Soudan in 1894 and again in 1904, and this produced census data for the Niger Bend showing a slave population ranging from 40 percent in the district of Bamba to 82 percent in the district of Ras-el-Ma.[13] However, these figures are not very reliable because the French lacked the personnel to carry out substantial data collection and because they had very limited, and often ill-conceived, knowledge of the societies they had recently come to rule. As we have

example: "If the Tuareg found something to their liking in a village, they did not hesitate to take it and the villagers would not dare raise a protest." Cercle de Gao, "Monographie du Cercle de Gao par le Capitaine LaCroix," 1905 (ANM FA 1D-39–1).

9 Interview, Youssouf Kakay, October 14, 2002, Kano. According to the colonial administration, Kano was a tributary village "belonging" to the Tuareg. Cercle de Tombouctou, "Rapport politique," July 1901 (ANM FA 1E 78–81).

10 Martin Klein, "Studying the History of Those who would rather Forget," *HA* 16 (1989): 209–17.

11 Interview, Youssouf Kakay, October 14, 2002, Kano.

12 Bonte, "Esclavage," 51.

13 In addition to these two extremes, 61 percent of the population of the district of Timbuktu were counted as slaves, and 75 percent of the district of Gao. See Martin Klein, *Slavery and Colonial Rule in French West Africa* (New York: Cambridge University Press, 1998), 252–4.

seen, French administrators brought with them ideas of race that affected the way that they understood social status in the Niger Bend. Perhaps more importantly, they gave credence to a variety of contested claims made by Sahelian interlocutors about the slave status of different people. The research of modern scholars has tended to replicate these colonial misperceptions, in part because colonial data provides the only source of census data, and because the diversity of servile-status positions has diminished over the course of the twentieth century. Even though it is certainly true that the majority of the population of the Niger Bend on the eve of the colonial occupation was potentially servile, percentages of between 50 and 75 percent for slaves in the area put forward by scholars are surely huge exaggerations.[14]

SORKO SERVILITY

A good example of how the French administration in the Niger Bend managed claims about slavery is the case of the Tengeregif leader Sobbo ag Fondogomo's failed attempt to gain control over the Sorko, the Songhay-speaking boatmen and fishers of the Niger River. In order to understand Sobbo's argument to the French, some historical background on the Sorko is necessary. According to Songhay oral traditions, the earliest inhabitants of the Niger River system were fishermen. Dispersed along the river and following seasonal patterns of migration in their boats, these river people long fulfilled an important occupational role in the Niger valley as transporters of goods and fishermen. River people on the Niger include several linguistically distinct groups, but in the Niger Bend, the main group is the Songhay-speaking Sorko. The origins of the

[14] Olivier de Sardan estimates the size of the slave population among the sedentary Songhay-Zarma further south along the Niger River in Niger to have included between two-thirds and three-quarters of the total population (*Les sociétés songhay-zarma (Niger-Mali): Chefs, guerriers, esclaves, paysans* [Paris: Karthala, 1984], 191). On the question of the percentage of slaves in different Tuareg societies, see Edmond Bernus and Suzanne Bernus, "L'évolution de la condition servile chez les Touaregs sahéliens" in *L'esclavage en Afrique précoloniale*, ed. Claude Meillassoux (Paris: F. Maspéro, 1975), 28–9. These estimates correspond roughly to neighboring areas such as the Sokoto Caliphate for which Paul Lovejoy and Jan Hogendorn give an approximation of the slave population on the eve of colonial conquest of 25–50 percent of the total population (*Slow Death for Slavery: The Course of Abolition in Northern Nigeria, 1897–1936* [Cambridge: Cambridge University Press, 1993], 1n). Martin Klein estimates that the slave population in the French Soudan at the end of the nineteenth century was between a quarter and a third of the total, and that slaves made up more than half of the population in Sahelian areas (*Slavery and Colonial Rule*, 253).

Sorko are obscure. Oral traditions collected by Jean Rouch suggest that they migrated into the region from the southeast, perhaps as far away as southern Chad.[15] This is not the place to go into the complicated details of the various migrations into the Niger valley, except to highlight the fact that local accounts concur that the earliest inhabitants such as the Sorko were gradually forced into subordinate relationships with more powerful peoples who came to the area after them.[16] The Sorko were one of the collective groups of slaves referred to as zanj in the forged nineteenth-century (Pseudo) "Ta'rikh al-fattash," discussed in Chapter 2.

Control over the Sorko was economically and strategically important for any state that sought to rule the Niger Bend. The Sorko provided the main means of transportation of goods and soldiers along the river. However, the degree of servility to which the Sorko were subjected was in direct proportion to the strength of the polity that controlled the region. One of the most important administrative positions in the Songhay Empire was that of the "commander of the boats" (So. hii-koy), whose responsibilities included management of Sorko transporters on the Niger.[17] The precise extent of the service provided by the Sorko to the rulers of the Songhay Empire is not known, but it appears that after the Moroccan invasion in 1591 and the destruction of the powerful Songhay state, the Sorko gained a greater measure of autonomy. In the nineteenth century, Amadu Lobbo claimed ownership of the Sorko as slaves of his state, but it is unclear how much success he had in enforcing this. Later in the nineteenth century, some Sorko apparently came under the authority of al-Hajj ʿUmar Tal and fought on the side of the Tukolor in the 1860s.[18] A number of Sorko communities claimed in the 1890s that they had continued to take orders from the Tukolor successor state based at Ségou until it was defeated by the colonial conquest.[19] Broadly, we know that claims could be made on Sorko labor and military service; but in the absence of a strong state, the Sorko were not enslaved in anything but a rhetorical sense.

[15] Jean Rouch, *Les Songhay* (Paris: Presses universitaires de France, 1954), 8.

[16] The most comprehensive treatment of the migrations into the Niger Valley is Boubou Hama, *L'histoire traditionnelle d'un peuple: les Zarma-Songhay* (Paris: Présence africaine, 1967); and *Histoire des Songhay* (Paris: Présence africaine, 1968).

[17] John Hunwick, *Timbuktu and the Songhay Empire: Al-Saʿdî's Taʾrîkh al-sûdân down to 1613 and other Contemporary Documents* (Leiden: Brill, 1999), 341.

[18] David Robinson, *The Holy War of Umar Tal: The Western Sudan in the Mid-nineteenth Century* (Oxford: Clarendon, 1985), 313.

[19] These were the Sorko from Bougoubéri, east of Timbuktu. "Rapport de Lieutenant Cauvin sur la tournée de recensement faite dans le Bingha, le Gourma et le Kissou du 3 février au 3 mars 1898," March 15, 1898 (ANM FA 1E 78–81).

The problem that arose in the first decade of colonial rule was provoked by these rhetorical claims of Sorko enslavement, and whether the Tengeregif would be allowed to "retain" control over them. Some groups of Sorko claimed that they had never lived under Tuareg authority and demanded their autonomy. One Sorko community that made this claim originated in the village of Bougoubéri (east of Timbuktu); its leaders claimed to have always recognized the authority of the Tukolor in Ségou. A French report in 1898 described the situation as follows: "[Sobbo] says that the Sorko of Bougoubéri belonged to his father alone because at that time, [the Tukolor of] Ségou exercised no authority in the country and the Tuareg were recognized as masters. Also, there existed a custom in which the Sorko belonged to the ruler of the country as property."[20] French officials were initially willing to recognize Sobbo's claims, but this presented some problems. There were Sorko families in most of the villages along the river, and as the French moved to free the Songhay-speaking villages from Tuareg domination, these Sorko could potentially act as a rear guard on behalf of Sobbo in order to gain authority over non-Sorko Songhay whom he claimed as his former tributaries. To solve this potential problem, French officials decided to allow Sobbo to exercise authority over four villages where the Sorko were concentrated (Kano, Minkiri, Bérégoungou, and Toya), and over any Sorko who were willing to move to one of these places. Otherwise, Sorko in other villages would fall under the authority of the Songhay village chief.[21]

Most Sorko decided not to move to the designated Sorko villages, and instead integrated further into the host societies where they lived. Sobbo sent out parties that attempted to force recalcitrant Sorko to move to the Sorko villages, and some were taken away by force. Other Sorko preferred to put themselves under Sobbo's authority because he was seen by some as less demanding than the Songhay village chiefs.[22] This is perhaps the reason that the local French administration reduced and finally eliminated Sobbo's power over the Sorko entirely.

Within a decade of the beginning of colonial rule, the Sorko largely disappeared from the colonial record.[23] Decades later in the 1940s, there

[20] "Rapport de Lieutenant Cauvin sur la tournée de recensement faite dans le Bingha, le Gourma et le Kissou du 3 février au 3 mars 1898," March 15, 1898 (ANM FA 1E 78–81).

[21] 1ère Territoire militaire, "Rapport politique," October 1901 (ANM FA 1E 78–81).

[22] Cercle de Tombouctou, "Rapport politique," March 1902 (ANM FA 1E 78–81).

[23] 1ère Territoire militaire, "Rapport Politique," November 1901 (ANM FA 1E 78–81); "Conditions imposées aux Touareg pendant la tournée de police du 1 mai au 3 juin 1907" (ANM FA IN 46).

was very little trace of the Sorko, even in the villages such as Kano and Minkiri in the Serere region east of Timbuktu where they were apparently the major part of the population.[24] When I visited these villages in 2002, most people professed to be unaware of this history of Sorko servility. A Sorko, I was told, was merely a person who has taken up the occupation of fishing, with no specific caste status distinct from other Songhay-speakers. (Indeed, "sorko" is the Songhay word for fisherman.) I had originally suspected that the people with whom I spoke were concealing slave pasts. However, I came to see with the help of my Songhay hosts that even if that was true in part, the Sorko had also been autonomous fishers and boatmen whose labor could be coerced at times by more powerful groups, but they were not slaves. The Sorko are sometimes recognized as the original inhabitants of the Niger valley and as such, they are accorded special powers as the masters of the magical world that some Songhay believe lies beneath the river. But in Songhay discourse, this is based on their autochthonous status rather than on a history of enslavement to Songhay, Fulbe, or Tuareg rulers.[25] Arguments about who was a slave were like other claims, open to contestation and rebuttal. We should not assume that because the language of slavery is so pervasive in the Niger Bend, everyone called a slave by someone else really was enslaved. The choice of language was active and calculated, but its intended results were not always realized.

THE COLONIAL POLITICAL ECONOMY OF SLAVERY IN THE NIGER BEND

French officials were initially quite cautious in their approach to the issue of slavery in the Niger Bend. In 1894, the year that French forces had definitively established their control in Timbuktu, the military commander of the town's colonial garrison wrote his initial thoughts on future policy regarding slavery: "Slavery is an age-old institution that forms the principal basis of the social organization of the peoples of

[24] A report written in 1941 states that the majority of the population of both of these villages was Songhay, originally from Goursougaye (Moreau, Cercle de Tombouctou, "Rapport de tournée effectuée du 24 septembre au 8 octobre 1941" [ANM FR 1E 42]). My oral research in these villages confirmed that this is still the local understanding.

[25] Interview, Youssouf Kakay, October 14, 2002, Kano. On the issue of Sorko magical powers, see Jean Rouch, *La religion et la magie songhay* (Paris: Presses universitaires de France, 1960), 10–11; Paul Stoller and Cheryl Olkes, *In Sorcery's Shadow: Memoir of an Apprenticeship among the Songhay of Niger* (Chicago: University of Chicago Press, 1987), 163–5; Jean-Marie Gibbal, *Genii of the River Niger*, trans. Beth Raps (Chicago: University of Chicago Press, 1994).

the Soudan, and although it is for us, as new conquerors, shocking to our ideas of liberty and civilization, we must tolerate it unless we want to bring about a complete disruption of the economy of the country."[26] Conservative attitudes toward slavery such as these reflected a larger ambivalence in French colonial thinking and practice that had developed in the second half of the nineteenth century after France abolished slavery in its colonial possessions in 1848. In particular, French administrators on the ground in the Algerian Sahara and in Senegal developed their own particular policies regarding slavery by which abolition was deployed to weaken indigenous enemies, but withheld when dealing with local allies.[27] In Senegal, this policy dates from the 1850s when the French governor, Louis Faidherbe, developed a policy compromise between the metropolitan ideals of abolition and what he perceived to be the realities on the ground in Africa. This allowed French officials to accept the existence of slavery in their African territories, while at the same time prohibiting slaveholding by French citizens. Faidherbe made French toleration of slavery into a political tool, conditional on political alliances. When France was at war with an African state, runaway slaves were received and freed; slaves who fled friendly states were returned to their masters.[28] The logic of this policy guided French action toward slavery across Africa during the period of colonial conquest. In areas along the desert edge such as the Niger Bend, where military conquest took much longer and where the French military itself played a much more important role in colonial administration because of the difficulty in "pacifying" hostile pastoralist groups, the political use of abolition remained an important tool of colonial administration throughout the colonial period.

The French regime in Soudan relied heavily on slave labor for its soldiers, porters, laborers on construction projects, domestic servants,

[26] Olivier de Sardan, *Sociétés*, 192.

[27] On Algeria, see Denis Cordell, "No Liberty, Not Much Equality, and Very Little Fraternity: the Mirage of Manumission in the Algerian Sahara in the second half of the Nineteenth Century," in *Slavery and Colonial Rule in Africa*, ed. Suzanne Miers and Martin Klein (Portland: Frank Cass, 1999), 38–56. On Senegal, see F. Renault, *L'abolition de l'esclavage au Sénégal: l'attitude d'administration française, 1848–1905* (Paris: P. Geuthner. 1972), Trevor Getz, *Slavery and Reform in West Africa: Toward Emancipation and Reform in Nineteeneth-century Senegal and Gold Coast* (Athens, OH: Ohio University Press, 2004).

[28] Martin Klein, *Slavery and Colonial Rule*, 28–9; Richard Roberts, "The End of Slavery in the French Soudan" in *The End of Slavery in Africa*, ed. Suzanne Miers and Richard Roberts (Madison, WI: University of Wisconsin Press, 1988), 284.

and concubines.[29] In 1905, the French Republic issued a decree abolishing enslavement and the sale, gift, or exchange of persons on French territory. The colonial administration in Soudan, however, had no intention of liberating slaves from their masters, at least not until an alternative system of labor had been put in place. Nonetheless, in some areas slaves themselves took the initiative and began to leave their masters. Beginning in 1905, a "slave exodus" occurred in the region of Banamba, north of Bamako, where there were large concentrations of slaves engaged in agriculture. By 1907, slave departures had spread to other areas of the Middle Niger and beyond. William Merlaud-Ponty, the governor of Soudan, issued a decree in 1908 that made all labor free and remunerated. He estimated that altogether 500,000 slaves had left their masters across the colony.[30]

The slave exodus was most dramatic where there were large concentrations of first-generation slaves such as in Banamba and Gumbu.[31] Those slaves who remembered a homeland someplace else were the most likely to take the opportunity to return home, usually in areas south of the Niger valley such as Buguni and Sikasso.[32] But many slaves had been born into slavery or were taken as young children, and these people had no homeland that they could return to. Consequently, many slaves remained in the area of their former masters and attempted to set themselves up as independent farmers or wage earners. Others negotiated with their former masters and stayed put, retaining their dependent and servile position.

In the Niger Bend, there was no significant slave exodus.[33] Part of the reason for this lies in the much harder line taken by the local colonial administration in the Niger Bend in opposing the end of slavery. But it was also because the nature of slavery and social hierarchy in this region was different. Many of the slaves in the Middle Niger had been enslaved in the recent past, often as a result of the military upheavals of the late nineteenth century. Few captives from these conflicts had been

[29] Roberts, "End of Slavery," 285.

[30] Klein, *Slavery and Colonial Rule*, 159–73; Roberts, "End of Slavery," 287–93.

[31] Richard Roberts, "The End of Slavery, Colonial Courts, and Social Conflict in Gumbu, 1908–1911," *CJAS* 34, no. 3 (2000): 684–713.

[32] Brian J. Peterson, "Slave Emancipation, Trans-local Social Processes, and the Spread of Islam in French Colonial Buguni (Southern Mali), 1893–1914," *JAH* 45 (2004): 425–9; Peterson, "Transforming the Village: Migration, Islam and Colonialism in French Southern Mali (West Africa), 1880–1960" (Ph.D. diss., Yale University, 2005), 32–60.

[33] Martin Klein cites some examples, but these are not extensive ("Slavery and French Rule in the Sahara." *Slavery and Abolition* 19, no. 2 [1998]: 73–90).

taken to the Niger Bend region. Most first-generation slaves in the Niger Bend were from adjacent areas or tributary communities and had been enslaved as children.

Those Tuareg and Arab groups allied with the French (such as the Kel Entsar, Tengeregif, and Kunta) were permitted to keep their slaves.[34] The only occasions in which French officials acted to free people that they generically referred to by the Songhay term "bellah" (Ta. iklan) were as punishment for open revolts. Thus, for example, after the defeat of the Iwellemmedan revolt led by Fihrun in 1916, some French officials were determined to weaken this Tuareg confederation by encouraging the bellah-iklan to break their ties with their Iwellemmedan masters. However, the colonial administration quickly backed off from this policy. Freeing the bellah-iklan would have certainly led to a much greater level of Tuareg resistance because it would have deprived the pastoralists of much of their workforce. Allowing pastoralist groups to keep control over servile populations within their own societies provided an important incentive for cooperation with the colonial authorities.

The ways that servile people were recruited into colonial service reveals the extent to which the colonial administration actually encouraged tighter control over them by pastoralist leaders. During the First World War, the French forcibly recruited large numbers of Africans into the military. In the Niger Bend, military recruitment for overseas service fell exclusively on blacks, both Songhay-speakers and pastoralist servile populations. Village chiefs sent the Songhay recruits, although it was not uncommon for eligible young men to flee to avoid the draft.[35] In 1918, French propaganda for voluntary enlistment actually attracted several "white" pastoralists who presented themselves for military service. They were rejected for racial reasons; among the pastoralist population, military recruitment for overseas service fell exclusively on the black bellah-iklan. Fear that recruitment of nonblack pastoralists would provoke rebellion, as well as overt colonial racism, determined French policy in this regard.[36]

The means by which bellah-iklan were recruited was often brutal. In 1918, ten recruits were drowned crossing the Niger River at Iloa (20 km from Timbuktu) when the canoe that was transporting them sank. They died because they were tied in groups of five by a rope around their necks

[34] Georg Klute, "Herren und Sklaven: Zur Frage der kolonialen Sklavenpolitik in Französisch-Westafrika" in *Macht der identität – identitäder macht. Politische prozesse und kultureller wandel in Afrika*, ed. H. Willer et al. (Münster: Lit, 1995), 241–53.

[35] Cercle de Tombouctou, "Rapport Politique," December 1915 (ANM FA 1E-78-81).

[36] Région de Tombouctou, "Rapport Politique," 2ème trimester, 1918 (ANM FA 1E-78-81).

while being taken to Timbuktu by a French officer. This small colonial scandal led to a French investigation that concluded with an indictment of the way Tuareg leaders delivered bellah-iklan "recruits" to colonial posts, comparing it to the slave trade within West Africa before colonial rule was established.[37]

The colonial state faced a similar dilemma in the economic domain. The Niger Bend was not an important economic zone in Soudan, let alone in the larger scheme of French possessions in West Africa. Colonial labor needs were filled most easily by a system of indirect procurement in which chiefs were required to provide a certain number of laborers. The continued control by pastoralist elites over servile members of their society served these interests. In the first decade of colonial occupation, French administrators developed a broad policy designed to encourage agricultural development in the Niger Bend based on freeing the Songhay-speaking sedentary population from the exactions of the Tuareg and encouraging pastoralists to sedentarize their servile people. There was great regional variation in the success of these objectives. The key factor in the regional differences in agricultural production was the nature of adjacent pastoralist power and the degree to which tribute was collected in an ordered and predictable manner. The "bread basket" of the Niger Bend in the second half of the nineteenth century and in the early decades of French rule was the lake region to the west of Timbuktu, and especially in the area around Lake Faguibine. Here, the Kel Entsar and Tengeregif ensured a sufficient level of security for extensive agriculture to occur. They also developed a more or less regular system of taxation or tribute with sedentary Songhay chiefs. By way of contrast, in the area along the Niger River to the east of Timbuktu where rival Tuareg groups had played out their hostilities by raiding riverine communities, sedentary people did not even eat grain. What little cereal they did grow was for Tuareg patrons or raiders, whereas the agriculturalists survived by fishing and gathering wild plant foods. Their lack of agricultural production and their inability to store food resulted in a catastrophe for the sedentary people of this region during the drought years of 1913–1916, when French administrators reported that more than half of the sedentary population east of Timbuktu had perished.[38]

[37] "Rapport de l'Inspecteur général Demaret," 1919 (ANM 1E 2361, Num. Sér. III).

[38] It is hard to know how accurate this figure is because famine victims migrated out of the region. The sedentary population along the river to the east of Timbuktu suffered terribly from the famine. In 1914, as the colonial administration in Timbuktu began to offer emergency food supplies to the destitute, an estimated 50 percent of the sedentary

The sedentarization of servile pastoralist populations in agricultural villages was long a dream of the colonial administration. In 1906, an administrator at Timbuktu was able to predict that "for a while, the Bellah will be the sharecroppers of the Tuareg, who are too keen on keeping them to molest or abandon them. Farming villages would create the first sites of sedentarization and would perhaps avoid, by their rational development, the crisis that threatens the nomads." Among the advantages that such a process might bring to the colonial administration was that colonial forces "would thus not have to face a [military] suppression [of the pastoralists] that would destroy their race, the only one capable of controlling the bush. Despite everything, [the pastoralists] are appealing [to us] because of their pride and attachment to their ancient customs from the old world of the nomad."[39] In only two areas of the Niger Bend did this policy produce any significant pastoralist-directed agriculture before the end of the First World War: around Lake Faguibine, where the Kel Entsar settled their servile people seasonally, and in the lake region of the Gourma, where the Kunta and others controlled more permanent agricultural villages.

It was the leaders of the Kel Entsar, Tengeregif, and Kunta who first understood the economic advantages that cooperation with the French offered them, and consequently the importance of putting their slaves to work as seasonal farmers. Among other pastoralist groups, servile people were sometimes put into existing agricultural villages on a seasonal basis, but most bellah-iklan who remained in their masters' service continued to fulfill traditional labor roles in pastoralist society, as animal herders or domestic laborers. There were, of course, ways in which servile people could leave their masters, even if only seasonally. New wage opportunities developed in towns such as Timbuktu where a large bellah-iklan population settled, and sharecropping opportunities existed to an extent in some Songhay villages. Beginning in the 1930s, significant new opportunities for wage labor arose in the Niger Bend when irrigation schemes were opened up at Diré and on Lake Oro. But even when servile people migrated to take up wage work or the petty

population had already perished. Cercle de Tombouctou, "Rapport Politique," July 1914 (ANM FA 1E-78–81); see also Andrew Clark, "Environmental Decline and Ecological Response in the Upper Senegal Valley," *JAH* 36, no. 2 (1995): 212–17.

[39] Capitaine Maziller, "Etude sur les populations de la Région de Tombouctou: Situation économique et agricole, sécurité et éléments de troubles intérieurs; Rezzous venus de l'extérieur, organisation de la lutte contre eux, sûreté à organiser," June 10, 1906 (ANM FA 1D-59–11).

commerce, their masters often followed and demanded a share of the wages for themselves.[40]

In an attempt to balance their two main political objectives in the Niger Bend, to ensure security and encourage at least moderate economic development, the French sought to divide the fertile floodplain of the Niger valley between the Songhay-speaking sedentary agriculturists and the pastoral nomads, assigning the tenure rights of lands worked by the slaves to their masters. In effect, French policy freed one segment of the tributary servile population from pastoral control while at the same time encouraging a landed relationship between pastoral overlords and their slaves.

SLAVEHOLDER RESPONSES

Slaveholders themselves were not pleased by limitations or changes imposed on their practices of slavery. Important chiefs sometimes argued with the colonial administration in Timbuktu about French policy on this issue. In one case, Sakib ag Assamsamo,[41] an important chief of the Tuareg Igawaddaran warrior-status group based in the eastern Gourma, wrote a letter to the French at Timbuktu in response to colonial charges that he had been engaged in selling slaves: "I saw your letter concerning the sale of the daughter of the slave girl by Ṭuja to a [Guwānīn] named al-Ḥawālī. Before this letter, and as far as I know ever since ancient times, the buying and selling of slaves has continued according to our wishes just like the buying and selling of cattle. There is no difference between the two." Not only did Sakib reject the idea that there could be anything wrong with trading slaves, but he professed not to know that this was French policy: "Nothing you have sent me before has indicated that you do not accept the buying and selling of slaves. No messengers have come to inform me of this, nor has any Tuareg mentioned to me that you do not accept the buying and selling of slaves."[42] Sakib ended the letter by telling the commander at Timbuktu that since the person who purchased the slave girl was not under Igawaddaran authority, Sakib could do nothing about it.

40 Jean Gallais, *Pasteurs et paysans du Gourma: La condition sahélienne* (Paris: CNRS, 1975), 93–94.

41 He died on October 1, 1936. Cercle de Gourma-Rharous, "Rapport politique, 3ème trimestre 1936" (ANM 1E 2959, Num. Sér. I).

42 Letter #1 from Sakib ag Assamsamo to the Commandant, Cercle de Tombouctou, no date (ART M13).

I have only found Sakib's side of the correspondence with the colonial officials in Timbuktu. However, it is clear that despite their acquiescence to slavery, the French administration was unhappy with news of continuing sales of slaves in the Gourma. Judging from the next letter that Sakib sent, colonial officials were even less pleased with his attitude of apparent defiance and professed ignorance of the policy outlawing the slave trade. Sakib began his response by saying that, "I saw your letter which suggested that I am a liar for claiming that I did not know that you, the French, do not accept the buying and selling of slaves. You did not inform me of this so I did not prohibit it." Apparently, the order to end slave trading had not been communicated orally: "If you had informed me of this, and I had heard it from your mouths, then it would have disheartened me that you have forbidden the selling of slaves... but I am a supporter of what you like and accept."[43]

Although the colonial government recognized that slavery persisted in the Niger Bend,[44] only the most egregious abuses of slaves rose to the level of concern for the colonial administration. Not only was Sakib accused by French officials at Timbuktu of condoning the continuing trade in slaves, but he was also arrested in 1909 after a complaint was lodged against him by a person identified in the colonial record as a "bellah" named Borazza, who belonged to the Tuareg Kel Ulli. Borazza testified that Sakib had burned out his eyes with hot irons.[45] When Sakib was brought to Timbuktu to answer these charges, he acknowledged having ordered this grizzly procedure; but he also justified it because the victim was, according to Sakib, an inveterate thief. Such punishments were, he said, customary among the Tuareg against rebellious or disobedient slaves.[46] The case was judged by the tribunal of the district of Bamba and Sakib was released with a fine of twenty head of cattle.[47]

There are many cases in the colonial records of violence by masters against their slaves, including killings. What I want to focus on here are the ways in which slavery was justified and defended in the colonial period by Sahelian elites. I will use Shaykh Bay's large collection of legal

[43] Letter #2 from Sakib ag Assamsamo to the Commandant, Cercle de Tombouctou, no date (ART M13).

[44] Fousset, "Réponse à la circulaire No.266 A.P/Z de 20 juillet 1931 sur le travail servile en A.O.F.," December 4, 1931 (ANM FR 2E-134).

[45] Letter from Capitaine Staup, Commandant, Cercle de Bamba to the Commandant, Région de Tombouctou, No.227, June 8, 1909 (ANM FA 1E 21–22).

[46] Région de Tombouctou, "Rapport politique," June 1909 (ANM FA 1E 78–81).

[47] Cercle de Bamba, "Rapport politique," September 1909 (ANM FA 1E 21–22).

opinions as the basis for this discussion. Shaykh Bay was the last great Kunta scholar of the Niger Bend. He maintained a correspondence with French officials from his base in the Adrar-n-Ifoghas at Telaya during the first three decades of colonial rule. Unfortunately, there are no dates given for his individual opinions so all that can be said is that these issues arose sometime between 1895 when he took control of the zwaya and 1929, when he died.[48] The advantage of using this collection is that there are almost a thousand legal opinions by the same author, so it presents a fairly full picture of the various issues that were directed to an important Muslim scholar in the early colonial period in the Niger Bend.

Shaykh Bay was also highly thought of by French officials, who sent him gifts of Islamic books, cloth, sugar, and tea.[49] He was awarded – and he accepted – the "croix de chevalier" from the colonial administration in 1921.[50] Shaykh Bay kept his distance from the French, remaining in his remote hamlet of Telaya, but he consistently praised the French in his correspondence with them for bringing peace to the region. He was more frank about his motives in letters exchanged with people not involved with the colonial regime. In one piece of correspondence included in his collection of legal opinions, he suggested that it was important to get along with the French-led military units operating in the desert. He wrote that "their leaders are mostly foreigners (Ar. majlūbāt) whom I seek to please because it is a matter of the weaker."[51]

There is little indication in the colonial account of Sakib's putting out the eyes of Borazza, but the punishment of slaves accused of theft was a common issue that recurs in the collections of legal opinions in the region. One way in which the issue was framed was in terms of whether the ḥudūd punishments prescribed in the shariʿa, such as amputation of the hand of a thief, could be applied to slaves. According to the eighteenth-century scholar al-Sharif Hama Allah, whose opinions on blacks I discussed in Chapter 2, slaves could be punished in this way under certain conditions.[52] The punishments sanctioned by the shariʿa, however, did not include burning out a slave's eyes as Sakib had ordered. In

[48] Some opinions may be from earlier than 1895.

[49] Letter from Shaykh Bāy al-Kuntī to the Gouverneur, Haut-Sénégal-Niger, received May 8, 1917 (ANM FA 78–81).

[50] Letter from Colonel Mangeot, Commandant, Région de Tombocutou to the Gouverneur, Soudan Français, December 16, 1921 (ANM FR 1E 42).

[51] Shaykh Bāy al-Kuntī, "Nawāzil Shaykh Bāy" (IHERIAB ms. 124), #820, f. 31.

[52] Sīdi ʿAbd Allāh b. al-Ḥājj Ibrāhīm al-ʿAlawī, "Nawāzil al-ʿAlawī" (IHERIAB ms. 490), #327, f. 188–89.

fact, the mutilation of a slave was considered by some legal authorities to lead automatically to manumission.[53] But slaveholders did use violence against their slaves. In Shaykh Bay's collection of opinions, there is a case drawn from the colonial context. The question asked of him was for a ruling on, "inflicting the hudud punishments on slaves in this time, because they [can] escape to the tyrant (Ar. ṭāghiya) if they are beaten. Should masters end this practice or not?"[54] The "tyrant" referred to in the question is the French. The question indicates that slaveholders recognized the challenge that the colonial presence presented in making it possible for slaves to leave their masters. This reality imposed potential constraints on the kind of discipline and violence that could be inflicted. In Shaykh Bay's answer, he says that "the overwhelming majority of the scholars make it a duty to inflict the hudud punishment on his slave when it is the hudud punishment for adultery and drinking [alcohol] which is below the [level] of the amputation of the thieves."[55] The hudud punishment for adultery could be either flogging or stoning to death; for drinking alcohol, the punishment is flogging. Presumably, Shaykh Bay means to sanction only the flogging punishments here.

One questioner asked Shaykh Bay "whether or not it is permitted to beat a slave for not improving in his work for his master?" Shaykh Bay responded that, "yes, it is permitted but in proportion to [the slave's] offense and what he deems to be proper, although forgiving him is better."[56] Beating slaves for misbehavior is equated with the education of the family. Shaykh Bay quotes the Qur'an: "Save yourselves and your families from a fire whose fuel is men and stones."[57] As such, disciplining domestic slaves is analogous to ensuring the respect for Islamic practice within the household among women and children. But in the very next opinion, Shaykh Bay says that at the current time, hudud punishments cannot be carried out because they cannot be equitably applied: "Know that the infliction of the hudud punishments is impracticable (Ar. muta'dhdhir) today and [the reason] for its impracticality is that the fairness of the judgment is corrupted by the money of the greedy."[58] It is not clear whether he means to tie the presence of corruption to the colonial occupation or to a more general decline of morals.

53 John Hunwick and Eve Troutt Powell, *The African Diaspora in the Mediterranean Lands of Islam* (Princeton, NJ: Marcus Wiener, 2002), 27–8.
54 Shaykh Bāy al-Kuntī, "Nawāzil Shaykh Bāy" (IHERIAB ms. 124), #851, f. 42.
55 Ibid., #851, f. 42.
56 Ibid., #852, f. 43.
57 Qur'an, 66:6.
58 Shaykh Bāy al-Kuntī, "Nawāzil Shaykh Bāy" (IHERIAB ms. 124), #853, f. 43.

The reason that the more severe hudud punishments such as amputation or capital punishment were not recommended for slaves was because the legal liability for crimes committed by slaves lay with their masters. One of the most common slave crimes committed in the Niger Bend was the theft of animals. According to Ibn Juzayy's (d. 1340) textbook of Maliki juridical principles, in cases involving crimes against property:

> It makes no difference whether the property belongs to a free person or a slave, for it is accountable to the person of the slave who committed the offense. His master has the option to hand him over against the value of the property he damaged or destroyed, or to redeem him for that. It makes no difference whether what was damaged or destroyed is equivalent to the price of the slave, or whether it is greater or smaller.[59]

The distinction is made between the liability of the master for the damages caused by the slave, and the slave's lack of liability, except in his person (Ar. raqaba). Shaykh Bay quotes Ibn al-Muqrī (d. 1433)[60] to explain the reasoning behind this rule:

> The root of the lack of liability for the crimes of slaves is because the slave intends [to commit] the wrong (Ar. fasād) so it is taken from his person (raqaba). His master is harmed and he did not commit the crime, while the slave does not suffer yet he is the one who committed the crime. For committing a sin, another carries [the burden] which the Sunna imposes, so he is required to be turned over.[61]

In the Sahel, there were specific local interpretations of this issue. Shaykh Bay quoted Sidi Muhammad b. Sidi al-Mukhtar al-Kunti (d. 1826): "Our shaykh, may God accept him, did not rule that [the slave] should be surrendered at all, but rather, if the crime had a fine [assigned to it] that was less than [the slave's] value, then the fine was to be paid from the amount of his crime."[62]

There is an interesting case that illustrates the property rights and liabilities of slaves. Whereas a slave is entitled to an equal share of what is produced or gathered together with free people, he is not liable for losses that might be suffered in the same way. Shaykh Bay quoted Sīdi Muḥammad b. ʿAlī al-Dāwūdī (d. 1538)[63] saying that "the slave does not

59 Hunwick and Powell, *African Diaspora*, 25.

60 Ismāʿīl b. Abī Bakr al-Muqrī (1363–1433) was a Yemeni scholar and jurist (GAL SII 254–5).

61 Shaykh Bāy al-Kuntī, "Nawāzil Shaykh Bāy" (IHERIAB ms. 124), #766, f. 7–8.

62 Ibid., #766, pp.7–8.

63 GAL SII 401.

suffer losses (Ar. lā yughramu) with the free person." He then explains this by citing an unnamed Sahalian antecedent:

> Some of the elders of the Kel Essuk issued a fatwa concerning some of the herders who were free and others who were slaves, and among them were young people and old people who united to slaughter a cow. Some of them went to guard the animals – these were the young ones – and some of the others were with the cattle. He who contributes (HAr. lawah)[64] is therefore among the partners in the loss. For those of free status, [the liability] is taken from their property; for those that are slaves, it is an issue for their masters, or they [must] be turned over to them.[65]

Shaykh Bay then explains the liability of slaves for theft as follows: "I say that there is no difference in that between the free and the slave because what is required of the free is in his liability (dhimma), and of the slave is in his person (raqaba), so his master chooses between surrendering and ransoming him."[66] The liability of masters for theft by their slaves was certainly an inconvenience and a source of economic losses for slaveholders. But it was also an important way in which social hierarchy was supported and perpetuated. Slaves were not only an asset to masters, but also a charge over which they had responsibility. To hold together the social hierarchy in the Niger Bend at the beginning of colonial occupation, slaveholders had to be able to discipline their slaves.

The corollary to the social hierarchy that slaveholders sought to defend was the fact that the local colonial administration made masters responsible for collecting taxes on behalf of their slaves. There is a specific set of question related to colonial taxes (Ar. itāwāt) that "the non-Muslims take from the Muslims."[67] Shaykh Bay was asked about how this tax should be collected, whether it should be imposed as a head tax or as a percentage of property, and whether colonial taxes could be paid out of the public treasury (Ar. bayt al-māl).[68] None of these questions deal with slaves specifically, but there are also a series of inquiries about whether Islamic taxes can be collected from slaves. Because taxes such as the "zakāt" and the "kharāj" were in principle paid into the public treasury, and because the treasury could be used to pay colonial taxes, these questions do bear on French demands. Shaykh Bay argues that the master is responsible for paying the kharaj for his slaves, which in this context refers to a general tax

64 Jeffrey Heath, *Hassaniya Arabic (Mali) – English – French Dictionary* (Wiesbaden: Harrassowitz, 2004), 129.

65 Shaykh Bāy al-Kuntī, "Nawāzil Shaykh Bāy" (IHERIAB ms. 124), #764, f. 4–5.

66 Ibid., #764, f. 4–5.

67 Ibid., #841, f. 37–38.

68 The answer was yes (Ibid., #843, f. 39–40).

rather than a specific land tax. The slave is also not responsible for paying zakat, which is a fixed tithe meant for the support of the poor. Shaykh Bay says, "know that the money of the slave is that which was given to him by his master or someone else, or given to him as charity and therefore is considered the dowry of the community (Ar. mahr al-umma).... This is his money from which no zakat can be taken.... When it does not derive from the master, the money is his money in every condition and provision."[69] According to the Maliki school, whatever money a slave possesses is meant for his or her manumission.[70]

The question of slave property was an issue raised by a number of questioners. Slaves are not allowed to bequeath according to Islamic law, and it is their masters who inherit whatever property they possess at their deaths. Shaykh Bay responded to the idea that slaves might be able to bequeath by an uncharacteristic outburst: "As for [slaves] bequeathing, they are acts of buffoonery (Ar. yatahārajūna) and the agitation of donkeys, and it is among the manifest abominations which are not permitted for Muslims."[71] But slaves could own their own property. In one case, a master claimed that he gave property to his slave to look after for him, but that there were no witnesses to the transaction: "The master said to the slave that the property belongs to him, and that the slave is a [only] storage place (Ar. maqarr) for the property." For Shaykh Bay, the inferior status of the slave, "that the slave is known as a non-being (Ar. ʿadam)," was a reason why the claims of the master in this case should prevail.[72] Slaves were, however, permitted to keep the part of their property that they earned on their own time. According to Shaykh Bay:

> His property is that which he possesses on the day of his freedom by the work of his own hand, or that he obtained his wages himself, so [in this case] his part is not for his master. There is a saying: What he does with his hand or by wages in the day of his master is for the master; but what he gives to him, or the alms that he receives, or in the case of the female, the dowry she receives, this is not for the master.[73]

In a similar way, the dowry of a married female slave belonged to her, and not her master.[74]

[69] Shaykh Bāy al-Kuntī, "Nawāzil Shaykh Bāy" (IHERIAB ms. 119), #241, f. 314.
[70] This is in Ibn Abī Zayd al-Qayrawānī, "al-Risāla," translated in Hunwick and Powell, *African Diaspora*, 30–1.
[71] Shaykh Bāy al-Kuntī, "Nawāzil Shaykh Bāy" (IHERIAB ms. 119), #352, f. 391–92.
[72] Shaykh Bāy al-Kuntī, "Nawāzil Shaykh Bāy" (IHERIAB ms. 121), #619, f. 655–56.
[73] Shaykh Bāy al-Kuntī, "Nawāzil Shaykh Bāy" (IHERIAB ms. 124), #880, f. 55–56.
[74] Shaykh Bāy al-Kuntī, "Nawāzil Shaykh Bāy" (IHERIAB ms. 122), #690, f. 58–59.

THE MORALITY OF SLAVERY

The extent to which the historical practice of slavery in the Sahel was regulated by the rules of Islamic law is difficult to ascertain. Questions about slavery are certainly very common in the collections of legal opinions from the area, and this suggests that there was certainly a broad level of awareness about what the rules of piety demanded in the treatment of slaves. However, the relationship between slavery and Islamic law took on some new meanings in the context of the early colonial period. Even though most French officials sympathized with slaveholders and acted to constrain the paths to independence by slaves,[75] colonial occupation presented a challenge to long-standing slave systems. Sakib's arguments to his French interlocutors in defense of slavery were not very sophisticated, at least in the form that we have access to them. He argued that slavery was as natural in the Niger Bend as the possession and trading of livestock. It seems likely that many slaveholders shared this view.[76] But it was not the only defense available to slaveholders. Slavery is legitimate in Islamic law and as such, defenders of slavery could make reference to a very sophisticated canon of ideas that helped define and justify its practice under colonial rule.

Sakib claimed that slaves were like livestock; Shaykh Bay disagreed, but only because he thought that slavery could be a moral instrument of uplift for blacks. Shaykh Bay met with the French agronomist and explorer Georges Reynard de Gironcourt in the Adrar-n-Ifoghas during his visit to the Niger Bend in 1911–1912.[77] He provided the French researcher with a number of brief historical notices written in Arabic about different peoples in the region. One of them was about the blacks who had inhabited the Adrar before the arrival of the Tuareg and Arabs: "As for the nations of the blacks and a detailed exposition of their states in this land, only God Almighty knows about it. They have died and as such information about them has disappeared except for their vestiges.... They were nations included in the passage of time but they were not among those

[75] On the legal pathways for slaveholders in colonial Mauritania, see Charles Stewart, "A comparison of the exercise of colonial and precolonial justice in Mauritania," in *Nomades et commandants: Administration et sociétés nomades dans l'ancienne A.O.F.*, ed. Edmund Bernus (Paris: Karthala, 1993), 81–6.

[76] Jeremy Berndt, "Closer Than Your Jugular Vein: Muslim Intellectuals in a Malian Village, 1900 to the 1960s" (Ph.D. diss., Northwestern University, 2007), 57.

[77] P.F. de Moraes Farias, "A Letter from Ki-Toro Mahamman Gaani, King of Busa (Borgu, Northern Nigeria) about the 'Kisra' Stories of Origin (*c.* 1910)," *SA* 3 (1992): 116–17.

who wrote and chronicled their history to preserve it. Rather they were like beasts for which the only important thing is to eat and drink."[78] It was only the introduction of Islam, according to Shaykh Bay, that began the process of civilizing the blacks. Enslavement was one means of beginning this process.

In response to a question about the status of a child borne to a female slave girl who was married to another slave, but whose master continued to have sexual relations with her, Shaykh Bay explained how slaves in the custody of Muslims could not be equated with beasts:

> Be warned that having sex with a female slave who has a husband is a grave sin requiring repentance. It is impossible for her husband to accept, even if he is a slave, or like a slave, or even a non-slave. Know that the rights of both the slave and the free are equal, and for both, violating their inviolability is not permissible. God has assigned to the master only those things from the slave that are known in [the rules for] the proper conduct in sales, or gifts, or in disciplining [the slave] commensurate with his offense. [The master] does not own [the slave] himself as he owns beasts (Ar. dawābb). Therefore, it is not permissible for him to kill him, nor to cut off his limbs, nor to hit him, nor to insult him wrongfully, nor to coerce his wife [into having sex with him]. He who presses [his slave] in any [of these ways] does so unlawfully and must [therefore] repent.[79]

That there are rules that regulate the social relationship between masters and slaves is a theme that Shaykh Bay returnes to again and again in his opinions. To further his point, he cited a hadith of the Prophet Muhammad:

> A man came and said "O Prophet of God, if I have some property and if I have a servant and if I become angry, can I decide to scold and hit him?" The Prophet of God, may God bless him and grant him peace, said: "Balance his offences with your punishment. If they are equal, then it is not to your benefit or to your detriment; but if the punishment is greater [than the offence], it will count as something taken out of your account on the Day of Judgment." So then the man said: "Alas! It is taken from my account." [The Prophet] then said: "[Excessive punishment] counts [against you]. Have you not heard the word of Almighty God? "We shall set up scales of justice for the Day of Judgment."[80]

[78] "Manuscrits arabes, ou copies, relatifs à l'histoire et aux traditions de l'Afrique intérieure, recueillis par Georges de Gironcourt au cours de sa mission archéologique au Soudan français (1911)" (Bibliothèque de l'Institut de France, Paris, Côte 2406, pièce 95). Printed with French translation in Charles Grémont, "Les Touareg Iwellemmedan (1647–1898): Un ensemble politique de la Boucle du Niger" (Ph.d. diss., Université Paris 1, 2007), 505–7.

[79] Shaykh Bāy al-Kuntī, "Nawāzil Shaykh Bāy" (IHERIAB ms. 119, #340), f. 384–87.

[80] Qur'an 21: 47; Shaykh Bāy al-Kuntī, "Nawāzil Shaykh Bāy" (IHERIAB ms. 119), #340, f. 384–87.

Shaykh Bay then cited another hadith: "He who falsely accused an innocent slave, will face the hudud punishment on the Day of Judgment unless it turns out that [his accusation was correct]."[81]

Just as there were strict rules regulating the punishments of slaves, Islamic law imposed conditions on masters as well. One of the clearest sites where this is evident is in the numerous questions about parentage of children born to slave women. We have already discussed cases of enslaved blacks claiming to be free Muslims, and the injunction by scholars from Ahmad Baba to Shaykh Bay that a newly enslaved person's claims to be wrongly enslaved should be considered credible in certain conditions. Those questions had to do with the status of the slave and the possibility that blacks could be free Muslims. A similar set of questions were sent to Shaykh Bay concerning wrongly enslaved women who were captured by pastoralist warriors in raids, and whose juridical status was therefore that of the mustaghraq al-dhimma. One question asks about a man "who bought an unlawfully acquired slave girl with his good money, and he had sex with her; and then it was explained to him after this that she is an unambiguous free person."[82] The questioner asks whether the child of the union should be linked to the man as his progeny, and whether the woman should be considered an "umm walad," or "mother of a child," which would allow her to later gain the status of a freed slave. Shaykh Bay said, in reference to the man who acquired the slave, that "if he knew that she was unlawfully acquired, then he is a fornicator and should receive the hudud punishments." Even if he only learned later that the female slave was acquired illegally, he acquires the status of usurper (Ar. ghāṣib) himself unless he immediately refunds the proceeds of the sale and returns the slave. If a child results from their sexual union, he is obliged to recognize the child and marry the woman: "Whether he received her as a gift or purchased her without knowing that this slave girl was obtained unlawfully, if he causes her to bear a child, the child is linked to him and he must pay a dowry."[83] Similarly, another questioner asked Shaykh Bay whether the child of a female slave acquired from a person or group whose juridical status is mustaghraq al-dhimma can be attributed to the master who had sex with her. To this creative effort to use the status of mustaghraq al-dhimma to evade the responsibility that masters had to their female slaves to free them once they had given the

[81] Shaykh Bāy al-Kuntī, "Nawāzil Shaykh Bāy" (IHERIAB ms. 119), #340, f. 384–87.
[82] Ibid., #348, f. 390–91.
[83] Ibid., #348, f. 390–91.

master a child, Shaykh Bay responded categorically: "Such a master, perpetrates a shameful, disgraceful affair, and as such we are afraid of the way of truth! But the child is linked to him because of the spurious argument raised concerning their properties."[84]

In one case, a questioner asked about a child presented to him by his female slave who was married to another slave. The questioner admitted to having had sex with his slave, but claimed that he could not have fathered the child. Shaykh Bay listed the conditions that would need to have been fulfilled for this man to have been cleared of parentage. However, instead of letting the questioner off the hook in this way, Shaykh Bay quotes the Prophet Muḥammad to admonish the questioner: "Woe to women who make people enter [a house] which does not belong to them or to God in any way; God will not invite her to enter His paradise. Woe to the man who disavows his child, expecting that God, in His power and majesty, will hide [the child] and his disgrace from the heads of neighboring families and others on the Day of Judgment."[85] It is the second line that is directed at the questioner. The crux of the matter, though, is that if it is possible that the master impregnated his slave, the child is judged to be his:

> If some of the aforementioned conditions are met, even if the slave sleeps with his wife and then you slept with her until her pregnancy became evident, and then you had sex with her in secret after this while she was in this state, and then [the slave] returns and sleeps with her again before the appearance of the pregnancy, the primary [person responsible for the pregnancy] is you – this is what the texts demonstrate.[86]

If the child belongs to the master, he is obliged to free the mother who now assumes the status of the umm walad.

If many of the issues discussed above are focused on correct behavior by masters toward their slaves, there is a still more explicit set of arguments that attach moral significance to the existence of slavery itself. Shaykh Bay did not say anything at all about a direct colonial challenge to the institution of slavery, but he did expend considerable energy connecting slavery to the historical role of people like the Kunta in bringing Islam to blacks. Shaykh Bay reiterated the ethical value of the kind of social and racial hierarchy that existed in his conception of the Sahel. It is the duty of slaveholders to teach their slaves about Islam and to wean them off non-Muslim customs that made them legitimate targets

[84] Ibid., #349, f. 391.
[85] Ibid., #340, f. 384–87.
[86] Ibid., #340, f. 384–87.

of enslavement in the first place. Even when slaves move away from their masters, or after their manumission, this ethics insists on the responsibility of the masters to guide them in their social lives. I think that the morality of slavery is meant to apply more broadly to the historical role imagined by pastoralist clerical groups such as the Kunta in bringing Islam to West Africa.

Many collections of legal opinions include some version of the question: Is it incumbent upon masters to educate their slaves about Islam, and to force them to be practicing Muslims? In the Kunta tradition, the answer to this question was made by the great shaykh, Sidi al-Mukhtar al-Kunti (d. 1811), in response to the query: "Is it sufficient for the master to exhort his slaves to Islam or must he force them? Is it incumbent upon him and why?" Sidi al-Mukhtar's response was that:

> It is not sufficient just to propagate but instead it is necessary that he force them [to become Muslims] whether they are non-believers (Ar. majūs) or idolaters (Ar. wathaniyīn). They should be forced without killing them by beatings and threats. If [the slave] is led to Islam, and he is corrected in the recitation of the Muslim credo, then it is also necessary to force them to learn their religion including issues of purity, prayer, and fasting. He should not speak to them about work during the period of learning the [essential] texts.[87]

Shaykh Bay made precisely the same point and said that there is no scholarly disagreement about this issue. The slave must "know what God permits and what he forbids," because in this way he will be able "to claim the rights that God has put in place for him."[88] In another question, he was asked whether in the particular conditions of pastoralist life, slaves should be forced to pray in the congregational Friday prayer. Shaykh Bay acknowledged the differences between religious customs among pastoralists and sedentary people, and the fact that pastoral life makes congregational prayer difficult because there are often an insufficient number of worshippers for it to be officially constituted. However, he insisted that it is a duty for everyone in pastoralist society to perform "the ʿid prayer [in the two major Muslim feasts] which is required of every Muslim. It is a duty for women, men, slaves, travelers, and those who are old enough to pray among the youth."[89]

Another questioner asked whether "the husband is required to educate the slaves of his wife just like his own slaves, or is that her obligation?"

[87] Sīdi al-Mukhtār al-Kuntī, "al-Ajwiba al-muhimma" (IHERIAB ms. 1476), f. 38.
[88] Shaykh Bāy al-Kuntī, "Nawāzil Shaykh Bāy" (IHERIAB ms. 118), #173, f. 218.
[89] Ibid., #179, f. 229.

Shaykh Bay's answer is that it is the wife's obligation because she is the provider (Ar. muqaddima):

As for the extent of the education that you teach the slave and the people of the family (Ar. ahl), it is a duty for him to struggle to do this, whether [he instructs them] himself or employs an agent to represent him. He should withdraw [the slaves] from work for a period of time in order to educate them about what is required in matters of their religion, just like the text of all of the scholars indicates....

He should set forth the principles (Ar. qawāʿid) of the articles of faith (Ar. ʿaqāʾid) in a simplified form. He does not mention that which is not conceivable in [the slave's] mind but instead provides him with satisfying proofs until the ideas are firmly embedded in him. It is not done according to the way of the kalām theologians, and he is not asked in the beginning about what are the principles of faith. Instead he must acknowledge his Lord according to the singularity of [God's] existence, and His Prophet according to the mission of prophethood. However, by demonstrating to him the truth about the difference between the Creator and His creation, and that Muhammad is a creature born from two parents and chosen by his Lord over all of His creation, and that He sent him to the two worlds so that he reached prophethood and that God his Lord took him [i.e. when he died], [the slave] will learn what his belief requires of him from the Resurrection and the sureness of the comfort of the grave or its torment [i.e. for having been a sinner]. It is a question of the Malikis for each person to be responsible, and the destiny of the believers is to go to heaven, and the infidels to the fire.[90]

Shaykh Bay said that it is a common practice of "masters to leave their slaves untended like livestock." He uses the term "bidʿ," which means "religious innovations," to describe this attitude, indicating that it is not consistent with correct Islamic practice. Arguing that these requirements for educating slaves can be found in a number of Kunta writings, he then cites what he calls a well-known poem that rhymes in the Arabic letter rāʾ (al-Qaṣīda al-rāʾiya), composed by Ḥabīb Allāh b. Sīdi al-Mukhtār al-Kuntī:

And preserve the right of the slave; for indeed
It is affirmed in matters of religion; so be patient and steadfast
And teach them the matter of the creeds; for indeed
It is incumbent upon you; so lead them to the well
And do not disregard them as if they were livestock; for indeed
They are human beings and everyone is under the intractability of the command
So first, the Day of Judgment is presented
For his slaves, as they yearn for recompense.
As for adversaries who ask about their rights,

[90] Shaykh Bāy al-Kuntī, "Nawāzil Shaykh Bāy" (IHERIAB ms. 125), #940, f. 22–26.

Asking how he could put down his basket for the sake of goodness?
But we are only under the grasp of His palm
Which turns us away from what He wishes in the matter.
So he is not defeated by that subjugation without a command,
And they are set forth in the protective hole of the embers.[91]

Shaykh Bay's principal argument is that God commands that the whole family be educated and practice Islam correctly. He finds further support for this position in one of Usman dan Fodio's writings called the "Rulings of the Foundation" ("Aḥkām al-Ass"), which he quoted at length:

> Among the matters which have become a general necessity in this country is the way that many of the scholars in this land act in neglecting their wives, girls, and slaves as if this were an act of kindness to not do what God has made a duty for them. They must [teach] them the credo, and the ruling about their ritual ablution before prayer, and [how to avoid] forbidden religious innovation. Instead, they treat them like a vessel (Ar. wiʿāʾ) that they work with until it breaks, after which they throw it away on the dung heap, which is [the same as] any place of impurity. Is it any wonder how they leave their wives, daughters, and slaves in the darkness of ignorance and error?[92]

If masters fulfill their obligations toward their slaves by educating them as Muslims, Shaykh Bay also required them to allow their slaves to live in dignified ways. This especially concerns female slaves. Slaves require the permission of their masters to marry. Shaykh Bay reported that he had participated in discussions with scholars of the Kel Essuk about the marriage of female slaves. He said, "it suddenly struck some of the lesser scholars (Ar. ṭalaba) that there was a rank of nobility required for marrying, and they preferred to leave [slaves] alone to move around like the beasts."[93] Shaykh Bay explains that marriage for slaves is a good thing because male slaves have "readily apparent needs." Not only does marriage provide an outlet for natural (male) slave sexuality, it also, he says, makes slaves happier. However, if slaves marry without having obtained the permission of their owners, Shaykh Bay says that those marriages are void and considered to be adultery:

[91] wa-ḥāfiẓ ʿalā ḥaqqi al-raqīqi fa-anna-hu * man awakkad amr al-dīni fa-iṣbir wa-ṣābir
wa-ʿallim-hum amra ʾl-diyānati anna-hu * yuḥiqqu ʿalay-kum wa-iḥmilū-hum ʿalā ʾl-bir
wa-lā tahmilū-hum ka-ʾl-bahāʾimi anna-hu * banū Ādam wa-ʾl-kull taḥt ʿaṣīy al-amr
fa-awwal mā yulqā-hu yawm ḥisābi-hi * ariqqāʾu-hu ama yahinūna bi-ʾl-ajr
wa-amā khuṣūm yusʾalūna ḥuqūqa-hum * yuqūlūna sall-hu kayfa lam yadaʿ li-ʾl-khayr
wa mā naḥnu illā taḥta qabḍati kaffi-hi * yaṣrifu-nā fī-mā yushāʾu min al-amr
fa-yukhṣamu ʿinda dhālik qahran bi-lā amran * wa-yulqūna fī qaʿr ḥāmiyat al-jamr
(Ibid., #940, f. 22–26).

[92] Ibid., #940, f. 22–26.

[93] Shaykh Bāy al-Kuntī, "Nawāzil Shaykh Bāy" (IHERIAB ms. 122), #687, f. 52–53.

It is not lawful for any [slaves] to marry without the permission of his master or an owner of a portion of him. If this happens anyway, then it is for the master to authorize or nullify it. If he wants to nullify it, he has to nullify it in a divorce [which is irrevocable], and he has to nullify it at a Maliki mosque by two proclamations of divorce in order to break off [the relationship that] is between them so that [the slave] does not hold out any hope.... All of this is well-known and it is the view of Abū 'l-Farj from the scholars of the Maliki madhhab, and most of the community, that the marriage of the slave without the permission of his master is immoral (Ar. fāsid). If the master authorizes [the marriage], this comes from the hadith of Abū Dāwūd,[94] [which states that] a slave can only marry with the permission of his people and his followers.[95]

For Shaykh Bay, the morality of slavery lay in its ability to raise slaves from infidelity to Islam. For this to work, however, masters had to be vigilant in their oversight.

THE STAIN OF SLAVERY

The manumission of slaves is considered a pious act that will bring rewards in the next world. However, a manumitted slave was expected to maintain a relationship with his or her former masters in a form of clientship called "walāʾ," in Arabic. It is in the structures of the post-emancipation relationships between former masters and freed slaves that the racial difference that stands at the beginning of enslavement reappears at the end. For Shaykh Bay, the act of manumission completes the transformation begun in the moral act of enslavement. One questioner asked whether in the current circumstances, manumitting slaves is better than giving alms. In his answer, Shaykh Bay responded that it is an act of piety to free a Muslim slave because such an action is evidence of religious redemption: "Manumission is better because it bears witness from those who are hidden and proclaims what he denies.... [The slave's] being is atonement for killing in a military conflict."[96]

One questioner asked about the relationship between a master and his manumitted slave. Shaykh Bay responded:

He is his brother, so what remains between brothers are good deeds (Ar. mabarra), and the aspects of the ties of contiguous kinship (Ar. ṣilat al-raḥim) that is permanent between them. That is, if the emancipated slave is a rightly-guided person. When there is no discourse like this for [the emancipated slave], he goes and lives where he likes, and he does with himself and his property as he wishes. There is

[94] Hadith collector, died 889.
[95] Shaykh Bāy al-Kuntī, "Nawāzil Shaykh Bāy" (IHERIAB ms. 119), #347, f. 389–90.
[96] Shaykh Bāy al-Kuntī, "Nawāzil Shaykh Bāy" (IHERIAB ms. 124), #881, f. 56.

nobody to protest about it, or about the need to restrict him or prevent him from going where he wishes. This is a matter subject to numerous grave offenses. It is in the authenticated hadith: "Your sparks (Ar. sharār) that are not manumitted freely, they glow for him in the end." [The Prophet Muhammad] said: "Any of them who manumit [their slave] should then employ him. If [the emancipated slave] wants to leave them, they should claim him as their slave."[97]

The manumitted slave is subject to a number of defects on his freedom. One of the questions that appears in Shaykh Bay's collection touches on the issue of inheritance for freed slaves. What can manumitted slaves bequeath? Shaykh Bay responded:

Know that you are, when you manumit your slave, still there for him and that he continues to have restrictions on his legal competence. He becomes like a cousin according to the indication of [the Prophet's] statement: "Clientage (walā') is [a form] of kinship (Ar. luḥma) like the kinship of lineage (Ar. nasab). He can not be sold and he can not be given as a present."[98]

The principle of inheritance in this case, however, is that the manumitter, or the larger community of Muslims, inherits from the slave, whereas his inferior social status means that he does not inherit from them: "The gist is that the manumitted slave … is brought by the manumitter … to the rank of the cousin on the paternal side, enjoying paternal relations (Ar. ʿaṣaba) in blood money (Ar. ʿaql), in which each one of them acts on behalf of the others. The manumitter … inherits from the manumitted slave but not the other way around."[99]

The manumitted slave is not permitted, according to the Sunan of Ibn Mājah (d. 887), to lead others in prayer. When a freed slave comes to prayer, he should pray at the back, behind the others. Shaykh Bay explained his interpretation of this hadith as follows:

The people have become accustomed to [the manumitted slave's] subjugation and his coercion so that when he is raised by his manumitter, it is reprehensible (Ar. munkar). This is my opinion on this hadith. In other hadiths, that presence is among the greatest offenses other than being afraid that if he is a fool who makes his foolishness apparent [to others], then his manumitter has a right with regards to trusteeship (Ar. wilāya) not different from that over a child who is owed his expenses until he is able to work and he is employed just as his sons are employed. It is not forbidden when it is in return for expenses. If he exceeds [this] and acts unjustly, [God] will know those who oppressed anyone in the hereafter where it will be turned upside down.[100]

97 Ibid., #879, f. 54–55.
98 Ibid., #901, f. 64–65.
99 Ibid., #901, f. 64–65.
100 Ibid., #879, f. 55–56.

Shaykh Bay says, "it is best that he who is manumitted is in the inviolable custody (Ar. riʿāya) of his manumitter and from this there is no separation for anything other than an obvious excuse. He is his big brother rather than his father."[101] However, the freed slave is obliged to remain in the relationship with his former master:

> It is a true [hadith] according to the tradition of the Prophet, that he who makes claims upon he who is not his father or depends on those who are not his masters, is cursed by God, the angels and the people together. God does not accept he who beats [people] and is not honest on the Day of Judgment. The entrusted person (Ar. mutawallin) who is without his masters is denied their favor (Ar. niʿma) upon him.[102]

So even after achieving freedom, the manumitted slave requires the intervention of his masters in order to assume a place in the next world.

The traces of slavery are also evident in a question about whether female slaves can cover themselves for reasons of modesty. Shaykh Bay said, "the slave girl is most deserving of protection because she is degraded and venal, so if the slave is not among them because of the paucity of clearness of her origins, then we turn to the nobility of her sons and the fact that they are accepted despite all of their baseness. So you should preserve her modesty and you should take care of her completely."[103] In response to a question about whether a female slave who had been taken as a concubine still owed her master the daily domestic labor of other slaves, Shaykh Bay responded by explaining the difference in status between slaves, freed slaves, and free people. After saying that the concubine still owes her master all the daily labor that other domestic slaves do, he turned to the case of the umm walad, the mother of her master's child:

> As for the umm walad, there is a flaw (Ar. shāʾiba) in her freedom, and although she has the utmost level of inviolability, she is below the wife in this. As such, he is owed more service from her than a free woman, but less than that required of a female slave. He can veil her, and this is desirable but not required, and she can wrap herself in it to avoid any doubt if it is a necessary matter. Respect for her is required as long as she avoids scandalous actions. Keeping the lineage name [of her master] is required [for the umm walad], whereas the slave girl is a despised (Ar. mumtahina) and trite (Ar. mubtadhal) interposing outsider.[104]

We must understand the flaw in the freedom of the manumitted slave as a result of the fact of his or her original enslavement.

[101] Ibid., #879, f. 55–56.
[102] Ibid., #879, f. 55–56.
[103] Shaykh Bāy al-Kuntī, "Nawāzil Shaykh Bāy" (IHERIAB ms. 125), #935, f. 18.
[104] Shaykh Bāy al-Kuntī, "Nawāzil Shaykh Bāy" (IHERIAB ms. 119), #372, f. 420–21.

CONCLUSION

The ideological structure of the racist argument is as follows: If the basis of the imagined relationship connecting Muslims and blacks lies in the original moment of encounter with ʿUqba b. Nafiʿ's jihad, and if the enslaveability of blacks is the result of that first meeting, then it is also true that the stain of original unbelief adheres to the person who passes through the system of slavery and becomes a Muslim. Even as a free person, the disabilities of blackness are retained, and the freed slave finds herself in a permanent relationship as a junior client. Shaykh Bay did not address the question of whether this disability was transgenerational. This would not be justifiable in the strict terms of personal status law. But it is clear that others did make the connection between race and inferior social status, and that blackness stood for a slave past in Sahelian societies. I will discuss some of the reactions of those defined as blacks in the following chapters; for now, I want only to point out that there was a pushback that suggested an argument that all free Muslims were in principle equal. A manumission document written in Timbuktu in 1925 seems to argue against these postemancipation conditions limiting freedom. It invokes the manumitted slave's status as a free Muslim, with no stain of slavery remaining, and it invokes the slave's color – his blackness – as an illegitimate argument for his social inferiority. The document says:

> [The emancipated slave] responds that the true vestiges and [remaining] reality [of his enslavement] is in the freedom of Muslims as their right and duty. Nothing of the traces of slavery remains upon him and the only bondage is the road of ardent desire for He who loves him [thus] releasing him. Whosoever disputes his change [of status] after hearing of it follows the example of those who oppress because of his color – God is all hearing and all knowing.[105]

This document makes no mention of the colonial presence in Timbuktu, but it is the product of the changed circumstances of French occupation that made necessary this contestation of the racial basis of slavery. The arguments that blacks can be full Muslims are as old as Ahmad Baba's famous response to the questioner from Tuwat at the beginning of the seventeenth century. But here is evidence that those defined as blacks contested the argument that their blackness was a marker of inferior status as Muslims. Race was not only a way of defending social privilege; it also became a tool for fighting against it.

[105] Alfa San b. Muḥammad al-Suyūṭī, manumission document, 1925 (IHERIAB ms. 16489).

7

Defending the River

Songhay Arguments about Land, c. 1893–1940

"THE RIVER BELONGS TO US, THE BUSH BELONGS TO GOD"

Whatever their difficulties and frustrations in administering pastoralist groups, French administrators admired the noble stratum among the Arabs and Tuareg. Their opinion of the sedentary, mostly Songhay-speaking people of the Niger Bend was almost exactly the opposite. Described as passive, racially degenerate, cowardly, and dishonest, the sedentary population was seen as ignoble by French officials. In the official publication on behalf of Soudan Français on the occasion of the colonial exposition in Paris in 1931, the Governor General of French West Africa echoed almost exactly the racial ideas of the nineteenth-century race polemist Arthur de Gobineau:

> By the way that they appear today, the Songhay could not have played the brilliant role attributed to them in the history of the Soudan. In reality, that history took place in their land, but only involved them in a passive way. The Songhay have never constituted a people of warriors or rulers, with the exception of some Sorko clans which have always had the instincts of pillagers and conquerors. The so-called Songhay Empire was from beginning to end governed by Berber and Soninké princes, to say nothing of the periods when it paid tribute to the Mandingos, Mossi, and the Tuareg. The rare powerful rulers who gave some prestige to that empire depended for their power on an army recruited from other places. The mass of the Songhay people are composed of farmers, fishers, and merchants, who are defenseless and of mediocre intelligence, and were endlessly at the mercy of invasions, raids, and revolutions which descended to the banks of the river from the lower to the middle Niger until the French conquest.[1]

[1] Gouverneur-Général de l'Afrique Occidentale Française, *Le Soudan* (Paris: Société d'éditions géographiques, maritimes et colonials, 1931), 23–4.

This perception, based in part on the reality of indigenous power relations in the immediate precolonial period, helped structure the nature of colonial domination and the perpetuation of inequality between pastoralists and sedentary peoples.

What happened to Songhay speakers during the period of colonial rule was quite distinct from the processes that helped shape Tuareg and Arab interactions with French officials. Instead of encouraging the further development of a self-conscious elite stratum among Songhay-speakers whose power would be based on the continuing control over servile labor, as was the policy toward Tuareg and Arab pastoralists, the colonial state showed little interest in cultivating Songhay allies. Colonial ideas about black inferiority translated into a double burden for Songhay-speaking sedentary people; on the one hand, they were forced to fulfill a greater share of colonial demands for forced labor, military conscription, and taxes, and on the other, they found themselves at a colonially-sanctioned disadvantage when in competition over resources with pastoralist groups. Yet despite these disadvantages, the French regime substituted itself for the pastoralist domination over Songhay-speaking sedentary people. The change in pastoralist-sedentary relations produced a shift in the trajectories of racial discourse among all the peoples of the Niger Bend.

The elite stratum that did exist among Songhay speakers before the arrival of the French was a landowning class. There was a wide variety of agricultural land tenure systems in the Niger Bend, ranging from highly concentrated, quasi-feudal sharecropping systems to village-level communal tenure arrangements that produced relatively little inequality in access to land. For an elite stratum to have consolidated among the Songhay, the colonial state would have had to encourage and support the quasi-feudal tenure systems that did exist, and make it colonial policy to recognize such arrangements in other locations where they did not. Indeed, for political reasons connected to the larger policies associated with "la politique des races," French officials did initially identify a racially distinct elite among Songhay-speakers. However, the relative weakness of this class compared to their Tuareg and Arab counterparts, and the lack of a military threat posed by the Songhay to the colonial position, rendered this strategy less important.

The ideas of Songhay-ness that emerged in the twentieth century were both ethnic and racial. The collective label "Songhay" appears in Sahelian Arabic sources in the early-sixteenth-century text of al-Maghili's replies to Askia Muhammad. Ahmad Baba referred to the Songhay in his "The ladder of ascent" written at the beginning of the seventeenth century, and the term is repeated many times in the mid-seventeenth-century chronicles the "Ta'rikh al-sudan" and the "Ta'rikh al-fattash." In these uses, the term Songhay meant all free or noble Songhay-speakers (So. borochin).[2] There are a complex of related Songhay languages and cultures along the Niger valley from Djenné in the west all the way to the Dendi areas of the present-day republic of Niger and Northern Benin. Different groups within this larger linguistic-cultural complex identify themselves with a variety of historical migrations into – and within – the Niger Bend, and in terms of the participation of their ancestors in one way or another in the last thousand years of the region's history.

Songhay-speaking societies were, like others in the Sahel, socially stratified with significant servile populations. As was the case among the speakers of Arabic, Tamashek, and Fulfulde in the Niger Bend, Songhay speakers distinguished between noble and servile people within their own societies using color-coded labels.[3] The elite stratum among the Songhay did not consider itself to be black. Many Songhay-speakers claim to be descended from an original traveler from Yemen who settled in the Niger Bend, killed a local fish deity, and married a local princess.[4]

[2] In Songhay, there is no difference between "free" and "noble." John Hunwick makes a slightly narrower argument that in the "Ta'rikh al-sudan," the term Songhay (Ar. ahl sughay) refers to the ruling elite of the Songhay Empire (*Timbuktu and the Songhay Empire: Al-Sa`dī's Ta'rîkh al-sûdân down to 1613 and Other Contemporary Documents* [Leiden: Brill, 1999], 2n.)

[3] In contemporary Hassaniyya Arabic, the terms "whites" and "blacks" (bīḍān/sūdān) are used to distinguish between Arabic-speakers who are free in status and those who have a slave past. A different Hassaniyya word for blacks (kwār) is used to identify non-Arabic speaking (or ethnically distinct) Africans (Urs Peter Ruf, "Ending Slavery. Hierarchy, Dependency and Gender in Central Mauritania" [Ph.D. diss., University of Bielefeld, 1998], 38; Catherine Taine-Cheikh, "La Mauritanie en noir et blanc. Petit Promenade linguistique en Hassaniya," *Revue du Monde Musulman et de la Méditerranée* 54 [1989]: 90–105). In contemporary Tamashek usage, color-based terminology is invoked to distinguish internal social status and to denote those who are termed blacks (kawalnen), whether they are of servile origin within Tuareg society or non-Tuareg-speaking blacks (Baz Lecocq, "'That Desert is Our Country': Tuareg Rebellions and Competing Nationalisms in Contemporary Mali (1946–1996)" [Ph.D. diss., University of Amsterdam, 2002], 12; Lecocq, *Disputed Desert: Decolonisation, Competing Nationalisms and Tuareg Rebellions in Northern Mali* (Leiden: Brill, 2010), 97–9; Jeffrey Heath, *Dictionnaire touareg du Mali: tamachek-anglais-français* [Paris: Karthala, 2006], 333). The Fulbe use a notion of color in their categories of social status, distinguishing between a red noble class (wodeebe) and the less noble, or ignoble, blacks (baleebe) (Hallasy Sidibé, Mamadou Diallo, and Coumbel Barry, "Pulaaku et crise d'identité: le cas des Fulbe wodeebe (Peuls rouges) de la région lacustre de l'Issa-Ber au Mali," in *Peuls et Mandingues. Dialectique des constructions identitaires*, ed. Mirjam de Bruijn and Hans van Dijk [Paris: Karthala, 1997], 226–8).

[4] This is in the "Ta'rikh al-sudan" (Hunwick, *Timbutku*, 5–6).

Others claim to be descended from Muslim Arabs, just like their pastoralist neighbors.[5] The "blacks" (So. gaabibi, harbibi) on the other hand, were described to early colonial researchers as a servile caste of people whose slave origins continued to impose on them a burden of service to noble Songhay-speakers.[6] These claims need to be understood as racial arguments about the obligations of certain people to others much like claims to Sorko servility made by Amadu Lobbo and Sobbo ag Fondogomo, rather than as an accurate description of social facts. However, it is also true that racial markers are found even in many place names in the Niger Bend where the terms white (So. korey) and black (So. bibi) appear. The best-known example is Sankoré, the name of the famous medieval mosque-university in Timbuktu, whose etymology is from "white masters" (So. san-korey). In important ways, high-status Songhay-speakers made the same kinds of racial arguments as others in the Sahel, privileging social status and lineage as more important than anything we might designate as ethnic.

Claims to be "nonblack" have not entirely disappeared from the Songhay-speaking world of the Niger Bend. It remains an oft-heard refrain among people who claim to be descended from the Arma and those who trace their ancestry to the family of the Prophet Muhammad. Nonetheless, as I will demonstrate in this chapter, the socioeconomic basis of racially distinct social strata among Songhay-speakers was significantly undermined by the imposition of colonial rule. The most significant issue around which debate occurred in Songhay-speaking communities was over access to, and control over, agricultural land. Contestation over land was an issue that was both internal to Songhay-speaking communities and directed against pastoralist actions and claims over pastures. Today, many Songhay-speakers argue that the whole of the Niger valley belongs to them, based on the premise that the Songhay are the autochthonous first inhabitants of the area and that they are the people who have put the land to work as farmers. Tuareg and Arab claims to land are often rejected because, according to many Songhay, pastures cannot be owned.

5 Like many of the Arabo-Berber groups in the Sahel, these claims to Arab descent were generally older and less prestigious compared to the Sharifian lineages of groups such as the Kunta. However, there were also people among Songhay-speakers who claimed to be sharif, although usually they were small in number and often were unable to make the same elaborate genealogical connections that groups like the Kunta could.

6 Auguste Dupuis-Yacouba, *Essai de Méthode pratique pour l'étude de la langue songhoï ou songaï* (Paris: E. Leroux, 1917), 23. Jean-Pierre Olivier de Sardan identified these people as either freed slaves or slaves of the fifth generation (*Concepts et conceptions songhay-zarma* [Paris: Nubia, 1982], 144).

They argue that pastoralists degrade rather than develop the land that they use. This is the meaning of the popular Songhay expression, "the river belongs to us; the bush belongs to God" (So. "isa-di yer se; ganji-di yerkoy se"), which became a kind of Songhay motto during the civil war in the first half of the 1990s.

ETHNICITY AND RACE IN THE NIGER BEND

Songhay is a complex of related languages as well as an ethnic appellation.[7] Although race and ethnicity are deeply intertwined among Songhay-speakers, it is helpful to try to unravel them for conceptual clarity. In the context of the Niger Bend, I use the term ethnicity to refer to ideas of belonging and difference that attach to language. In different social and historical contexts, ethnicity can, of course, mean very different things. Most broadly, it refers to a perception of shared origin. In the Niger Bend, there are four principal language groups that are the basis of ideas of ethnic belonging today. Much of the discussion of race so far in this book has focused on distinctions of social status, both within single linguistic groups and across languages. At a general level, it seems to me that race, to a much larger extent than ethnicity, is used to codify social difference in an effort to naturalize inequality. But ethnicity can also do this, especially when it takes on racial qualities.

Max Weber made a distinction between what he called "caste structure" and "ethnic coexistence" in his typology of power relations involving people who consider themselves to be ethnically distinct. A "caste" system is the extreme outcome of differences in social status in a society when status is perceived to be "ethnic." Social inequality is naturalized by belief in blood relationships, and as a consequence, exogenous marriage and social intercourse are discouraged. Weber cited the Jews

[7] Songhay is classified as a Nilo-Saharan language. There are four major Songhay languages in Mali, each of which includes significant dialectical variations: Koyra Chiini (spoken in Timbuktu and upriver from Timbuktu along the Niger), Koroboro Shenni (spoken downriver from Timbuktu and often referred to as the Songhay of Gao), Djenné Chiini (spoken in Djenné), and Humbori Senni (spoken in Hombori). The two largest languages, and the ones I encountered in my research, are Koyra Chiini and Koroboro Shenni. The principal dividing line between these two Songhay language complexes is east and west of Timbuktu, although they are intermixed to some extent in the area west of Timbuktu because of relatively recent migrations. On the distribution of Songhay languages, see Robert Nicolaï, *Les dialects du Songhay: contribution à l'étude des changements linguistiques* (Paris: Société d'études linguistiques et anthropologiques de France, 1981). On the Songhay languages of Mali, see Jeffery Heath, *A Grammar of Koyra Chiini: The Songhay of Timbuktu* (Berlin: Mouton de Gruyter, 1999), 1–5.

as the paramount historical example of such a "caste" group: "A 'status' segregation grown into a 'caste' differs in its structure from a mere 'ethnic' segregation: The caste structure transforms the horizontal and unconnected coexistences of ethnically segregated groups into a vertical social system of super- and subordination." For Weber, this involved a process of racialization: "In their consequences they differ precisely in this way: ethnic coexistences condition a mutual repulsion and disdain but allow each ethnic community to consider its own honor as the highest one; the caste structure brings about a social subordination and an acknowledgement of 'more honor' in favor of the privileged caste or status group."[8]

In his study of ethnic conflict, Donald Horowitz used Weber's ideas to distinguish between what he called ranked and nonranked ethnic systems. In ranked systems, the relation between ethnic groups is hierarchical, with one superordinate and the other subordinate. For Horowitz, the boundaries of ranked ethnic groups coincide with class divisions:

> Mobility opportunities are restricted by group identity. In such systems, political, economic, and social status tend to be cumulative, so that members of Group B are simultaneously subordinate in each of these ways to members of Group A. Relations between groups entail clearly understood conceptions of superordinate and subordinate status. Interactions partake of caste etiquette and are suffused with deference... In unranked systems, on the other hand, parallel ethnic groups coexist, each group internally stratified.[9]

It is in social contexts that exhibit the characteristics of Weber's "caste structure" and Horowitz's "ranked ethnic systems" that race becomes most explicit.

Horowitz was interested in the dynamics of ethnic relationships and the typologies of conflict that ethnic systems produce. He argued that "ranked" ethnic systems lead to particular kinds of ethnic conflict: "Subordinate groups can attempt to displace superordinate groups; they can aim at abolition of ethnic divisions altogether; they can attempt to raise their position in the ethnic hierarchy; or they can move the system from ranked to unranked."[10] The most common outcome is the last one, in which formerly subordinate groups develop elites that lead them into a measure of collective autonomy and prestige

8 Max Weber, *From Max Weber: Essays in Sociology* (New York: Oxford University Press, 1958), 189.

9 Donald Horowitz, *Ethnic Groups in Conflict* (Berkeley: University of California Press, 1985), 22–3.

10 Ibid., 34.

that they had not formerly known and also into competition with their former masters.[11]

There is no perfect fit with an ideal-typical model, but the ways in which Songhay-speaking sedentary people and the pastoralists in the Niger Bend have represented their relationship on the eve of the French occupation resembles Horowitz's ranked ethnic system and Weber's idea of a caste structure. It was colonial policy to liberate Songhay-speaking sedentary people from pastoralist domination; although this occurred unevenly, it did produce very real changes. The endemic conflict that occurred in the colonial period over access to the fertile land that pastoralists and agriculturalists shared in the floodplain of the Niger valley can be understood then as part of a struggle over the changing nature of pastoralist-sedentary relations. As this shift occurred, ethnic labels became more important because the colonial state came to regulate access to resources using them. But as the mechanisms of power that bound sedentary people to pastoralist overlords was broken in the first decades of colonial occupation, racialized conceptions of social status began to expand into a larger kind of ethno-racial consciousness.

FROM PASTORALIST TO FRENCH DOMINATION

The earliest colonial administrators in the Niger Bend believed that the Songhay-speaking sedentary population would welcome the French as liberators from the deprivations of their Tuareg and Arab overlords. So grave was the situation where Tuareg domination was most pronounced that, according to French officials, whole areas had been depopulated of sedentary people. The most dramatic example of this was thought to be in the regions of Kissou and Killi, to the southwest of Timbuktu, where one French report written in 1895 estimated that there were ruins of three thousand villages and only three hundred that were still occupied.[12] Because the ability of colonial forces to exercise control over the areas of the Niger Bend was so limited in the first decade of the French presence, there were many raids on sedentary villages by pastoralist groups that had not accepted French authority. Local French officials interpreted these raids as evidence that the black sedentary population had long been brutalized by pastoralists.

[11] Ibid., 34.

[12] "Rapport du Sous-Lieutenant Jacobi sur la région du Kissou parcourue pendant la reconnaissance," August 20, 1895 (ANM FA 1E-78–81).

The image of Tuareg domination predated the colonial occupation. European travelers to the Niger Bend in the nineteenth century portrayed the nomad-sedentary relationship in stark terms. Mungo Park reported that the blacks "are looked upon by the Moors as an abject race of slaves, and are treated accordingly."[13] In the nineteenth century, other European travelers to the West African Sahel made similar observations. Reporting on his trip down the Niger River from Djenné to Timbuktu in 1828, the French adventurer René Caillié described the Tuareg as "a nomad people who live on the shores of [the Niger River]; they have the gift of creating fear, and they live at the expense of the unfortunate blacks, whom they have made into tributaries."[14] After having stopped at the village of Koura [about twenty kilometers northeast of Diré], Caillié described the relationship between the Songhay-speaking sedentary people and the Tuareg as follows: "The black inhabitants of this village came to sell us some milk. We gave them millet in exchange because they often lack provisions although they grow lots of rice; but they are continually robbed and harassed by the Sourgous [Tuareg],[15] who have made them into tributaries and forced them into feeding them by their misfortune."[16] When the German traveler Hienrich Barth passed through the Niger Bend area in 1853 and 1854, he noted the degraded condition of local black people and their fear of the Tuareg, whom he called the "tormentors" of the blacks.[17] Barth described the Aribinda region of the Gourma as beset with conflict: "The inhabitants belong chiefly to the Songhay race, but there are also a great many Tawarek [Tuareg], or rather Tawarek half-castes, who live here peaceably, though in general the Tawarak and the inhabitants of these districts are engaged in almost uninterrupted warfare with each other, the former always pushing more and more in advance and threatening to overrun the whole of this region of Negroland."[18] Barth traveled through the region when the Fulbe authority of the Hamdullahi Caliphate was at its height. However, even when traveling in areas under Tuareg domination, such as along the river east of Timbuktu, he did not describe any kind of Tuareg administration. Instead, he noted that

[13] Mungo Park, *Travels in the Interior Districts of Africa*. ed. Kate Ferguson Marsters (Durham, NC: Duke University Press, 2000), 162.

[14] René Caillié, *Journal d'un voyage à Temboctou et à Jenné, dans l'Afrique central* (Paris, 1830), 2:281–2.

[15] Caillié uses the Songhay term "Sourgou" for the Tuareg.

[16] Ibid., 2:287.

[17] Hienrich Barth, *Travels and Discoveries in North and Central Africa* (New York, 1859), 3:439.

[18] Ibid., 3:212.

villagers had abandoned their former locations for safer ground on protected islands in the river.[19]

Early colonial reports are full of descriptions of displaced Songhay communities, fortified villages, and above all, the overwhelming fear that Songhay villagers felt for the Tuareg. The lasting impression that one gets from reading the early colonial documents is that Tuareg domination was little short of chaos: "The history of the Tuareg tribe before our occupation is one of raids against neighboring tribes and against the sedentary people."[20] In a lengthy notice written in 1897 on the history of the territory that had become the administrative district of Goundam, the French author described the period between 1864 and 1894 as a "calamity," when the area was under the domination of the Tengeregif: "Under the guise of tax collection, the Tuareg would take anything that suited their fancy, including clothes, animals and cereals. One is even assured that on Fridays, some of them would wait for the inhabitants at the door of the mosque to strip them of their clothes."[21] Indeed, some Songhay-speaking people today recount that Tuareg tribute collection was effectively a form of pillage, and that their ancestors would hide valuables by burying them in the sand, or that household items such as blankets were made with intentional faults to make them less attractive to the Tuareg.[22]

There can be little doubt that Songhay-speaking people found themselves in greatly reduced position vis-à-vis pastoralist groups in the nineteenth century than in previous times when, for example, the Songhay Empire had controlled the Niger Bend. But the principal causes of insecurity in the nineteenth-century Niger Bend were the upheavals of political power and the invasions of the area by the Fulbe of the Hamdullahi Caliphate and the Tukolor of al-Hajj ʿUmar Tal. It was in areas where the fighting and raiding between competing powers was most concentrated that depopulation occurred. According to the accounts of people living in the Kissou region today, the main reason that sedentary people reconstructed villages in more secure locations was because of Tukolor slave raids, not Tuareg depredations.[23] Even according to the colonial sketch of the history of Goundam cited earlier, there was a regular annual tax imposed on sedentary people. In Goundam, if this report

19 Ibid., 3:439.

20 Région de Tombouctou, "Note sur les tribus nomades, 2ème Partie – Région Tombouctou," 1897 (ANM FA 1D 59–7).

21 "Notice sur le Cercle de Goundam," January 1, 1897 (ANM FA 1D 59–18).

22 Interview, Oumar Bilali, October 27, 2002, Moricoïra.

23 Ibid.

is to be believed, the annual tax on the town was 100 eighty-kilogram sacks of rice or millet, 100 full outfits of clothing, and 100,000 cowries.[24] The Songhay word for these sacks of grain that the Tuareg took as an annual tax is "suuni." A suuni is in fact a kind of large basket made out of reeds, and Songhay informants told me that each family head was responsible for filling one suuni with grain each year. All the suunis of a given village were stored together in an enclosure called a "kali," and when the Tuareg came to collect their tribute, the villagers would load the grain onto canoes and transport it to the site that the Tuareg requested.[25]

It seems likely that there was a great deal of regional variation in the regularity of Tuareg tax collection depending on the degree of hegemony a particular Tuareg group exercised. But however harsh Tuareg tribute demands were, they were not, in most cases, outright pillage. Both Tamashek-speaking tributaries and Songhay-speaking villagers recognized it as a tax (Ta. tiwse; So. alkaasu/alkaashi), exchanged for protection and in recognition of the authority of Tuareg power.[26] As one village chief in the Kissou told a French official in 1895, "before your arrival, the Tuareg demanded a tax that was often very difficult, but they had no interest in entirely ruining the country so that the inhabitants would be forced to flee." This had changed, according to the chief, because, "today, they feel that you will stay in the country, that they will not be able to force you out of it, that their incursions will become more and more rare. They don't have any interest anymore in managing us and thus they destroy all that they find and take with them all the captives that they come across in the floodplains." It was the colonial occupation, the chief said, that had produced the repeated incidents of pillage: "They reproach

[24] "Notice sur le Cercle de Goundam," January 1, 1897 (ANM FA 1D 59–18).

[25] Interview, Ibrahim Abdou Maïga, October 2, 2002, Kano. This unit, alternatively called a sunu or suniya, appears in older documents from Timbuktu. See Hunwick, *Timbuktu*, 159; Michel Abitbol, *Tombouctou et les Arma: de la conquête marocaine du Soudan nigérien en 1591 à l'hégémonie de l'Empire du Macina en 1833* (Paris: G.P. Maisonneuve et Larose, 1979), 56; cited in Ghislaine Lydon, *On Trans-Saharan Trails: Islamic Law, Trade Networks, and Cross-Cultural Exchange in Nineteenth-Century Western Africa* (Cambridge: Cambridge University Press, 2009), 257–8. Also, Auguste Dupuis-Yacouba, *Industries et principales professions des habitants de la région de Tombouctou* (Paris: E. Larose, 1921), 143. It varied in size, according to these texts, from 48 to 60 kg. In the Songhay communities in the eastern Niger Bend, the tribute in grain paid to the Tuareg Iwellemmedan was calculated in terms of leather sacks called "hawgara" in Songhay (Charles Grémont, "Les Touareg Iwellemmedan (1647–1898): Un ensemble politique de la Boucle du Niger" [Ph.d. diss., Université Paris 1, 2007], 297–8)

[26] Grémont, "Touareg Iwellemmedan," 378–81.

us for our alliance with you and take advantage of us when you are too far away to protect us."[27]

Songhay-speaking sedentary people did not welcome the French invasion of the Niger Bend. Although French forces encountered the greatest initial resistance from Tuareg groups such as the Tengeregif and Iwellemmedan, there were also battles fought against sedentary communities. While on its march from Ségou to Timbuktu in 1893–1894, for example, the military column led by Joffre met its first combat at the Songhay town of Niafunké on January 10, 1894, where a hundred Songhay fighters were killed by Joffre's troops.[28] Once French rule had been established, the Songhay-speaking sedentary population was obliged to pay taxes to the colonial state and to stop paying tribute to Tuareg groups. Deprived of a significant source of income, many Tuareg groups responded by pillaging villages that had once paid them tribute. The colonial reports of the first decade of the French occupation are filled with incidents of pastoralist raids on sedentary villages. In many communities where the French could offer no effective protection, sedentary people were forced to continue providing their annual tribute to their Tuareg overlords while at the same time paying colonial taxes.[29] This double burden provoked a migration of many Songhay-speaking people to more secure areas; for those who remained behind, it augmented their already considerable poverty and reduced many sedentary people to a diet of food they could gather because all the cereals that they grew were used to pay colonial taxes or pastoralist tribute. Even if colonial explanations of such behavior tended to emphasize what they considered to be a poor work ethic among sedentary people, French descriptions of the desperate poverty of many Songhay speakers in the early colonial period are sometimes vivid. For example, one colonial report in 1902 described the situation of the sedentary population in Bamba as follows:

> The poor inhabitants of many villages, anticipating the difficulties and suffering that payment of the tax will cause, are deserting their land and migrating to the district of Timbuktu to avoid the misery that has befallen them ... All the gaabibis [blacks], the people of the river who have a deep-rooted laziness, would like to use this simple method of changing administrative districts at the moment they

[27] "Rapport du Sous-Lieutanant Jacobi sur la région du Kissou parcourue pendant la reconnaissance," August 20, 1895 (ANM FA 1E-78-81).

[28] Letter from Commandant Joffre to the Gouverneur, Kayes, February 13, 1894 (ANM FA B 84). On these battles, see also Louis Frèrejean, *Objectif ... Tombouctou. combats contre les Toucouleurs et les Touareg* (Paris: L'Harmattan, 1996), 239–40.

[29] Cercle de Bamba, "Rapport politique," année 1901 (ANM FA 1E 21–22).

have to pay their taxes. Hating all work, they do not grow anything and instead live off of cram-crams [a wild grain][30] and water lilies that their women collect. They live in poor huts made of straw so it costs them nothing to leave.[31]

The one demand that was repeated again and again by Songhay-speaking villagers was for the French administration to maintain a presence in their area to prevent pastoralist raids.

Clearly, French officials understood that in order to break pastoralist independence, they would have to end the support that Tuareg groups received from within the sedentary population.[32] As one colonial report described the goals of this policy:

There is not, among the Tuareg and Arabs who live in the Northern Region, a single tribe that we would be able to make into an ally or friend. All that we can ask of them is the peace which our power obliges them to accept. The only natives who really have an interest in changing their master are the blacks who live along the river. They are not, in reality, as miserable and craven as they first appeared. The people of Boïa, Rhergo, Ouaraï, Bamba and Dongoï are very capable of becoming, in a few years and with our support, a serious counterweight to Tuareg influence.[33]

But the Songhay-speaking sedentary people did not always see their interests in this way, and while the arrival of the French occupation did eventually take them out from under the domination of the Tuareg, the colonial state exacted new demands in taxes, forced labor, and conscription that were often harsher than the demands made on them by the Tuareg. On several occasions when Tuareg groups threatened to revolt, the colonial administration discerned active support among Songhay-speaking communities for the rebels and open hatred for the French.[34] Songhay-speaking communities were subordinate to Tuareg power on the eve of colonial conquest. But pastoralist-sedentary conflict grew as the French attempted to break the pastoralist dominance over Songhay people, thus beginning the shift from a ranked ethnic system in the Niger Bend to the direction of an unranked one.

30 "Cenchrus biflorus," also known as "Indian sandbur," is a ubiquitous grass in the Sahel that produces a burr with edible grains (Ta. wazzaj; So. daaney).

31 Cercle de Bamba, "Rapport politique," December 1902 (ANM FA 1E 21–22).

32 Interview, Hamey Shoumaïgal, October 15, 2002, Minkiri. Charles Grémont found the same thing in interviews further east around Gao ("Touareg Iwellemmedan," 399–401).

33 Région de Nord, "Rapport Politique," 1ère trimestre 1898, July 14, 1898 (ANM FA 1E 78–81).

34 Cercle de Tombouctou, "Rapport de tournée de l'administrateur Bonamy, Commandant le cercle de Tombouctou," April 4, 1916 (ANM FA 1E 81).

SONGHAY SOCIAL CATEGORIES: CHANGE AND CONTINUITY

One of the principal changes that occurred in the Songhay world under colonialism was the erosion of certain social categories within Songhay society. In the main, this was because colonial domination was a heavy burden on all sedentary people in terms of taxation, forced labor requirements, and military conscription. As in the administration of pastoralist groups, the colonial regime initially identified indigenous power structures and sought to coopt Songhay-speaking elites. Thus, in the first decades of colonial rule, considerable attention was paid to the genealogies of colonially sanctioned village chiefs and canton heads.

One of the principal tasks of the colonial administration in its first years was the collection of information on the composition of the population that had come under its control. Each of the administrative districts of the Niger Bend produced studies of this sort within the first decade of the beginning of the colonial occupation. The focus, unsurprisingly, was on understanding the complicated political and social structure, as well as the history, of Tuareg and Arab groups. Attention was also paid to the Songhay-speaking sedentary population. Local French officials were preoccupied with social status and paid special attention to distinctions between nobles, vassals, and slaves. In many of these early reports, there was a basic distinction made between a remnant nobility known as the Arma, whose members claimed to be the descendants of the Moroccan army that defeated the Songhay Empire in 1591, and the Songhay gaabibi (blacks), who were understood to be the descendants of the older Songhay-speaking population that had been reduced to servile status by Arma domination in the seventeenth and eighteenth centuries. In more sophisticated colonial reports, the category of Songhay gaabibi was further subdivided into the "pure" Songhay who were thought to be the descendants of the main free population of the Songhay Empire, and the gaabibi proper, who were identified as either the original black population of the Niger Bend that had been made into slaves long ago by the Songhay, or the descendants of slaves more generally. According to a census carried out in 1906 for the region of Timbuktu, there were 7,000 Arma and 45,000 Songhay gaabibi in the sedentary population. Twenty thousand of the Songhay gaabibi were "pure" gaabibi, and 25,000 "pure" Songhay.[35]

[35] Capitaine Maziller, "Etude sur les populations de la Région de Tombouctou: Situation économique et agricole, sécurité et éléments de troubles intérieurs; Rezzous venus de l'extérieur, organisation de la lutte contre eux, sûreté à organiser," June 10, 1906 (ANM FA 1D 59–11).

The distinction between Arma and Songhay gaabibi reflected a local discourse of racial difference. Local French administrators noted that although both groups were Songhay-speakers, the Arma considered themselves to be of Arab descent and therefore nonblack. The term Arma is derived from the Arabic "rumāh," or "riflemen," which was a term used to describe the invading Moroccan soldiers in 1591. According to a typical colonial description of the Arma, "they are the descendants of the Moroccans who, having occupied Timbuktu, intermarried with Songhay women. They form the superior class of the population."[36] Distributed throughout the northern part of the Niger Bend in areas that had been under the control of the Arma Pashalik that was established after the Moroccan invasion, they represented a noble class for the French, "the intelligent portion of the population."[37] By contrast, the gaabibi were characterized as ignoble and as slaves: "These blacks, who have been subjected to centuries of slavery by their masters, have and will continue to carry the mark of slavery, which is in the veritable flesh of slaves. They are a little bit stupid, fearful and dishonest; physically, they are animal-like in general."[38] The main center of Arma concentration was the town of Timbuktu, although there were also Arma groups in Goundam, Diré, Dongoï, Bamba, Bourem and Gao.

Whereas the French emphasized the blackness of the Arma because of their intermarriage with local women, Sahelian constructions of the Arma recognized their foreign descent. Thus, in Aḥmad Bābīr's "The Gems of the splendid ones in the history of the blacks" ("Jawāhir al-ḥisān fī akhbār al-sūdān"), a history of the Niger Bend written in postcolonial Timbuktu, the Arma are referred to as "mixed tribes," incorporating people from every "tribe," including "Spaniards, Christians, Jews and Muslims."[39] In another Arabic history of the Niger Bend written in 1941–1942 by the Timbuktu merchant and bibliophile Aḥmad Bul-ʿArāf al-Tiknī (d. 1955), and who was himself of more recent southern Moroccan origin,[40] the Arma population of Timbuktu is described as white in origin. However, Ahmad Bul-ʿAraf argued that their status as whites had been greatly diminished by the fact that they have lost the knowledge of their precise genealogies:

They do not know their origins for the most part, and no person from the Draa Valley, or the Atlas Mountains, or Fes is mentioned. The meaning of this is that

[36] "Notes sur Tombouctou, Songhais, Touaregs, Divers," 1902 (ANM FA 1D 59–9), f. 9.

[37] Ibid., f. 42.

[38] Ibid., f. 43.

[39] Aḥmad Bābīr al-Arawānī, *Jawāhir al-ḥisān fī akhbār al-sūdān*, ed. al-Hādī al-Mabrūk al-Dālī (Benghazi: Dār al-kutub al-waṭaniyya, 2001), 69.

[40] For a discussion of the large Tikna lineage see Lydon, *Trans-Saharan*, 170–9.

> the army of Mawlay [Aḥmad al-Mansūr] took soldiers from every tribe, and when they entered the land of the blacks... they got mixed up in this country ... and they have all been transformed into blacks except for some of them who have a reddish color with thin arms and legs, which is proof of their Arab-ness; but they do not speak Arabic for the most part.[41]

The weakness of the Arma claims to be nonblack, according to the Moroccan-descended Ahmad Bul-ʿAraf, lay not so much in their current skin color, which is black, but in their inability to connect themselves with known and accepted genealogies of nonblacks.

At the beginning of the colonial period, Songhay-speaking people who claimed to be Arma clearly had a distinct idea of themselves that connected nobility with foreign origins and with a past of political and economic power. To the extent that the Arma could exercise some authority over non-Arma Songhay-speaking people, they were useful to the local French administration that on a few occasions imported Arma families to take over the role of chiefdom in troublesome villages to the east of Timbuktu (in Millala and Bougoubéri).[42] But the limits of Arma power were soon apparent and the colonial administration largely gave up the idea of imposing them as chiefs. There were, however, villages that identified themselves as Arma and that attempted to use French sympathy for "aristocratic" groups to claim lost historical rights over other Songhay-speaking people.

In the first decade of the twentieth century, two villages along the Tassakant (the branch of the Niger that leads to Goundam from west of Timbuktu) became embroiled in a conflict over ownership of agricultural land. The Arma-controlled village of Dongoï claimed that the land cultivated by the neighboring village of Niambourgou, whose inhabitants are described as Songhay in colonial documents, belonged to Dongoï. The people of Dongoï argued that during the Arma Pashalik, all cultivated land had been taken over by the state, and that the Songhay-speaking sedentary population had paid an annual rent for the right of cultivation.[43] Because the agricultural land in the Tassakant had come

[41] Aḥmad Bul-ʿArāf al-Tiknī, *Izālat al-rayb wa-ʾl-shakk wa-ʾl-tafrīṭ fī dhikr al-muʾalifīn min ahl al-takrūr wa-ʾl-ṣaḥrāʾ wa-ahl shinqīt*, ed. al-Hādī al-Mabrūk al-Dālī (Benghazi: Dār al-kutub al-waṭaniya, 2000), 53–4.

[42] Cercle de Tombouctou, "Rapport politique," August 1908 (ANM FA 1E 78–81).

[43] This case does not reflect the general situation of Arma power. The actual appropriation of land was limited to the most fertile agricultural areas in the Niger Bend, where Arma groups put slaves to work in cultivation. One of the areas that the Arma of Timbuktu claimed to own and used in this way was the lake region of the Gourma, especially Lake Garou and Lake Do. Hienrich Barth passed through this area in the 1850s and noted the slave-based agricultural system employed by the Arma of Timbuktu (*Travels*, 3:473–8).

under the ownership of the Arma of Dongoï, and because in the past, the inhabitants of Niambourgou had recognized this right by paying rent, Dongoï sought to have the colonial authorities enforce this obligation on Niambourgou farmers. Although the people of Niambourgou recognized the historical precedent of having paid rent in the past, they invoked a different historical tradition of land rights based on occupation and continuous cultivation. They argued that Niambourgou had long ago ceased to pay for their land, and that under the traditional land tenure system of the Niger Bend, which stipulates, according to most versions, that after ten years of continuous cultivation by a nonkinsman and sixty years by a kinsman, the ownership of the land reverts to the cultivator.[44] Colonial officials eventually settled the dispute by siding largely with the people of Niambourgou because Dongoï could not demonstrate that any rent had been paid in recent years. However, the local French administrator did insist that Dongoï be allowed to hold rights over a small amount of land to mollify the Arma there.[45] Similar disputes occurred in other areas with Arma groups, but because the Arma offered relatively little in the way of political power or authority over other Songhay-speaking people, and because the French were keen to see the agricultural economy extended, most Arma claims were rejected by the colonial administration.

The largest part of the Songhay-speaking population of the Niger Bend was described as Songhay gaabibi. There is a great deal of confusion in colonial documents about what exactly is meant by the label gaabibi. In one document, the term gaabibi is used to refer to all the servile people of the Niger Bend, including the Tamashek-speaking bellah-iklan and the Arabic-speaking ʿabīd and ḥarāṭīn.[46] This usage is perhaps not as inappropriate as it at first seems, because the term gaabibi is a racial one, literally meaning "black body." Since the discourses on racial difference in the nineteenth century were in large part organized around grades of social status and used to make arguments about service owed to nobility, the wider meaning of the term gaabibi, as it is used in this document, probably did reflect contemporary usage by "noble" speakers of Songhay. In any case, gaabibi was a term widely used in Songhay to describe people who were accorded servile origin. In another

44 It would be better to describe this as the traditional normative understanding of land tenure in the Niger Bend because there were, in fact, a significant variety of tenure systems in practice. For an analysis of some of these differences, see A. de Loppinot, "Régime foncier des indigènes dans le cercle de Goundam," *BCEHS-AOF* 3, no. 1 (1920): 64–78.

45 Cercle de Goundam, "Rapport politque," August 1911 (ANM FA 1E 40).

46 "Notes sur Tombouctou, Songhais, Touaregs, Divers," 1902 (ANM FA 1D 59–9), f. 6.

document, the gaabibi are described as those who do agricultural work. This reflected the French impression that except for the Arma, the entire Songhay-speaking sedentary population had been reduced to the level of servile people under Tuareg domination, and that consequently, there was little difference between "pure" Songhay and gaabibi. According to this view, they had become so mixed as to make it impossible to tell one from the other.[47]

Another colonial definition of the gaabibi was that they were "slaves who had the choice to leave their masters."[48] In this case, the document refers to a category of people often called "captifs de case," or those people in Songhay-speaking society who had been born into slavery and could not be sold, at least theoretically. These people were known by the Songhay term "hosso" ("horso" in Songhay dialects downriver) and although they were considered slaves, they were slaves of a higher order, with more rights than those who had been purchased or captured. A hosso was socialized into the larger family unit that he or she was a part of and held certain rights over his or her noble relations.[49] Also, like so many other lower-status people in the Songhay world, the hosso were believed to have special access to magical powers and technical (artisanal) knowledge.[50] The American anthropologist Horace Miner reported that in 1940, all the barbers, butchers, and masons in Timbuktu were gaabibi, although he did not give any precise information on the origins of these people except to divide the Songhay-speaking population of Timbuktu town between Arma and gaabibi.[51]

One of the main problems in attempting to uncover the social meaning of the term gaabibi is that it appears to have been used only in juxtaposition to the Arma, and probably mainly by the Arma themselves. Dupuis-Yacouba, a Frenchman who came to Timbuktu as a missionary for the White Fathers in the 1890s before leaving the Church, marrying locally,

47 Région de Nord, "Rapport politique," 2ème semestre, 1899 (ANM FA 1E 78–81).

48 "Rapport du Sous-Lieutanant Jacobi sur la région du Kissou parcourue pendant la reconnaissance," August 20, 1895 (ANM FA 1E-78–81).

49 "Rapport du chef de Bataillon Mazillier, Commandant la Région de Tombouctou, sur l'attitude des Touaregs de l'Ouest et la nécessité d'une prochaine repression," October 1906, No. 33C (ANM FA 1E 78–81).

50 Jean-Pierre Olivier de Sardan, *Les Sociétés songhay-zarma (Niger-Mali): chefs, guerriers, esclaves paysans* (Paris: Karthala, 1984), 40–3. On the particular magical attributes over which people who are at times referred to as gaabibi, see Boubou Hama, *L'histoire traditionnelle d'un peuple: les Zarma-Songhay* (Paris: Présence africaine, 1967), 16.

51 Horace Miner, *The Primitive City of Timbuktu*, Revised Edition (New York: Doubleday, 1965), 54–62.

and becoming a long-time teacher in Timbuktu,[52] reported that the gaabibi were the remnants of the Songhay population in the Niger Bend that had not fled south after the Moroccan invasion and were thereby made into servile clients of the Arma.[53] What Depuis-Yacouba reported on, however, were not definitive accounts of the origins of the gaabibi, but arguments about racialized status that he heard in his inquiries in Timbuktu. The difficulty that colonial-era writers had in pinning down the meaning of the term gaabibi stems from the fact that it was part of a contested semantic terrain in the early colonial period, as different people made claims on others using Sahelian racial language. For the people of the Niger Bend, differences between noble and servile, nonblack and black, were of great consequence in the early colonial period because they led directly to colonial claims to taxes and labor that were borne almost exclusively by blacks.

As the distinctiveness of Arma status diminished over time under colonial rule, the use of the term gaabibi seems to have faded. In towns such as Timbuktu where there was a large Arma population, the term gaabibi still retains a certain vague sense of servile or lower-status Songhay person today. But in areas where there was not a significant Arma population, such as in the Serere (to the east of Timbuktu), my attempts to elicit information about the former meaning of the term gaabibi were difficult. One informant said that the gaabibi were the same as the bellah-iklan, slaves of the Tuareg.[54] The general consensus was that the term gaabibi simply referred to all black people and that it did not have any connotation of slavery except in the minds of the pastoralists. In the Serere, informants said that it was a name given to the Songhay-speaking population by the Tuareg who thought that all black people were inferior and could be used like slaves.[55] One might suspect that people of servile origin would deny it to an outsider, and this is true to some extent. For the most part, however, the people with whom I talked were quite open about the existence of slavery in their communities, and I often met Songhay-speaking people who claimed to be descended from slaves (So. "bañña," "hosso"). Gaabibi is a term that is too vague to have had any meaning outside of the direct relationship

52 On his life see William Seabrook, *The White Monk of Timbuctoo* (New York: Harcourt, Brace and Co., 1934); Owen White, "The Decivilizing Mission: Auguste Dupuis-Yakouba and French Timbuktu," *French Historical Studies* 27, no. 3 (2004): 541–68.

53 Auguste Dupuis-Yacouba, *Essai de Méthode pratique pour l'étude de la langue songhoï ou songaï* (Paris: E. Leroux, 1917), 23.

54 Interview, Youssouf Kakay, October 14, 2002, Kano.

55 Interview, Hamad Amar, October 15, 2002, Mandiakoy.

with the Arma, and even here, it was a targeted racial label that had come to mean less and less to those for whom it was meant to apply. By the early colonial period, if not long before, the invocation of the term gaabibi was an elite Songhay (or Arma) racial argument about social status and slavery. Like other racial arguments, we should understand that these were contested claims that did not necessarily translate directly into social reality.

CONFLICT OVER LAND

The principal economic goal of the colonial regime in the Niger Bend was the development of agricultural production. This was, along with weakening the Tuareg, the principal reason for the French policy of freeing the Songhay-speaking sedentary population from pastoralist domination. The initial enthusiasm for agriculture development was slowly tempered as the colonial administration began to see the economic value of animal husbandry. As colonial policy became more sympathetic to pastoralist interests after the First World War, sedentary agricultural people found their interests constrained by a colonial regime that now sought to manage a mixed pastoral and agricultural economy in the Niger valley. The main pressure on sedentary-pastoralist relations was the expansion of land under cultivation into areas used to graze animals in the dry season when they came to the river, and the increases in the size of herds that frequently led to crop damage on agricultural land. Both pastoralists and agriculturalists had very different ideas about rights to land, and it was around these issues that both groups tended to come into conflict. The long-term consequences of this process are clear: Claims over land became a central issue in Songhay arguments about their place in the Niger Bend. It was, therefore, no accident that the name given to the militias formed by Songhay-speaking people during the recent civil war in northern Mali was "Ganda-koy," which means "owners of the land."

Ironically, French officials believed that because the economy of the Niger Bend was so underdeveloped under pastoralist hegemony, there would be no problem created by expanding cultivated land. Increased agricultural production required security for the Songhay-speaking sedentary population. According to one influential colonial official writing in 1906:

> The nomad is only a destroyer according to the agricultural population. He attacks the trees and bushes that he prunes and cuts down to allow his sheep and goats to graze. While the nomad occupies himself with raising animals and struggles to increase his herds of goats, sheep, camels and cattle, the sedentary person

> does his best to enlarge some corners of flooded land where he plants some millet, rice, and in certain regions, wheat. The production of grain could be extended greatly if the population was large enough to push the nomad back into the bush and develop all the land that could be cleared and planted... For the development of the population, one should have no doubts; a miserable population, malnourished, brutalized by the yoke of the nomads, which is still on them, cannot grow. The extension of agriculture and an effective protection must go together.[56]

Ten or fifteen years into the colonial occupation, the security problem for Songhay-speaking sedentary people had shifted away from a defense against pastoralist raids of pillage to the protection of crops from incursions of grazing animals.

There was, of course, nothing new in the antagonism between sedentary and pastoral people in the Niger Bend over the actions of grazing animals. The cycle of semi-nomadic movements follows the seasons as animals are taken to different areas of pasturage determined by the ecology of the Niger Bend. For part of each year, at the end of the dry season before the rains come in June or July, pastoralists bring their animals to the Niger River (or its branches) to graze on a deep-water grass known as "burgu" (Echinochloa stagnina).[57] The burgu can be cut and fed to animals. It becomes directly accessible to herds once the level of the river begins to drop sufficiently to enable them to stand and graze. In most years, this occurs in February. Some pastoralists bring their animals to the river as early as November, but the principal moment in which sedentary-pastoralist conflict occurs is between February and June. There are a number of structural problems that lead to conflict, but the most important one is that agricultural crops, especially rice, are grown in areas of the Niger floodplain where burgu is found. Consequently, animals grazing on burgu tend to do damage to rice fields by eating or trampling the agricultural crops. Sedentary people also use burgu as food and, in the past, to make a fermented drink. Conflict with pastoral groups was sometimes provoked when sedentary people harvested significant amounts of burgu for their own alimentation.[58]

56 Capitaine Maziller, "Etude sur les populations de la Région de Tombouctou: Situation économique et agricole, sécurité et éléments de troubles intérieurs; Rezzous venus de l'extérieur, organisation de la lutte contre eux, sûreté à organiser," June 10, 1906 (ANM FA 1D 59–11).

57 "Burgu" is a Songhay word, but the French administration adopted it, as "bourgou," to describe this grass. A version of the same word is used in Tamashek (Ta. berju). The French also employed the term "bourgouthière" to describe the areas where burgu grew. I call these "burgu paddies." The grass is also known as "hippo grass" in some other places in the world.

58 Jean Gallais, *Pasteurs et paysans du Gourma. La condition sahelienne* (Paris: CNRS, 1975), 56–8.

Pastoralist-sedentary relations have often been seen as symbiotic, and there certainly were (and still are) elements of the relationship between the pastoral and agricultural peoples of the Niger valley that meet this description. For example, Tuareg groups often left young animals with sedentary people during the period of the year when they migrated to areas away from the river, and this allowed agricultural people to supplement their diet with milk.[59] Songhay-speakers also recall that they obtained animals as gifts from pastoralists, which allowed them to build up small herds of their own.[60] But the relationship, whether symbiotic or otherwise, was always structured by inequalities of power. The colonial occupation changed the relations of power between agricultural and pastoral people in the Niger Bend, and attempted to set Songhay-speaking sedentary people on a more equal footing with their pastoralist neighbors. Whereas in the nineteenth century, pastoral destruction of sedentary crops could pass largely unchallenged, under colonial rule, it would not. As Songhay-speaking communities became more autonomous vis-à-vis the pastoralists, they also became more militant in protecting their interests and in asserting their claims to floodplain land. Many writers who have worked on the Tuareg have described the colonial regime as prosedentary in its policies. Tuareg groups, according to this line of argument, saw their "traditional" access to floodplain grazing land curtailed and regulated by the colonial state, and this worked to their long-term disadvantage.[61] In a sense, the colonial empowerment of Songhay-speaking agricultural people did weaken the Tuareg; but the colonial state was, on the whole, much more sympathetic to pastoralist interests than most writers acknowledge. From the perspective of Songhay-speaking people, the colonial state was highly biased toward the pastoralists, and in no area was this clearer than in the colonial assignment of proprietary rights over riverine grazing lands to nomadic groups.

[59] This is a veritable trope used today by Tuareg and Songhay people in presenting a picture of harmonious relations between themselves in the past (interview, Hamad Amar, October 15, 2002, Mandiakoy). See also the recent collection of local testimonies by Charles Grémont, André Marty, Rhissa ag Mossa, Younoussa Hamara Touré, *Les liens sociaux au Nord-Mali. Entre fleuve et dunes. Récits et témoignages* (Paris: Karthala, 2004), 84–9.

[60] Gallais, *Pasteurs*, 58.

[61] See Gallais, *Pasteurs*, 49; Gallais, "Essai sur la situation actuelle des relations entre pasteurs et paysans dans le Sahel ouest-africain," in *Etudes de Géographie tropicale offertes à Pierre Gourou* (Paris: Mouton, 1972), 301–13; F. Camel, "Les relations touaregs/sédentaires à travers le regard du colonisateur français," in *Touaregs et autres Sahariens entre plusieurs mondes. Les Cahiers de l'IREMAM* 7–8, ed. Hélène Claudot-Hawad (Aix-en-Provence: CNRS, 1996), 199–214; Hélène Claudot-Hawad, "Honneur et politique: les choix stratégiques des Touaregs pendant la colonization française," in *Touaregs, exil et résistance*, ed Claudot-Hawad, REMMM 57 (1990): 11–49.

Before we consider the nature of pastoralist-sedentary conflict over land, and the way that the colonial state attempted to regulate it, I want to briefly examine the land tenure structures in Songhay-speaking communities and how these systems changed under French rule. With several exceptions, the basic proprietary rights to agricultural land remained in the hands of individual villages under the various political formations that followed one another before the arrival of Europeans. The main exception to this was in the case of villages composed largely of slaves, or in those taken over and occupied by Fulbe forces from the Hamdullahi Caliphate in the nineteenth century, such as Saremayou and Minéssengué, on the edge of the Binga region.[62] For the most part, however, powerful forces in the Niger Bend contented themselves with the collection of tribute or taxes from Songhay-speaking villages without getting involved in managing the land tenure system or claiming the land for themselves. Certainly, the dominant Tuareg and Arab pastoralist groups never attempted to claim property rights over agricultural land cultivated by Songhay-speaking people. Pastoralist groups considered all land, including cultivated land, to be common. Rights to land use were based, in theory, on need; in practice, however, pastoralist land use in the nineteenth century followed the fortunes of different pastoralist groups in terms of military power. It is important to remember that most Tamashek- and Arabic-speakers were also themselves tributary to the most powerful pastoralist groups, forced to pay powerful overlords for rights to graze their animals on good land.[63]

In theory, the Songhay system of land tenure is based on the principle of first occupation, so that the land belongs to the person or group who first cultivated it, and this right of property is transmissible to descendants. Thus, it is common in Songhay villages to be told that the land that the villagers cultivate was empty when their ancestors arrived at the site. In the villages of the Serere, the claim made by current occupants is that they were the first to cultivate the area.[64] In reality, one can often trace particular systems of land ownership to a conquest or displacement of some kind. There are a variety of Songhay tenure systems in which this is part of the "traditional" structure of land distribution. But even

62 Abitbol, *Tombouctou*, 126–34.

63 Grémont, "Touareg Iwellemmedan," 298–9.

64 The dispersion of villages in the Serere from a single initial migration by Songhay-speakers from the east is described as colonization of uncultivated land, although this does not mean necessarily that land was unused by pastoralists for example (Interview, Yacouba al-Mouhali, October 17, 2002, Moyadji Koira).

in instances such as those in the Serere, where the current inhabitants claim proprietary rights based on the principle of first occupancy, this proves not to be historically accurate when one snoops around elsewhere in the Niger Bend. Other people recount that they were forced to leave the Serere because of a conquest by the ancestors of the current inhabitants. One of the ways that this process of displacement can be traced is by following the repetition of village names in the Niger Bend.[65] The place name "Koura," for example, is the name of several villages along the Niger River southwest of Timbuktu. There was once a village of Koura in the Serere east of Timbuktu, before its inhabitants were forced to migrate upriver because of the arrival of the ancestors of the current inhabitants during the nineteenth century. The original migrants settled in several different places, and in each gave their new village the name Koura. Another new Koura was established in the immediate wake of the colonial occupation as people from the established villages of Koura claimed new agricultural land made accessible and secure by the French presence.[66] Another good example of this is the village of Bourem-Sidi Amar, east of Diré, and Bourem-Inali, southeast of Timbuktu, where the populations are the descendants of migrants who came from the larger and older village of Bourem to the east during the nineteenth century, and who have continued to maintain relations with the "mother" village by marriage ties. In the case of the different Bourems, the inhabitants have maintained their distinct Songhay language from the east (Koroboro shenni) despite being surrounded by speakers of Western Songhay (Koyra chiini). In a sense, these people consider themselves to be, first and foremost, people of Bourem (So. Burem-boro-diyo).[67]

In some villages, the fact of conquest is recognized by the assertion that the first inhabitants conferred their rights to an outsider as a present. A good example is Fatacara on Lake Télé, northwest of Goundam. According to its traditions, the site was first occupied by Sorko fishers who did not practice agriculture. At the beginning of the eighteenth century, a stranger named Koundoum arrived, and he was given control over all the agricultural land because the fishermen had no use for it. Koundoum then went to Timbuktu where he presented the Arma ruler

[65] I am indebted to Abdoulaye Ali Maïga, originally from Kano in the Serere, for pointing me in this direction (Interview, Abdoulaye Ali Maïga, October 29, 2002, Diré).

[66] "Rapport du Lieutenant Cauvan sur la tournée de recensement faite dans le Bingha, le Gourma et le Kissou du 3 février au 3 mars, 1898," March 15, 1898 (ANM FA 1E-78-81).

[67] Interview, Muhamane Alkaidi, October 27, 2002, Bourem-Sidi Amar.

with gold and silver so as to be officially recognized by the Pashalik as the owner of the land. As Fatacara grew into a moderately important agricultural center, Koundoum and his descendants divided up the land each year in return for service and a portion of the harvest. This system, which we may think of as an "aristocratic" regime of land tenure, survived into the colonial period.[68] But it provoked considerable problems because of disputes over the position of village chief and repeated complaints about abuses of his power in the distribution of land. In a letter written to the colonial administration in 1930, a villager named Issa M'Bodji sought to have the village chief removed:

> Amadou [M'Bodji, the village chief] married a woman from Tioki, and since he married that woman, he does not live in Fatacara anymore. He only comes to divide up the land for the people who rent it; each of these people gives him a calf and one or two donkeys according to the quality of the land. As for the money that we give him, we do not know exactly how much. You yourselves [the French] have said that each person who has to pay a tax must have a field in order to pay his taxes. Amadou does the opposite; there are people in our village, whose names are listed below, who have paid him to be able to have fields to cultivate and he takes their goods and instead of giving them a field, he rents it to someone else.[69]

The local French administrator eventually removed Amadou M'Bodji from his position as chief a year later, in 1931, but this only provoked more outrage from his family and supporters. The main problem seems to have been a shortage of agricultural land and the fact that the village chief was profiting from his position as proprietor by selling and renting parts of the village land for his own benefit. The M'Bodji family that controlled the chiefdom of Fatacara, like other elite Songhay-speaking groups that ruled other villages, had begun to consider itself on a par with pastoralist elites to whom the French administration had assigned land tenure rights to encourage the settling of Arab and Tuareg servile people for the purposes of agriculture. As in so many other colonial contexts in Africa, the French sought to prevent the development of private property in land. The tendency of Songhay-speaking elites in villages with "aristocratic" systems of land tenure[70] to treat the land they controlled as private property that could be rented or sold to anyone willing to pay, including those not connected to the village, was strongly resisted by the colonial administration.

[68] De Loppinot, "Régime foncier," 67–8.

[69] Letter from Issa M'Bodji, Fatacara, to the Commandant, Cercle de Goundam, 8 February 1930 (ACG).

[70] Another prominent example is the case of most of the villages in the Tioki region such as Ata and Tindirma.

The only context in which this tendency for the emergence of a landholding elite was tolerated by French officials was when it occurred among Tuareg or Arab groups, in which case it was strongly encouraged because it provided a set of material interests that bound pastoralist elites to the colonial state. Songhay-speaking elites did not offer the same potential political threat and consequently, their efforts to solidify the material basis of their elite status by private land holdings were not supported. By removing the village head in Fatacara and forcing a new, more equitable annual sharing out of land that was overseen by the French administration, the "aristocratic" structure of land tenure that had operated in Fatacara, and which had been abused by its beneficiaries, was undermined.[71]

In a letter written to the French administration in Goundam in 1937 by a member of the former chief's family living in Bamako, the historical rights to the land and the chiefdom by this family were asserted in a slightly different way than I explained earlier:

By every letter, my family informs me that it is the victim of the plotting of Abadi Yattara, chief of the village of Fatacara (District of Goundam). Insofar as the facts reported to me are correct, it is very clear that they are of a nature that seriously damages my interests, because to take away farm land from a cultivator is to condemn him to death... I must say to you above all, that Abadi Yattara fulfills the function of chief against all legality... Only his trickery could have induced the [French] commander of the district to make such an error, because his good faith was abused when they made him the chief. He never belonged to a family that could pretend to lead the village. The command of the village of Fatacara was held by my forefathers and here is how:

The first chief of the village was Mody,[72] originally from Goumbou, who arrived in the region of Goundam (Lake Télé) to look for pasturage. He purchased [the land] from the pasha of Timbuktu, because at that time, all of the region was under the domination of the Almoravids,[73] including the land which forms the village in dispute and its surroundings.

Mody died, and for his successor as chief of the village [these were the following]:

Moudou, his son;
Mekene, son of Moudou;
Mahamane, son of Mekene;

[71] Cercle de Goundam, "Rapport sur la vérification des terrains de Fatacara," June 2, 1930 (ACG).

[72] Oral accounts today refer to the founder by the name of Koundoum, based on the name of his purported origin (in this letter, "Goumbou").

[73] This is, of course, inaccurate historically. The letter writer means the domination of the Arma. The Almoravids arose as a major power in the eleventh century in present-day Mauritania, greatly reduced the power of the Empire of Ghana, and captured Morocco, from where they became an important dynasty controlling Islamic Spain as well as much of North Africa.

Bania, son of Mahamane;
Ousmane, son of Bania;
Bodji, son of Ousmane;
Mahamane, son of Bodji [and father of the letter writer];
Gallo, brother of Mahamane;
Amadou, brother of Gallo;
Consequently, I appeal to your elevated and uncontested spirit of justice, and I beg of you very respectfully to please ask the chief Abadi Yattara to return the farm land to its proper owners who have held it for centuries.[74]

What we see in Fatacara is an example of how French policy toward Songhay-speaking sedentary people initially sought to organize its rule through an alliance with local elites, but how this policy gave way to a more pragmatic approach to local Songhay authority designed to prevent the consolidation of a Songhay landholding elite. As a consequence, it was hoped that social tensions within Songhay-speaking communities would thereby be reduced. Fatacara is also an example of how the older status structure in the Songhay-context – at least at the village level – began to break down under colonial rule. It shares much in common with Igillad complaints and rhetoric that I discussed in Chapter 5.

The most productive agricultural area in the Niger Bend in the late nineteenth and early twentieth centuries was the floodplain of Lake Faguibine, a large seasonal lake that sometimes fills with water during the annual flood of the Niger. There are three main Songhay villages on the southern shore of the lake (M'Bouna, Bintagoungou, and Toucabango). These villages were subordinate to Tuareg power in the nineteenth century, but because of their position in the middle of a pastoralist milieu, and because of the nature of the agricultural economy of the Faguibine, which required a well-organized distribution of cultivable land each year because of the variability of the annual flood, a Songhay-speaking elite held considerable power over not only their own villagers but also over pastoralist groups that wished to put servile people under their control to work in order to cultivate grain. At the beginning of the colonial occupation, the French were astonished to find that the people responsible for allotting agricultural land to both Songhay-speakers and the Tuareg were the chiefs of the Songhay villages. The land in the western half of the lake was under the authority of the chief of the village of M'Bouna, Baba Mahadio.[75] This role for the chief of M'Bouna had been assigned

74 Letter from Ali Mahamane Bodji, Bamako, to the Commandant, Cercle de Goundam, September 5, 1937, (ACG).

75 Born c. 1860; became chief of M'Bouna in 1894; died 1923.

by the Tengeregif, under whose suzerainty M'Bouna found itself.[76] The French thought it bizarre that "a black chief of low origin" would hold authority over neighboring Tuareg and Arab groups in dispensing agricultural land.[77] According to French reports, Baba Mahadio treated all the cultivable land of the western half of Lake Faguibine as his own personal property, and he operated a kind of sharecropping system in which half of the harvest was owed to him.[78] The colonial interest in encouraging pastoralist groups to sedentarize their slaves so that they could become agricultural producers led the colonial administration to change this system of land management, taking over the role themselves in 1901 of dividing up the land each year.[79]

French management of the arable land in Lake Faguibine changed the relationship between pastoralist and sedentary people by dispossessing the Songhay elite of its important role as the ultimate arbiters in matters of agriculture. This is still remembered bitterly by local people.[80] Interestingly, the Songhay-speaking elites in the Faguibine area claim a genealogy connecting them with either Arab or Soninke origins, not Songhay ones.[81] This reflects the distinctive character and history of the Songhay-speaking communities around Lake Faguibine, but it also supports the hierarchical structure of Songhay society in the area today, which, although diminished, is much more marked than in other Songhay areas. Part of the reason for this is that slavery played a much more important role in the Songhay-speaking communities of the Faguibine than in most other areas of Songhay concentration, and because, with pastoralist support, the Songhay-speaking elites in the communities of the Faguibine have been able to keep a tighter hold on the scarce resource of arable land in this very inhospitable area.[82]

76 Poste de Ras-el-Ma, "Rapport politique," 1ère trimestre 1988 (ANM FA 1E 66).

77 Ibid.

78 Poste de Ras-el-Ma, "Rapport politique," January 1899 (ANM FA 1E 66).

79 Territoire de Ras-el-Ma, "Rapport politique," February 1901 (ANM FA 1E 66).

80 Interview, Oumar Kasey, Alamir Baba, Mahamadou Sahibou, November 3, 2002, M'Bouna.

81 Interview, Oumar Kasey, Alamir Baba, Mahamadou Sahibou, November 3, 2002, M'Bouna; Interview, Ibrahim Sall, October 31, 2002, Bintagoungou; Interview, Abdarahman Hamma al-Madan, November 4, 2002, Toucabangou.

82 The land tenure system in the Songhay communities around Lake Faguibine is best described as patriarchal, with a number of families in each village owning agricultural land that they divide up among their extended family members and outsiders willing to rent the land (Interview, Ibrahim Sall, October 31, 2002, Bintagoungou; also, de Loppinot, "Régime foncier," 70).

DIVIDING UP THE RIVER

The loss of control by Songhay-speaking elites over land in the Niger valley benefited the pastoralists. French officials rewarded the Kel Entsar for their loyalty to the colonial cause by giving them the land on the north shore of Lake Faguibine, where they settled their bellah-iklan on a seasonal basis to grow grain. The area of Lake Faguibine was the first place in the Niger Bend where the colonial administration became active in regulation and managing land issues. In other places, they did attempt to settle land disputes as Songhay-speaking communities expanded their agricultural production and where pastoralists refused to respect sedentary land claims. French officials began the process of demarcating areas of the floodplain, assigning specific pieces of land to sedentary villages and others to specific groups of pastoralists. At the beginning of the colonial period, they also forbade pastoralists from camping on the outskirts of villages because of the damage that animals did to villagers' crops. What follows is one of many examples of the sort of situation that developed between Songhay-speaking villages and pastoralists once colonial rule was firmly established:

> The relations between the people of Goïrum [east of Timbuktu] and the Irreganatan [a Tuareg warrior-status group] who, contrary to the orders given in 1907, are camped on the outskirts of this village, are more and more strained, to the point that a serious conflict could erupt between them. A man from the village received a hard blow to the head from a [Tuareg's] sword; another man suffered serious contusions, and the village chief was also hit seriously on the head. The affair could not be judged by the Tribunal of Timbuktu because the Tuareg who committed these acts of aggression had left the area.[83]

The main problem as far as Songhay-speaking sedentary people were concerned was that the Tuareg did not respect them, or the colonial orders that were meant to protect them. The colonial reports are filled with examples:

> A certain number of conflicts between Tuareg and sedentary people was indicated by Mr. Dufan, commissioner of native affairs, during his census-taking in the villages of the east. Lieutenant Moaligou has been sent to be with him by the commander of the Region in order to resolve these problems on the spot and to remind the nomads in general, and the Tuareg in particular, to observe our treaties demarcating the land and prohibiting them from being on the outskirts of villages. This officer found some of the nomads' animals, most often those of the Tuareg, in the fields where millet has begun to grow.[84]

[83] Cercle de Tomboutou, "Rapport politique," April 1908 (ANM, 1E 78–81).
[84] Ibid.

By the 1920s, the colonial administration had become much more sympathetic to pastoral land needs and, as a consequence, began to devote much more attention to the problem of regulating different and conflicting land usage between pastoralist and agricultural communities. By the early 1940s, the French had formalized colonial mediation into official land conventions, which were then signed by the competing parties. There were different kinds of colonial conventions, managing different land-use conflicts. Among the pastoralists, a major source of conflict between different groups was the issue of ownership and use of wells. Most important of all, however, was controlling the grazing lands that pastoralists could use. One example of a convention regulating intrapastoralist problems was signed in 1939 between Ouadan ag Baber, the head of the Igawaddaran I,[85] and Baidegui, head of the Kel Ulli, both Tuareg groups:

> Conforming to the convention already passed in 1927 by the two chiefs designated above, in the presence of the administrator Mourgues, it is agreed that the Kel Ulli of Baidegui will have the right to use the burgu paddies located on the islands of Dangouma and Banigoungou, on the north side [of the river] as well as the burgu paddies located in the place called Oueygoungou, in a part of the floodplain touching the left bank of the Niger; the Igawaddaran I, will have the usage of Banigoungou-Gourma [on the south side of the river], the islands of Tintaberek, and Banguel. It is agreed that the Kel Ulli must no longer cross the river, nor penetrate into the burgu paddies reserved for the Igawaddaran. Likewise, the Igawaddaran agree not to bother the Kel Ulli on the territory attributed to them.[86]

By 1946, all the pastureland of the district of Gourma-Rharous had been formalized into conventions, and each pastoral clan was given rights over certain areas.[87]

Another important issue was the management of conflict between different sedentary communities over agricultural land. The extension of agricultural production was not always in areas adjacent to villages. In fact, many villages decamp during the agricultural season to work in their lands that may be dozens of kilometers away. The issue of propriety often

[85] When the French arrived in the Niger Bend, a conflict between two clans had led to the division of the Igawaddaran into two separate groups (Igawaddaran I, led by Sakhaoui, and the Igawaddaran II, led by Sakib). In time, the French gave up on their attempts to mediate in this conflict or to forcibly reconcile the two groups, and the two sections of the Igawaddaran were recognized as separate "tribal" groups for administrative purposes.

[86] Cercle de Tombouctou, Subdivision de Gourma-Rharous, "Convention," March 19, 1939 (ACT).

[87] Cercle de Tombouctou, Subdivision de Gourma-Rharous, "Convention," July 10, 1946 (ACT).

surfaced in cases of this sort when different Songhay communities shared the same land. A sense of the dynamics of this process can be gleamed from a 1936 convention attempting to regulate one such dispute:

> Alidji Boubakar, chief of the village of Kagha;
> Faranfarou Lougoueye, chief of the village of Bérégoungou;
> who have requested a judgment on the conflict which divides the two localities over the subject of pasture land and rice paddies on the Island of Goya where the inhabitants of Kagha have been established for approximately thirty years. They would like to extend their agricultural activities onto new land. First of all, it is accepted that the village of Kagha, Kunta in origin, cannot claim rights to the land before the [colonial] conquest because Goya, like Bérégoungou, occupied the site at this time. To get to the origin of the dispute, one must recall the fact that Lougoueye Hama Sorko, chief of Bérégoungou, and father of the current chief, had authorized certain inhabitants of Kagha to establish themselves on the Island of Goya, although nobody sought to dispute his ultimate ownership of the land. These few inhabitants of Kagha were soon followed by others who now consider the land to be theirs. Bérégoungou does not request the expulsion of the inhabitants of Kagha but simply that a division of the land be made that determines definitively the rights of the two villages.[88]

The convention divided the land of the island between the two communities, assigning legal rights to each of the competing groups.

Part of the problem for Songhay-speaking sedentary agriculturalists was that land closer to home had been given to pastoralist groups, and this had been the cause of some of the attempts to gain lands further afield. In the case of the previously mentioned village of Kagha, the fertile floodplain land adjacent to the village had been partly assigned to the Tuareg Kel Temulayt:

> The burgu paddy of Teïteïkaïna located 2 km to the east of the village of Kagha and of a surface area of 20 hectares, is a place of common pasturage for the pastoralists of the Kel Temulayt tribe and the village of Kagha. This burgu paddy will in no case be transformed into agricultural land for the sole benefit of the sedentary people. No work of irrigation, no management in view of creating rice fields will be undertaken on it.[89]

In other cases, fertile floodplain land was assigned to pastoralist groups to be cultivated by their servile bellah-iklan. Thus, the village of Aglal was forced to cede part of its floodplain land to the Kel Temulayt in 1942, so that it could be farmed by Kel Temulayt bellah-iklan.[90] In another case,

[88] Cercle de Tombouctou, "Décision No. 90," September 21, 1936 (ACT).
[89] Cercle de Tombouctou, "Convention," April 8, 1946 (ACT).
[90] Cercle de Tombouctou, "Convention," April 2, 1942 (ACT).

the village of Bellassao-Djinguina was forced to allow the Arab Barabish to install their slaves and haratin in the adjacent Island of Inarata.[91]

CONCLUSION

The colonial policy of mapping the river and demarcating land was not accepted as legitimate by either pastoral or agricultural communities, who had very different and mutually exclusive ideas about land ownership. The result was that conflict between pastoralist and Songhay-speaking communities over land increased in the 1940s and 1950s as available fertile floodplain land became an increasingly scarce resource. Whereas elite pastoralist groups came to see the advantage that accrued to them in possessing agricultural land that they put into cultivation using the labor of the servile people whom they still controlled, Songhay-speaking communities never accepted these arrangements as legitimate. The differences in interests and traditions of land ownership shaped the increasing divide between Songhay and pastoralist people.

New strategies for social mobility arose based on individual holdings of land, or access to land that was (always) recognized in Islamic law as heritable property. As servile people from pastoralist groups increasingly sought independence from their masters, there was a pool of labor available for landowners to exploit, making ownership of land an especially important basis of wealth accumulation and status. This is especially true in the period after the Second World War, when the French regime embarked on several significant irrigation projects at Lake Oro and at Diré, and even more so after independence, when various Western donors brought new land under irrigation, especially at the Korioumé project not far from Timbuktu. In a sense, the old land-holding Arma elite has reconstituted itself using access to the state, credit provision, and other means to acquire land worked by others.[92]

My purpose here has been to outline the most important changes that the colonial occupation provoked in the Songhay-speaking milieu in terms of its relationship to fertile land. I argue that the mobilization of race in the anticolonial politics after the Second World War, and in postcolonial northern Mali, was undergirded by struggles over land that

91 Cercle de Tombouctou, "Convention," April 24, 1941 (ACT).

92 For a parallel story in a similar context, see Peter C. Bloch, "An Egalitarian Development Project in a Stratified Society: Who Ends Up With the Land?" in *Land in African Agrarian Systems*, ed. Thomas J. Bassett and Donald E. Crummey (Madison, WI: University of Wisconsin Press, 1993), 222–43.

began before 1940. Since the Second World War, the basis of Songhay ethnic politics has been increasingly based on proprietary claims over the Niger River. To be a Songhay came to be defined as a person of the river (So. "isa-boro")[93] Songhay arguments about historical rights over the entire river absorbed notions of autochthony from African nationalists during the anticolonial struggle in the 1950s. This has further strengthened already existing Songhay claims to be the first occupants of the land, or at least earlier occupants than the so-called "nomads." For Songhay-speakers, it was they, and only they, who had developed the river and who had cultivated its banks. The pastoralists were latecomers and destroyers of civilized sedentary economic and social activity. As outsiders, the pastoralists had no rights over the Niger valley, and any claims that they could make were procured illegitimately through their unholy alliance with the Europeans. Songhay ideas about ethnicity and race emerged as an argument about unequal treatment and access to land when compared to pastoralists. In Songhay eyes, the realization of full autonomy was blocked by the pastoralist-French alliance, and they found themselves on the receiving end of racial discourses that justified their inequality compared to the Tuareg and Arabs. It was in response to the use of race against them that Songhay-speaking people began to develop ideas of a racialized geography of the Niger Bend, in which only blacks were the legitimate inhabitants.

[93] Interview, Youssouf Kakay, October 14, 2002, Kano.

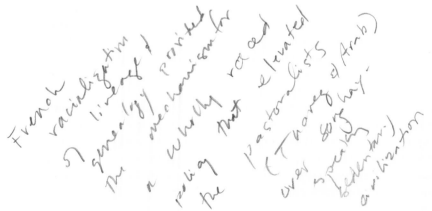

PART FOUR

RACE AND DECOLONIZATION, C. 1940–1960

PRELUDE

In Part Four, I explore the racial rhetoric that animated local politics after the Second World War. There were two racial leitmotifs that emerged in the process of decolonization. One was embarrassment by French administrators, and outrage by black-African anticolonial leaders, at the fact that racialized slavery continued to exist among the pastoralist peoples of the Niger Bend, epitomized by the slavery of the Tamashek-speaking bellah-iklan. The other issue that drove local politics was the emergence of a racialized nationalism in certain elite Tuareg and Arab circles. As the eventuality of decolonization became clearer in the mid-1950s, the issue of racial separatism from blacks was raised as a rallying cry by several influential Arab and Tuareg political leaders. In the single chapter in Part Four, I trace the ways in which the politics of decolonization became a politics of race in the Niger Bend.

The process that would lead to decolonization began during the Second World War, when Charles de Gaulle convened a conference in Brazzaville in 1944 to prepare the ground for the postwar colonial reforms that France would need to make to ensure its ability to hold onto its territories in Africa. The Brazzaville reforms were designed to improve the economic and social welfare in the colonies, and to allow greater African political representation. Beginning with the founding of the French Union in 1946, there were a series of elections throughout Soudan that eventually culminated in the "yes" vote in the 1958 referendum to remain inside the reformed French Community. Initially, there was a very limited franchise with a double electoral college, but at each step, more and more people were permitted to participate. Full electoral rights were not achieved until

1956.[1] The two most important political groupings in Soudan were the Parti Progressiste Soudanais (PSP), which was broadly more conservative, drew much of its support from chiefs and other well-placed people, and was initially favored by the colonial administration; and the Union Soudanaise-Rassemblement Démocratique Africain (US-RDA), which eventually prevailed, winning the 1956 elections to the French National Assembly and leading the colony to independence in 1960.

The continued existence of slavery among pastoralist groups in the colonial Niger Bend was the result of deliberate French policy toward Tuareg and Arab groups to ensure their loyalty, and the successful arguments made by slaveholders about the need to retain the institution of slavery. By the 1940s, it was clear to many colonial administrators and slaveholders alike that slavery could not survive indefinitely, especially with the prospect of a more liberal legal and political framework in postwar Soudan. What made the issue of continued slavery so much more explosive in the Niger Bend than elsewhere in the colony was the fact it was so deeply racialized there. People defined as black in pastoralist societies could not easily escape their racial status while remaining ethnically (or linguistically) Tuareg or Arab. Anticolonial activists from elsewhere in Soudan were quick to recognize racial differences within Tuareg and Arab societies, even if they did not understand much about the complex range of social positions different people could occupy. For example, Mali's first president and the leader of the US-RDA, Modibo Keita, worked as a teacher in the village of Kabara near Timbuktu in 1951. Like others from outside the region, he blamed the French for allowing the pastoralist elites to continue holding slaves.[2] He used the label of feudalism in US-RDA political campaigns to describe Tuareg and Arab social hierarchy, and argued that throwing off the colonial yoke would require breaking the feudal system and freeing the slaves.[3]

The emergence of racial nationalism among certain Arab and Tuareg leaders drew on the wealth of racial ideas already discussed in this book. But arguments were formulated in new ways that drew on the experience

[1] Tony Chafer, *The End of Empire in French West Africa: France's Successful Decolonization?* (New York: Berg, 2002), 147.

[2] Amadou Seydou Traoré, *Modibo Kéïta: Une référence, Un symbole, Un patrimoine national* (Bamako: Librairie Traoré, 2005), 79.

[3] Naffet Keïta, "De l'identitaire au problème de la territorialité: L'OCRS et les sociétés Kel Tamacheq du Mali," in *Mali-France. Regards sur une histoire partagée*, ed. GEMDEV, Université du Mali (Paris: Kathala, 2005), 104–5; Pierre Boilley, "Un complot français au Sahara? Politiques françaises et représentations maliennes…" in *Mali-France. Regards sur une histoire partagée*, ed. GEMDEV, Université du Mali (Paris: Kathala, 2005), 168–9.

and rhetoric of "modernization" as it was deployed by agents of the colonial state beginning in the 1930s. The prospect of losing control over slaves, and the serial conflicts over land with Songhay-speaking sedentary agriculturalists in the Niger valley, fed a certain anxiety about the future place of the Tuareg and Arabs. Also, the connections between people in the Niger Bend and the larger Arabophone Middle East provided access to models of nationalism that could be manipulated in the context of French decolonization. There was an attempt in the 1950s to separate off the Niger Bend from soon-to-be-independent Mali as a new, French-controlled Saharan colony in which white Tuareg and Arabs would retain demographic and political dominance. The new territory was to be called the Organisation commune des régions sahariennes (OCRS). In the end, these proposals came to little; however, the campaign for the OCRS, and the resentment it spawned among those who would form Mali's first postcolonial government, led directly to the first Tuareg rebellion in 1963 and its indiscriminate repression by the Malian army.

Start w/ his argument now about French involved the state in racialized genealogies.

8

The Racial Politics of Decolonization, c. 1940–1960

MODERNIZING THE KEL ENTSAR

From the French perspective, the one Tuareg group in the Niger Bend that was the most enlightened and forward-looking was the Kel Entsar. Like their great rivals the Tengeregif, they had fought the French in the 1890s, had suffered from bloody French reprisals, and had lost their leaders to French bullets. But even more than the Tengeregif, who were never fully trusted, the Kel Entsar were crucial French allies in the military defense of the territory against the raids of the Saharan "grands nomades" who often targeted the area around Lake Faguibine where the Kel Entsar were concentrated. When the Kel Entsar chief N'Gouna was killed by the French in 1898, the colonial administration refused to install his son, Muhammad, as chief of this important clerical confederation.[1] Instead, they appointed N'Gouna's brother, Allouda,[2] who was suspected by many Kel Entsar of having betrayed his brother to the French. The Barabish chronicle discussed in Chapter 4 repeats this claim:

> In this year [1898] Allouda, the brother of N'Gouna, had made the choice of joining the Christians. In the second half of the year, N'Gouna rode until he reached the Kel Entsar at the site of Faguibine Immajarān. His brother approached him with all the Kel Entsar and N'Gouna struck his brother, reprimanding him for having joined the Christians without being ordered to. So [Allouda] informed the Christians and the soldiers approached [N'Gouna] unbeknownst to him until

[1] Born c. 1865.

[2] Or Loudar; his real name was Muḥammad Mawlūd ag Muḥammad Aḥmad (c. 1850–1914).

they had surrounded him. He looked left and right but there was no way to escape. So the soldiers said to him: "Come with us to Timbuktu."[3]

N'Gouna escaped on the way to Timbuktu but was quickly tracked down and killed. Allouda's betrayal of his brother to the French remained part of local historical memory and continued to motivate opponents of the Kel Entsar leadership throughout the colonial period.[4] When Allouda died in 1914, the French appointed his administrative assistant, Attaher, who was from a nonchiefly lineage, as the leader of the Kel Entsar.[5] Attaher also stood accused of betraying N'Gouna in 1898, in league with Allouda. But Attaher was a useful chief from the French point of view. He managed to provide a significant counterweight to his Tengeregif rival, Sobbo ag Fondogomo, which the French found especially valuable during the First World War. When Attaher died in 1926, his son, Muhammad ʿAli ag Attaher, assumed the position of chief at the young age of twenty . The local French administration had to apply all its powers of persuasion to make the Kel Entsar accept this unpopular decision.[6]

The lack of legitimacy in the eyes of many Kel Entsar must have been a factor in the approach Muhammad ʿAli took to exercising his power. He saw himself as part of a new generation of leaders among the pastoralists of the Niger Bend, and he was one of the first chiefs to champion "modernizing" reforms that he hoped would help reinvigorate his people. Muhammad ʿAli made two trips to France as chief, once to attend the colonial exposition held in Paris in 1931, and a second time to attend a colonial development conference in the winter of 1934–1935. In both

[3] "Taʾrīkh Azawād fī ʾl-akhbār al-Barābīsh wa ḥurūbi-him maʿ al-rakībāt wa-ḥajār Afūghās wa-Idnān wa-dhikr baʿḍ akābiri-him mithl Sīdi b. Muḥammad b. Amhammad wa-Muḥammad b. Amhammad wa-Maḥmūd b. Daḥmān wa-dakhūl al-nasārā fī Tinbuktū wa-ghayr dhālak" (IHERIAB ms. 279), f. 24.

[4] The French administrators based in Goundam spent a lot of time dealing with these intrigues. They were well aware of the questions of the legitimacy of the Kel Entsar leadership. See Gaston Mourgues, Commandant, Cercle de Goundam, "Rapport sur les déclarations faites à l'Administrateur-adjoint Tanguy par Ousman ag Rhalala, marabout des Kel Antessar, contre le chef de tribu Muhamed Ali ag Attaher," No.54/C, November 17, 1938 (ACG).

[5] Al-Tahir ag al-Mahdi ag Muhammad ag Habda (c. 1868–1924). On the clan differences between Allouda and Attaher, see Florence Camel, "La construction coloniale d'une élite touarègue. Le cas des Kel Intessar, Soudan français (fin du XIXe siècle – années quarante)," in *Elites du monde nomade touareg et maure. Cahiers de l'IREMAN* 13–14, ed. Pierre Bonte and Hélène Claudot-Hawad (Aix-en-Provence: CNRS, 2000), 61–70.

[6] Gaston Mourgues, Commandant, Cercle de Goundam, "Rapport sur les déclarations faites à l'Administrateur-adjoint Tanguy par Ousman ag Rhalala, marabout des Kel Antessar, contre le chef de tribu Muhamed Ali ag Attaher," No.54/C, November 17, 1938 (ACG).

FIGURE 4. Muhammad ʿAli ag Attaher (source: ACG).

FIGURE 5. Muhammad ʿAli ag Attaher with two bellah-iklan servants, France, 1934–1935 (source: ACG).

instances, he requested that the French government send him to the meetings.[7] These trips made a big impression on his sense of the wider world and of the "backwardness" of his own people. In his letters to the French administrator in Goundam (the administrative district responsible for the Kel Entsar) written from Paris in January 1935, he offered an autocritique: "We Tuareg have a very bad character and terrible customs."[8] Although Muhammad ʿAli carried out all of his correspondence with the colonial state in Arabic, he became a great advocate for French-language education for the children of Kel Entsar nobles. He encouraged the French to establish schools to serve the pastoralist population, and he valued them so much that he sent two of his younger brothers to attend, including his eventual successor, Muhammad al-Mahdi. For many Kel Entsar, accepting French education was a step too far. In a letter he wrote to the commander of Goundam in 1936, he admitted that his travels in France had changed the perception of him by others: "Since my return from France almost half the people in my tribe are suspicious of me. They say that I lost my spirit in France and that all I think about now is how to transform them into Frenchmen."[9]

In 1939, Muhammad ʿAli sent a kind of manifesto for the modernization of the Kel Entsar to the governor of Soudan. He called this document the "Project for the program to follow by me and my successors to introduce French civilization in the Tuareg milieu."[10] In this document, Muhammad ʿAli proposed that all "nomad" children go to French-language school. Understanding that there would be resistance to such a project, he said that he would begin by sending the children of the best, most noble families to set the example: "I am sure that if these children can be made to understand French, the others will blindly follow their example without trying too hard to understand the reasons behind it. In order to have children from good families I will promise to their parents that the children will learn French and Arabic at the same time. I know that the parents are afraid of losing their first tradition which is Quranic education." French

[7] Muhammad ʿAli requested that he be allowed to participate in this exposition, and that the colonial state pay for his voyage (Cercle de Goundam, "Rapport politique," 4ème trimestre 1930 [ANM FR 1E 18]).

[8] Muhammad ʿAli, letter to Commandant, Cercle de Goundam, January 6, 1935 (ACG).

[9] Letter from Muhammad ʿAli ag Attaher to Commandant, Cercle de Goundam, 1936 (ACG).

[10] "Projet de Programme à suivre par moi et mes successeurs pour introduire la Civilisation Française dans les milieux touareg," August 10, 1939 (ACG). The letter is in a file with Telegram-letter, P. Le Floch, Commandant, Cercle de Goundam, to the Gouverneur, Soudan Français, August 16, 1939 (ACG).

FIGURE 6. Muhammad ʿAli ag Attaher with two bellah-iklan servants, ship captain, headed to France, 1934 (source: ACG).

efforts at training nobles from pastoralist groups such as the Tuareg had been largely unsuccessful to that point. A mobile, so-called nomad school was developed to try to accommodate colonial education with pastoralist lifestyles. Muhammad ʿAli argued that this had been a mistake: "I want a school to be built which will not be a nomad school like in previous times, but one that is fixed on a site of our choice near our agricultural fields. I will then create a reserve of good pasture land for the student's cows. The children will be fed very easily with milk and grains." The advantage of having a fixed location for the school was that "the children will see agricultural crops at the site and, under the direction of their teachers, they will learn agriculture." With the knowledge of farming, Muhammad ʿAli proposed an ideal of Tuareg yeoman farmers supported by Tuareg veterinarians, doctors, and teachers: "We will then have engineers who will work on irrigation schemes for our lands and the value of our country will thus be increased." The biggest fear that Muhammad ʿAli harbored was the eventual loss of control over Tuareg slaves, who performed all agricultural work. Training the Tuareg as farmers "will permit them to give up all the bellah who will certainly abandon them in the end because of civilization."

Among the larger objectives of the 1939 manifesto was an effort to improve the "bad customs" of the Kel Entsar: "We have noticed a considerable regression in the reproduction of the nomadic people. We are getting less numerous because of ourselves." The cause for the purported decline in population was that "our customs of marriage are exaggerated and go well past what is necessary. To have a wife you must give a dowry of fifteen to forty head of livestock. The young and the poor families are thereby prevented from marrying, and they are the most numerous." Such prohibitive costs led young Kel Entsar away from the institution of marriage altogether: "They would never want to marry a black woman, or a Moor, which they would consider to be dishonorable. These are the races that do not ask for very much in the way of a dowry. The youths can do nothing but lead a life of debauchery. I call the attention of the Administration to this point which makes us afraid that we will disappear in the future." Another problem that Muhammad ʿAli identified was female obesity: "We have a custom which hinders reproduction even more. We force our female children to become fat at a young age and as they grow up they become enormously obese. Too much fat prevents reproduction." Not only did female obesity hinder Tuareg population size, but it also rendered women useless in the "modernization" project that Muhammad ʿAli proposed: "This fatness makes the woman incapable of doing anything that requires the least effort. She cannot work. All these customs are not ancestral but habits acquired in recent times. It is only after having consulted friends in different countries who affirmed it for me, that I was able to raise this problem with the Administration."[11] Muhammad ʿAli had taken up this issue since returning from his first trip to France in 1931. It was also perceived as a problem by the local colonial administration in the 1930s. For French officials in Goundam, for example, the apparent lack of fecundity of the "white race" in the Niger Bend threatened its very existence.[12]

This modernization project reflected ten years of exposure and encouragement from local French officials such as Gaston Mourgues, and to the impression made by trips to France and North Africa. But it was also about very local, Kel Entsar politics. Muhammad ʿAli said at one point, "my situation resembles that of France in 1789 at the moment of the French Revolution. The neighboring chiefs are constantly pushing those whom I administer against me, so that they can get rid of me. They will be afraid to turn away from the old customs which they will be made to lose. I do not hesitate. I commit myself. God knows, and France will know, that I only want what is best for my Tuareg race." The manifesto ended with a flourish of praise for the French colonial project:

> Do not say that in acting this way, the Tuareg will hate France. No and No. If we want to return to the first step made by France at the moment of the conquest, we see that many of our fathers died fighting against France. After them, we knew the happiness that France brought us. It is too late for them to benefit from that tranquility, from that peace, from that justice. France gave its own children in death, expending them so that we might be raised up and learn to live happily. We, who are the children of those who have died; we thank France forever and will always acknowledge it. Now it is the turn of our children. We must make a greater effort to not allow our children to grow up like weeds. We want to make our children go up the steps of French civilization, and in this way our children will thank France all the more.[13]

In 1946, Muhammad ʿAli voluntarily resigned his position as chief of the Kel Entsar confederacy in favor of his brother, Muhammad al-Mahdi. He left Soudan in 1948 and traveled in Europe, the Middle East and Africa, for the next fifteen years. As we will see, he became actively involved in wider Tuareg nationalism in the 1950s, and ended up as a fierce critic of French colonialism.

[11] Muhammad ʿAli ag Attaher, "Projet de Programme."
[12] Cercle de Goundam, "Rapport politique," 2ème trimestre 1933 (ANM FR 1E 18).
[13] Muhammad ʿAli ag Attaher, "Projet de Programme."

Even after he had fallen out with the colonial administration, Muhammad ʿAli stuck to his modernizing agenda. In a letter to his brother from Mecca in Saudi Arabia written in 1956, he wrote, "I have learned that you have created a school at Ras-el-Ma [on the western edge of Lake Faguibine]. I suspect that this decision will only bring reproaches and failures without any advantage for the students in the future. It will only discourage the teachers from the cause by moving far away from the sedentary population. Right now, nothing good will come from schools if they are not those of the towns." Just as he had argued in 1939 in his manifesto, sedentarization and agriculture were essential features for the future of the Kel Entsar: "There is no good reason to put the schools far from the sedentary population because the children of the nomads are wild people. If they are left with their wildness, they will grow up with it. They will never serve civilization. Bring together the schools beside the markets, roads, and fields and this will give the students the idea to sedentarize and will remove from them their independence and divisiveness."[14] Muhammad ʿAli recognized that education was the solution to the diminishing value of high birth among nobles in the Niger Bend. In a letter that he wrote to the commander of Goundam from Libya on the eve of independence in 1959, seeking the administration's help with several Kel Entsar students, he said, "you know well that in the current moment that there is no recognition for the father, or nobility, or the kindness of someone because of ignorance. It is only education that can raise someone for his life."[15] In his old age, Muhammad ʿAli argued that his encouragement of education among the Kel Entsar was a means of resistance to colonial rule.[16] And indeed, he was responsible for sending many young Kel Entsar to study in both French schools and in the Arab world as well.

"THE BELLAH QUESTION"

Part of Muhammad ʿAli's motivation for his modernization project was based on his recognition that slavery could not be maintained indefinitely. By the end of the Second World War, it had also become clear to many

[14] This is quoted from the French translation of this letter made by the colonial administration. I have not been able to locate the Arabic original (Letter from Muhammad ʿAli ag Attaher to Muhammad al-Mahdi, July 28, 1956, Mecca [ACG]).

[15] French translation of a letter from Muhammad ʿAli ag Attaher to the Commandant, Cercle de Goundam, Libya [no original], translation September 24, 1959 (ACG).

[16] Mohamed Ali ag Attaher, "La scolarisation moderne comme stratégie de résistance," *Revue du Monde Musulman et de la Méditerranée* 57 (1990): 91–7.

colonial officials that the continued practice of slavery among the pastoralist Tuareg, Arabs, and Fulbe was a potential political problem that could no longer be ignored. The French administration worried that the loss of control over servile populations by the elite stratum of pastoralists would destroy the political and social settlement that colonial occupation had ushered in. They also knew that it was a powerful issue for anticolonial forces in Soudan, and more broadly in the French Union. Slavery was an issue that brought race to the forefront of the politics of decolonization.

Almost from the beginning of its occupation, the colonial administration had encouraged pastoralist groups such as the Kel Entsar and Kunta to settle their slaves in agricultural villages for at least part of the year to grow grain. The policy met with some success in the Lake Faguibine region and in the lacustrine region of the Gourma. The colonial state had also had some success at sedentarizing Tamashek-speaking bellah-iklan in two large agricultural development projects that involved irrigation and resettlement of families as laborers. The first was at Diré, where a cotton colonization scheme was initiated in the early 1920s by the businessman Marcel Hirsch who founded the Compagnie de culture cotonière du Niger (CICONNIC). For a variety of technical and labor reasons, the project failed and had to be taken over by the Office du Niger in the early 1930s.[17] In its first stages, labor had been recruited from all over Soudan and was organized in gangs under the direction of European foremen; however, by 1926, a system of sharecropping was put in place to organize production.[18] After the collapse of CICONNIC, an entirely new workforce had to be recruited for the 1930–1931 season, but none of the families moved to the scheme willingly. By 1936, the colonial administration on the ground at Diré reported that they had managed to put 570 hectares of cotton into cultivation, in addition to 356 hectares of rice and 570 hectares of wheat.[19] There were 415 families settled and enrolled in the project in 1937 and at least as many more waiting to be given a place.[20]

[17] Jean Filipovich, "Destined to Fail: Forced Settlement at the Office du Niger, 1926–45," *JAH* 42, no. 2 (2001): 248n.

[18] Emil Schreyger, *L'Office du Niger au Mali: la problématique d'une grande enterprise agricole dans la zone du Sahel* (Wiesbaden: Steiner, 1984), 32–5; Monica van Beusekom, *Negotiating Development: African Farmers and Colonial Experts at the Office du Niger, 1920–1960* (Portsmouth, NH: Heinemann, 2002), 35.

[19] Letter from Gaston Mourgues, Commandant, Cercle de Goundam to the Contrôleur de la Société d'Etudes et de Colonisation, Koulouba, January 24, 1936 (ANM 1D 57, Num. Sér I).

[20] Richard Roberts, *Two Worlds of Cotton: Colonialism and the Regional Economy in French Soudan, 1800–1946* (Stanford, CA: Stanford University Press, 1996), 118–62.

The other major irrigation scheme was run by the Office du Niger on Lake Oro. Work began in 1940 on a dam at Tonka, where a channel connects the lake to the Niger River. The first agricultural season on the irrigated land was in 1942. As at Diré, labor was provided by a system of sharecropping in which whole families of bellah-iklan, Fulfulde-speaking rimaybe, and other subalterns established households near the new lands.[21] A new village called Yourmi was built beside the irrigated fields. Because of the importance of bellah-iklan settlers to the irrigation scheme at Lake Oro in particular, the colonial administration was keen to maintain strict control of bellah-iklan movements and prevent them from migrating out of the administrative districts of the Niger Bend. Whether at these irrigation schemes, or in towns of the Niger Bend where bellah-iklan settled to take up wage work or petty commerce, their masters usually paid regular visits to demand a share of the crop or wages for themselves.[22]

Colonial officials in the Niger Bend did not react well to the changes in administration promised at the Brazzaville Conference in 1944. In January 1945, the governor general of French West Africa sent a circular to all the administrative districts in the colonies explaining the changes that were imminent after the war and soliciting local responses.[23] In his response, Jean Raynaud, the commander of the district of Goundam, highlighted the problem that slavery would pose for political reforms in the Niger Bend:

> This issue of the servants also deserves our attention, because evidently the present system, about which we have not brought any real change in over fifty years cannot last forever even if the administration doesn't intervene directly. A slow evolution is occurring. Numerous are the bellah who have left their masters to seek refuge first in the freedom villages (villages de liberté) and then later in the districts far to the south. It is my opinion that we have an interest in avoiding as much as possible the crisis that will explode any day now among the servants, a crisis which could provoke the total disintegration of the nomadic tribes. To avoid this, it is necessary that the evolution of the bellah be made to take into account their aspirations and the vital needs of the nomadic tribes.[24]

Raynaud then listed the objectives of French policy toward the bellah-iklan, which he said should include a strict colonial surveillance and

[21] Vincent Joly, *Le Soudan Français de 1939 à 1945: Une colonie dans la guerre* (Paris: Karthala, 2006), 314–17.

[22] Jean Gallais, *Pasteurs et paysans du Gourma. La condition sahelienne* (Paris: CNRS, 1975), 93–4.

[23] Gouverneur-Général de l'A.O.F., "Circulaire," January 17, 1945 (ART B44).

[24] Telegram-letter, Cercle de Goundam to the Gouverneur, Soudan Français, March 1, 1945, No. 13/C (ACG).

control, and an insistence that the bellah-iklan be registered and taxed according to the Tuareg clan to which they belonged, even if this meant splitting up bellah-iklan families so that the wife and children would be registered and taxed in one clan and the husband in another. Where an individual slave belonged was entirely dependent on the identity of his or her master.

Raynaud's hope was that the changes in the status of the bellah-iklan would occur within Tuareg society, under noble Tuareg supervision. Others were less worried about the political ramifications of ending slavery, but more concerned about the economic consequences. Paul Laîne, for example, in an audit of administrative practice in the Gourma region carried out in 1944, argued that "the Tuareg are not who they were and will not be who they are now. The warrior adventures ... have left the great solitude and entered into the domain of legend." Instead of rebellion, the Tuareg "think of their herds and would also like to have agricultural lands."[25] Laîne elaborated on the strategic steps needed to manage the changing social system among the Tuareg in another report written in 1945. In it, he proposed that the Tuareg groups in the Gourma should be regrouped under fewer chiefdoms, and that economic development in the region should focus on pastoralism rather than agriculture: "Far from favoring this extension of agriculture on the banks of the river, we should limit it. It is the cause of annoyances and losses from the real richness of the country, the herds." Laîne thought that the old colonial order based on a separation between sedentary and pastoralist populations, and the continuing servility of the bellah-iklan to their pastoralist masters, could not be sustained. He hoped that more economically logical development initiatives would sustain Tuareg pastoralists, with or without their slaves.

After the Second World War, there were a number of incidents in which bellah-iklan groups absconded with animals entrusted to them by their masters, claiming that their actions were legitimate because their masters had stolen from them. Such events often provoked counterraids by masters against bellah-iklan groups, and the resulting disorder caused the French administration to become very concerned about what they called "the bellah question."[26] By the late 1940s, the colonial administration

[25] Paul Laîne, "Rapport au Gouverneur: La situation dans la Subdivision de Gourma-Rharous," Koulouba, April 17, 1944, No.25/AA (ANM FR 2D15).

[26] Baz Lecocq, "'That Desert Is Our Country': Tuareg Rebellions and Competing Nationalisms in Contemporary Mali (1946–1996)" (Ph.D. diss., University of Amsterdam, 2002), 51; Martin Klein, "Slavery and French Rule in the Sahara," *Slavery and Abolition* 19 (1998): 80–2.

was forced to regulate more and more conflicts between masters and "servants," to use the euphemism employed by French administrators.

A growing appreciation of the bellah-iklan as industrious hard workers who would be necessary for the economic development of the Niger Bend region began to appear in colonial correspondence after the war. For example, in a letter from the commander of Timbuktu to the governor of Soudan in 1949, the administrator in the Niger Bend wrote that "the real question for us here is not so much the white Tuareg, but rather the bellah, those black Tuareg who constitute more than three-quarters of the total population of the Gourma, and who, by their mixing (métissage) and their hard life, have managed to constitute a selective race, very solid and prolific. The Tuareg on the other hand have less and less children and refuse to adapt to current life and to the necessary work." This was a strange reversal of decades of French racial sentiment in the Niger Bend that had romanticized the Tuareg noble warriors for so long: "The bellah, who is happy with very little, works to constitute his herd, because he has become a herder who knows the animals perfectly. He is forced to endure more and more bad things, and more and more difficulties from his masters who abuse him, pressuring him and looking to get the maximum out of him." The masters were aided in this by their "clerics" who "know how to adapt the precise rules of Quranic law to the needs of the cause. This is why we are continually forced to resolve the numerous differences between masters and servants."[27]

However, it was only at the very end of the colonial period, well into the process of decolonization and Africanization of the administration, that steps were finally taken to address the division and allotment of property between masters and bellah-iklan. It is in this process that we see one of the ways in which the racialized category "bellah" did so much social work in the Niger Bend by keeping servile dependants in place for so long. Local French administrators hoped that bellah-iklan families could be constituted within the framework of continuing relations with Tuareg masters, and that bellah-iklan groups would slowly accumulate property, which would give them greater autonomy. The administration began to give identity cards to bellah-iklan families rather than list them as dependants of their masters, and this meant that individual bellah-iklan could be taxed separately. But by far the thorniest problem was the provision for bellah-iklan property rights. The colonial administration

[27] Letter from the Commandant, Cercle de Tombouctou to the Gouverneur, Soudan Français, "Sur la situation politiques actuelle des Tribus du Gourma Ouest," No.31/C, May 6, 1949 (ART 1E 10).

arrived at a formula for providing bellah-iklan herders with a small number of animals from their masters' herds (three head of cattle and thirty goats), and for an annual remuneration for bellah-iklan who continued to work for their masters as herders (a heifer for every twenty head of cattle, ten sheep for every hundred herded).[28] In practice, however, bellah-iklan-master relations could not be managed directly by the colonial state; instead, various negotiations occurred between masters and slaves about the terms of continued service.

Philippe Loiseau, the deputy commander of Timbuktu, writing in 1956, noticed that there were two conditions that had to be met by masters in order to keep their bellah-iklan working for them. Masters could not beat or abuse their slaves, and masters had to be rich. If one of these conditions was not met, the bellah-iklan would leave: "I was able to notice that rich but brutal masters have seen their bellah lost in the bush and disobeying them, sometimes taking with them all the animals confided to them. This is what happens in the family of the chief of the tribe who does not manage to make contact with more than half of his slaves. It is the same with financially ruined families."[29] Loiseau wrote that there was a fundamental problem in attempting to assign property to bellah-iklan because they are slaves: "In effect the strict rule is that the animals belong to the master and the bellah, being a thing, cannot possess anything. If the bellah becomes a person, the animals must all return to the master, who forces them to do this in any case."[30] As I explained in Chapter 6, this was not theoretically true under Islamic law, because slaves are permitted to own property under certain conditions. In the legal tradition of the Sahel, slaves were not juridically "things." Again and again during the 1950s, bellah-iklan groups claimed that significant portions of herds that they were looking after belonged to them, not to their masters. These claims were often challenged by masters, but it is clear that many bellah-iklan made arguments drawn from Sahelian traditions of some limited property rights for slaves. This was part of a larger set of claims that some slaves could make on the moral discourse that was sometimes used to justify slavery as redemptive of original unbelief.[31]

[28] Baz Lecocq, "The Bellah Question: Slave Emancipation, Race, and Social Categories in Late Twentieth-century Northern Mali." *CJAS* 39, no. 1 (2005): 51–2.

[29] Letter from Philippe Loiseau, Commandant, Cercle de Tombouctou, to the Subdivision de Gourma Rharous, July 4, 1956 (AMI sér.BO).

[30] Ibid.

[31] However, these choices were limited. See Sean Hanretta, *Islam and Social Change in French West Africa: History of an Emancipatory Community* (New York: Cambridge University Press, 2009), 217–26.

Whether as slaves or freed slaves, there was no right to bequeath; masters stood to inherit the property of a slave or freed slave. This was true across the region in servile communities among all linguistic groups. Because the colonial state sided with masters in cases of inheritance from slaves, it represented one of the biggest grievances against the colonial regime by servile people.[32] Shaykh Bay had called the idea of slaves bequeathing their property to their own descendant "buffoonery and the agitation of donkeys."[33] Loiseau proposed a compromise as part of the colonial administration's attempt to constitute bellah-iklan families: "As for what concerns the attribution of property in livestock at the death of the bellah, it is for the tribunal to leave one part of the goods of the deceased for his children, the other part returns to the master. The bellah family will therefore be entirely established in this second stage."[34] The possibility of bequeathing property to descendants was the key to the long-term possibilities of autonomy and economic independence for those servile people who remained in the Niger Bend. But it was only in the postcolonial period that the state recognized this right and denied the claims of masters to their slaves' property.

When Muhammad ʿAli became aware of the reforms proposed in the 1950s to address the so-called bellah question, he feared that Kel Entsar land would be turned over to the bellah-iklan who worked it. In a letter that he wrote from Saudi Arabia in 1955 to his brother and chief of the Kel Entsar, Muhammad al-Mahdi, Muhammad ʿAli insisted that under no circumstances was their land to be given to the bellah-iklan:

> I have learned that the bellah have the right to fields and that you are sharing the fields with them. I want you to know that only my children will inherit my field and not any bellah who was bought for money. If you ever give away my fields, I will write to the Minister of the Colonies, care of the French Ambassador in Saudi Arabia. You know very well that I spent a year and a half at Lake Oro doing nothing but raising the value of the agricultural economy of my country. Paris and Dakar promised me assistance ... but nothing came in the end![35]

This critique of French colonialism for its failures of development would become Muhammad ʿAli's refrain as he developed a full-blown politics of racial separatism in the late 1950s.

[32] Jeremy Berndt, "Closer Than Your Jugular Vein: Muslim Intellectuals in a Malian Village, 1900 to the 1960s" (Ph.D. diss., Northwestern University, 2007), 288–91.

[33] Shaykh Bāy al-Kuntī, "Nawāzil Shaykh Bāy" (IHERIAB ms. 119), #352, f. 391–92.

[34] Letter from Philippe Loiseau, Cercle de Tombouctou, to the Subdivision de Gourma Rharous, July 4, 1956 (AMI sér. BO).

[35] Letter from Muhammad ʿAli ag Attaher to Muhammad al-Mahdi ag Attaher, Taif, Saudi Arabia, July 9, 1955 (ACG).

SLAVE TRADE TO ARABIA

The struggle between masters and slaves to redefine their relationship provoked a certain level of conflict and violence in the postwar Niger Bend, which the colonial administration struggled to manage. The issue of slavery was also used as a tool for political mobilization by anticolonial activists of the US-RDA in local election campaigns in the Niger Bend.[36] But the most dramatic role that slavery played in the era of decolonization was in the accusation that the Tuareg were involved in a slave trade of their bellah-iklan to Saudi Arabia. The issue first appeared publicly when an interview was published in the Dakar-based weekly newspaper *Afrique Nouvelle* in 1954 with a young bellah-iklan man from Gourma Rharous named Awad el Djoud. Awad claimed that he had been taken by Muhammad ʿAli to Saudi Arabia for the pilgrimage in 1948, and that he was later sold as a slave in Mecca. According to his testimony, Awad lived for several years as a slave before escaping and managing to return, after much suffering, to Soudan. Awad's story brought the issue of slavery to the forefront of politics in Soudan, and it helped generate international attention on the trafficking of black Africans into slavery in Saudi Arabia.[37]

Awad claimed that he had been taken into the service of Muhammad ʿAli as a boy. On the overland pilgrimage trip across Africa to the Red Sea, he said that he had been well treated and that he and Muhammad ʿAli had eaten "out of the same bowl." However, after accomplishing the pilgrimage in 1950, Awad reported that Muhammad ʿAli sent him to the house of Prince ʿAbd Allāh al-Fayṣal, where he was expected to work in order to pay off the cost of his trip. Muhammad ʿAli went to Egypt, claiming that he would return to Saudi Arabia to pick up Awad for the return trip to Soudan. But according to Awad, he was never paid for his work and was later told that he had been sold as a slave to the prince. Four of his companions on the trip were also sold as slaves. After three years, in 1953, Awad testified that his Saudi master "turned me over to his assistant in order to sell me on the slave market of Jeddah. They drove me there in a truck and made me enter a large, dark room in which there where many men and women. I stayed there for many hours but then I

[36] For electoral details and local instances of violence, see Bruce S. Hall, "Bellah Histories of Decolonization, Iklan Paths to Freedom: The Meanings of Race and Slavery in the Late-colonial Niger Bend (Mali), 1944–1960," *IJAHS* (forthcoming).

[37] Baz Lecocq, *Disputed Desert: Decolonisation, Competing Nationalisms and Tuareg Rebellions in Northern Mali* (Leiden: Brill, 2010), 116–27.

FIGURE 7. Awad el Djoud, Bamako, 1955 (source: *Paris Match*, June 25, 1955).

decided to escape." After asking to be allowed outside to smoke a cigarette, Awad fled. Eventually, he stowed away on a boat leaving Jeddah for Port Sudan, from where he managed to return to Soudan Français. The Nouvelle Afrique reporter asked him whether he had been maltreated by his master. He responded, "if you are docile and do not try to escape, you are not maltreated. But I saw my master use a club to beat a slave to death who was suspected of theft and wanting to escape."[38] In another article published in the French magazine *Paris Match* nine months later, Awad explained that before his transfer to the slave market and his escape, he had been well-treated by his Saudi owner and had been married to one of the prince's female slaves named Farah.[39]

Two weeks after its first article, *Afrique Nouvelle* published a follow-up on August 18, 1954 about the overland slave trade to Saudi Arabia from the Spanish Sahara and Mauritania. The article revealed that the Tibesti region in northern Chad was an important gathering point and market

[38] "La route des esclaves noires commence à Villa Cisneros et aboutit à la Mecque," *Afrique Nouvelle* (August 4, 1954).

[39] Georges de Caunes, "Il y a encore des marchands d'esclaves," *Paris Match* (June 25, 1955).

where slaves taken from West Africa, Cameroon, and Uganda were sold. Apparently, a rifle could be exchanged there for three female slaves, and a box of ammunition for two mature males. From Tibesti, smugglers then took the slaves across the Red Sea in small boats to evade the authorities, and once in the large towns of the Hijaz, sold them to local buyers.[40] The *Paris Match* article in 1955 connected the slave trade to Saudi Arabia with the continuing servility of many people in French-ruled West Africa. It reported that there were "hundreds of thousands of black men who are not entirely slaves but they are called servants." The article singled out the bellah-iklan as the worst case: "Closest to the slave is the bellah, the do-it-all man of the Tuareg. In an agreement made between two tribes one frequently finds enumerations of this kind: The tribe of X ..., cedes to the tribe of Y ..., ten male camels, ten female camels, and six bellah. A camel is exchanged today for ten to twelve bellah." If not entirely responsible for this state of affairs, the colonial administration was, according to *Paris Match*, aware of the issue: "The French administrators have chosen to favor a policy of important chiefs in Black Africa, and as such they discreetly close their eyes to these facts."[41]

In November 1954, the issue of the African slave trade to Saudi Arabia was raised in the parliament of the French Union. Inquiries were launched in the Niger Bend, and Awad el Djoud brought a complaint against Muhammad ʿAli to the labor tribunal in Bamako, seeking unpaid wages of more than one million francs for the entire period of his service between 1940 and 1952.[42] The colonial administration in the Niger Bend worried that if Awad won his case, "every bellah would be in his rights to formulate the same kind of claims against the chief of the tent that he lives in."[43]

As early as 1953, the colonial administration suspected that Muhammad ʿAli and other Tuareg pilgrims had been involved in trafficking slaves for sale in Saudi Arabia. Inquiries were made in the Niger Bend and with French consuls in Jeddah and Khartoum about the whereabouts

40 "Le Tibesti, gare de triage," *Afrique Nouvelle* (August 18, 1954).

41 De Caunes, "Il y a encore des marchands d'esclaves," 96.

42 The case was heard by the Tribuanl du Travail in Bamako on November 30, 1955. He claimed unpaid wages of 83,304F55 for work between April 1, 1940 and April 30, 1952, with an additional 1,000,000F00 for damages and interest. His total claim was for 1,083,304F55. Letter from François Perhirin, Commandant, Cercle de Goundam to the Gouverneur, Soudan Français, 105/C, November 10, 1955 (ACG). Awad had first made his complaint against Muhammad ʿAli once he reached Niamey, but the case was forwarded to Bamako. Letter from Gouverneur, Soudan Français to the Commandants, Cercles de Gao, Goundam, Tombouctou, 216/C, April 29, 1954 (ACG).

43 Letter from Perhirin to Gouverneur, Soudan Français, November 10, 1955 (ACG).

of the five bellah-iklan who had left with Muhammad ʿAli in 1948. The commander of Goundam reported that according to his information, Muhammad ʿAli had indeed sold these bellah-iklan as slaves, although he also pointed out that Awad had been able to send money and clothes to his mother in Rharous.[44] According to a series of interviews with returned pilgrims in Goundam, there were many black Africans living in difficult circumstances in Arabia, but everyone denied or claimed not to know anything about a slave trade there.[45]

Muhammad ʿAli did not return to Soudan to face these charges, but he did defend himself in letters, claiming that Awad was a liar and an opportunist. In a letter written to one of his brothers named Muḥammad al-Mukhtār in January 1955, and intercepted by the French, he said, "a friend in Bamako wrote to me last August after having read in a newspaper that a certain Awaṭṭan [Awad] claimed that I have been selling slaves in Mecca. I was astonished." Muhammad ʿAli argued that it was not possible because of the colonial government's close involvement with the Muslim pilgrimage: "Let me inform you Muhammad al-Mukhtar that every year the government sponsors its friends among the Muslim scholars and chiefs to make the pilgrimage. Here is the story of the slave (ʿabd) Awattan [Awad]: All the pilgrims saw him. He was paid by the Saudis and his master al-Ḥājj ag Hakūnkūn saw him himself when he was in Rharous." He claimed that it was André Michel, the French commander of Goundam, who had encouraged Awad to lodge his complaint. The real reason that Awad had left Saudi Arabia was a sexual relationship he had carried on with a concubine of the sultan. Awad's wife became jealous and threatened to inform her master about it: "How could I have forced Awattan [Awad] to leave Goundam or Bamako without him lodging a complaint against me? How could anyone believe that I sold him such a long time ago and he never lodged a complaint with the French consulate? How could anyone believe that I sold him when on our way to Mecca, he sometimes stayed a month behind me?"[46] It is important to

[44] He also pointed out that he had received completely contradictory information. Four of the five bellah-iklan were reported to have left Muhammad ʿAli's service in Khartoum in 1952. The other four bellah-iklan were two married couples: 1. Ousman ag Hameye, 33 years old, Sittelher oualet Aljoumarat, 30 years old; 2. Banhassan ag Alhad, 25 years old, Mamma oualet Oumarou, 25 years old. Letter from the Commandant, Cercle de Goundam to the Gouverneur, Soudan Français, 13/C, February 26, 1953 (ACG).

[45] Letter from François Perhirin, Commandant, Cercle de Goundam to the Gouverneur, Soudan Français, 109/C, November 27, 1955 (ACG).

[46] Letter from Muhammad ʿAli ag Attaher to Muhammad al-Mukhtār, January 31, 1955 (ACG).

note that Muhammad ʿAli referred to Awad as a slave (ʿabd). He made no effort to deny his slave status, only that he could not have sold him in the circumstances presented.

In another intercepted letter written in October 1955 to his brother Muhammad al-Mahdi, Muhammad ʿAli again blamed André Michel for the affair with Awad. He said that Awad was working in Mecca and earning money. His master, al-Hajj ag Hakunkun, who was a Tuareg Igawaddaran from Gourma Rharous, came to Mecca on the pilgrimage and stayed with Awad, who gave him money to help with his trip. At that time, al-Hajj ag Hakunkun explained that Awad had left his mother when he was eight years old to go to work for the head of the police force (goum) in Rharous. Only after that man left the country did Awad fall on hard times. Muhammad ʿAli wrote that he first saw Awad when he came to him as a beggar. He did not have proper clothes or shoes, and his hair was unkempt. Muhammad ʿAli's son Mustafa al-Kayri took pity so they looked after him and fed him. Because he could make the children laugh, they called him General Awad instead of his real name, which was Awaṭṭan. When Muhammad ʿAli was preparing to go to Mecca in 1948, Awad asked to come with him as far as Gourma Rharous so that he could see his mother. When the boat reached Gourma Rharous, Muhammad ʿAli reported that he gave Awad clothes to give to his parents. Instead of staying in Gourma Rharous, however, Awad hid on the boat and was not discovered until Gao, where he was made to get off. But he took advantage of a colleague of Muhammad ʿAli's and managed to get himself to Niamey where he begged Muhammad ʿAli again to take him on the trip to Mecca. He promised that once in Mecca, he would find work and pay back the price of the trip. Afterward, he went and worked for the Saudi minister of the interior.

Muhammad ʿAli told his brother that he had read the article in *Paris Match*:

> I do not want to respond because if I ever reply, I will be forced to write in the magazine and many nations will have a bad impression of France. I have some legal agreements made by my grandfather and Commander Joffre allowing us to own the bellah who were with us, and freeing those who were not. They were freed but then they came back to us on their own account. I do not understand how I have been accused [of this action] because of my bellah who are outside of French territory. There are more than 100 bellah who have come by themselves and there are more bellah who work for us. They have come by different routes... These bellah have visited different countries and they know that they are French, but nevertheless they call themselves slaves and work for the owners. I do not

understand why I stand accused because it is sufficient to say to a bellah that you are free, after which he can go where he wants.[47]

Awad el Djoud's case against Muhammad ʿAli was eventually sent to the labor tribunal in Gao, which ruled in May 1956 that Awad had not proven that he was enslaved in the Niger Bend or in Saudi Arabia.[48]

Whether Awad's version of the story was true or not, it made the issue of slavery in the Niger Bend even more prominent than it had been. In March 1956, the US-RDA newsletter, *L'Essor*, published a note suggesting that slave trading was occurring in Goundam: "Is the only existing slave market in Africa found in Goundam? The sinful slave trade continues to operate there. The most recent case is that of a young bellah and his sister who belonged to the same master who had just sold her against her will."[49] The commander of Goundam carried out an inquiry into this case and reported that this was simply a case of bellah-iklan changing the family to which they were attached. He could find no proof of a sale of slaves.[50] However, his report hardly dispelled the notion that the bellah-iklan had little control over their lives.

By 1956, with the passing of the *loi cadre* that gave a certain level of autonomy to Soudan within the French Union, and with the definitive victory in legislative election in 1956 of the US-RDA, the administration continued to follow news of the slavery and the slave trade to Saudi Arabia. Emigration of bellah-iklan from the Soudan was forbidden if there was any indication of coercion, and Tuareg and Arab requests to make the pilgrimage were treated with greater suspicion. For example, the Tuareg Kel Essuk were accused of involvement in the slave trade. Like the Kel Entsar, the Kel Essuk are a clerical-status lineage, and a number of their members had migrated to Arabia at the beginning of the colonial period. These emigrants had assimilated into Arabian society, but they maintained links with their fellows back in Soudan. The commander of Gao reported that there were many clandestine departures of Kel Essuk pilgrims. He wrote that the relations with people in Saudi Arabia "[seem] to have incited some [Kel Essuk] to give themselves over to the fruitful commerce in unfree persons."[51] In February 1958, a Kel

47 Letter from Muhammad ʿAli ag Attaher to Muhammad al-Mahdi ag Attaher, Mecca, October 19, 1955 (ACG).

48 "Extrait des minutes du Tribunal du Travail de Gao, Aouat Aliou contre Mohamed ag Attaher," May 23, 1956 (ACG).

49 "Vente d'esclaves à Goundam," *L'Essor* no.1977 (March 29, 1956).

50 Letter the from Commandant, Cercle de Goundam to the Gouverneur, Soudan Français, No.49/C, May 9, 1956 (ACG).

51 Letter from J. Bertin, Commandant, Cercle de Gao, to the Ministeur de l'Intérieur, No.119/C, March 26, 1959 (AMI sér. BO).

Essuk man named Ismail ag Mohamed Lamine was arrested by the police in Maradi while he was attempting to illegally cross the Nigerian border in a truck, bringing twenty-eight slaves with him to Mecca. Among them were six women and eighteen children, of which a number were less than six years old.[52]

The principal African official who reported on the question of the slave trade in Saudi Arabia was an Arabic- and French-speaker named Abdoul Wahab Doucouré, who had studied at Zaituna University in Tunisia and later worked for the Ministry of the Interior.[53] In 1958, he reported that he had learned about the sale of a man named Zoubéirou Bakrou who was originally from Upper Volta but had lived in Mecca for twelve years. He had been sold three years before by another man from Upper Volta. Zoubéirou Bakrou protested to the Saudi authorities that neither he nor any member of his family was a slave. The Saudi officials demanded that the seller provide proof that Zoubéirou was his slave. When the seller returned to Dori, he sent the testimony of twelve people attesting to the fact. Even as far away as Saudi Arabia in the 1950s, the echo of Sahelian arguments about race and status reverberated. When Abdoul Wahab Doucouré met with Zoubéirou, he was given the names of others who had been sold as slaves, as recently as a month before the discussion took place. None of those who had been sold were in Mecca any longer. According to Zoubéirou, "in Mecca, there are other sellers who are usually Moors or Tuareg who claim the right of property over all the blacks from French West Africa who are abandoned here in Arabia for a long time."[54]

In 1958, Muhammad ʿAli was again accused of trading in slaves in Saudi Arabia. This time, the Saudi government demanded to see proof of the slave status of those he held, and because Muhammad ʿAli was unable to provide it, the prisoners were released.[55] One of those imprisoned in this way wrote a letter to Modibo Keita, the head of the US-RDA government in Soudan:

> We address our complaint to you after having first addressed it to God. We are originally from the district of Goundam. We came to carry out our religious duty

[52] Ibid.

[53] Louis Brenner, *Controlling Knowledge: Religion, Power and Schooling in a West African Muslim Society* (Bloomington, IN: Indiana University Press, 2001), 104; Benjamin Soares, *Islam and the Prayer Economy: History and Authority in a Malian Town* (Ann Arbor: University of Michigan Press, 2005), 226.

[54] Letter from Abdoul Wahab Doucouré, fonctionnaire du Ministère de l'Intérieur, to the Ministre de l'Intérieur, July 19, 1958 (AMI sér. BO).

[55] Abdoul Wahab Doucouré, "Rapport sur le trafic d'esclaves," July 1, 1960 (AMI sér. BO).

> in 1957. We met Muhammad ʿAli who promised us assistance; he would provide us with a place to stay for free, he said. He brought us to a house belonging to Abdel Aziz Haidani where we were kept, and he demanded our passports. We refused and we then rented a house in the Daraʿa neighborhood. A few days later, Abdel Aziz Haidane, Muhammad ben Saleh, the representative of Muhammad Ali, and the men of the police came to arrest us. We were taken to prison in Mecca where they submitted us to all sorts of atrocities. The goal of this torture was to make us admit that we are slaves. Over seven months, they dispersed us. Some were sent to the prison of Jeddah. They prevented us from doing the prayer. We did not eat or drink and we were forbidden from saying "lā ilāh illā-llāh." ("there is no god but God," part of the Muslim credo.)[56]

The letter writer said that he knew the names of twenty-three victims of Muhammad ʿAli's slave trading. During his trip to the Hijaz in 1960, Abdoul Wahab Doucouré reported that there were hundreds of people from Soudan, almost all of them from the Niger Bend, who were held as slaves in Arabia.[57] It is clear that there was a slave trade to Saudi Arabia in the 1950s,[58] and that it was legitimized according to old Sahelian claims to immutable slave status for blacks.

IRREDENTIST DREAMS, MUHAMMAD MAHMUD OULD AL-SHAYKH, AND THE OCRS

In 1944, the western Mauritanian region of the Hodh (the district of Néma) was removed from the administrative control of Soudan and transferred to Mauritania.[59] The colonial government in Dakar argued that the largely Arab population of this region would be easier to administer in Mauritania than in Soudan, which was predominantly black.[60] As it became clear by the early 1950s that political reforms would lead to greater autonomy and self-rule in Soudan, the future place of the Niger Bend, with its Arab and Tuareg populations, was called into question. Should the Niger Bend remain in the black-majority Soudan, or should it be joined to another territory?

56 The letter is attached to Doucouré, "Rapport sur le trafic d'esclaves."

57 Abdoul Wahab Doucouré, "Compte rendu de la Mission effectuée en Arabie Saoudite au cours du pèlerinage 1960" (AMI sér. BO).

58 Lecocq, *Disputed Desert*, 117. The final abolition of slavery in Saudi Arabia accurred in 1962. See Suzanne Miers, *Slavery in the Twentieth Century: The Evolution of a Global Problem* (Walnut Creek, CA: Altamira, 2003), 347–50.

59 Joly, *Soudan Français*, 547.

60 Cédric Jourde, "Dramas of Ethnic Elites Accommodation: The Authoritarian Restoration in Mauritania" (Ph.D. diss., University of Wisconsin, 2002), 128–9.

Beginning in 1951, a campaign was launched in France by the journal *Hommes et Mondes* to create a French-ruled Saharan territory that would not participate in the devolution of political authority underway in the colonies of North and sub-Saharan Africa. In 1952, a proposal was made in the French national parliament and in the parliament of the French Union to hive off the Saharan regions of French West Africa, French Central Africa, and Algeria to create a new territory called "Afrique Saharienne Française." The campaign only attracted wider French political interest when oil was discovered in Hassi-Massaoud in the Algerian Sahara in 1956. By December 1956, a law was passed in France to create new framework that would bring together Mauritania, southern Algeria, and the Saharan regions of Soudan, Niger, and Chad into something called the "Organisation commune des régions sahariennes" (OCRS). However, these territories were not to be detached from their original administrative homes, as some proponents of the project had envisioned. Instead, the OCRS was meant to promote social and economic development in the Sahara. Largely rejected by the countries that administered these territories, the OCRS survived only until 1962, when Algeria won its full independence.[61]

Saharan irredentism was primarily motivated by French economic interests in the potential petroleum and mineral wealth of the region. However, political and social arguments were also put forward about safeguarding the interests of the people of the Sahara and ensuring that they would not be incorporated into the black African-dominated territories where the Tuareg and Arab pastoralists would constitute small minorities.[62] Quite understandably, African political leaders from the French colonies that stood to lose their Saharan territories were quite unhappy about the potential dismemberment of their soon-to-be independent countries.[63] Advocates of a Greater Morocco that would include Mauritania and part of the Niger Bend also opposed it. There was, however, an African constituency that supported the creation of the French Saharan territory and the continuation of French colonial rule. One of

[61] Pierre Boilley, "L'Organisation commune des régions sahariennes (OCRS): une tentative avortée," in *Nomades et commandants: Administration et sociétés nomades dans l'ancienne A.O.F.*, ed. Edmund Bernus, Pierre Boilley, Jean Clozel, and Jean-Louis Triaud (Paris: Karthala, 1993), 215–39.

[62] Pierre Boilley, "Un complot français au Sahara? Politiques françaises et représentations maliennes," in *Mali-France. Regards sur une histoire partagée*, ed. GEMDEV, Université du Mali (Paris, Kathala, 2005), 167.

[63] For some of the comments made by African deputies in the French parliament, see Boilley, "L'Organisation commune," 224. For comments made in African Territorial Assemblies, see André Salifou, *La question touarègue au Niger* (Paris: Karthala, 1993), 38.

the most important representatives of this group was an Arab intellectual and politician from Timbuktu named Muḥammad Maḥmūd ould al-Shaykh.[64] (d. 1973).

Ould al-Shaykh was a highly controversial person in both his politics and in his relations with other scholars in Timbuktu. Originally from Arawan, he was one of the most prominent Islamic intellectuals in Timbuktu, who "took knowledge from many scholars and from whom many scholars also took knowledge."[65] He was appointed qadi for the people of Arawan residing in Timbuktu in the early 1930s and he participated in a number of debates with other scholars in the city. He was famous for his wit and his learning, but also for his quick temper and sometimes cantankerous nature. According to a colonial report in 1935, Ould al-Shaykh was a person "whose pretention in the religious domain knows no limits, and who wants to reign as master of the scholars of the town of Timbuktu."[66] As a result, the colonial administration faced calls for his removal from the office of qadi for the people of Arawan as early as 1935. He famously refused to pray behind one of his former teachers who, unlike Ould al-Shaykh, was understood to be black. This teacher was a renowned scholar named al-Shaykh Abī ʾl-Khayr b. ʿAbd Allāh b. Murzūq who also traced his ancestry to Arawan.[67] I have proposed elsewhere that the reason Ould al-Shaykh refused to pray behind al-Shaykh Abi ʾl-Khayr was because of his blackness.[68] We have seen that Shaykh Bay argued that manumitted slaves should pray behind others, not in front of them.[69] To Ould al-Shaykh, a black man from Arawan had a slave past. This is certainly how many people in Timbuktu today interpret the event. It is perhaps for this reason that al-Shaykh Abi ʾl-Khayr made a claim that he was in fact descended from Fulbe ancestors, and therefore not black at all.[70] However, I do not have any hard evidence about Ould al-Shaykh's motives. Shahid Mathee has proposed that the roots of this incident lay in a personal disagreement between the two over a matter of

64 He died in 1973.

65 Maḥmūd b. Muḥammad Dadab (known as Ḥammū al-Arawānī al-Tinbuktī), "Kashf al-ḥāʾil fī ʾl-taʿrīf bi-kutub al-fatāwā wa-ʾl-nawāzil" (unpublished manuscript given to me by the author), 273.

66 Chasal, Commandant, Cercle de Tombouctou, "Rapport politique 1è trimestre 1935," April 10, 1935 (ANM FR 1E-42).

67 He died in 1976. Maḥmūd b. Muḥammad Dadab, "Kashf al-ḥāʾil," 273.

68 Bruce Hall, "Mapping the River in Black and White: Trajectories of Race in the Niger Bend, Northern Mali" (Ph.D. diss., University of Illinois at Urbana-Champaign, 2005), 260.

69 Shaykh Bāy al-Kuntī, "Nawāzil Shaykh Bāy" (IHERIAB ms. 124), #879, f. 55–56.

70 "Maktūb fī dhikr taʾrīkh ahl al-ḥill wa-waqāʾiʿ-hum maʿa ʾl-sūdān" (IHERIAB ms. 6248). I thank Shahid Mathee for this reference.

marriage.[71] But it is a remarkable statement about how unpopular Ould al-Shaykh was with his contemporaries that he was intentionally left out of Ahmad Babir's biographical dictionary of Timbuktu scholars entitled "The eternal good fortune" ("al-Saʿāda al-abadiyya").[72]

Ould al-Shaykh led the campaign for the OCRS in the Niger Bend. He spent much of 1957 and 1958 traveling around the region gathering signatures for a petition he had written on behalf of the people of the Niger Bend. More than three hundred, mostly Arab and Tuareg notables, but also some Songhay, signed the letter. The colonial police in Gao claimed that Ould al-Shaykh and his allies used racial arguments selectively in their efforts to collect signatures: "Among the nomads, the propagandists [for the OCRS] use arguments with a racial character that invoke fear of blacks." Ould al-Shaykh "argues that the [postcolonial] government will consist uniquely of blacks. He conveys to his partisans a propaganda in favor of the OCRS in which the blacks will not be the majority. He does not hide his intention in the case of a failure of the OCRS to demand that the populations of the white race of the Niger Bend be attached to Mauritania or Niger." One of the other issues deployed in the campaign was "the current fact that masters are subject to claims made on their property by bellah. Among the sedentary people, he goes to the chiefs, and to those with axes to grind."[73]

According to the local colonial administration, the Tuareg and Arabs of the Niger Bend felt politically trapped in the late 1950s. The issue "which preoccupies the chiefs is their future situation with regards the black sedentary government of Soudan. They do not have any sympathy for it and they are sure that the inverse is true. They feel blocked; they see the proof in the fact that the French authorities have not intervened, and that no nomads have been designated for the information mission to the Sahara." French observers thought that the Tuareg and Arabs were increasingly behind the OCRS solution: "A politico-administrative Saharan organization would safeguard their interests and their traditional way of life. But they also know that the government in Bamako, like the [US-RDA] Party and the unions, would not agree to a solution that appears more or less like a concession of territory, and would mean losing the [Saharan] territory and the benefits hoped for from the development of the desert." On

[71] Personal communication. Shahid Mathee.

[72] Mawlay Aḥmad al-Bābīr, "al-Saʿāda al-abadiyya fī ʾl-taʿrīf bi-ʿulamāʾ Tinbuktu al-bahiyya" (IHERIAB ms. 15).

[73] Brigade mobile de police de Gao, "Renseignments," No.113/C, July 30, 1958 (ACG).

a visit to Timbuktu in 1957, Modibo Keita made it clear that the Soudan would not cede its Saharan regions. During this visit, Ould al-Shaykh "organized a little demonstration for the arrival, bringing together several partisans under a banner saying "Vive le Sahara Français." Then, receiving an audience from Modibo Keita along with his Barabish ally Mahmud ould Dahman, he explained the desire of the Saharans to be granted a special status. The next day, he tried without success to present a petition demanding the incorporation of Timbuktu into the Saharan territory."[74]

In the open letter and petition that he sent to the French government in Paris in 1958, Ould al-Shaykh claimed that the people of the Niger Bend strongly desired to be incorporated into the proposed French Saharan territory:

> We assure you of our formal opposition to being incorporated into an autonomous or federalist system of Black Africa or North Africa. Our interests and aspirations could in no case be properly defended as long as we are attached to a territory represented and governed by a black majority, which is an ethnic group whose interests and aspirations are not the same as ours.[75]

For Ould al-Shaykh, and for many other Arab and Tuareg leaders in the Niger Bend, the paramount threat in the 1950s was the imminent end of French colonial rule and subsequent incorporation into an independent republic run by blacks.[76] His reference to North Africa reflects his alliance with French proponents of the OCRS and his active opposition to Muhammad ʿAli and the proponents of a Greater Morocco, who were quite numerous in the Arabophone communities of the Niger Bend.[77] Muhammad ʿAli later accused Ould al-Shaykh of being a French spy sent to North Africa to keep tabs on his political associations.[78]

It is clear that Ould al-Shaykh's activities were sponsored directly by French colonial officers on the ground in the Niger Bend, who hoped to

74 Délégation de la Boucle du Niger, Territoire du Soudan Français, "Bulletin Mensuel de Renseignements," September 1957 (ACG).

75 Quoted in Boilley, "L'Organisation commune," 225. The full text of this letter is published in Hélène Claudot-Hawad, *Le politique dans l'histoire touarègue. Cahiers de l'IREMAN* (Aix-en-Provence: CNRS, 1993), 133–53.

76 André Bourgeot, "Sahara: espace géostratégique et enjeux politiques (Niger)" in *Afrique noire et monde arabe: continuités et ruptures*, ed. Emmanuel Grégoire and Jean Schmitz (La Tour-d'Aigues: Aube, 2000), 40; Bourgeot, *Les Sociétés touarègues. nomadisme, identité, resistances* (Paris: Karthala, 1995), 356. For a slightly different take on this see Claudot-Hawad, *Le politique dans l'histoire touarègue*, 81–2.

77 Lecocq, "That Desert," 62–4.

78 Mohamed Ali ag Attaher, "Scolarisation moderne," 96–7.

forestall independence. Local political reports of the colonial administration in the 1950s often referred to the travels of Ould al-Shaykh in the area, his use of government airplanes, and his meetings with local dignitaries and French officials. Much of this support came from the French military, as did the French support for the OCRS. Colonial civilian administrators were often much less enthusiastic. After attending a conference in Paris in 1958, the French high commissioner in Dakar intervened to prevent Ould al-Shaykh from being flown directly back to Timbuktu in a French military plane: "The inconvenience of the activity of this character and the facilities which have been accorded to him by certain authorities, have not escaped me. Also, having learned that, during his last trip to Paris, Muhammad Mahmud plotted to obtain transport directly to Timbuktu by military plane, I intervened with the departmental authorities and managed to succeed in aborting this project."[79] Ould al-Shaykh's status and influence were often subjects of discussion by civilian colonial administrators in the Niger Bend who felt that he had been accorded too much support by their military counterparts.[80]

It would be a mistake, though, to see Ould al-Shaykh as just a French puppet. His project reflected the deep misgivings of Arab and Tuareg elites about the changes threatened by decolonization. Ould al-Shaykh played an important role in articulating the problems faced by these elites, and in constructing an overtly racial means of understanding them. Contrary to what has been said about him by his detractors,[81] he was a first-rate intellectual in his milieu of Timbuktu, trained in the Islamic sciences, and active for much of his life in the traditional field of Islamic law, both as

[79] Letter from the Haut-Commissariat de la République, A.O.F., Dakar, to Madeira Keita, Ministère de l'Intérieur, Soudan, October 3, 1958 (ACG).

[80] The support for Ould al-Shaykh is discussed in Pierre Boilley, *Les Touaregs Kel Adagh. Dépendances et révoltes: du Soudan français au Mali contemporain* (Paris: Karthala, 1999), 295–7.

[81] He was referred to as the "Qadi of Timbuktu" in many French administrative documents. Clearly, his supporters in the colonial administration had an interest in exaggerating his importance and authority. It was sometimes pointed out, rightly, in colonial correspondence by those administrators who were less sympathetic, that he was not the qadi of Timbuktu, but the qadi of the "Ahl Arawān" in Timbuktu – mostly Arab merchants resident in Timbuktu, who, like Ould al-Shaykh, traced their origin back to the Azawad town of Arawan. The colonial administration gave official recognition to a qadi for each of the communities resident in Timbuktu. That Ould al-Shaykh was not the single qadi of Timbuktu – an office that did not exist at the time – does not mean that he was a charlatan, as one of André Bourgeot's footnotes seems to indicate: "The 'cadi' of Timbuktu never had a religious function, as his name seems to indicate. A handy man for the military commanders of the Cercle de Timbuktu, he was equally an informant" ("Sahara," 39).

an adjudicator and as an exegete. He taught himself French, which he learned to speak quite well. He was also highly regarded in Timbuktu as an Arabic poet. In 1938, he composed and translated into French a poem in praise of France:

> The price of the hearts of free men is the good deed. Authority on the basis of the good deed is a known thing.
> The recognition of a good deed is equally a good deed; Recognizing good deeds is a habit of the virtuous.
> Here among the French there is a government which performs good deeds publically and secretly, in justice and in policy, by mercy and kindness, with benevolence and respect.
> Her compassion and her benevolence have satisfied all Muslims in every country.
> Before her coming, our countries were in a state of anarchy and misery.
> Peace was something unknown and unimaginable there.
> Fighting and pillage, war and the abduction of women and children into captivity.
> The stealing of goods, the rape of our women, and sale of free men.
> Our lands were unproductive and famine reigned.
> Education was devalued and scholars were despised.
> [...]
> God brought the French for the good of the fearful peoples; they arrived to get rid of injustice and polygamy.[82]

In 1956, an influential French intelligence officer named Marcel Cardaire undertook a study of the political, economic, and familial connections between the inhabitants of the different parts of the Sahara.[83] He took Ould al-Shaykh along as his travel companion and interpreter. The long report that Cardaire produced emphasized the interconnectedness of the Saharan population from one side of the desert to the other, based in large part on family connections, genealogies, and migration histories. Cardaire (and Ould al-Shaykh) concluded that the Saharans were united by so many deep connections that they should properly be understood as a singular people requiring one administration. In the preface to the report, he wrote, "it is true, in effect, that these files will sometimes be difficult to read, with some of the genealogies, the lists of families, the detailed histories in some cases, and the endless loading down [of details]. But the family ties that appear here are more than elsewhere in the name

[82] Poem by Muḥammad Maḥmūd ould al-Shaykh sent to Colonel Bertrand, Commandant, Cercle de Tombouctou (ART 4E 37). I thank Shahid Mathee for this document.

[83] Cardaire had previously worked with Amadou Hampâté Bâ. See Gregory Mann, "Fetishizing Religion: Allah Koura and French 'Islamic Policy' in Late Colonial French Soudan (Mali)," *JAH* 44, no. 2 (2003), 270; Brenner, *Controlling Knowledge*, 60.

of a common ancestor. In addition, the awareness that these people have of belonging to the same group, when it is the case, is extraordinary."[84]

If a genealogical-historical study of the population of the Sahara could demonstrate that the core population of the proposed Saharan territory belonged under the same administration, the problem of borders remained. The colonial administration began making contingency plans about where borders might be located. In the case of the Niger Bend, where a very large percentage of the population relied on access to the Niger floodplain, finding a border was very difficult. The idea proposed by French administrators was to separate the black Songhay population from the Tuareg and Arabs that were to be included in this new territory; the servile bellah-iklan and haratin were to remain with "their masters" in the OCRS. Any border that excluded the Songhay from the OCRS would also exclude many pastoralists because they both shared the same larger space. Thus, proposals to make a border five kilometers north of the Niger River, for example, would simply have dispossessed most pastoralists of important dry-season grazing lands and left many others entirely outside of the proposed colonial territory. Many of the French administrators on the ground realized how impossible such a project was in the Niger Bend, and communicated their objections.[85]

For Ould al-Shaykh, the solution to the problem of borders lay in a "Greater OCRS," which would include the entire Niger Bend. One of the ways he sought to justify this was by arguing that the Niger Bend belonged to the Saharan white population by virtue of its past. He wrote a comprehensive history of the Niger Bend and the Azawad, entitled "The book of the interpreter" ("Kitāb al-Turjumān"), to demonstrate the truth of this assertion.[86] The work is long for a local history at 136 manuscript pages, and scholarly in its extensive and critical use of historical references. It is a text in the traditional style, and at first glance not especially remarkable except perhaps for the fact that there is a long and favorable discussion of the benefits brought to the region by the French colonial occupation, not unlike the sentiments he displayed in the poem quoted earlier in the chapter. However, the text does introduce a new synthesis of older material, and a new arrangement, to some extent, of well-known information from

84 "Etude de sahara de Marcel Cardaire, 1956" (ACG). See Lecocq, "That Desert," 55–8.

85 For example, a letter from the Commandant of the Cercle de Goundam to the Governor in Bamako described several different possibilities for borders in his district, none of which accomplished the goal of dividing nomads from the Songhay population without excluding the nomads from the OCRS (Letter, April 6, 1957, No.38C [ACG]).

86 Muḥammad Maḥmūd b. al-Shaykh al-Arawānī, "Kitāb al-turjumān fī taʾrīkh al-ṣaḥrāʾ wa-ʾl-sūdān wa-bilād tinbuktu wa-shinjīt wa-arawān" (IHERIAB ms. 762).

older works of local history.[87] The way that Ould al-Shaykh rearranged the older material allowed him to produce a history that supported his larger political objectives, namely that the Niger Bend belonged to the whites. A full elaboration of the different ways in which he constructed his new historical synthesis in this text is not possible here. However, an example helps illustrate the larger point. Ould al-Shaykh gave the standard account of the founding of Timbuktu, following the tradition laid down in numerous texts and current in the oral traditions, in which the Imaghsharen Tuareg established a campsite at a place named for a slave woman called Buktu. The etymology of Timbuktu is thus "tin-buktu," or "place of Buktu" in Tamashek. In describing the way in which Timbuktu came to be populated, and the origins of the different people who moved to the town during its early history, Ould al-Shaykh wrote that the inhabitants were Arab and Tuareg. He then discussed how people came from different places in North Africa (Egypt, Morocco, Tuwat, Ghadames, etc.), and how different mosques and neighborhoods came to be built. What is interesting here is what is left out from older texts. There is no mention of early black immigrants to Timbuktu from Wagadoo mentioned in the written histories that Ould Cheikh clearly relied on in other places.[88] Nor is there any discussion of the black inhabitants in the town's history. This omission served Ould al-Shaykh's purposes in that it rendered Timbuktu white. As race entered into the politics of decolonization, we begin to see the geographical space of the Niger Bend itself turned into the object of racialized contestation. Such arguments were new in the 1950s, and they clearly followed the emerging logic of the nation state. Since it was impossible to find a way of dividing the Niger Bend between black and white, it seems almost inevitable with hindsight that the attempts to do so would plant the seeds of larger racial conflict.

THE RACIAL SEPARATISM OF MUHAMMAD ʿALI AG ATTAHER

Muhammad ʿAli and Ould al-Shaykh were enemies. When the slave trading charges were brought against him, Muhammad ʿAli accused Ould

87 Part of this is a formula in the writing of a new work that covers old ground, but because Ould al-Shaykh was such a polarizing figure in the local milieu of Timbuktu, where much of what he discusses in his work is known from older texts, he had to go further in justifying his book.

88 Compare, for example, Ould al-Shaykh's "Kitāb al-Turjumān," f. 3–4 with the passage from the "Ta'rikh al-sudan" concerning the same issue (Abderrahman ben Abdallah ben ʿImran ben ʿAmir Es-Saʿdi, *Tarikh es-Soudan*, ed. and trans. O. Houdas (Paris: Adrien-Maisonneuve, 1964 [1900], 21–6 [Arabic text]).

al-Shaykh of being in league with French officials in the Niger Bend to ruin his name.[89] By 1957, the French commander of Goundam, who had taken a lead role in monitoring his correspondence, noticed that Muhammad ʿAli had changed his tone when writing to people in the Niger Bend. After 1955, he no longer addressed the slave trading accusations or spoke in detail about the failures of the colonial regime in providing development for the Tuareg. Instead, he announced that he would soon be returning home and indicated that he hoped to come with arms and troops ready to fight for Tuareg freedom. He also accused his brother and current chief of the Kel Entsar of being too close to the French. The commander of Goundam reported that "during the pilgrimage [to Mecca] of 1956, he said openly to pilgrims who visited him that a "vote" would take place between Muslims and pagans, and that those who "voted" badly, even his own brother, would be punished. He encouraged the pilgrims to return to their country, telling them that Islam would come to their aid." He was also reported to be circulating a letter on behalf of the Sultan of Morocco advocating the project of a Greater Morocco.[90]

Muhammad ʿAli opposed the OCRS plan and rejected the legitimacy of the petition that Ould al-Shaykh was circulating in 1957 and 1958. But if anything, Muhammad ʿAli's approach was much more radical and explicitly racial than anything Ould al-Shaykh advocated. In a typed and photocopied letter that he sent to many notables in the Niger Bend in 1959 from Tripoli, Libya, he wrote:

> I have heard that the blacks (zunūj) of Mali have demanded independence from France because the time of French rule in our country has been completed. However, the day of freedom and independence will only come when all the nations (shuʿūb) know the principles of freedom and are able to reach self-rule themselves with their own state. I do not understand how you could accept from France that you should be incorporated with the idolatrous blacks of Mali. I inform you that in my capacity as representative (wakīl) of our country before my emigration, I never accepted that the government of Mali be placed above us because that would be something strange for he who was below us in the past, and with whom we share no religion or customs or parentage, that he should be raised [above us] by French colonialism.... I have written to the president of their government, Modibo Keita, informing him that I do not agree to live in this huge tumult (ḍajja) if he does not leave our country to rule over itself.[91]

[89] Letter from Muhammad ʿAli ag Attaher to Muhammad al-Mahdi ag Attaher, Mecca, October 19, 1955 (ACG).

[90] Letter from François Perhirin, Commandant, Cercle de Goundam, to the Gouverneur, Soudan Français, February 6, 1957 (ACG).

[91] Letter from Muhammad ʿAli ag Attaher, Tripoli, Libya, 1959 (AMI sér. BO).

The language used in this letter is not derived from the intellectual context of the Sahel. It is true, as we have seen, that the term "zanj" (blacks) does appear in local texts such as the (Pseudo) "Ta'rīkh al-fattash." But zanj is the form of the collective noun used in the nineteenth-century Sahelian context (sing. "zanjī"); nowhere, to my knowledge, does the more Middle Eastern and modern collective noun "zunūj" appear.[92] The much more common Arabic word for blacks in the Sahel was "sudan." Did Muhammad ʿAli consider the term "zunuj" to be less racial and more neutral? Or was this a term he picked up while in the Arab world? A reader of this letter in the Niger Bend would likely have had the same reaction to the term "shuʿūb" for "nations," which, although it appears in the Qur'an,[93] was certainly more a part of the lexicon of Arab nationalism than the variety of terms used in the Niger Bend for "people" (ahl, qawm, nās, qabīla). It is certainly the case that some readers of Arabic in the colonial Niger Bend were well versed in the literary and journalistic debates animating the larger Arab world. But this could not represent more than a relatively small minority, even in the late 1950s.

The introduction of new terminology is even clearer in a letter Muhammad ʿAli wrote to French president Charles de Gaulle in 1959. In this letter, Muhammad ʿAli argued that the white nomads of the Niger Bend only accepted French domination because of certain promises that were made to them. He said that his racial brothers will never accept the rule of Mali, and that he was prepared to support their cause by all means at his disposal. He asked de Gaulle to help the white nomads to free themselves from the tutelage of Mali and to attach themselves to Mauritania:

> To his eminence, the President de Gaulle, president of the esteemed French Republic. After the greetings appropriate to your eminence, know that the Tuareg race (jins) was entirely self-reliant and self-governing until the coming of the French occupation to this country. As historic battles bear witness, the Tuareg race did not accept this by its choice until they had been conquered. There is no shame in that because in war there is a victor and a vanquished. After the French government was established in the country of the Tuareg, it informed them that it had come to teach and train them in the matters of modern civilization (al-madanīya al-ḥadītha). After that, they would leave them to their own affairs. If they wanted, they could remain as part of France or, if they did not desire this, they could separate from France. It is their right to self determination (taqrīr maṣīr), after which there would be [ties of] cooperation and friendship between them.[94]

[92] John Hunwick, "Some Notes on the Term 'Zanj' and its Derivatives in a West African Chronicle," *RBCAD* 4 [1968]: 41.

[93] Qur'an 49:12.

[94] Letter from Muhammad ʿAli ag Attaher to President Charles de Gaulle, no date. Attached in a letter from the Cercle de Goundam to the Ministère de l'Intérieur, December 22, 1959 (ACG).

The use of the term "jins" to talk about a Tuareg race is new. This is a very clear borrowing from the contemporary intellectual milieu of the Arabic-speaking Middle East. Muhammad ʿAli continues his letter:

> This is the pact (ʿahd) which was agreed for our country by General Joffre in the name of the French Government when it established its rule over our country in Timbuktu and all of the Tuareg country. Permit me, your honor Mr. President, to remind you ... that joining the Tuareg nation (shaʿb) to the government of Mali is unjust and it is not what General Joffre agreed to. It is the opposite of those who ruled over us before the French government, and the Tuareg will never accept the present position of their country which is divided between the government of Mali and the government of Niger. The principle, according to the French government when it decided to leave the Tuareg country, is that it should not disperse them between different peoples with whom the Tuareg people [do not share the same] race (ʿunṣur), religion, or language.[95]

In the last line quoted, he introduced "ʿunṣur," another new word for race, this one more connected to the twentieth-century term "racism."

If the Tuareg can never accept Mali, Muhammad ʿAli tells de Gaulle that he must fulfill the French promise to them and allow them to join Mauritania: "It would be better for France to fulfill the promise made to the Tuareg by which they leave them with the freedom of self-determination by themselves or, at the very least, join them to the Islamic Republic of Mauritania which has ties of race (ʿunṣurīya), religion, and language to the Tuareg country." The stakes were extremely high, and Muhammad ʿAli raised the specter of racial annihilation: "I personally am the chief Muḥammad ʿAlī al-Ṭāhir al-Anṣārī, and I am ready, if the French government helps me, to unify this race (jins) whose destruction is threatened unless we refuse to entwine one race (jins) with another that is not the same." He then made the argument that the example of the British in Nigeria provided a good model. As he relates it, the British had prevented the better-educated Yoruba from ruling over the Hausa in northern Nigeria: "We in our turn would hold the French government in all friendship and honor if it separated us from the blacks (zunūj) of Mali and Niger."[96]

In another letter written in May 1960, by which time there was no question of detaching the Niger Bend from Mali, Muhammad ʿAli sounded a slightly different tone: "As for the tracts opposed to inclusion in Mali, a Mali newly given birth by the colonialists who, after having killed our nation which was alive and well in 1894 and after, we have fought against

[95] Ibid.

[96] Ibid.

France, it will be impossible for us to accept Senghor after Louveau." He continued, "if it is only between us and the blacks (Soudanais). These are our brothers with whom we can get along. Understanding is indispensible between us and our black neighbors." In this more pragmatic vein, he returned to an older idea of race much more familiar to the people of the Niger Bend than in the letters discussed earlier:

> My brother, we are like the Palestinian people upon whom the domination of the Jews was imposed. As for us, we will never accept domination imposed over us. The nomads who pretend to accept this are gutless hypocrites. The future will bring about a humiliating denial from them. As for what concerns Gao and Timbuktu, they constitute half of our people. Their inhabitants can rule and manage [those territories] because they are Armas and Songhays. They have ruled in the past under the authority of the Moroccans and we cannot deny them or push them aside. With the Arma and Songhays, we have the same religion and the same customs and the same blood – Arab blood. As for Muhammad Mahmud [ould al-Shaykh], he is not on our side but instead on the side of the miscreants and the liars and the spies. He has neither religion nor nation and he only asks for bad things for Muslims.... I will defend the Arab Muslim nation with my last breath.[97]

If the Arma and Songhay can rule, it is because they can claim genealogical connection to Arab ancestors. As such, in the terms of racial thinking in the Niger Bend, they are not black. It is a remarkable change of tactics, if not position.

Like Ould al-Shaykh, Muhammad ʿAli also offered a historical sketch that supported his claims for racial separatism, although it is in no way comparable in its seriousness or depth. Like Ould al-Shaykh's "The book of the interpreter," Muhammad ʿAli made genealogical arguments to define the Niger Bend and to whom it should belong. His document is called, "The claims of the country of Arab Timbuktu." Under the subheading "Arabism in our country," he wrote:

> Our people make up 3 million inhabitants who are all Arab in origin according to ancient history.
>
> 1. The Himyarites who emigrated from Yemen in the time of Queen Saha and crossed Libya, Tunisia, and Morocco, and then settled in West Africa with their Arab brothers the Sanhaja.
> 2. The Quraysh, Khalradz [?] and the Ansar who emigrated from Andalusia to avoid Christian domination and came and settled in Mauritania and Timbuktu. They were given the name Tuareg by those in Timbuktu to differentiate them from their Sanhaja brothers, long since islamicized.[98]

[97] Letter from Muhammad ʿAli ag Attaher to Abd al-Rahman b. Zacou, Libya, May 21, 1960 (AMI sér. BO). In French, no Arabic original. Sent by Abdoul Wahab Doucoure.

[98] Ibid.

Under the subheading "Nationalist struggle of the Tuareg," Muhammad ʿAli argued that, "over the course of the Arab Islamic centuries, the Tuareg struggled for national unity. They founded the largest empire which extended from contemporary Morocco to Mauritania and Timbuktu." This is a reference to the eleventh-century Almoravid Empire. However, the power of the Almoravids weakened over time, which allowed France to conquer the Arabs of the Niger Bend in 1894: "France claimed to have come to transfer civilization and science. But from its arrival, [France] robbed us of our dignity and our nation and imposed on us its traditions.... The pilgrimage was forbidden to us, as was having any contact with our Arab brothers. The madrasas were closed down. During France's rule, it did nothing to improve the economic or cultural level of the people." Worse than this, France divided the people with illegitimate borders: "They found it better to divide our nation between Soudan, Mauritania, and Niger.... If we keep silent about the French crimes in the economic and cultural domain, we cannot shut up about the unity of our nation." Muhammad ʿAli ended the historical sketch with a demand: "Our people are energetically opposed to the French policy which will destroy our racial unity. I demand in the name of our people that our borders of 1894 be respected. I demand complete independence. It is agreed that Mali will be independent along with Niger this coming July. I will never recognize the independence of those two countries in their current form."[99]

THE POSTCOLONY IN TWO COLORS?

The projects of Muhammad ʿAli and Ould al-Shaykh did not come to pass. For those Tuareg and Arabs who remained in Soudan, an accommodation had to be reached with the soon-to-be independent Malian government. Although the PSP remained important in local politics in the Niger Bend, it was much diminished at the colonywide level. In the late 1950s, many Tuareg leaders who had been members of the PSP joined the US-RDA in hopes of gaining influence in the new postcolonial state. The Kel Entsar chief, Muhammad al-Mahdi, was one important person who did this, much to the annoyance of his brother Muhammad ʿAli. When Muhammad ʿAli sent his letter to de Gaulle, he posted a copy to Muhammad al-Mahdi with a sarcastic comment appended to it: "I send to your highness (ḥaḍrat-kum) this reminder which I sent to President de Gaulle, president of France. We will regret it if we are forced to live with

[99] Ibid.

the blacks (zunūj)."[100] However, there was a new cadre of Tuareg intellectuals, often from the Kel Entsar, who had gone to colonial schools and sought to represent Tuareg interests to the nascent US-RDA government. In a series of letters, these writers sought a place at the new Malian table for the Tuareg. They made clear that race was the fundamental division in the new Mali, but they also offered up the possibility of interracial friendship between blacks and whites.

In a letter written to the minister of the interior by Muhammad ag Mahmoud, director of the school for "nomads" at Timbuktu, he put the case for political representation clearly: "Today, in the name of the nomads, I will tell the truth. It is perhaps a shocking truth, but it is a necessary truth for the accomplishment of the ideals of the Soudan without obstacles. It is a truth, Mr. Minister, that you were yesterday, and will be tomorrow, in lands that belong to the nomads." From this starting point, the Tuareg and Arabs demanded "to be in the majority on the political, governmental and administrative chessboard of the Niger Bend." The other main issue was development. Muhammad ag Mahmoud said that the Tuareg required schools, wells, Tamashek-language programs on the radio, drug dispensaries, and respect for land rights:

> These are the conditions made by the nomads. If they are not respected by their black brothers, the consequences will be unfortunate. It is regrettable but it is necessary to say it. If, as one wishes, the black brothers give their word of honor and promise to respect them, the egoists will see against them, and despite them, that the whites and blacks of Soudan will march hand in hand, singing the national anthem, and hand in hand, showing to the saboteurs, and to the racists, that nothing can be confirmed about whether Adam and Eve were white or black.[101]

The rhetoric of racial brotherhood was often used in addressing the Malian authorities. For example, in a letter from a person named Hamama ag Attaher at Ras-el-Ma, addressed to all the people of Bamako and Dakar in 1959, he included a couple of lines antiracial poetry at the end:

> People are from the same place without exception,
> Their father is Adam and their mother Eve.
> If you bring honor to the name of a lineage,
> Indeed we trace our ancestry to the clay and the water.[102]

[100] Letter from Muhammad ʿAli ag Attaher to Muhammad al-Mahdi ag Attaher, December 22, 1959 (ACG).

[101] Letter from Mohamed ag Mahmoud, Directeur, l'école campement Tombouctou, to the Ministre de l'Intérieur, no date (AMI sér. BO).

[102] al-nāsu min jihati al-tamthīli iʿfāʾ * abū-hum adamun wa-al-ummu ḥawwāʾ
wa-ʾin ataytu bi-fakhr min dhūʾi nasabin * fa-ʾinna nasabta-nā al-ṭīn wa-ʾl-māʾ (Letter from Hamama ag Attaher, Ras-el-Ma, to the people of Bamako and Dakar, October 13, 1959 [AMI sér. BO]).

The clay and the water are the substances from which God created human beings.[103]

Part of the rhetorical strategy of these Tuareg intellectuals was to claim a part in the anticolonial struggle. A Kel Entsar teacher in Tin-Attène, for example, wrote in 1959 to the minister of the interior, telling him that the Kel Entsar had opposed the OCRS plan and that "we react against all anti-Africanist politics, by the example of the propaganda of the French officers for the OCRS in the nomad milieu."[104] In a letter written in 1961, Zeini ag Hamoutfa claimed that "we are in agreement that the nomad population of the Niger Bend participated in the expulsion of the enemy and the destruction of the chimera of the OCRS. From this fact, their rights in the nation must be presented. We want a government of two colors in which the sedentary people and the nomads will figure together in both Mali and in the three districts which the nomads want (Goundam, Timbuktu, Gao)." This government of "two colors" would include a minister responsible for the "nomads," a director of the cabinet who was a "nomad," and ambassador posts for the Tuareg and Arabs. He also complained that "some Kel Entsar returning from Mecca were arrested in Bamako, accused of having sold slaves. It appears that this is without any basis, this sale of bellah." But even it were true, he said, "these Kel Entsar left for Mecca under the colonial regime and if there was a transaction, it was under the colonial administration. These arrests constitute a gross indignity in the Kel Entsar tribe which demands their release and return."[105] Zeini argued that it was in the lack of political representation for the Tuareg and Arabs that one could speak of the true racism in Mali.

In another letter written later in 1961, Zeini argued that "the nomadic populations are for the principle of a government of two colors. They want the nomads to participate in political power. In Mauritania, there are two black ministers; in Niger, there are two ministers who are nomads. Those two republics take account of colors in forming their governments." The demands for a government of "two colors" was usually accompanied by recriminations and claims that it was the Tuareg and Arabs who were suffering from racism directed at them. In the same letter, Zeini wrote that "the struggle against racism must be persistent. In Timbuktu the nomads do not have their rights. Racism is evident every day. During the

[103] Qur'an, 15:26.

[104] Letter from Leini [Zeini ag Hamoutfa?], teacher at Tin-Attène (Tombouctou) to the Ministre de l'Intérieur, October 15, 1959 (AMI sér. BO).

[105] Letter from Zeini ag Hamoutfa, Timbuktu, to Madeira Keita, Membre du bureau politique national US-RDA, Bamako, August 31, 1961 (AMI sér. BO). For a discussion of this letter and others like it, see Lecocq, "That Desert," 106–10.

inauguration of the Malian army, Fort Bonnier [in Timbuktu] was given the [new] name of a sedentary Songhay despite the fact that Colonel Bonnier was killed by a Tuareg named [Sobbo ag Fondogomo] and Fort Bonnier should be named Fort [Sobbo]."[106]

CONCLUSION

Muhammad ʿAli remained in exile in Morocco until 1964 when he was extradited to Mali, where he was imprisoned until 1977;[107] Ould al-Shaykh was arrested shortly after independence. He remained in prison until the successful military coup d'état brought Moussa Traoré to power in 1968. According to the Malian government, Ould al-Shaykh's arrest was greeted with "wild enthusiasm." The Malian commander of Timbuktu reported that "this man was unanimously recognized as one of the best educated people in the district, but he put his knowledge in the service of bad things. It appears over the course of different conversations that his name still inculcates terror."[108] The Malian administrator may have been right in his appraisal of the popular feeling toward Ould al-Shaykh in Timbuktu, but this was certainly not a view shared universally. Zeini ag Hamoutfa argued in late 1961 that it would improve political unity in the Niger Bend if Ould al-Shaykh was released from prison. After all, he said, Ould al-Shaykh's project for the OCRS had been entirely sponsored by the French and represented no interest in the Niger Bend. Zeini proposed a simple solution: "The politics of [Ould al-Shaykh] do not exist anymore because the qadi in question was in the service of France for money. As such, if Mali gives him money, [Ould al-Shaykh] might be gentle with our young republic. In any case, no one is for the politics of Muhammad Mahmud ould al-Shaykh."[109]

Things were not so simple. Race had been mobilized as a defining argument in the politics of decolonization in the Niger Bend. Both blacks and whites held racial grievances about the other. Both saw in the other a major obstacle to the achievement of the moral order to which their politics were directed. It was perhaps not inevitable that this would lead to

[106] Letter from Zeini ag Hamoutfa, Timbuktu, to the Secretaire Général de l'US-RDA, December 10, 1961 (AMI sér. BO).

[107] Lecocq, "That Desert," 155; Lecocq, *Disputed Desert*, 214. He died in 1994.

[108] Letter from the Commandant, Cercle de Tombouctou to the Ministère de l'Intérieur, No.42, July 3, 1962 (AMI sér. BO).

[109] Letter from Zeini ag Hamoutfa to the Secretaire Général de l'US-RDA, December 10, 1961 (AMI sér. BO).

violence, but that is what happened in 1963 when Tuareg rebels in Adrar-n-Ifoghas launched a revolt against the Malian state. This conflict, and the brutal and indiscriminate suppression of the rebellion by the Malian army, ensured that the seeds sown over centuries would continue to bear fruit for many decades thereafter.

Conclusion

RACE IN THE POST COLONY

The racilialized violence that has plagued the Sahel and other parts of Africa since the achievement of political independence in the 1950s and 1960s needs to be understood as a product of the African intellectual traditions that inscribe these actions with meaning and coherence. There is no question that colonial rule played an important part in instrumentalizing African racial distinctions through the mechanisms of bureaucratic statecraft. But the existence of African discourse about racial difference is not, at root, the result of borrowing European racial theory. Such a framework often suits a particular kind of postcolonial politics and academic writing, which sees in colonial rule the source of many contemporary ills. But at least for the Sahel, this approach founders against the fact that racial thought existed long before Europeans arrived in the area, and that it retained a large measure of continuity and coherence from the precolonial past under colonial rule.

The purpose of this book is not, however, to argue that Africans in the Sahel were isolated from intellectual developments elsewhere in the world. If anything, what I have demonstrated is the extent to which people in the Sahel participated in a larger, cosmopolitan network connected by shared literacy in Arabic and faith in Islam.[1] As such, Sahelian racial thought cannot be understood as "traditional" any more than it can be

[1] Not unlike the Sanskrit or Latin cosmopolitanisms described by Sheldon Pollock, "Cosmopolitan and Vernacular in History," *Public Culture* 12, no. 3 (2000): 599–606; John Hunwick has called Arabic "the Latin of Africa" (*West Africa, Islam, and the Arab World* [Princeton, NJ: Marcus Wiener, 2006], 53).

deemed a Middle Eastern or European borrowing. Sahelian intellectuals made active choices in reshaping concepts and practices derived from both local and transregional sources. But this occurred in particular historical context, as arguments and claims designed to affect social and political configurations in the Sahel itself.

It is important to emphasize that the presence of racial modes of thought in the Sahel does not alone explain the forms of racialized violence that have occurred in the region in the postcolonial period. As the literature on the Rwandan genocide makes clear, there is a complex relationship between racial ideas and violence. Just as it would be difficult to construct a credible explanation of recent Rwandan history without taking account of the role played by racist ideology in framing that conflict and in motivating the most violent participants in the genocide, we cannot understand conflict in the Sahel without this history.[2] Racial categories matter when they can be called on and developed by people to frame problems, define opponents, and mobilize support. Appeals to race, however, are always arguments made about the world that are not wholly shared or agreed on by everyone in a particular milieu. As Scott Strauss found in his research on Rwandan genocide, relatively few Hutu participants in the killing took seriously the so-called Hamitic hypothesis of the Tutsis as foreign Nilotics, racially distinct from Hutu autochthones.[3] This is purported to be the core racial idea in Rwanda, introduced by colonial writers, taught to Rwandans by church and state institutions, and inscribed in colonial and postcolonial law.[4] As such, racial antipathy is not atemporal; it has to be invoked by people who wish to argue for it and use it for some purpose.

It would be difficult not to conclude that racial discourse has grown in importance in Mali since the end of colonial rule in 1960. Race has been at the center of the relationship between the Malian state and the Tuareg and Arab populations in the Niger Bend. According to Baz Lecocq, racial arguments played a significant role in the two civil wars fought in northern Mali in 1963–1964 and 1990–1995: "The conflict between the

[2] Scott Strauss, *The Order of Genocide: Race, Power, and War in Rwanda* (Ithaca, NY: Cornell University Press, 2006), 8–9, 129–35.

[3] Ibid., 132–3.

[4] Timothy Longman, *Christianity and Genocide in Rwanda* (New York: Cambridge University Press, 2010), 59–66; Mahmood Mamdani, *When Victims Become Killers: Colonialism, Nativism, and the Genocide in Rwanda* (Princeton, NJ: Princeton University Press, 2001), 76–102; Christopher Taylor, *Sacrifice as Terror: The Rwandan Genocide of 1994* (Oxford: Berg, 1999), 55–97.

Malian state and the [Tuareg and Arabs] forms part of a problem that haunts all of the Sahel, a problem often seen by foreign experts as one of ethnicity, but locally phrased in terms of race."[5]

Mali's first president, Modibo Keita, often made use of racial ideas in defining the newly independent country, especially when he spoke about what he thought of as authentic African culture, which he called "la personalité africaine."[6] Keita did not accord a place to Tuareg and Arab pastoralists in the "black-African" civilization that he sought to make the basis of the Malian nation. Among the goals of the Malian government in the early 1960s was to "achieve African unity and independence … that will permit the irresistible extension of black African culture."[7] Even in efforts to take account of the diversity of Mali, blackness was made central to the national project. For example, in a speech in 1961 to the National Assembly, Keita remarked that:

> Mali, which was a melting pot of African, Berber and Arab cultures, will continue to carry out the role of connecting link without losing its own qualities. We shall thus build the solid core of a well-rounded civilization. Cultural decolonization can only be accomplished, however, through an unshakable resolve to affirm ourselves as Africans, to observe and judge the men and the institutions of Africa solely with African eyes and brains.[8]

This was a racial rhetoric directed at the former colonial metropole, at white Europeans and those who might imitate them. Such sentiments fit easily into a racial narrative of colonial emancipation that was widespread in Africa in the 1960s. From the standpoint of the Niger Bend, however, such language carried different meanings. For the Tuareg and Arabs especially, it was exclusionary. It suggested to them that to be Malian was to be African, and to be African was to be black.

The new Malian government approached the Niger Bend as a backward territory in dire need of modern reforms. There was a fundamental perception among those who led Mali to independence that the Tuareg and Arabs were both inveterate racists and slaveholders.[9] In a meeting

[5] Baz Lecocq, "'That Desert Is Our Country': Tuareg Rebellions and Competing Nationalisms in Contemporary Mali (1946–1996)" (Ph.D. diss., University of Amsterdam, 2002), 301.

[6] Modibo Diagouraga, *Modibo Keita: un destin* (Paris: L'Harmattan, 1992), 154. On this point, see also Francis G. Snyder, "The Political Thought of Modibo Keita," *Journal of Modern African Studies* 5, no. 1 (1967): 83–4.

[7] Diagouraga, *Modibo Keita*, 62.

[8] Modibo Keita, *A Collection of Speeches, September 22, 1960–August 27, 1964* (Moscow: [no publisher], 1965), 33.

[9] Lecocq, "That Desert," 51–2.

with Tuareg leaders in 1959 during the transition to self-government, the first African commander of the district of Timbuktu, H. Sangare, felt compelled to tell his interlocutors that the colonial period had ended and that from now on, the US-RDA government of Mali would guarantee the right to property of every individual, without distinction for social status. The government would not return lands to noble Tuareg that had only recently been assigned to liberated bellah-iklan by the colonial administration. Local Tuareg would have to adapt to this new reality.[10] In 1962, Bakary Diallo, the first Malian governor of the Niger Bend region (based in Gao), announced that "nomad society, as it is left to us by the colonial regime, undoubtedly poses us problems in light of the objectives of our socio-political program.... Our objective is to know the problems which we, in reference to the colonial regime, will call the Nomad problem."[11] Although its policies were not always effective, the Malian government attempted to reduce or end altogether the political power of Tuareg and Arab chiefs, regulate the movement of herds across national borders, and definitively free the bellah-iklan.

The first Tuareg rebellion began in 1963 in the Adrar-n-Ifoghas among the Tuareg Kel Adagh. One of the main motivations of the rebels was unhappiness at being included in the newly independent Mali. The ostensible goal was Tuareg independence. According to a government interrogation of a captured rebel named Amouksou ag Azandeher in October 1963, racial grievance was a motivation for the rebellion: "We nomads of the white race, can neither conceive nor accept to be commanded by blacks whom we always had as servants and slaves.... We Ifoghas, do not accept or conceive of the equality between races and men Mali wants to impose on us, starting with taking our imghad and bellah away from us."[12] The rebellion was started by a small group of no more than a few dozen men who hoped to raise the profile of Tuareg discontent at having been included in postcolonial Mali. They hoped that Algeria or France would intervene on their behalf. But the international help never materialized. Baz Lecocq estimated that no more than 250 lightly armed men, using camels for transport, were involved in the rebellion on the rebel side.[13] Some Kel Adagh chiefs supported the rebel cause, although others sided with the Malian government. Muhammad ʿAli ag Attaher was a

[10] Cercle de Tombouctou, "Procès-verbal de la séance de travail," November 23, 1959 (AMI, sér BO).

[11] Quoted by Lecocq, "That Desert," 74.

[12] Quoted in Ibid., 134.

[13] Ibid., 136–7.

prominent political supporter of the revolt from his base in Morocco. But the conflict did not spread to other parts of northern Mali.

The Malian army responded with the camel-mounted goum units inherited from the colonial state, whose members were mostly Arab and Tuareg. Over the course of the conflict, many members of the goum defected to the rebels, and the government was forced to send in hundreds of regular troops from southern Mali in largely ineffective motorized units. Frustrated by its inability to defeat or capture the rebels, the Malian army quickly turned to anti-insurgency tactics that targeted the civilian population. Civilians fled to Algeria, but those who remained were rounded up into camps. Wells were poisoned, and many important religious and political notables were executed. The Malian government declared the rebellion over in August 1964.[14]

The brutality used by the Malian army to put down the rebellion made a deep mark of racial grievance on many Tuareg and Arabs in northern Mali. It confirmed what many had feared in the 1950s about being incorporated into a black-ruled postcolonial country. It is also important to recognize, however, that the actions and language of Tuareg rebels acted to confirm what many black Malians thought about the inveterate anti-black racism felt by Arabs and Tuareg towards them. Baz Lecocq has argued that:

> Both sides were equally obsessed with race.... Both used racial discourses. One could safely say that [the 1963–1964 conflict] was the result of relations between two different political elites based on mutual distrust and negative preconceived stereotyped images. While the Keita regime perceived the [Tuareg] as white, anarchist, feudal, lazy, proslavery nomads who needed to be civilized, the [Tuareg] elite saw the Malian politicians as black, incompetent, untrustworthy slaves in disguise who came to usurp power.[15]

The memory of the events of 1963–1964 in the Adrar-n-Ifoghas has often been cited as a direct cause of the second Tuareg rebellion that began in 1990 and drew in the whole Niger Bend region.

The second Tuareg rebellion was in some ways motivated by the same kinds of grievances as the first one, compounded by strong feelings of vengeance toward the Malian state. Huge changes transformed northern Mali in the years between 1964 and 1990. Above all, the catastrophic droughts of the early 1970s and mid-1980s destroyed pastoralist herds, wiping out wealth that had been accumulated over decades. It also caused

[14] Ibid., 129–68.
[15] Ibid., 301.

devastation for the sedentary farmers of the Niger valley who saw their crops fail. A military coup brought Moussa Traoré to power in 1968. The Traoré regime largely ignored the north; very little investment in infrastructure or social development was undertaken there.[16] Many Tuareg and Arabs left Mali to seek opportunities in Algeria, Mauritania, Libya, and elsewhere. Among the consequences of these changes in Tuareg and Arab societies was a breakdown of the traditional social hierarchy and political authority of chiefs. In exile, many Tuareg and Arab Malians also developed a more coherent set of political complaints against the Malian state, which some turned into a program for political independence in the 1970s.[17] The second rebellion was organized from Algeria and Libya, as a Tuareg and Arab national liberation movement.

In 1990, the second rebellion was launched in both Mali and Niger. This time, the rebels were much more sophisticated militarily, and the Malian army suffered a string of demoralizing defeats. In Mali, Moussa Traoré's government quickly sought to negotiate with the rebels, and an agreement was reached at Tamanrasset in southern Algeria in January 1991, which imposed a ceasefire and promised to devolve power to the northern regions. But at that point, the rebel movement split into factions of those prepared to accept a future within Mali and those hardliners who would not. After the Tamanrasset agreement, the hardliners extended the Malian conflict from the Adrar-n-Ifoghas region to the towns of the Niger valley and the Gourma region of the Niger Bend. Moussa Traoré was overthrown in March 1991 by a military coup that was instigated by a popular uprising in Bamako. The new regime negotiated another agreement with the rebels, called the National Pact in 1992, which promised, among other things, to integrate rebels into the Malian army and make special investments in the north. However, the conflict continued as Tuareg and Arab civilians were targeted for assassination by the Malian army, and rebels launched attacks on black civilians in the towns of the Niger valley. In 1994, a black militia was formed among the Songhay that called itself the "Mouvement Patriotique Ganda Koy," which invoked the idea of autochthonous "owners of the land" (So. ganda-koy). Its goals were to defend the black population of the Niger valley from Tuareg and Arab rebel attacks. Its political rhetoric focused on the

[16] Mohamed Tiessa-Farma Maïga, *Le Mali: de la sécheresse à la rébellion nomade: Chronique et analyse d'un double phénomène du contre-développement en Afrique sahélienne* (Paris: L'Harmattan, 1997).

[17] Pierre Boilley, *Les Touaregs Kel Adagh. Dépendances et révoltes: du Soudan français au Mali contemporain* (Paris: Karthala, 1999), 400–4.

elimination of the racially irredeemable "nomads" from the Niger Bend altogether. By the later stages of the conflict, large numbers of Tuareg and Arab civilians had fled to neighboring countries as refugees, and most of the towns in northern Mali had been racially cleansed of their Arab and Tuareg populations.

A report on the conflict produced for the United Nations Institute for Disarmament Research (UNIDIR), attempted to provide a balanced overview of the course of events that had led to the civilian displacements along racial lines: "Throughout this period, the violence continued in the North, persecuting nomad and sedentary populations, Touareg and Songhay and Bozo and Arab and Gabero [Fulbe] in more or less equal proportions." Rebels attacked camps for displaced civilians, and both official and nongovernmental relief organizations were forced to stop sending their agents outside of the main towns, or to freeze their programs altogether: "The reaction of certain army units was unfortunate.... Unable to catch the real bandits, they turned to killing and looting any available 'red skin.' All Touareg and Arab shops in Gao were looted. Summoned to a meeting in Léré, Touareg leaders were simply executed. The elite of the FIAA [Front Islamique Arabe de l'Azawad, a rebel group] was imprisoned in the barracks in Timbuktu, and killed." In this state of insecurity, "thousands of Touaregs and Arabs fled the towns and abandoned their livelihoods, becoming displaced persons and de facto dependents of the rebel movement. Some of those who were driven out of their homes, retaliated against their black neighbours. Mainly thanks to army indiscipline, the seeds of civil war were sown."[18]

The main aim of the UNIDIR report was to show that the racial violence – the killing of "red skins" and the "retaliation against black neighbours" – was a consequence of the indiscipline of the Malian army. There is no question that the army's brutality against civilians was instrumental in the extension of racial violence among northern Malian combatants during the civil war, as it had been in the first Tuareg rebellion in 1963–1964. But it is difficult to see how the racial aspect of the violence can so easily be explained away as a consequence of something else. The implication of the UNIDIR study is that either racialized violence is somehow latent, even natural, among people as different as Tuareg, Arabs, and Songhay if the right spark lights the dry tinder; or that it developed mechanically

[18] Robin-Edward Poulton and Ibrahim ag Youssouf, *A Peace of Timbuktu: Democratic Governance, Development and African Peacemaking* (Geneva: United Nations Institute for Disarmament Research, 1998), 62.

out of community solidarity as a response to aggression. In this sense, the analysis makes the common assumption in African contexts of the instrumentality of racial or ethnic identities in the context of weak and retreating states.[19] But the racial dimension of the conflict in northern Mali was neither natural nor a mechanical reaction to aggression. Invoking racial difference was an active choice, whether it was made by leaders of the Malian army, Tuareg rebels, or Ganda Koy militiamen. In a context such as northern Mali, making arguments about race had become easy and commonplace. It is, therefore, hardly surprising that race would be invoked as part of the postcolonial civil conflict that has plagued northern Mali. As we now know, racial ideas were extremely deep and well developed in the intellectual history of this region over centuries.

ARGUING AGAINST RACE?

The more difficult argument to make in the Sahel is a nonracial one. As I have argued, there have always been intellectuals in this region prepared to offer explicitly antiracial arguments, usually in response to others who had invoked race. From Ahmad Baba's rejection of the idea of a reserve pool of black slaves at the beginning of the seventeenth century, to Sidi al-Mukhtar al-Saghir al-Kunti's recognition of the Hamdullahi Caliphate as a Muslim state in the middle of the nineteenth century, to Hamama ag Attaher's letter to the people of Bamako and Dakar in 1959, we have seen examples of Sahelian arguments against race. What these antiracial arguments share in common is a rejection of the meanings ascribed to difference rather than a rejection of difference altogether. In this way, they are not like a certain kind of academic approach to race, which seeks to reveal the incoherence of racial distinctions themselves. In Mahmood Mamdani's recent book on Darfur, he argues at length that racial difference is not real (by which he means "biological") in Sudan. The people who are today called Arabs and Africans are, in fact, descended from the same people: "In the riverine Sudan, Arab was an identity of power. But not all Arabs wielded power or were even identified with power. Arabs came from different historical experiences, as varied as former slave-owning merchants and former slaves. A minority had immigrant origins, but the vast majority was native in origin."[20] Further, he argues that "to be an

[19] Crawford Young, "Deciphering Disorder in Africa: Is Identity the Key?" *World Politics* 54, no. 4 (2002): 536.

[20] Mahmood Mamdani, *Saviors and Survivors: Darfur, Politics, and the War on Terror* (New York: Pantheon, 2009), 101.

Arab is thus to be a member of any one of contemporary political communities called 'Arab.' Arab is, above all, a political identity – one that is tribal, not racial. To be an Arab is to be a member of an Arab tribe."[21] Mamdani wrote this book to make an intervention in the larger international debate about the conflict in Darfur. He contends that American activists have applied a false racial dichotomy to the Sudanese context, derived from American ideas about race. In this sense, Mamdani's argument is anti-foundational, seeking to demystify and delegitimize the category of race in the interests of preventing its misuse.[22] As such, race in Sudan is not really about biological difference, or the distinction between foreign migrants and autochthones, but about cultural and political identity.[23]

This kind of approach can serve useful political purposes, but it is far from an honest account of the uses of racial discourse in Sudan. Mamdani's book fails to address the Sudanese reality that racial difference is an extremely important idiom by which politics, law, and social life in Sudan are defined. Race has also been at the center of the arguments made by the different parties to the conflict in Darfur.[24] To suggest that race is not real in Sudan does very little to help us understand how racial language has become such an important means by which difference is defined in that country, by Sudanese. Objective physiological difference does not determine culture, intelligence, occupation, or social status. But that does not mean that racial difference is not real in Sudan, or Rwanda, or the Sahel. An effective antiracial argument must take account of difference even as it demystifies it.

Postcolonial Malian intellectuals have often been more frank in recognizing the reality of racial difference in Mali, even as they have attempted to show that such divisions need not be the basis of conflict. The Malian writer Yambo Ouologuem's controversial novel "Le Devoir de violence" is a good example of an antiracial argument that works as an exposé, describing in detail the ugliness of racialized violence over the long

21 Ibid., 108

22 Gaurav Desai, *Subject to Colonialism: African Self-Fashioning and the Colonial Library* (Durham, NC: Duke University Press, 2001), 11n.

23 Alex de Waal makes a similar argument about the malleability of racial identities in Sudan (*Famine That Kills: Darfur, Sudan*. Revised Edition [New York: Oxford University Press, 2005], 48). See also Julie Flint and Alex de Waal, *Darfur: A Short History of a Long War* (New York: Zed Books, 2005), 4–5.

24 Sharif Harir, "Racism in Islamic Disguise: Retreating Nationalism and Upsurging Ethnicity in Darfur," in *Never Drink From the Same Cup: Proceedings of the Conference on Indigenous Peoples in Africa, Tune, Denmark, 1993*, ed. H. Veber et al. (Copenhagen: IWGIA and the Centre for Development Research, 1993), 291–311.

history of the Sahel.[25] As Christopher Wise has pointed out, many critics make the mistake of reading this novel as vulgar and self-hating, feeding a European image of Africa as savage.[26] Although Ouologuem clearly intended to burst the historical mythologies of African nationalism, the way he portrays race in "Le Devoir de violence" is as a tool of domination and violence used by Sahelian rulers against people defined as lowly blacks (la négraille). This approach reflects quite closely the intellectual history of race in the Sahel that I have presented in this book. Cheick Oumar Sissoko's 1999 film "La Genèse" is another example of an antiracial argument made without denying the validity of difference. In the wake of the civil war in the 1990s, Sissoko used the biblical story of Jacob and Esau (Genesis 33–37) to dramatize the ways that conflict develops between pastoralists and farmers. By remaining so faithful to the biblical text, "La Genèse" shows us the possibility of reconciliation between world-weary patriarchs, but also, by its genealogical logic, the inescapable consequences of conflict on future relations. Shot in the Niger Bend at Hombori, the film captures Sissoko's sense of the tragedy of racial conflict in northern Mali.

Finally, Albakaye Ousmane Kounta's novel "Les sans repères" (2006) is an example of an antiracial argument directed at the mentality of racial superiority associated with slavery in the Sahel.[27] "Les sans repères" is a story of a young southern Malian boy kidnapped and sold into slavery in the Niger Bend during the late 1950s or early 1960s. Violently abused and overworked by his Arab master,[28] the young slave nonetheless bears his misfortune with great dignity. The novel's plot is based on the mistaken identity of the young slave, who turns out to be of noble descent. After eventually freeing himself during the catastrophic drought of the early 1970s, he marries the daughter of his former master and then, in a twist of fate, is asked to save his master's life by donating his own blood. It turns out that the master and slave are descended from the same southern Malian family. The way out of the racial box in "Les sans repères" is genealogical. The enslaved boy never returns his master's abuse with even

[25] Yambo Ouologuem, *Bound to Violence*, trans. Ralph Manheim (New York: Harcourt Brace Jovanovich, 1971).

[26] Christopher Wise, "Introduction: A Voice from Bandiagara," in *Yambo Ouologuem: Postcolonial Writer, Islamic Militant*, ed. Christopher Wise (Boulder, CO: Lynn Rienner, 1999), 2–3.

[27] Albakaye Ousmane Kounta, *Les sans repères* (Brinon-sur-Sauldre: Editions Grandvaux, 2006).

[28] Albakaye Ousmane Kounta, personal communication. The novel does not reveal his ethnic identity.

a word of protest. He is handsome and intelligent, honest and loyal. We learn at the end of the novel that the reason that he does not behave like a slave is because of his honorable blood and lineage.[29]

These efforts to argue against race in postcolonial Mali run up against deeply engrained ideas about fundamental differences between nobles and slaves, pastoralists and farmers, Muslims and non-Muslims, and blacks and nonblacks. It is for this reason that antiracial arguments made in "Les sans repères" and "La Genèse" draw so heavily on the same genealogical logic out of which race has been made and remade in the Sahel for centuries. Such a choice can contribute to reinscribing the structures of lineage on the social imagination, but it also strikes me as the most effective tactic in contesting racism in the Sahel. These are not full antiracial arguments. Masters and slaves are fundamentally different in principle, according to Kounta's novel; it is just that physical appearances do not fully reveal who has been rightly and wrongly enslaved. The wrongful enslavement of the boy in "Les sans repères" does not suggest that slavery itself is wrong. Ahmad Baba made precisely this argument when he said that enslavement was only valid against those groups that could not be counted among the Muslims. Such arguments may strike us as less than fully satisfying. But it is almost certainly the case that the most effective answers to the challenge of racial discourse will be found within the intellectual framework of Mali and the larger Sahel, not outside of it.

[29] The plot of a wrongfully enslaved (Muslim) overcoming his predicament using honor, piety, and integrity appears in the Nigerian Hausa novel by Abubakar Tafawa Balewa, *Shaihu Umar*, trans. Mervyn Hiskett (London: Longmans, 1967).

Index

cycles of, 260
and relations with sedentary people, 212–13, 247–51, 261
pax gallica, 178, 208
Périer, Jean, 117
political treaties, 185. *See also* Barābīsh, Ḥammādi, Iwellemmedan, Kunti
ʿahd (pact), 96–7, 146, 149, 154, 204–5, 309
amān (safe conduct), 154–60, 197, 204–5
bayʿa (allegiance), 98–101, 200
negotiations, 152–9
submission, colonial demands for, 138–9, 140–1, 154, 185
politique nomade. *See* colonial administration
Ponty, William. *See* Merlaud-Ponty, William (d. 1915)
Pratt, Mary Louise, 16, 20

race labels. *See* Bambara, bellah-iklan, Fulbe, Sorko
bīḍān, 2, 12, 103
gaabibi, 244, 253–4, 256–9
harbibi (ar-bi), 72, 74, 102, 244
kuhl, 67, 243
sūdān, 2, 27, 40, 41, 45–55, 58, 67, 73–4, 80–7, 103–4, 243, 308
zanj, 71, 72, 74, 102, 215, 307–8
zunūj, 307–8, 309, 312
Rafʿ sha'n al-ḥubshān, 51. *See also* al-Suyūṭī, ʿAbd al-Raḥmān
raiding, 144, 287. *See also* ʿĀbidīn al-Kuntī, Barābīsh, Kunta, Rgaybāt, Shaʿāmba
and colonial countermeasures, 145, 152–3
against colonial forces, 139–43, 149–50, 165–70
and *les grands nomades*, 140–1, 276
and mustaghraq al-dhimma, 76–7, 90–5, 232
and Sahelian pastoralists, 140
and sedentary villages, 140
against sedentary villages, 32, 168–70, 212–13, 221, 247–52
Raising the status of the Ethiopians. *See* Rafʿ sha'n al-ḥubshān
Ras-el-Ma, 138, 213, 284, 312
Raynaud, Jean, 286–7
Renan, Ernest (d. 1892), 112, 123
Rgaybāt, 141, 152, 165, 168
Rhergo, 252
Rio Oro. *See* Saqiat al-Hamra
Roberts, Richard, 96, 219, 285
Robinson, David, 207–8
Rouch, Jean, 215
Rwanda, 317, 324

Saad, Elias, 24
safe conduct (amān). *See* political treaties
Saʿīd b. Ibrāhīm al-Jirārī, 81, 86
Saint-Simonians, 118–19
Sakhawi (Sakhaoui), 164, 197, 269
Sakib ag Assamsamo (d. 1934), 164, 223–4, 225, 269
Salifou, André, 3
Samori Touré (d. 1900), 134, 135
Ṣanhāja, 41–4, 48, 53, 77, 310
Saqiat al-Hamra, 106, 165, 168, 292
Sard al-kalām fīmā jarā baina-nā wa-baina ʿAbd al-Salām, 104. *See also* Muhammad Bello
Saremayou, 185, 262
Second World War, 174, 178, 208, 272, 273, 284
Ségou, 28, 101, 132, 134, 215, 216
Senegal, 105, 207, 218
Senegal River valley, 28, 32, 67
Serere, 141, 217, 258, 262
Shaʿāmba, 141, 152, 165
Shamanamas, 161
Shaykh Bāy al-Kuntī (d. 1929)
and Aḥmad Bābā al-Tinbuktī (d. 1627), 84–5
and clientship for manumitted slaves, 237–9
and colonialism, 164, 225, 226, 228–9
and education of slaves, 233–7
and female slaves, 232–7
and goods from the blacks, 89–90
and inheritance for slaves, 229, 290
and Iwellemmedan, 159–60, 164
and mustaghraq al-dhimma, 90, 159–60
and prayer, 238–9, 300
and punishment of slaves, 225–7
and ritual purity, 89–90
and Shaykh Zayni b. ʿAbd al-ʿAzīz al-Jubīhī (d. 1936), 170
and slave marriages, 232–3
and slavery, 225–8, 229, 230–2
and slaves' claims to be Muslim, 84–5
and slaves' liability for crimes, 227–8
and taxes, 228–9
and umm walad, 232–3, 239

BOOKS IN THIS SERIES *(continued after page iii)*

1 *City Politics: A Study of Léopoldville, 1962–63*, J. S. LaFontaine
2 *Studies in Rural Capitalism in West Africa* , Polly Hill
3 *Land Policy in Buganda,* Henry W. West
4 *The Nigerian Military: A Sociological Analysis of Authority and Revolt, 1960–67,* Robin Luckham
5 *The Ghanaian Factory Worker: Industrial Man in Africa,* Margaret Peil
6 *Labour in the South African Gold Mines,* Francis Wilson
7 *The Price of Liberty: Personality and Politics in Colonial Nigeria,* Kenneth W. J. Post and George D. Jenkins
8 *Subsistence to Commercial Farming in Present Day Buganda: An Economic and Anthropological Survey,* Audrey I. Richards, Fort Sturrock, and Jean M. Fortt (eds.)
9 *Dependence and Opportunity: Political Change in Ahafo,* John Dunn and A. F. Robertson
10 *African Railwaymen: Solidarity and Opposition in an East African Labour Force,* R. D. Grillo
11 *Islam and Tribal Art in West Africa,* René A. Bravmann
12 *Modern and Traditional Elites in the Politics of Lagos,* P. D. Cole
13 *Asante in the Nineteenth Century: The Structure and Evolution of a Political Order,* Ivor Wilks
14 *Culture, Tradition and Society in the West African Novel,* Emmanuel Obiechina
15 *Saints and Politicians,* Donald B. Cruise O'Brien
16 *The Lions of Dagbon: Political Change in Northern Ghana,* Martin Staniland
17 *Politics of Decolonization: Kenya Europeans and the Land Issue 1960–1965,* Gary B. Wasserman
18 *Muslim Brotherhoods in Nineteenth Century Africa,* B. G. Martin
19 *Warfare in the Sokoto Caliphate: Historical and Sociological Perspectives,* Joseph P. Smaldone
20 *Liberia and Sierra Leone: An Essay in Comparative Politics,* Christopher Clapham
21 *Adam Kok's Griquas: A Study in the Development of Stratification in South Africa,* Robert Ross
22 *Class, Power and Ideology in Ghana: The Railwaymen of Sekondi,* Richard Jeffries
23 *West African States: Failure and Promise,* John Dunn (ed.)

24 *Afrikaners of the Kalahari: White Minority in a Black State*, Margo Russell and Martin Russell
25 *A Modern History of Tanganyika*, John Iliffe
26 *A History of African Christianity 1950–1975*, Adrian Hastings
27 *Slave, Peasants and Capitalists in Southern Angola, 1840–1926*, W. G. Clarence-Smith
28 *The Hidden Hippopotamus: Reappraised in African History: The Early Colonial Experience in Western Zambia*, Gwyn Prins
29 *Families Divided: The Impact of Migrant Labour in Lesotho*, Colin Murray
30 *Slavery, Colonialism and Economic Growth in Dahomey, 1640–1960*, Patrick Manning
31 *Kings, Commoners and Concessionaires: The Evolution and Dissolution of the Nineteenth-Century Swazi State*, Philip Bonner
32 *Oral Poetry and Somali Nationalism: The Case of Sayid Mahammad 'Abdille Hasan*, Said S. Samatar
33 *The Political Economy of Pondoland 1860–1930*, William Beinart
34 *Volkskapitalisme: Class, Capital and Ideology in the Development of Afrikaner Nationalism, 1934–1948*, Dan O'Meara
35 *The Settler Economies: Studies in the Economic History of Kenya and Rhodesia 1900–1963*, Paul Mosley
36 *Transformations in Slavery: A History of Slavery in Africa*, Paul E. Lovejoy
37 *Amilcar Cabral: Revolutionary Leadership and People's War*, Patrick Chabal
38 *Essays on the Political Economy of Rural Africa*, Robert H. Bates
39 *Ijeshas and Nigerians: The Incorporation of a Yoruba Kingdom, 1890s–1970s*, J. D. Y. Peel
40 *Black People and the South African War, 1899–1902*, Peter Warwick
41 *A History of Niger 1850–1960*, Finn Fuglestad
42 *Industrialisation and Trade Union Organization in South Africa 1924–1955*, Stephen Ellis
43 *The Rising of the Red Shawls: A Revolt in Madagascar 1895–1899*, Stephen Ellis
44 *Slavery in Dutch South Africa*, Nigel Worden
45 *Law, Custom and Social Order: The Colonial Experience in Malawi and Zambia*, Martin Chanock
46 *Salt of the Desert Sun: A History of Salt Production and Trade in the Central Sudan*, Paul E. Lovejoy

47 *Marrying Well: Marriage, Status and Social Change among the Educated Elite in Colonial Lagos*, Kristin Mann
48 *Language and Colonial Power: The Appropriation of Swahili in the Former Belgian Congo, 1880–1938*, Johannes Fabian
49 *The Shell Money of the Slave Trade,* Jan Hogendorn and Marion Johnson
50 *Political Domination in Africa,* Patrick Chabal
51 *The Southern Marches of Imperial Ethiopia: Essays in History and Social Anthropology*, Donald Donham and Wendy James
52 *Islam and Urban Labor in Northern Nigeria: The Making of a Muslim Working Class*, Paul M. Lubeck
53 *Horn and Crescent: Cultural Change and Traditional Islam on the East African Coast, 1800–1900,* Randall L. Pouwels
54 *Capital and Labour on the Kimberley Diamond Fields, 1871–1890,* Robert Vicat Turrell
55 *National and Class Conflict in the Horn of Africa,* John Markakis
56 *Democracy and Prebendal Politics in Nigeria: The Rise and Fall of the Second Republic,* Richard A. Joseph
57 *Entrepreneurs and Parasites: The Struggle for Indigenous Capitalism in Zaïre,* Janet MacGaffey
58 *The African Poor: A History,* John Iliffe
59 *Palm Oil and Protest: An Economic History of the Ngwa Region, South-Eastern Nigeria, 1800–1980,* Susan M. Martin
60 *France and Islam in West Africa, 1860–1960,* Christopher Harrison
61 *Transformation and Continuity in Revolutionary Ethiopia,* Christopher Clapham
62 *Prelude to the Mahdiyya: Peasants and Traders in the Shendi Region, 1821–1885,* Anders Bjørkelo
63 *Wa and the Wala: Islam and Polity in Northwestern Ghana,* Ivor Wilks
64 *H. C. Bankole-Bright and Politics in Colonial Sierra Leone, 1919–1958*, Akintola Wyse
65 *Contemporary West African States,* Donald Cruise O'Brien, John Dunn, Richard Rathbone (eds.)
66 *The Oromo of Ethiopia: A History, 1570–1860,* Mohammed Hassen
67 *Slavery and African Life: Occidental, Oriental, and African Slave Trades,* Patrick Manning
68 *Abraham Esau's War: A Black South African War in the Cape, 1899–1902*, Bill Nasson
69 *The Politics of Harmony: Land Dispute Strategies in Swaziland,* Laurel L. Rose

70 *Zimbabwe's Guerrilla War: Peasant Voices*, Norma J. Kriger
71 *Ethiopia: Power and Protest: Peasant Revolts in the Twentieth Century*, Gebru Tareke
72 *White Supremacy and Black Resistance in Pre-Industrial South Africa: The Making of the Colonial Order in the Eastern Cape, 1770–1865*, Clifton C. Crais
73 *The Elusive Granary: Herder, Farmer, and State in Northern Kenya*, Peter D. Little
74 *The Kanyok of Zaire: An Institutional and Ideological History to 1895*, John C. Yoder
75 *Pragmatism in the Age of Jihad: The Precolonial State of Bundu*, Michael A. Gomez
76 *Slow Death for Slavery: The Course of Abolition in Northern Nigeria, 1897–1936*, Paul E. Lovejoy and Jan S. Hogendorn
77 *West African Slavery and Atlantic Commerce: The Senegal River Valley, 1700–1860*, James F. Searing
78 *A South African Kingdom: The Pursuit of Security in Nineteenth-Century Lesotho*, Elizabeth A. Eldredge
79 *State and Society in Pre-colonial Asante*, T. C. McCaskie
80 *Islamic Society and State Power in Senegal: Disciples and Citizens in Fatick*, Leonardo A. Villalón
81 *Ethnic Pride and Racial Prejudice in Victorian Cape Town: Group Identity and Social Practice*, Vivian Bickford-Smith
82 *The Eritrean Struggle for Independence: Domination, Resistance and Nationalism, 1941–1993*, Ruth Iyob
83 *Corruption and State Politics in Sierra Leone*, William Reno
84 *The Culture of Politics in Modern Kenya*, Angelique Haugerud
85 *Africans: The History of a Continent*, John Iliffe
86 *From Slave Trade to 'Legitimate' Commerce: The Commercial Transition in Nineteenth-Century West Africa*, Robin Law (ed.)
87 *Leisure and Society in Colonial Brazzaville*, Phyllis Martin
88 *Kingship and State: The Buganda Dynasty*, Christopher Wrigley
89 *Decolonization and African Life: The Labour Question in French and British Africa*, Frederick Cooper
90 *Misreading the African Landscape: Society and Ecology in an African Forest Savannah Mosaic*, James Fairhead and Melissa Leach
91 *Peasant Revolution in Ethiopia: The Tigray People's Liberation Front, 1975–1991*, John Young
92 *Senegambia and the Atlantic Slave Trade*, Boubacar Barry
93 *Commerce and Economic Change in West Africa: The Oil Trade in the Nineteenth Century*, Martin Lynn

94 *Slavery and French Colonial Rule in West Africa: Senegal, Guinea and Mali*, Martin A. Klein
95 *East African Doctors: A History of the Modern Profession*, John Iliffe
96 *Middlemen of the Cameroons Rivers: The Duala and Their Hinterland, c.1600-c.1960*, Ralph Derrick, Ralph A. Austen, and Jonathan Derrick
97 *Masters and Servants on the Cape Eastern Frontier, 1760–1803*, Susan Newton-King
98 *Status and Respectability in the Cape Colony, 1750–1870: A Tragedy of Manners*, Robert Ross
99 *Slaves, Freedmen and Indentured Laborers in Colonial Mauritius*, Richard B. Allen
100 *Transformations in Slavery: A History of Slavery in Africa, 2nd Edition*, Paul E. Lovejoy
101 *The Peasant Cotton Revolution in West Africa: Côte d'Ivoire, 1880–1995*, Thomas J. Bassett
102 *Re-Imagining Rwanda: Conflict, Survival and Disinformation in the Late Twentieth Century*, Johan Pottier
103 *The Politics of Evil: Magic, State Power and the Political Imagination in South Africa*, Clifton Crais
104 *Transforming Mozambique: The Politics of Privatization, 1975–2000*, M. Anne Pitcher
105 *Guerrilla Veterans in Post-war Zimbabwe: Symbolic and Violent Politics, 1980–1987*, Norma J. Kriger
106 *An Economic History of Imperial Madagascar, 1750–1895: The Rise and Fall of an Island Empire*, Gwyn Campbell
107 *Honour in African History*, John Iliffe
108 *Africans: History of a Continent, 2nd Edition*, John Iliffe
109 *Guns, Race, and Power in Colonial South Africa*, William Kelleher Storey
110 *Islam and Social Change in French West Africa: History of an Emancipatory Community*, Sean Hanretta
111 *Defeating Mau Mau, Creating Kenya: Counterinsurgency, Civil War, and Decolonization*, Daniel Branch
112 *Christianity and Genocide in Rwanda*, Timothy Longman
113 *From Africa to Brazil: Culture, Identity, and an Atlantic Slave Trade, 1600–1830*, Walter Hawthorne
114 *Africa in the Time of Cholera: A History of Pandemics from 1817 to the Present*, Myron Echenberg

Made in the USA
Monee, IL
20 February 2020

22082528R00210